LITERACY AND LEARNING

ADVANCES IN LEARNING AND BEHAVIORAL DISABILITIES

Series Editors: Thomas E. Scruggs and
Margo A. Mastropieri

Recent Volumes:

ADVANCES IN LEARNING AND BEHAVIORAL DISABILITIES VOLUME 23

LITERACY AND LEARNING

EDITED BY

THOMAS E. SCRUGGS
George Mason University, Fairfax, VA, USA

MARGO A. MASTROPIERI
George Mason University, Fairfax, VA, USA

Emerald

United Kingdom – North America – Japan
India – Malaysia – China

Emerald Group Publishing Limited
Howard House, Wagon Lane, Bingley BD16 1WA, UK

First edition 2010

British Library Cataloguing in Publication Data
A catalogue record for this book is available from the British Library

ISBN: 978-1-84950-776-9
ISSN: 0735-004X (Series)

CONTENTS

LIST OF CONTRIBUTORS

Stephanie Al Otaiba	College of Education and the Florida Center for Reading Research, Florida State University, FL, USA
Faye Antoniou	Department of Psychology, University of Athens, Greece
Amy L. Boelé	School of Education, University of Colorado at Boulder, CO, USA
M. Susan Burns	College of Education and Human Development, George Mason University, Fairfax, VA, USA
Mary Beth Calhoon	Department of Educational Psychology and Special Education, Georgia State University, GA, USA
Cesare Cornoldi	Department of General Psychology, University of Padua, Italy
Yojanna Cuenca-Sanchez	College of Education and Human Development, George Mason University, Fairfax, VA, USA
Francesco Del Prete	Department of General Psychology, University of Padua, Italy
Julian Elliott	School of Education, Durham University, UK
Michael Faggella-Luby	Department of Educational Psychology, University of Connecticut, CT, USA
Anna Gallani	Department of General Psychology, University of Padua, Italy

Tamara Genarro	College of Education and Human Development, George Mason University, Fairfax, VA, USA
Simon Gibbs	School of Education, Communication and Language Sciences, Newcastle University, UK
Alison Gould Boardman	School of Education, University of Colorado at Boulder, CO, USA
Patricia Sampson Graner	Center for Research on Learning, University of Kansas, Lawrence, KS, USA
Anne W. Graves	Department of Special Education, San Diego State University, San Diego, CA, USA
Nancy Irby	College of Education and Human Development, George Mason University, Fairfax, VA, USA
Julie K. Kidd	College of Education and Human Development, George Mason University, Fairfax, VA, USA
Janette K. Klingner	School of Education, University of Colorado at Boulder, CO, USA
Richard Kubina	Department of Educational and School Psychology and Special Education, Pennsylvania State University, PA, USA
Solveig-Alma Halaas Lyster	Department of Special Needs Education, University of Oslo, Norway
Linda Mason	Department of Educational and School Psychology and Special Education, Pennsylvania State University, PA, USA
Margo A. Mastropieri	College of Education and Human Development, George Mason University, Fairfax, VA, USA

Sara Mills	College of Education and Human Development, George Mason University, Fairfax, VA, USA
Ana Miranda	Department of Developmental and Educational Psychology, University of Valencia, Spain
Susana Padeliadu	Department of Special Education, University of Thessaly, Greece
Anna Maria Re	Department of General Psychology, University of Padua, Italy
Thomas E. Scruggs	College of Education and Human Development, George Mason University, Fairfax, VA, USA
Francesco Sella	Department of General Psychology, University of Padua, Italy
Georgios D. Sideridis	Department of Psychology, University of Crete, Greece
Manuel Soriano	Department of Developmental and Educational Psychology, University of Valencia, Spain
Elizabeth Swanson	Meadows Center for Preventing Educational Risk, The University of Texas, TX, USA
Jeanne Wanzek	Florida Center for Reading Research and School of Teacher Education, Florida State University, FL, USA

RESPONSE TO INTERVENTION: TREATMENT VALIDITY AND IMPLEMENTATION CHALLENGES IN THE PRIMARY AND MIDDLE GRADES

Stephanie Al Otaiba, Mary Beth Calhoon and Jeanne Wanzek

ABSTRACT

The primary purpose of this chapter is to describe intensive multi-component reading interventions for use in Response to Intervention (RTI) implementation within elementary and middle schools. In early elementary grades, RTI has a focus on prevention through effective classroom instruction and increasingly powerful early interventions to meet student needs. By contrast, in middle school, the focus of RTI shifts to remediation and the provision of interventions with the power to help more students to be able to read on grade level. First, we provide an overview of RTI and explain the notion of treatment validity within RTI implementation. Next, we describe a kindergarten study that illustrates how the intensity of delivery may impact expected outcomes at Tier 2 and

Literacy and Learning
Advances in Learning and Behavioral Disabilities, Volume 23, 1–28

ISSN: 0735-004X/doi:10.1108/S0735-004X(2010)0000023003

then summarize research on extensive interventions for the primary grades. Then we summarize remedial interventions for older students and examine the percent of older students whose reading could be normalized by focusing on a newly developed intensive middle school remedial intervention that incorporates code- and meaning-focused instruction in a peer-mediated format. Finally, we will discuss RTI challenges and implementation issues.

Poor reading instruction leads to poor reading achievement for far too many students in this country (Snow, Burns, & Griffin, 1998; Vellutino et al., 1996). It is very troubling that over a third of American fourth graders perform below "basic" on the reading comprehension section of the National Assessment of Educational Progress (NAEP; National Center for Educational Statistics, 2007). Furthermore, scores remain markedly lower for minority students, many of whom live in poverty (e.g., 53% of Blacks and 50% of Hispanics at fourth grade performed below basic). Even with reading difficulties as the predominant reason for referrals to special education, intervention support in the elementary grades has historically been delivered as remediation rather than as prevention with students qualifying for services as "reading disabled" only after demonstrating failure in the form of an IQ-achievement discrepancy.

As students transition to middle school, chronic and persistent reading difficulties exist for a substantial portion of the student population (McCardle & Chhabra, 2004). Meanwhile, reading difficulties become increasingly difficult to remediate and students' motivation is impacted (Fletcher & Foorman, 1994; Kennedy, Birman, & Demaline, 1986; Morgan & Fuchs, 2007) as reading difficulties become associated with lower self-esteem, discipline problems, a higher likelihood of dropping out of school, and adjudication (Juel, 1996). Unfortunately, the poor quality of both general education literacy instruction and remedial special education reading instruction provided to adolescents with reading disabilities (RD) exacerbates their self-esteem difficulties and awareness of their own intractable reading problems (Bat-Hayim, 1997; Ryan, 1982; Vogel & Forness, 1992). Researchers find these adolescent students struggling to read and comprehend even the simplest of course assignments (Klingner, Vaughn, Hughes, Schumm & Elbaum, 1998). Thus, even if they graduate, their opportunities for employment are severely limited.

RESPONSE TO INTERVENTION (RTI) AND TREATMENT VALIDITY

In recognition of the need to improve reading instruction and subsequently to improve life long opportunities for children, the Individuals with Disabilities Educational Improvement Act (IDEIA) (2004) allows school districts to use a Response to Intervention (RTI) approach "that determines if the child responds to scientific, research-based intervention as a part of the evaluation procedures" for learning disabilities (Pub. L. No. 108-446 § 614 [b][6][A]; § 614 [b] [2 & 3]). To date, RTI is perceived mostly as a general education initiative, at least in part because the overarching goal of RTI is to prevent (or at least reduce the incidence) of reading disability through early intervening services. In fact, IDEIA provides for 15% of Part B funds to be used for early intervention in general education.

Fuchs and colleagues (Fuchs & Fuchs, 1998; Fuchs, Fuchs & Speece, 2002) proposed that for RTI to have "treatment validity," RTI should not only reduce the incidence of students identified as reading disabled by focusing on prevention, but also maximize the outcomes of students after their identification with RD through effective remedial education. Prevention provides children who are at risk for reading difficulties with evidence-based instructional services immediately, rather than waiting for children to fall farther behind. Students who are significantly behind in expected outcomes and do not catch up even with additional interventions may then be identified as reading disabled Then remediation in special education should continue to provide even more highly individualized extensive intervention and ongoing assessment of student success in the intervention to inform whether the student can return to less-intensive general education supports, or whether continued or even more intensive or individualized special education supports are needed.

Formative assessments, in the form of ongoing progress-monitoring tools, are one metric that can determine the efficacy of prevention and remediation efforts. These assessments are a check that most students at a school, or within a particular grade level or classroom, are successful, ensuring that an individual student's learning difficulty is not related to poor quality instruction. Further, these assessments ideally are used to assist teachers in appropriate grouping for instruction or in individualizing intervention efforts in an aptitude by treatment interaction fashion that takes into account data regarding students' strengths and weaknesses (cf. Jimerson, Burns, & Van Der Heyden, 2007). In addition, formative assessments may help gauge when students have responded well enough to interventions that they may exit intervention or when their response indicates a need to continue additional intervention. Torgesen (2000) suggested another way to judge responsiveness is to calculate the percentage of students who are "normalized," meaning that their reading scores on a nationally normed test are within normal limits. In other words, students with standard scores below 85 at the end of an intervention are considered "not normalized" and need to continue intervention.

Currently researchers have tested a variety of RTI models, however, the research has been predominantly focused on primary grades (K-3) when arguably, RTI systems may have the most traction because learning to read is a goal of core reading programs and because reading problems are less severe (and, therefore, may be more malleable). It is relatively easier to reduce the number of students with reading difficulties through early intervention than to remediate persistent chronic reading difficulties of students who have not learned to read in the primary grades (Francis, Shaywitz, Stuebing, Shaywitz, & Fletcher, 1996; Jenkins & O'Connor, 2002; Juel, 1988; Torgesen, 2000). Researchers have suggested that in the primary grades, it is expected that Tier 1, or classroom instruction, should help roughly 80–90% of students read on grade level by ensuring that they receive evidence-based classroom core reading instruction provided by a well-trained general education classroom teacher for a minimum of about 90 min/day (Batsche, Curtis, Dorman, Castillo, & Porter, 2007). Then, well-implemented Tier 2 interventions should help most of the 10–20% who did not make adequate progress in the initial classroom instruction, leaving perhaps 5% (or less) of the overall student population who require more intensive interventions.

Tier 2 interventions typically involve supplemental small-group instruction for 2–5 days/week for roughly 15–30 min provided by classroom teachers, reading specialists, or even well-trained and supervised paraprofessionals or community tutors. Tier 3 interventions typically increase in intensity by providing intervention more frequently, for longer periods of time, and/or in smaller instructional groups. Tier 3 may be either a blend of general and special education or purely special education, regardless it must be responsive to individual child's needs and intensive (e.g., an hour or more of extensive intervention per day provided in very small group or individual sessions by experts (O'Connor, Fulmer, Harty, & Bell, 2005; Vaughn, Linan-Thompson, & Hickman, 2003)). As students enter interventions, their progress is monitored more frequently in order to individualize intervention, plan homogeneous small groups, and gauge treatment validity. Ideally, Tier 3 interventions should help all but 1–3% of students read on grade level. However, these guidelines have been developed largely for the elementary grades. To our knowledge, there are no analogous recommendations for middle school.

RTI IMPLEMENTATION IN ELEMENTARY SCHOOL

A Volunteer-Implemented Tutorial: The Importance of Intensity at Tier 2

Al Otaiba, Schatschneider, and Silverman (2005) directly compared the impact of intervention dosage – two versus four 30-min sessions/week (mean of 72 vs. 36 sessions distributed across 20 weeks). The intervention, Tutor-Assisted Intensive Learning Strategies (TAILS), was investigated through a randomized field trial conducted in four high poverty schools (Al Otaiba et al., 2005). Within the 12 participating classrooms, students were randomly assigned to receive tutoring for 2 or 4 days/week or to a control condition that received small-group storybook reading 2 days/week. A total of 73 (of the 243 kindergartners in these classrooms) met eligibility criteria of naming less than two letters correct per minute or naming less than three letter-sounds correct per minute. About 80% of the students were African American and a similar proportion received free and reduced lunch.

Although RTI was not being implemented in the four participating schools, TAILS could be conceptualized as a Tier 2 intervention that supplemented children's existing explicit classroom core reading program. TAILS is based on principles of direct instruction (i.e., Carnine, Silbert, & Kame'enui, 1997), has a clear scope and sequence, follows a model-lead-test format, and includes cumulative review and practice. Adult (nonteacher) tutors (trained for 13 h) followed scripted lessons that included 10–15 min of phonological awareness and phonics instruction, and fluency practice in game-like formats that increased in difficulty from letter-sounds to connected text. Then, tutors read aloud to children for 10–15 min using dialogic reading strategies (Beck, McKeown, & Kucan, 2002; Lonigan, Anthony, Bloomfield, Dyer, & Samwel, 1999). Fidelity of TAILS implementation was consistently above 85%.

Standardized reading tests were administered (at pre-, mid-, and post-treatment) as were weekly curriculum-based progress-monitoring measures. There were no significant differences between groups during pretreatment; initial language scores of participants (Peabody Picture Vocabulary – Revised, $M = 77.75$; SD $= 12.90$) were relatively lower than their initial word reading scores (Word Identification, $M = 84.77$; SD 7.73). Students in the 4-day TAILS condition demonstrated significantly greater growth on word reading, word attack, and passage comprehension than students in either the 2-day or control condition on three reading measures. The magnitude of effects were large (favoring students in the 4-day vs. control condition – these were .79, .90, and .83, on word identification, passage comprehension, and basic reading skills, respectively). Furthermore, despite their impoverished language and alphabetic skills at the start of kindergarten, most students achieved grade-level reading scores. A relatively small number of students (9.6%) ended the study with a standard score below 85 on word identification and word attack (three of these students were in the 4-day condition, three were in the control condition, and one student was in the 2-day condition).

In summary, findings from this study demonstrated that it is feasible to use volunteers as tutors in a Tier 2 intervention if it is provided 4 days/week and with fidelity. In light of the severely limited resources within schools, this is encouraging. Nevertheless, additional follow-up study of these students is warranted to learn whether TAILS participation in kindergarten ensured a strong reading trajectory. Further, learning more about the characteristics of the students who did not reach grade level at the end of the study and learning whether this unresponsiveness could have been predicted at an earlier point in the study would inform RTI implementation procedures related to moving students to more intensive layers of intervention provided by a certified teacher.

What Are The Promising Extensive Interventions For Use In RTI Implementation In Primary Grades?

Wanzek and Vaughn (2007) recently synthesized the research on extensive early reading interventions (defined by them as interventions provided for 100 or more sessions). Thus, their findings have ramifications for RTI implementation in that they reported the successfulness of Tier 3-type interventions. Additionally, they compared effect sizes related to intervention components taught, duration, intensity (group size), and training of interventionist. Furthermore, they described how effective interventions were when used in an RTI framework, that is, when delivered to students who had not benefited from either Tier 1 or less-extensive Tier 2 intervention(s).

Encouragingly, Wanzek and Vaughn (2007) reported positive findings, in most of the 18 studies they reviewed, for students with RD and with reading difficulties. Consistent with other meta-analyses of early reading instruction and intervention (National Reading Panel, 2000; Snow et al., 1998; Snow, 2002), higher effect sizes were found for interventions that included a component of explicit teaching of decoding. Larger effects were found for 1:1 intervention group size, but as noted by the authors, no studies directly compared effects based on group size and relatively few studies used small group formats.

The RTI hold that intervening earlier is more powerful than later was supported by the synthesis findings; effects were stronger for first grade interventions than for students who received intervention in second or third grade. The authors indicated this finding could be partly due to the confound related to second and third graders already having relatively severe reading problems (students had identified learning disabilities). Another possible explanation was that researchers may have purposefully (or through screening measurement error) over-served students – the "false positives" – who may not have required such an extensive intervention rather than those children with the most severe reading disabilities. Only two reviewed studies described the efficacy of an extensive intervention for students who had not benefited sufficiently from a previous intervention (Vadasy, Sanders, Peyton, & Jenkins, 2002; Vaughn et al., 2003); nevertheless, Vadasy et al. reported relatively large effects ranging from .56 to .92 and Vaughn et al. reported large pre- to postgains.

Another important question was whether effect sizes were consistently higher for word reading skills compared with reading comprehension or reading fluency. In seven of the 12 studies that provided sufficient data for calculation of effect sizes, comprehension was a dependent measure. Findings were equivocal: in only one study Jenkins, Peyton, Sanders, & Vadasy (2004), the effect size for comprehension (.86 on the Woodcock Reading Mastery Test – Revised (WRMT-R)) was higher than word reading (ranging from .35 to .83) or reading fluency (.56). In two other studies, effect sizes on the WRMT-R were also large (.74 and .81), but the magnitude of these effects was comparable to effect sizes on word reading measures (Morris, Tyner, & Perney, 2000; Vadasy, Sanders, & Peyton, 2005). In the remaining four studies (Gunn, Biglan, Smolkowski, & Ary, 2000; Gunn, Smolkowski, Biglan, & Black, 2002; Mathes et al., 2005; Torgesen, Wagner, & Rashotte, 1997; Torgesen et al., 1999; Vadasy et al., 2002), word reading effects were moderate to large, by comparison comprehension effects were small (.30 or lower, ranging from –.05 to .30). Oral reading fluency was also assessed in four of these investigations and in two studies fluency effects were moderate and comparable to average word reading effects (Jenkins et al., 2004 (.56); Vadasy et al., 2005 (.50)). In the other two studies, fluency effects were small and markedly lower than average word reading effects (Gunn et al., 2000, 2002 [.27]; Mathes et al., 2005 [.26 on CRAB-R and .00 on WJ-III fluency]).

Wanzek and Vaughn (2007) noted the need for additional research on types of intervention for students whose response to typically effective interventions is low and who require not just extensive, but highly intensive interventions. As a result, the findings provide initial guidance for considering appropriate Tier 3 interventions, but additional investigation regarding Tier 3 intervention development to meet the needs of elementary students with severe reading disabilities is warranted.

RTI IMPLEMENTATION IN MIDDLE SCHOOL

Clearly, students who have not learned to read on grade level in the primary grades will still need high-quality individualized reading instruction in middle school. However, in middle school, the reading instructional focus shifts from reading to learning, not only in literature courses but also in content areas. This instruction largely focuses on comprehension, rather than decoding instruction, even for multisyllable words. There are few remedial reading programs that provide specific, intensive, and explicit reading instruction; furthermore, little empirical research exists to guide optimal grouping or intensity of instruction (deBettencourt, Zigmond, & Thorton, 1989; Klingner et al., 1998; Zigmond & Baker, 1995). Moreover, students with RD spend very little of their school day reading, with studies reporting between 0 and 17.4 min/day of connected text reading across settings (Swanson, 2008). When it does occur, reading instruction is not as intensive as the extensive interventions we just described that benefited students in primary grades. By contrast, instruction is likely provided in a whole-class (or within a large group of up to 20 students) rather than a small group or individualized format and may not explicitly address multiple components of phonics, fluency, and comprehension (Moody, Vaughn, Hughes, & Fisher, 2000; Swanson, 2008; Vaughn, Moody, & Schumm, 1998).

Subsequently, students' reading levels frequently stagnate or fall even further behind for every year spent in special education (McIntosh, Vaughn, Schumm, Haager, & Lee, 1993; Vaughn, & Klinger, 1998; Zigmond & Baker, 1995; Zigmond et al., 1995). For example, Hanushek,

Kain and Rivkin (1998) found that special education students increased their test scores at only .04 SD/year, which is negligible.

What are The Promising Extensive Interventions for RTI Implementation with Older Students?

There is converging evidence from meta-analyses and research syntheses of the special education literature regarding which intervention components (NRP, 2000) lead to improved academic outcomes specifically for students with learning disabilites (LD) (Gersten et al., 1998; Elbaum, Vaughn, Hughes, & Moody, 2000; Mastropieri & Scruggs, 1996; Swanson, 1999b; Swanson & Hoskyn, 1998; Vaughn, Gersten, & Chard, 2000). However, Swanson (1999a) cautioned that younger students were associated with higher effects on word recognition variables in comparison to middle school or older students.

The critical elements of instruction that produced the strongest effects included small group interactive instruction, extended practice and feedback, sequenced tasks presented in order of difficulty to ensure student success, and instruction that showed students how to be metacognitive (think aloud, self-question, or problem-solve) while reading text. Notably, Swanson did not find that severity of reading disability moderated treatment effects on word recognition or comprehension.

As we compare the extensiveness of interventions within the Edmonds et al. (2009) older reader synthesis to Wanzek and Vaughn's (2007) early grade synthesis, it is a concern that the comprehension interventions for older students were far less extensive. The average number of intervention sessions was only 23 h (number of sessions varied widely from 2 to 70). Therefore, even though 13 of the 19 interventions were provided by teachers, none of these studies would have provided what Wanzek and Vaughn considered nearly as "extensive" as the intervention studies they reviewed. Furthermore, it is a concern that among the 29 studies Edmonds et al. reviewed, only two incorporated critical elements of strong research designs (randomly assigned students to condition, reported treatment fidelity, and student outcomes on standardized assessments of reading [Abbott & Berninger, 1999; Allinder, Dunse, Brunken & Obermiller-Krolikowski, 2001]).

A Remedial Multicomponent Intervention: Individual Differences in RTI

One program that is more extensive than those reviewed by Edmonds et al. (2009) and has been empirically tested as an intensive remedial reading program with adolescents is the Reading Achievement Multi-Modular Program (RAMP-UP; Calhoon, 2003). RAMP-UP incorporates multiple components of literacy instruction within a delivery system of reciprocal class wide peer tutoring (CWPT). As is typical in CWPT, teachers divide their students into pairs and then using scripted lessons, train students how to provide and receive verbal instructions, feedback, and step-by-step explanations for each individual reading component (linguistics skills, spelling, fluency, reading comprehension, etc.) within RAMP-UP.

For example, within the linguistics component, students learn a form of segmenting and telescoping that focuses on phonetic and orthographic awareness (Carnine, Silbert, Kame'enui, & Tarver, 2004), modified for older students with RD. The scope and sequence of these skills range from simple phonetics (i.e., speech–sound identification, vowel and semivowel patterns, phoneme counting, phonetic transcription) and phonology (i.e., phonemes and minimal pairs, phonetic variation, systematic variation in speech sound production, sequencing, syllables [vcv, vccv, x, ble]) to more complex English orthography and morphology (i.e., word origins and historical layers of English orthography, Latinate ending, Romance language spellings, orthographic conventions). Metacognitive strategy instruction (in this case, a word-attack strategy) or a "Procedural Facilitator" is explicitly taught and applied each time students' learn a new linguistics skill (Baker, Gersten, & Scanlon, 2002). Furthermore, students are trained to use written signals (i.e., c = consonant, ∧ = peak, ĕ = lax sound for the letter e, ē = tense sound for the letter e) for each linguistics skill to supports word attack. Calhoon combined the procedural facilitator and the signaling system as metacognitive cues to support students' strategy use.

The comprehension portion of RAMP-UP directly integrates partner reading from Peer-Assisted Learning Strategies (PALS) developed by Fuchs, Fuchs, Phillips, Hamlett, and Karns (1995), which incorporates: *Partner reading*, student-centered guided oral reading designed to develop fluency; *Paragraph shrinking*, designed to develop comprehension through summarization and main idea identification (Fuchs, Fuchs, Mathes, & Simmons, 1997); and *Prediction relay*, designed to extend *Paragraph shrinking* to larger chunks of text and asks students to make and confirm or disconfirm predictions.

In later iterations of RAMP-UP, Calhoon added a spelling and a fluency component. The spelling component was designed to reinforce linguistic skills knowledge (Adams, 1990; Chall, 1996; Snow et al., 1998; Templeton & Morris, 1999). The "Working with Words" instructional sheets used in spelling instruction, systematically address specific spelling patterns and mirror skills taught during linguistics lessons (e.g., double vowels, silent "e," Latinate endings). In linguistics and spelling paired lessons, students are presented with an opportunity to synthesize information into a comprehensive understanding of word patterns, rules, and expectations (Carreker, 2005). The fluency component was based on the *repeated reading technique* developed by Stahl, Heubach, and Cramond (1997). Working with their partner, students read a passage for 1 min, set a goal to increase the number of words read correctly, and then reread the same passage (controlled text that integrates the linguistics and spelling skills) for 1 min (Beck & Juel, 1995; Samuels, Schermer, & Reinking, 1992).

Each instructional component (linguistics skills, spelling, reading fluency, and reading comprehension) of RAMP-UP was developed as a separate, stand-alone instructional unit. This innovative design of RAMP-UP allows the creation of multiple instructional versions or modules from the four components. Each module, depending on the arrangement or organization of the components, permits a specific emphasis or dosage of instruction to be placed on a different component(s). In two studies, Calhoon and colleagues (Calhoon, 2005; Calhoon, Sandow, & Hunter, in press) have shown impressive gains using different modular versions of RAMP-UP.

The first study compared RAMP-UP to a contrasting intervention; both were conducted daily for 31 weeks, 45 min/day, for a total of 85 h of instruction. This was a pretest/posttest design with classrooms randomly assigned to condition. Participants were 38 6th-grade students with RD (Letter-Word Identification, $M = 78.97$. $SD = 9.51$; Passage Comprehension, $M = 78.13$, $SD = 10.56$); approximately 66% of students were Hispanic, 29% were Caucasian, and 5% were African American. This initial study of RAMP-UP used the first module developed termed, *Alternating* module (Calhoon, 2005). In other words, students received linguistics instruction 3 days/week (e.g., Tuesday, Wednesday, and Thursday), and on the remaining weekdays (Monday and Friday) students received comprehension strategy instruction. Students in the contrast condition participated for 3 days/week in a teacher-directed program that provided phonics, spelling, vocabulary, fluency, and reading comprehension in every lesson (Saxon Phonics Intervention; SPI; Simmons, 2001). On the remaining 2 days, students were trained using the SRA Skill Acquisition program, which is a teacher-directed reading comprehension program. As a result, in this contrast condition, students received approximately 10 h more of comprehension instruction than in RAMP-UP. Fidelity of both conditions was consistently above 90%.

Reading subtests of the Woodcock–Johnson Achievement Test III (WJ-III; Woodcock, McGrew & Mather, 2001) were administered pre- and posttreatment. At pretreatment, there were no significant differences in reading performance between conditions. Note that the sample as a whole had initial scores that were markedly lower on Letter-Word Identification ($M = 78.97$, SD = 9.51), Reading Fluency ($M = 79.50$, SD = 6.15), and Passage Comprehension ($M = 78.13$, SD = 10.55) than on Word Attack ($M = 87.34$, SD = 7.96). Students in the RAMP-UP condition demonstrated significantly greater growth than students in the contrast condition on all but the Reading Fluency subtest; in fact there were no significant gains in either condition on fluency. Moreover, the magnitude of effects favoring students in the RAMP-UP were large on Letter-Word Identification (1.10), Word Attack (.99), and Passage Comprehension (.94)

While overall the group-mean gains are impressive for RAMP-UP, given our interest in RTI for this chapter, it is worthwhile to explore the magnitude of individual differences in response to both interventions based upon students' initial risk. Table 1 shows students separated into an at-risk group (pretest scores below 85) and a not-at-risk group for each measure; then shows the magnitude of growth (RTI) on each subtest by treatment condition. To judge the magnitude of RTI, we have used an heuristic of growth >15 standard score points as "excellent," between 11 and 14 as "very good," between 5 and 11 as "good," and <5 as marginal, because this represents the standard error for the WJ-III.

So, for example, looking at Table 1, 4 of the 12 RAMP-UP students at risk (due to initial scores below 85 on Letter-Word Identification) demonstrated very good response to treatment (they grew more than 11 standard score points), 4 showed good response (they gained between 5 and 10 standard score points), and 4 showed marginal response (they gained <5 standard score points). The table also shows that overall the magnitude of response was greater for students when their pretreatment score was below 85 on that particular measure. Thus, conceivably some students were regressing to the mean.

It is also readily apparent from Table 1 that the magnitude of growth for students in the RAMP-UP condition was stronger than for students in the contrast condition. Overall, a higher percentage of at-risk students in the RAMP-UP than in the contrast condition made gains of 5 or more standard scores on Letter-Word Identification, Word Attack, and Passage Comprehension. Examining these individual RTI trends in conjunction with the higher group effect sizes for RAMP-UP demonstrates that RAMP-UP is a promising Tier 2 intervention because it can help to close the gap relative to

Table 1. Standard Score Gains by Condition.

	At Risk at Pretest (<85 SS).				Not At Risk at Pretest (>85 SS)			
	Condition				Condition			
	RAMP-UP		Contrast		RAMP-UP		Contrast	
Woodcock–Johnson III, Letter-Word Identification – age standard score gains								
	$N = 12$		$N = 13$		$N = 6$		$N = 7$	
	n	%	*n*	%	*n*	%	*n*	%
<5	4	33	9	69	3	50	7	100
5–10	4	33	4	31	2	33	0	0
11–15	1	8	0	0	0	0	0	0
>15	3	25	0	0	1	17	0	0
Woodcock–Johnson III, Word Attack – Age Standard Score Gains								
	$N = 2$		$N = 6$		$N = 16$		$N = 14$	
	n	%	*n*	%	*n*	%	*n*	%
<5	0	0	2	33	3	19	9	64
5–10	2	100	2	33	9	56	5	36
11–15	0	0	1	17	3	19	0	0
>15	0	0	1	17	1	6	0	0
Woodcock–Johnson III, Spelling – Age Standard Score Gains								
	$N = 16$		$N = 15$		$N = 2$		$N = 5$	
	n	%	*n*	%	*n*	%	*n*	%
<5	9	56	5	33	1	50	4	80
5–10	3	19	6	40	1	50	1	20
11–15	3	19	3	20	0	0	0	0
>15	1	6	1	7	0	0	0	0
Woodcock–Johnson III, Reading Fluency – Age Standard Score Gains								
	$N = 14$		$N = 17$		$N = 4$		$N = 3$	
	n	%	*n*	%	*n*	%	*n*	%
<5	14	100	13	76	4	100	2	67
5–10	0	0	3	18	0	0	1	33
11–15	0	0	1	6	0	0	0	0
>15	0	0	0	0	0	0	0	0

Table 1. *(Continued).*

Woodcock–Johnson III, Passage Comprehension – Age Standard Score Gains								
	$N=11$		$N=13$		$N=7$		$N=7$	
	n	%	*n*	%	*n*	%	*n*	%
<5	1	9	7	54	5	71	6	86
5–10	3	27	5	38	1	14	0	0
11–15	6	55	1	8	1	14	1	14
>15	1	9	0	0	0	0	0	0

national norms in phonological decoding and comprehension skills for many students. However, not all students made adequate RTI; a relatively small number of students in the RAMP-UP condition ended the study with a standard score below 85 on Letter-Word Identification ($N=6$, 33%), Word Attack ($N=0$), and Passage Comprehension ($N=6$, 33%) compared to students in the contrast condition, Letter-Word Identification ($N=14$, 70%), Word Attack ($N=5$, 25%), and Passage Comprehension, ($N=13$, 65%).

Furthermore, it is noteworthy that more than half of the students in the RAMP-UP condition with initially weak comprehension scores improved their comprehension to such a degree that they would likely be able to read well enough to understand texts in their general education content area courses. Recall that these students received 10 h less of comprehension instruction than students in the contrast condition, whose instruction was all teacher-directed. Furthermore, 12 of the students in RAMP-UP achieved comprehension scores above 85 at posttest, while only seven students in the contrast condition ended the study with scores above 85. In the context of RTI, this suggests that some of the RAMP-UP graduates may have been able to better access the general education curriculum within their content area courses.

A second study, also conducted by Calhoon and colleagues (in press) compared the efficacy of the original *Alternating* module with two new modules: *Additive* and *Integrated* (Calhoon et al., 2009). Each new module added the instructional components of spelling and fluency to the existing linguistic and comprehension components provided in the original module. However, whereas the *Integrated* module (see Table 2) was similar to the *Alternating* schedule, the *Additive* module provided a markedly different schedule (see Table 3). Classrooms were randomly assigned to the three modules; each module of RAMP-UP provided 97 hs of instructional time

Table 2. Organization of Components for Integrated Module.

Integrated Module				
Monday	Tuesday	Wednesday	Thursday	Friday
Comprehension	Linguistic skills Fluency Spelling	Linguistic skills Fluency Spelling	Comprehension	Linguistic skills Fluency Spelling

Table 3. Organization of the Components for the Additive Module.

Additive Module			
1st–7th weeks	2nd–7th weeks	3rd–7th weeks	4th–7th weeks
Linguistic skills	Linguistic skills Spelling	Linguistic skills Spelling Fluency	Spelling Fluency Comprehension

across 26 weeks implemented daily in the same CWPT format for 45 min during students' resource Language Arts class time. The participating 90 students with RD were in 6th through 8th grades, and approximately 34% of the students were Caucasian, 30% were African American, 26% were Hispanic, and 10% were Asian. Fidelity of RAMP-UP implementation in all three modules was consistently above 86%.

There were no significant pretreatment differences among the conditions on any of the WJ-III reading subtests, AIMSweb Oral Fluency (ORF) Passages (PsychCorp, 2009), or the Gray Silent Reading Test (GSRT; Wiederholt & Blalock, 2000). As in the prior study, pretreatment scores for this impaired reader sample were very low (Letter-Word Identification: $M = 78.75$, SD = 8.31; Word Attack: $M = 81.38$, SD = 8.61; Reading Fluency: $M = 80.49$, SD = 8.25; ORF: $M = 68.17$, SD = 26.43; GSRT: $M = 67.36$, SD = 11.71). Posttreatment findings demonstrated that all students in all three modules made significant gains on linguistics; the sample averages at posttreatment were (Letter-Word Identification, $M = 83.89$, SD = 9.50; Word Attack, $M = 92.62$, SD = 6.61) fluency (Reading Fluency, $M = 83.89$, SD = 8.57; ORF, $M = 97.06$, SD = 31.82) and reading comprehension (GSRT, $M = 81.74$, SD = 19.19). Table 4 shows the mean effect sizes by module comparisons on these subtests.

Table 5 shows the magnitude of RTI for students in the at-risk group (pretest scores below 85) and Table 6 shows students not at-risk on each

Table 4. Effect Size Comparisons across Modules.

Measures	Modules		
	Integrated vs. alternating	Additive vs. alternating	Additive vs. integrated
Letter-Word Identification	−.11	.87	1.08
Word Attack	.02	.69	.59
Reading Fluency	.52	.51	−.12
Gray Silent Reading Test	−.17	.49	.64

particular measure by treatment condition. To judge the magnitude of RTI, we again applied our heuristic of growth >15 standard score points as "excellent," between 11 and 14 as "very good," between 5 and 11 as "good," and <5 as marginal, because this represents the standard error for the WJ-III. Once again, as in the prior study, the magnitude of RTI was more often very good or excellent among students who started the study at risk on a given measure. Next, we notice that across the three modules, decoding gains were very strong, as were the silent reading comprehension gains. A comparison of RTI across the modules reveals that the *Additive* module appeared associated with the most robust RTI as measured by the WJ-III Letter-Word Identification and the Reading Fluency subtests, as well as by the GSRT.

Swanson (1999a) suggested there is a low probability of obtaining high effect sizes on phonological skill variables for older students in comparison with younger students. In sharp contrast, the large number of students who made "very good" and "good" gains in phonological skills in both RAMP-UP studies indicates these phonological skills can be dramatically increased for older students with RD, if the intervention provided is intensive and extensive enough to impact these skills. Furthermore, it is interesting to note, the RAMP-UP modules (*Additive* and *Alternating*) that provided the heaviest emphasis on phonological decoding skills produced the largest effect sizes and percentage of standard score gains in comprehension for these older students with RD. Findings from both RAMP-UP studies begin to lend support to the importance of providing intensive phonological decoding instruction at the middle school level, and the generalization of phonological decoding instruction into better gains of comprehension skills.

This second study also showed greater gains on fluency than did the first study of RAMP-UP. Two types of reading fluency assessments were

Table 5. Standard Score Gains by RAMP-UP Modules for Students At Risk.

Students At Risk at Pretest (<85 Standard Scores)						
Modules						
	Alternating		Integrated		Additive	
Woodcock–Johnson III, Letter Word Identification – Age Standard Score Gains						
	$N=17$		$N=22$		$N=25$	
	n	%	*n*	%	*n*	%
<5	10	59	14	64	6	24
5–10	4	24	5	23	7	28
11–15	2	12	2	9	8	32
>15	1	6	1	5	4	16
Woodcock–Johnson III, Word Attack – Age Standard Score Gains						
	$N=18$		$N=19$		$N=19$	
	n	%	*n*	%	*n*	%
<5	1	6	1	5	1	5
5–10	8	44	7	37	3	16
11–15	4	22	6	32	4	21
>15	5	28	5	26	11	58
Woodcock–Johnson III, Reading Fluency – Age Standard Score Gains						
	$N=24$		$N=21$		$N=21$	
	n	%	*n*	%	*n*	%
<5	11	46	10	48	14	67
5–10	9	38	10	48	5	24
11–15	2	8	0	0	2	19
>15	2	8	1	4	0	0
Gray's Silent Reading Test – Age Standard Score Gains						
	$N=26$		$N=29$		$N=28$	
	n	%	*n*	%	*n*	%
<5	12	46	11	38	5	18
5–10	4	15	4	14	2	7
11–15	1	4	7	24	4	14
>15	9	35	7	24	17	61

Table 6. Standard Score Gains by RAMP-UP Module for Students Not At Risk.

Not At Risk at Pretest (>85 Standard Scores)						
Modules						
	Alternating		Integrated		Additive	
Woodcock–Johnson III, Letter-Word Identification – Age Standard Score Gains						
	$N = 12$		$N = 8$		$N = 6$	
	n	%	*n*	%	*n*	%
<5	7	58	8	100	2	33
5–10	3	25	0	0	1	17
11–15	1	8	0	0	3	50
>15	1	8	0	0	0	0
Woodcock–Johnson III, Word Attack – Age Standard Score Gains						
	$N = 11$		$N = 11$		$N = 12$	
	n	%	*n*	%	*n*	%
<5	4	36	7	64	3	25
5–10	4	36	3	27	4	33
11–15	2	18	0	0	3	25
>15	1	9	1	9	2	17
Woodcock–Johnson III, Reading Fluency – Age Standard Score Gains						
	$N = 5$		$N = 9$		$N = 10$	
	n	%	*n*	%	*n*	%
<5	4	80	8	89	6	60
5–10	1	20	1	11	4	40
11–15	0	0	0	0	0	0
>15	0	0	0	0	0	0
Gray's Silent Reading Test – Age Standard Score Gains						
	$N = 3$		$N = 1$		$N = 3$	
	n	%	*n*	%	*n*	%
<5	0	0	1	100	0	0
5–10	0	0	0	0	1	33
11–15	0	0	0	0	1	33
>15	3	100	0	0	1	33

measured in this study, the WJ-III Reading Fluency and the ORF, and students showed relatively good response on both types of measures. Deno, Fuchs, Marston, and Shin (2001) suggested that promising growth for older students with RD in the area of oral fluency is .50 words/week. It is important to note that students were given ORF passages at their grade level (i.e., 6th grade students read 6th grade passages, 7th grade students read 7th grade passages, and 8th grade students read 8th grade passages). Encouraging for RAMP-UP and its use as a Tier 2 intensive program is that 28 students in the *Additive*, 29 in the *Integrated*, and 22 in the *Alternating* modules made gains of more than .50 words correct per minute (wcpm) per week, 18 students in the *Additive*, 17 in the *Integrated*, and 11 in the *Alternating* modules made gains of more than 1.0 gains in wcpm per week, and three students in the *Additive*, five in the *Integrated*, and one in the *Alternating* modules made gains of more than 2.0 gains in wcpm per week on the ORF measure. After treatment, students' ORF wcpm scores ranged from 18 to 184, with 55.60% of the students reading over 100 wcpm at grade level, while at the beginning of treatment only 12.10% of the students read at this rate on grade-level passages.

Nevertheless, as may not be surprising given the intractability of RD, a number of students did not "catch up" to national norms, Letter-Word Identification ($N = 44$, 48.90%), Word Attack ($N = 10$, 11.10%), Reading Fluency ($N = 54$, 60%), ORF ($N = 86$, 95.60%), Spelling ($N = 59$, 66%), and GSRT ($N = 53$, 58.90%), emphasizing the need for more intensive and explicit instruction in special education classrooms (Snow et al., 1998; Adams, 1990; Chall, 1983, 1996).

CHALLENGES AND RTI IMPLEMENTATION ISSUES

Research on RTI implementation and treatment validity continues. To date, a majority of the research on multiple tiers of intervention has been implemented by researchers. Those of us with classroom experience, as well as research experience, understand the research to practice division far too well. As research on RTI continues, the need to examine RTI through school implementation in both urban and rural areas, as well as large and small school districts, is needed. Some guidance is available from schools that have already implemented RTI models for two decades in Iowa and Minnesota (Ikeda et al., 2007; Marston et al., 2007). The National Institute of Child Health and Development has funded four large multidisciplinary centers to examine RTI. Their findings may be followed on the following websites: for Colorado: http://ibgwww.colorado.edu/cldrc/olson.html, for Florida: http://www.fsuld.org/, for the Northeast: http://www.readingresearch.kennedykrieger.org/ldrc.html, and for Texas: http://www.texasldcenter.org/.

We close this chapter examining several areas of challenge for schools as RTI is implemented. Future research and implementation studies should provide additional guidance to schools in these areas.

Time Needed for Intervention

In both elementary and secondary schools, educators may struggle with finding instructional time for providing reading interventions, particularly Tier 3 interventions. However, schools that have implemented RTI models note the importance of providing sufficient amount of time for intervention at the elementary level. In Washington's Kennewick School District (Fielding, Kerr, & Rosier, 2007) where it has taken a decade to increase the proportion of third graders reading on a basic level from 74% to 90% within the District's 13 elementary schools, school leaders attributed their success to a school-wide commitment to change that is reflected in the following quotation: "Direct instructional time is proportional to their [children's] deficiency. The greater the need, the more time they get." (p. 25). Further, they caution that "catch up growth" requires more time and better quality instruction. Ikeda and colleagues cautioned that in *most* schools within the Iowa Heartland district, "interventions were not sufficiently rigorous to impact reading performance" (p. 265).

Finding the time to implement interventions is also even more of a scheduling challenge at middle school. Struggling readers may be placed in a resource Language Arts class, where it is difficult to provide remedial reading instruction and the Language Arts curriculum, or students could be provided the opportunity of voluntarily taking an extra period of reading instruction during an elective class (e.g., band, music, art) to supplement their English Language Arts class. Further exacerbating this time challenge, initial research suggests that even when these elective class sizes are kept small (e.g., five students), older struggling readers may require more time and more individualized instruction to accelerate learning outcomes (Calhoon et al., in press; Vaughn et al., in press). Therefore, meeting student literacy needs as well as content needs in all subjects is a particular challenge in the upper grades (Calhoon & Hunter, 2010).

Resources

In addition to time for intervention, securing intervention providers can be a challenge for many schools. Interventions using peer tutoring in general and special education classrooms or utilizing trained community volunteers (Calhoon, 2005; Calhoon et al., in press; Al Otaiba & Foorman, 2008) have shown promise for helping a substantial number of students reach grade-level outcomes, and subsequently at distinguishing responders and poor responders who need more intensive help (Calhoon, 2005; Calhoon et al., in press; Calhoon & Hunter, 2010; Swanson, 1999a, 1999b; Swanson & Hoskyn, 1998). Basic adult-tutoring and reciprocal-peer-tutoring, such as implemented with the TAILS and RAMP-UP programs procedures are cost-effective, feasible, and easily implemented. Thus, these intervention setups may be appropriate for implementation of the less-intensive Tier 2 interventions. However, there is a need to allocate specialized personnel who are highly trained to deliver well-implemented Tier 3 programs and more importantly to ensure that special education remains specialized.

Data-Based Interventions and Longitudinal Tracking of RTI

Marston et al. (2007), who have conducted RTI research in Minnesota's public schools, emphasized that even though progress-monitoring systems are now part of their school district's culture, there is a critical need at the school system level to connect data to interventions. There is a general agreement that RTI models should begin with "what works," in other words using evidence-based standard treatment protocols, but, if students make insufficient response, then intervention should be increasingly differentiated based on progress monitoring (Case, Speece, & Molloy, 2003; O'Connor et al., 2005; Speece & Case, 2001; Vaughn et al., 2003). Using data to address students' difficulties is a critical part of individualizing instruction through a formative or problem-solving fashion (Marston, Muyskens, Lau, & Canter, 2002; Reschly, Tilly, & Grimes, 1999). Further study is needed in school systems to help teachers use data to make instructional decisions for students with insufficient response to intervention. In addition, there is a dearth of information for schools to access in terms of how to setup databases and decision-making models that use data across grade levels to make appropriate decisions within an RTI model.

Need for Procedural Guidelines Regarding "Adequate" Response and Movement Across Tiers

There has been little agreement about what constitutes "adequate" response to instruction and intervention (Al Otaiba & Torgesen, 2007). This lack of agreement is an important issue because it determines who gets intervention and who does not. In the present chapter, we have focused on one method: normalization (following Torgesen, 2000, we considered students reading below the 85 standard score as not having normal or grade-level reading). In a recent paper, titled "What We Need to Know about Responsiveness to Intervention (and Shouldn't Be Afraid to Ask)," Fuchs and Deshler (2007) described normalization and four additional methods that researchers have used to define unresponsiveness: (1) median split in reading slope (e.g., Vellutino et al., 1996 calculated slopes of growth during treatment and students whose slope was below the median were considered unresponsive; (2) scoring below cut-points or end of year benchmarks (e.g., scores associated with "risk" on a criterion referenced progress-monitoring measures such as the Dynamic Indicators of Basic Early Literacy Skills or DIBELS measures used by Good, Simmons, & Kame'enui, 2001); (3) dual discrepancy (e.g., scores that are initially below a normative cut point and a treatment slope that is below that of a peer group as proposed by Fuchs and Fuchs, 1998); or (4) slope discrepancy (e.g., treatment slope below that of peer group used in Fuchs, Fuchs, & Compton, 2004). It is also a concern for the psychometric accuracy of RTI as a means of identifying students with LD because each method may identify different children as needing help (Al Otaiba et al., 2008; Schatschneider, Wagner, & Crawford, 2008).

Furthermore, none of these methods have yet been replicated in middle schools, so even less is known about defining unresponsiveness or selecting appropriate dosages/levels of intensity. Thus, schools have little guidance about "what works" or even if it works, what proportion of students are likely to respond, etc. We argue that students at the middle school level may often need more than one dose of remedial reading (more than 1 year), particularly if the goal is to help them read fluently enough to independently comprehend grade-level reading.

In summary, knowledge is growing about RTI implementation both in terms of prevention and remediation, but more knowledge is needed to ensure its treatment validity. We are reminded of the concern Scruggs and Mastropieri (2002) conveyed regarding eliminating one system of identifying learning disabilities for another in "On Babies and Bathwater: Addressing the Problems of Identification of Learning Disabilities." At this time, as RTI implementation is rapidly scaling up, we echo their concern; certainly more research is needed to continue to tackle the major issues of identification of learning disabilities within this RTI framework, namely overidentification, variability, and specificity.

ACKNOWLEDGMENT

This work was supported in part by (a) a Multidisciplinary Learning Disabilities Center Grant P50HD052120 from the Eunice Kennedy Shriver National Institute of Child Health and Human Development and (b) a grant from the Eunice Kennedy Shriver National Institute of Child Health and Human Development Grant 1 RO3HD048988.

REFERENCES

Abbott, S. P., & Berninger, V. W. (1999). It's never too late to remediate: Teaching word recognition to students with reading disabilities in grades 4–7. *Annals of Dyslexia*, *49*, 223–250.

Adams, M. J. (1990). *Beginning reading instruction in the United States*. Washington, DC: Office of Educational Research and Improvement.

AIMSweb: Progress Monitoring and RTI System. (2009). http://www.aimsweb.com. PsychCorp; TX: Pearson Publishing.

Allinder, R. M., Dunse, L., Brunken, C. D., & Obermiller-Krolikowski, H. J. (2001). Improving fluency in at-risk readers and students with learning disabilities. *Remedial and Special Education*, *22*(1), 48–54.

Al Otaiba, S., Connor, C., Petscher, Y., Greulich, L., Folsom, J., & Meadows, J. (2008). Response to kindergarten reading instruction. Paper presented at the Annual Society for the Scientific Study of Reading Conference, Asheville, NC.

Al Otaiba, S., & Foorman, B. (2008). Early literacy instruction and intervention. *Community Literacy Journal*, *3*, 21–37.

Al Otaiba, S., Schatschneider, C., & Silverman, E. (2005). *Tutor assisted intensive learning strategies in kindergarten: How much is enough? Exceptionality*, *13*(4), 195–208.

Al Otaiba, S., & Torgesen, J. (2007). Effects from intensive standardized kindergarten and first grade interventions for the prevention of reading difficulties. In: S. R. Jimerson, M. K. Burns & A. M. Van der Heyden (Eds), *The handbook of response to intervention: The science and practice of assessment and intervention* (pp. 212–222). New York: Springer.

Baker, S., Gersten, R., & Scanlon, D. (2002). Procedural facilitators and cognitive strategies: Tools for unraveling the mysteries of comprehension and the writing process, and for providing meaningful access to the general curriculum. *Learning Disabilities Research & Practice*, *17*(1), 65–77.

Bat-Hayim, M. L. (1997). Learning to learn: Learning therapy in a college classroom. *Annals of Dyslexia*, *47*, 203–240.

Batsche, G. M., Curtis, M. J., Dorman, C., Castillo, J. M., & Porter, L. J. (2007). The Florida Problem-Solving/Response to Intervention Model: Implementing a statewide initiative. In: S. R. Jimerson, M. K. Burns & A. M. VanDerHeyden (Eds), *Handbook of response to intervention* (pp. 378–395). New York: Springer.

Beck, I. L., & Juel, C. (1995). The role of decoding in learning to read. In: Consortium on Reading Excellence (Eds), *Reading research: Anthology, The Why? of reading instruction* (pp. 78–87). Novato, CA: Arena Press.

Beck, I. L., McKeown, M. G., & Kucan, L. (2002). *Bringing words to life: Robust vocabulary instruction*. New York: The Guilford Press.

Calhoon, M. B. (2003). *Reading Achievement Multi-Modular Program (RAMP-UP)*. Unpublished manual.

Calhoon, M. B. (2005). Effects of a peer-mediated phonological skill and reading comprehension program on reading skill acquisition of middle school students with reading disabilities. *Journal of Learning Disabilities, 38*(5), 424–433.

Calhoon, M. B. & Hunter, C. V. (2010). Delivering remedial reading instruction using two versions of the reading achievement multi-component Program (RAMP-UP). Manuscript in preparation.

Calhoon, M. B., Sandow, A., & Hunter, C. V. (in press). Re-organizing the instructional reading components: Could there be a better way to design remedial reading programs to maximize middle school students with reading disabilities' response to treatment? *Annals of Dyslexia*.

Carnine, D. W., Silbert, J., & Kame'enui, E. J. (1997). *Direct instruction reading*. New York: Prentice Hall.

Carnine, D. W., Silbert, J., Kame'enui, E. J., & Tarver, S. G. (2004). *Direct reading instruction* (4th ed.). New Jersey: Merrill Prentice Hall.

Carreker, S. (2005). Spelling instruction: Foundation of reading and ornament of writing. *Perspectives, 31*(3), 22–25.

Case, L. P., Speece, D. L., & Molloy, D. E. (2003). The validity of a response-to-instruction paradigm to identify reading disabilities: A longitudinal analysis of individual differences and contextual factors. *School Psychology Review, 32*, 557–582.

Chall, J. S. (1983). *Stages of reading development*. New York: McGraw-Hill.

Chall, J. S. (1996). *Stages of reading development* (2nd ed.). Fort Worth, TX: Hartcourt Brace.

deBettencourt, L. U., Zigmond, N., & Thorton, H. S. (1989). Follow-up of postsecondary age-rural learning disabled graduates and dropouts. *Exceptional Children, 56*, 40–49.

Deno, S. L., Fuchs, L. S., Marston, D., & Shin, J. (2001). Using curriculum-based measurement to establish growth standards for students with learning disabilities. *School Psychology Review, 30*(4), 507–524.

Edmonds, M. S., Vaughn, S., Wexler, J., Reutebuch, C., Cable, A., Tackett, K. K., & Schnakenberg, J. W. (2009). A synthesis of reading interventions and effects on reading comprehension outcomes for older struggling readers. *Review of Educational Research, 79*, 262–300.

Elbaum, B., Vaughn, S., Hughes, M. T., & Moody, S. W. (2000). How effective are one-to-one tutoring programs in reading for elementary students at risk for reading failure? A meta-analysis of the intervention research. *Journal of Educational Psychology, 92*(4), 605–619.

Fielding, L., Kerr, N., & Rosier, P. (2007). *Annual growth for all students, catch-up growth for those who are behind*. Kennewick, WA: The New Foundation.

Fletcher, J. M., & Foorman, B. R. (1994). Issues in definition and measurement of learning disabilities: The need for early intervention. In: G. R. Lyon (Ed.), *Frames of reference for the assessment of learning disabilities: New views on measurement issues* (pp. 185–200). Baltimore, MD: Paul H. Brookes.

Francis, D. J., Shaywitz, S. E., Stuebing, K. K., Shaywitz, B. A., & Fletcher, J. M. (1996). Developmental lag versus deficit model of reading disability: A longitudinal, individual growth curve analysis. *Journal of Educational Psychology, 88*, 3–17.

Fuchs, D., & Deshler, D. D. (2007). What we need to know about responsiveness to intervention (and shouldn't be afraid to ask). *Learning Disabilities Research & Practice, 22*(2), 129–136.

Fuchs, L. S., & Fuchs, D. (1998). Treatment validity: A unifying concept for reconceptualizing the identification of learning disabilities. *Learning Disabilities Research and Practice, 13*, 204–219.

Fuchs, L. S., Fuchs, D., & Compton, D. L. (2004). Monitoring early reading development in first grade: Word identification fluency versus nonsense word fluency. *Exceptional Children, 71*, 7–22.

Fuchs, D., Fuchs, L. S., Mathes, P. G., & Simmons, D. C. (1997). Peer-assisted leaning strategies: Making classroom more responsive to academic diversity. *The American Educational Research Journal, 34*, 174–206.

Fuchs, L. S., Fuchs, D., Phillips, N. B., Hamlett, C. L., & Karns, K. (1995). Acquisition and transfer effects of class wide peer students with varying leaning histories. *School Psychology Review, 24*(4), 604–620.

Fuchs, L. S., Fuchs, D., & Speece, D. L. (2002). Treatment validity as a unifying construct for identifying learning disabilities. *Learning Disability Quarterly, 25*(1), 33–45.

Gersten, R., Williams, J. P., Fuchs, L., Baker, S., Koppenhaver, D., Spadorcia, S., & Harrison, M. (1998). *Improving reading comprehension for children with disabilities: A review of research.* Final Report. Washington, DC: Special Education Programs (ED/OSERS).

Good, R. H., III., Simmons, D. C., & Kame'enui, E. J. (2001). The importance and decision-making utility of a continuum of fluency-based indicators of foundational reading skills for third-grade high-stakes outcomes. *Scientific Studies of Reading, 5*(3), 257–288.

Gunn, B., Biglan, A., Smolkowski, K., & Ary, D. (2000). The efficacy of supplemental instruction in decoding skills for Hispanic and Non-Hispanic students in early elementary school. *Journal of Special Education, 34*(2), 90–103.

Gunn, B., Smolkowski, K., Biglan, A., & Black, C. (2002). Supplemental instruction in decoding skills for Hispanic and Non-Hispanic students in early elementary school: A follow-up. *Journal of Special Education, 36*(2), 69–79.

Hanushek, E. A., Kain, J. F., & Rivkin, S. G. (1998). *Does special education raise academic achievement for students with disabilities?* Working Paper No. 6690, National Bureau of Economic Research, Cambridge, MA.

Ikeda, M. J., Rahn-Blakeslee, A., Niebling, B. C., Gustafson, J. K., Allison, R., & Stumme, J. (2007). The heartland area education agency 11 problem-solving approach: An overview and lessons learned. In: S. R. Jimerson, M. K. Burns & A. M. VanDerHeyden (Eds), *Handbook of response to intervention: The science and practice of assessment and intervention* (pp. 255–268). New York: Springer.

Individuals with Disabilities Educational Improvement Act (2004). Pub. L. No. 108-446 § 614 [b][6][A]; § 614 [b][2 & 3].

Jenkins, J., & O'Connor, R. (2002). Early identification and intervention for young children with reading/learning disabilities. Executive summary. Washington, DC: Special Education Programs (ED/OSERS), ERIC ED458757.

Jenkins, J. R., Peyton, J. A., Sanders, E. A., & Vadasy, P. F. (2004). Effects of reading decodable texts in supplemental first-grade tutoring. *Scientific Studies of Reading*, *8*(1), 53–85.

Jimerson, S. R., Burns, M. K., & Van Der Heyden, A. M. (Eds). (2007). *Handbook of response to intervention: The science and practice of assessment and intervention*. New York: Springer.

Juel, C. (1988). Learning to read and write: A longitudinal study of 54 children from first through fourth grades. *Journal of Educational Psychology*, *80*, 437–447.

Juel, C. (1996). What makes literacy tutoring effective? *Reading Research Quarterly*, *31*(3), 268–289.

Kennedy, M. M., Birman, B. F., & Demaline, R. E. (1986). *The effectiveness of Chapter I services*. Washington, DC: Office of Educational Research and Improvement, U.S. Department of Education.

Klingner, J. K., Vaughn, S., Hughes, M. T., Schumm, J. S., & Elbaum, B. E. (1998). Outcomes for students with and without learning disabilities in inclusive classrooms. *Learning Disabilities Research & Practice*, *13*, 153–161.

Lonigan, C. J., Anthony, J. L., Bloomfield, B. G., Dyer, S. M., & Samwel, C. S. (1999). Effects of two shared-reading interventions on emergent literacy skills of at-risk preschoolers. *Journal of Early Intervention*, *22*(4), 306–322.

Marston, D., Muyskens, P., Lau, M., & Canter, A. (2002). Problem solving model for decision-making with high-incidence disabilities: The Minneapolis experience. *Learning Disabilities Research and Practice*, *18*(3), 187–200.

Marston, D., Pickart, M., Reschly, A., Heistad, D., Muyskens, P., & Tindal, G. (2007). Early literacy measures for improving student reading achievement: Translating research into practice. *Exceptionality*, *15*(2), 97–117.

Mastropieri, M., & Scruggs, T. E. (1996). Current trends in science education: Implications for special education. In: M. C. Pugach & C. L. Warger (Eds), *Curriculum trends, special education, and reform: Refocusing the curriculum* (pp. 42–52). New York: Teachers College.

Mathes, P. G., Denton, C. A., Fletcher, J. M., Anthony, J. L., Francis, D. J., & Schatschneider, C. (2005). The effects of theoretically different instruction and student characteristics on the skills of struggling readers. *Reading Research Quarterly*, *40*(2), 148–182.

McCardle, P., & Chhabra, V. (Eds). (2004). *The voice of evidence in reading research*. Baltimore, MD: Brookes Publishing Company.

McIntosh, R., Vaughn, S. R., Schumm, J. S., Haager, D., & Lee, O. (1993). Observations of students with learning disabilities in general education classrooms. *Exceptional Children*, *60*(3), 249–261.

Moody, S. W., Vaughn, S. R., Hughes, M. Y., & Fisher, M. (2000). Reading instruction in the resource room: Set up for failure. *Exceptional Children*, *16*, 305–316.

Morgan, P. L., & Fuchs, D. (2007). Is there a bidirectional relationship between children's reading skills and reading motivation? *Exceptional Children*, *73*(2), 165–183.

Morris, D., Tyner, B., & Perney, J. (2000). Early steps: Replicating the effects of a first-grade reading intervention program. *Journal of Educational Psychology*, *92*(4), 681–693.

National Assessment of Educational Progress. (2007). The nation's report card. Washington DC: National Center for Education Statistics.

National Reading Panel. (2000). Report of the National Reading Panel. Washington, DC: National Institute of Child Health and Development (www.nationalreadingpanel.org).

O'Connor, R. E., Fulmer, D., Harty, K. R., & Bell, K. M. (2005). Layers of reading intervention in kindergarten through third grade: Changes in teaching and student outcomes. *Journal of Learning Disabilities*, *39*, 440–456.

Reschly, D. J., Tilly, W. D., III, & Grimes, J. P. (Eds). (1999). *Special education in transition: Functional assessment and noncategorical programming*.

Ryan, R. M. (1982). Control and information in the interpersonal sphere: An extension of cognitive evaluation theory. *Journal of Personality and Social Psychology*, *43*, 450–461.

Samuels, S. J., Schermer, N., & Reinking, D. (1992). Reading fluency: Techniques for making decoding automatic. In: S. J. Samuels & A. E. Farstrup (Eds), *What research says about reading instruction* (2nd ed., pp. 124–144). Newark, DE: International Reading Association.

Schatschneider, C., Wagner, R. K., & Crawford, E. C. (2008). The importance of measuring growth in response to intervention models: Testing a core assumption. *Learning and Individual Differences*, *18*, 308–315.

Scruggs, T. E., & Mastropieri, M. A. (2002). On babies and bathwater: Addressing the problems of identification of learning disabilities. *Learning Disability Quarterly*, *25*, 155–168.

Simmons, L. (2001). *Saxon phonics intervention*. Norman, OK: Saxon Publishers.

Snow, C. E. (2002). *Reading for understanding: Toward an R&D program in reading comprehension*. Arlington, VA: RAND.

Snow, C. E., Burns, M. S., & Griffin, P. (Eds). (1998). *Preventing reading difficulties in young children*. Washington, DC: National Academy Press.

Speece, D. L., & Case, L. P. (2001). Classification in context: An alternative approach to identifying early reading disability. *Journal of Educational Psychology*, *93*, 735–749.

Stahl, S. A., Heubach, K., & Cramond, B. (1997). *Fluency-oriented reading instruction (Reading Research 790)*. Athens, GA: National Reading Research Center.

Swanson, E. A. (2008). Observing reading instruction for students with learning disabilities: A synthesis. *Learning Disability Quarterly*, *31*, 115–131.

Swanson, H. L. (1999a). Instructional components that predict treatment outcomes for students with learning disabilities: Support for a combined strategy and direct instruction model. *Learning Disabilities Research & Practice*, *14*(3), 129–140.

Swanson, H. L. (1999b). Reading research for students with LD: A meta-analysis of intervention outcomes. *Journal of Learning Disabilities*, *32*, 504–532.

Swanson, H. J., & Hoskyn, M. (1998). A synthesis of experimental intervention literature for students with learning disabilities: A meta-analysis of treatment outcomes. *Review of Educational Research*, *68*, 271–321.

Templeton, S., & Morris, D. (1999). Questions teachers ask about spelling. *Reading Research Quarterly*, *34*, 102–112.

Torgesen, J. K. (2000). Individual differences in response to early interventions in reading: The lingering problem of treatment resisters. *Learning Disabilities Research and Practice*, *15*, 55–64.

Torgesen, J. K., Wagner, R. K., & Rashotte, C. A. (1997). Prevention and remediation of severe reading disabilities: Keeping the end in mind. *Scientific Studies of Reading*, *1*(3), 217–234.

Torgesen, J. K., Wagner, R. K., Rashotte, C. A., Lindamood, P., Rose, E., Conway, T., & Garvan, C. (1999). Preventing reading failure in young children with phonological processing disabilities: Group and individual responses to instruction. *Journal of Educational Psychology*, *91*, 579–593.

Vadasy, P. F., Sanders, E. A., & Peyton, J. A. (2005). Relative effectiveness of reading practice or word-level instruction in supplemental tutoring: How text matters. *Journal of Learning Disabilities*, *38*(4), 364–380.

Vadasy, P. F., Sanders, E. A., Peyton, J. A., & Jenkins, J. R. (2002). Timing and intensity of tutoring: A closer look at the conditions for effective early literacy tutoring. *Learning Disabilities: Research & Practice*, *17*(4), 227–241.

Vaughn, S., Wanzek, J., Wexler, J., Barth, A., Cirino, P. T., Fletcher, J. et al. (in press). The relative effects of group size on reading progress of older students with reading difficulties. *Reading and Writing: An Interdisciplinary Journal*.

Vaughn, S., Gersten, R., & Chard, D. J. (2000). The underlying message in LD intervention research. *Council for Exceptional Children*, *67*, 99–114.

Vaughn, S., & Klinger, J. K. (1998). Students' perceptions of inclusion and resource room settings. *Journal of Special Education*, *32*, 79–88.

Vaughn, S., Linan-Thompson, S., & Hickman, P. (2003). Response to instruction as a means of identifying students with learning/reading disabilities. *Exceptional Children*, *69*, 391–409.

Vaughn, S., Moody, S. W., & Schumm, J. S. (1998). Broken promises: Reading instruction in the resource room. *Exceptional Children*, *64*, 211–225.

Vellutino, F. R., Scanlon, D. M., Sipay, E. R., Small, S., Chen, R., Pratt, A., & Denckla, M. B. (1996). Cognitive profiles of difficult-to-remediate and readily remediated poor readers: Early intervention as a vehicle for distinguishing between cognitive and experiential deficits as basic causes of specific reading disability. *Journal of Educational Psychology*, *88*, 601–638.

Vogel, S. A., & Forness, S. R. (1992). Social functioning in adults with learning disabilities. *School Psychology Review*, *21*(3), 375–386.

Wanzek, J., & Vaughn, S. (2007). Research-base implications from extensive early reading interventions. *School Psychology Review*, *36*(4), 541–561.

Wiederholt, J. L., & Blalock, G. (2000). *Gray Silent Reading Test*. Austin, TX: Pro-Ed.

Woodcock, R. W., McGrew, K. S., & Mather, N. (2001). *Woodcock-Johnson III*. Itasca, IL: Riverside Publishing.

Zigmond, N., & Baker, J. M. (1995). Concluding comments: Current and future practices in inclusive schooling. *Journal of Special Education*, *29*(2), 178245–250.

Zigmond, N., Jenkins, J., Fuchs, L. S., Deno, S., Fuchs, D., Baker, J. N., et al. (1995). Special education in restructured schools: Findings from three multi-year studies. *Phi Delta Kappan*, *76*, 531–540.

THE ROLE OF CONTEXT IN THE ASSESSMENT OF "UNRESPONSIVENESS" WITHIN RESPONSIVENESS-TO-INTERVENTION: THE "RELATIVE SLOPE-DIFFERENCE DISCREPANCY MODEL" (RSDDM)

Georgios D. Sideridis, Susana Padeliadu and Faye Antoniou

ABSTRACT

*The purpose of the present study was to evaluate the role of context in the identification of learning disabilities (LD) within the responsiveness-to-intervention (RTI) model. In Study 1, using a sample of students with and without LD (*N = *167) and data from a reading assessment, we tested whether the decision making regarding literacy disabilities is significantly different if we take into account variability within the schools and school characteristics. Initially a logistic multilevel model was fit to the data to assess prevalence rates of LD identification. The validity of these*

Literacy and Learning
Advances in Learning and Behavioral Disabilities, Volume 23, 29–59

ISSN: 0735-004X/doi:10.1108/S0735-004X(2010)0000023004

estimates was substantiated by bootstrapping the sample's parameters using 1,000 replications and by evidencing negligible bias parameters. Subsequently, the relationship between reading ability and LD identification was established by means of a multilevel model including random effects. The significant slopes linking reading to LD identification (i.e., fluency and overall reading ability ratings by teachers) were predicted by cross-level interactions involving schools' location (rural, urban, and suburban). The results of Study 1 demonstrated the moderating role of school context, as the slopes linking fluency and reading achievement to LD placement were moderated by the area in which a school was located. Study 2 was designed to present a relative discrepancy identification model by taking into account information from the school (i.e., district). Using 29 students from one district, whose writing ability was evaluated three times within the semester, comparisons were made between a specific low-ability student and the rest of his/her class. Through fitting a multilevel model in which within-student and between-student variance was assessed, Study 2 demonstrated that the specific pattern of responsiveness of a target student can be tested against the norm of his/her school district in order to have a more sensitive relative criterion of what constitutes both responsiveness and the norm. Thus, by utilizing a multilevel framework that involves school characteristics into our assessment we demonstrated that decision making is much more informative and likely more "accurate" under the RTI model. Certainly more research is needed to verify the usefulness and applicability of the proposed "relative slope-difference discrepancy model."

The most important attribute one can possess at school is achievement. Achievement has the most important implications regarding one's academic and social standings, his/her psychological functioning (acceptance, rejection), etc., particularly so for students with learning disabilities (LD; Elias, 2004; Elksnin & Elksnin, 2004; Greenway & Milne, 1999; Grolnick & Ryan, 1990). Thus, decision making with regard to the presence or absence of LD has implications regarding one's functioning and well-being (Filippatou, Dimitropoulou, & Sideridis, 2009; Heath & Ross, 2000). The thesis of the present paper is to contribute information that may be useful in the valid identification of students with learning and other disabilities, particularly within the responsiveness-to-intervention (RTI) model (Ehren & Nelson, 2005; Fuchs, Mock, Morgan, & Young, 2003). Specifically the present paper will deal with the "unresponsiveness" aspect of the RTI model by presenting issues that affect responsiveness and a proposal to accommodate those issues.

IDENTIFICATION OF LEARNING DISABILITIES: THE RESPONSIVENESS-TO-INTERVENTION (RTI) MODEL

Historically, the IQ-achievement discrepancy posits that learning disabled students have a significant academic deficit, which is demonstrated by a significant discrepancy between a student's expected ability (for his/her age) and his/her actual ability, as demonstrated using normative criteria. This model has been with the field of LD for more than 30 years (since P.L. 94-142) and has been criticized on several grounds and for some has outlived its usefulness (for analytical discussions and critiques see Fletcher et al., 1998; Francis et al., 2005; Scruggs & Mastropieri, 2002).

Recently, the field has moved toward a noncategorical classification system that defines LD as an inadequate response to documented effective instruction (called the responsiveness-to-intervention (RTI) model; e.g., Fuchs & Fuchs, 2006; Fuchs et al., 2007; Hollenbeck, 2007). Specifically, the IDEA reauthorization (2004) suggested that "a local educational agency may use a process that determines if a child responds to scientific research-based intervention as a part of the evaluation procedures." (20 USC §§1400). The essence of this model is to rule out the hypothesis that poor instruction is accountable for low achievement (Burns, Appleton, & Stehouwer, 2005; Fuchs, Fuchs, & Hollenbeck, 2007; Sampson, Faggella-Luby, & Fritschmann, 2005). Fuchs et al. described that the RTI has two goals: (a) to classify students as having LD based on their inability to respond to effective instruction and (b) to provide effective instruction to students who need it, as early as possible. Based on the RTI model, a student is initially selected based on "unresponsiveness," that is, his/her inability to demonstrate adequate growth in academic subjects using Tier-1, traditional (effective) instruction (Mastropieri & Scruggs, 2005; Mellard, Byrd, Johnson, Tollefson, & Boesche, 2004). Subsequently, that student is subjected to a set of educational practices that have proved to be effective and his/her academic behavior is evaluated systematically with the expectation that the intensive instruction will lead to improved academic outcomes (Tier-2; see Marston, 2005). If this practice is yet not effective, then the student moves toward more intensive and systematic instruction in order to improve

(Tier-3 instruction; see Vaughn, Linan-Thompson, & Hickman, 2003). Lack of responding following Tier-3 would likely signal the presence of an LD.

However, with regard to the RTI, there is at least one important question posited by Compton (2006), "What type of criteria should be used to identify children who do not respond to validated secondary intervention?" (p. 170). The answer to this important question has implications regarding who, among students, will receive intensive instruction, how long will that instruction last, when it should take place, when it will be discontinued, and what criteria will signal discontinuation of the applied intervention. This concern is discussed in detail below.

How Is "Unresponsiveness" Evaluated?

What is the golden criterion, deviation from which constitutes a significant deficit? Should it be (a) the deviation between a child's score from his/her previous performance (Berninger & Abbott, 1994), (b) the deviation between a student's performance and the mean or slope of his/her class, (c) the deviation between a student's performance and the mean or slope of his/her school (See Fig. 1[1]), (d) the deviation of a student's performance from the norms (grand mean), (e) the deviation of a student's performance from an average based on an elaborate weighted model that involves personal and situational parameters, (f) the deviation between a student's performance and a specific learning profile, or (g) the meeting of critical benchmarks[2] (Good et al., 2001)? We believe that all of the above concerns *should* be placed within an ecological framework that takes into account information from the school itself.

For example, what would happen to a student whose performance is at the lowest 10th percentile among students in his/her school (School B, Fig. 2) and how would his/her performance be evaluated and judged if the same student were educated in a low-achievement school (School A)? Obviously, there would be a significantly lower probability for a low-achieving student in a high-ability school to be identified as having LD compared to the (high) probability of identification in the high-achieving school. Similarly, an average-ability student in a low-achieving school would have a high probability of being identified as having LD in a high-ability school. This concern is not addressed currently within the RTI, as information about the school or setting in which a student is educated are not weighted upon. Unfortunately, schools within or across districts may be very different not only at their mean level but also in their rate of

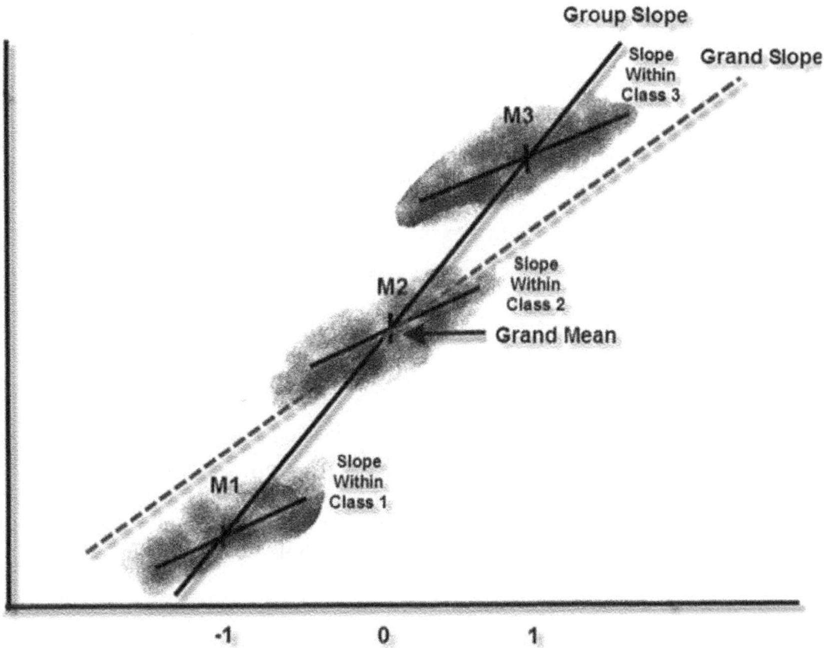

Fig. 1. The effects of type of centering on the prediction of a school outcome. Schools have equal slopes but differ in their mean levels.

growth in a given academic subject (see slopes of two different-ability schools in Fig. 3).

Currently, several important models have been proposed, but none of them involves (or weighs) information from the school or school district regarding students with LD identification or classification. For example, Fuchs and Fuchs (1998) have proposed the "dual discrepancy" model in which evaluations are based on both growth (slope of improvement) and mean-level improvement at the end of a treatment (see also Burns & Senesac, 2005). Torgesen et al. (2001) used standard scores (e.g., 10th percentiles) as a means of differentiation using normative assessments. Fuchs, Fuchs, and Compton (2004) proposed the "slope discrepancy" model in which academic achievement is measured periodically and then evaluated against a predefined standard. Good et al. (2001) suggested the need to meet specific learning milestones (benchmarks) that need to be defined both empirically and theoretically. Last, Vellutino et al. (1996) proposed a median split model in comparing the growth of a target student to the mean slope of his/her class.

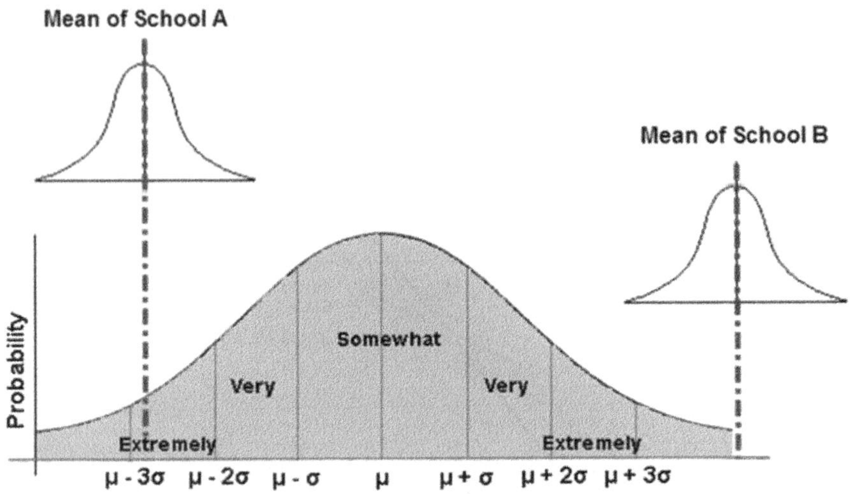

Fig. 2. Two examples of schools, a low-achieving (School A) and a high-achieving (School B) from the population of schools within a state.

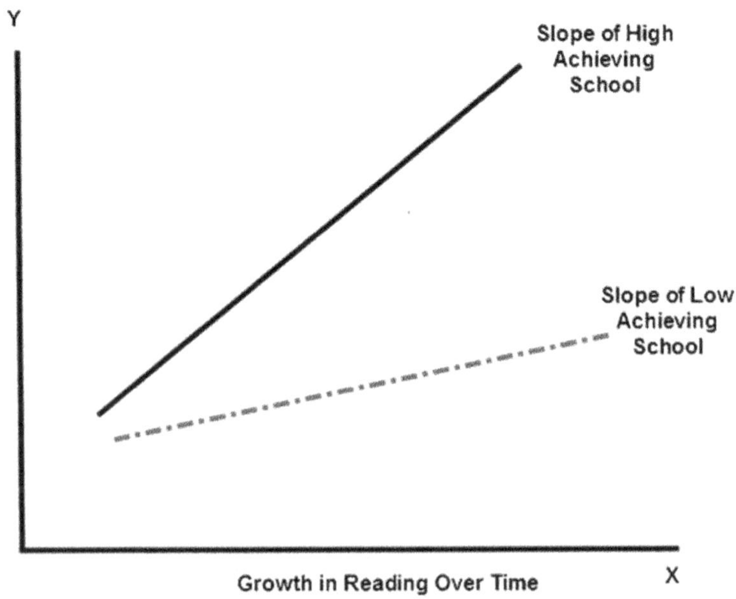

Fig. 3. Two examples of schools, a low-achieving and a high-achieving from the perspective of growth differences in reading.

Although the above models did not explicitly state inclusion of information from the school or district, several of the above researchers have commented on the need to do so. For example, Fuchs and Deshler (2007) suggested that the point of reference could potentially be a mean that would be computed from a data pool (norm) defined by same age peers from the same school or district (or nation) using multiple curriculum-based measurements (CBMs). Mastropieri and Scruggs (2005) raised concerns about the consistency of decision making across schools, districts, and states, and similar concerns were raised by Kavale, Holdnack and Mostert (2005) as an explanation of the different identification rates across states (see also Johnson, Mellard, & Byrd, 2005). The above concerns could be addressed using an ecological approach to LD identification.

The Importance of Context: An Ecological Perspective to the Identification of Learning Disabilities

Dean, Burns, Grialou, and Varro (2006) stated that "When considering a classification of LD and the need for special education services it would seem that more than the specific achievement standards within a given school or district should be taken into account to warrant the descriptor of ecological" (p. 161). Thus, an ecological approach may be particularly valuable in order to make the most informal decisions. According to the ecological perspective (Bronfenbrenner, 1986), in order to understand a child's behavior one needs to take into account all parameters of the child's environment (home, school, community, culture, etc.).

Within the school, for example, it is important to understand that a student's achievement is a function of the activities taking place in that school. For example, the provision of ample practice and reinforcement by teachers, the implementation of effective practices, adherence to the curriculum, the ability of teachers to manage challenging behaviors or keep a fast-paced lesson are only some factors that explain the achievement levels of the students. This is one explanation why classrooms and schools vary in their achievement level. That is, specific differences in context are likely accountable for the observed differences in mean achievement. Does it then make sense to evaluate students in the absence of context?

The Relative Achievement Discrepancy Model (Peterson & Shinn, 2002)

The purpose of the relative achievement discrepancy (RAD) model is to take into account information from the district or the school in order to make informed decisions about placement and identification. Peterson and Shinn (2002) described the (RAD) model as a means of drawing inferences about what constitutes deficient achievement by using information from a student's district or school (see also Deno, 1989; Shinn, 2002).

Peterson and Shinn (2002) added that there is no information about the adequacy of the RAD model. However, there is another consideration that may contribute to the need to adapt an RAD model. That consideration pertains to the regression to the mean phenomenon (Labouvie, 1982; Nesselorade, Stigler, & Baltes, 1980). Based on that model, individuals' repeated assessments of a construct tend to cluster around the mean of their (representative) distribution. In other words, students who lie further away from the mean tend to come closer with repeated testing. Thus, based on that consideration it is likely that students who are educated in a low-achieving school would likely cluster around the mean of their distribution and that effect would contribute to increased differences between schools. This consideration further strengthens the need to take into account the variability between classrooms, schools, or districts and the use of relative criteria in the identification of LD.

Purpose

The purpose of the present studies was twofold. First, to evaluate how context affects decision making regarding identification of LD, and secondly to propose an RAD model that would assist in defining "unresponsiveness," within the RTI model. Specifically, Study 1 tested the importance of educational context in drawing conclusions regarding deficits in achievement. Study 2 attempted to expand on the RAD (Peterson & Shinn, 2002) by presenting a multilevel model that would use "relative" achievement criteria in order to define "unresponsiveness" in LD.

Specifically, Study 1 attempted to provide answers to the following research questions:

1. What are prevalence rates of LD?
2. Are the prevalence rates of LD predicted by students' actual reading ability and teacher ratings of that ability?
3. Is the relationship (slope) between reading ability and LD identification moderated by the area in which a school is located?

STUDY 1: METHOD

Participants and Procedures

Participants were 167 students, out of which 149 were typical and 18 had been diagnosed as having LD through a state diagnostic team. There were 75 boys and 92 girls. All students came from state schools and identification of LD was based on the discrepancy between ability and achievement. Students came from general education/inclusive classrooms and were from grades 1 to 9 (elementary = 124, junior high school = 43). Students were Caucasian and represented three different nationalities. There were also 15 students who were bilingual.

Measures

Learning Disabilities Screening Scale for Teachers

Primary and secondary school educators who were well acquainted with students' skills and achievement were asked to fill in the Learning Disabilities Screening Scale for Teachers (Padeliadu & Sideridis, 2008). The educators rated 116 behaviors based on frequency (9-point Likert-type scale where 1 = always and 9 = never). The behaviors represented the following academic subjects: listening, speaking, reasoning, reading, writing, and mathematics. Each subscale contained 17–20 items representing the multidimensional nature of the problems that students with LD face as defined from the National Joint Committee on Learning Disabilities (see Hammill, 1990). For example, in reading, educators rate behaviors related not only to decoding, fluency, and comprehension, but also to reading comprehension strategy use (cognitive and metacognitive). For the present study's purposes, however, only the reading scale was used. Its internal consistency estimate was equal to 0.995.

Tests of Reading Achievement

Five constructs, related to decoding, fluency, morphology, syntax, and comprehension, comprised the reading instrument. This reading test was similar in principle and concept to the existing Test of Reading Performance (TORP; Padeliadu & Sideridis, 2000). The difference is that all items corresponded to the lexical, morphological, and syntactical level of each grade (3rd–9th).

Decoding

The ability of decoding is based on the usage of the orthographic and phonological strategy (dual-route hypothesis; Castles & Coltheart, 1993) as well as on semantic knowledge (Perfetti & Hart, 2001). Therefore, three subtests were implemented in order to evaluate the threefold elements of decoding. These subtests were the following.

Word Decoding. A list of 53 words, presented in ascending difficulty, assessed students' orthographic ability (Griffiths & Snowling, 2002) to correctly decode words with a meaning. These words ranged between 1 and 8 syllables. Students were asked to read aloud the real words. Any decoding errors such as missing or added letters/syllables, word replacements, and/or incorrect stressing were scored with a 0, while phonologically correctly read words were scored with a 1. A discontinuation rule involved five consecutive errors. The internal consistency (Cronbach's alpha) estimate of the scale was equal to 0.831.

Pseudoword Decoding. A list of 24 pseudowords, presented in ascending difficulty, assessed students' phonological strategy (Share & Stanovich, 1995) while decoding words without meaning. Syllables in pseudowords varied from 1 to 6. Students were asked to read the pseudowords accurately and to stress them appropriately. When students read items incorrectly (i.e., made mistakes in stressing, missed or added letters/syllables, and/or replaced part of the word that reminded them of an existing word) they received the score of 0; correct reading was linked to a score of 1. The discontinuation rule involved also five consecutive errors. Internal consistency (Cronbach's alpha) of the scale was 0.799.

Word and Pseudoword Decoding. In order to find out the amount that vocabulary knowledge supported decoding, students were asked to read aloud only the words with meaning derived from a pool of mixed words and pseudowords. Students had to correctly choose and decode aloud only the 18 words with meaning included within 32 items, which were presented in rows including 3 to 5 words and pseudowords. For each correctly chosen word, students were given 1 point, whereas a 0 signaled a failed item. Alpha reliability was 0.898.

Reading Fluency

Students were presented with an unfamiliar expository text of 279 words and were asked to read the words as accurately and fast as they could for one minute. After the lapse of time, students' score was evaluated by adding the words read correctly. For this construct, alpha reliability was 0.928.

Morphology and Syntax
Two grammar and two syntax subtests were included in the reading measure (Carlisle, 2003). Students were asked to transform words included in brackets into the correct grammatical form (the first two subtests) or to put words in the right order by the help of a picture (the last two subtests). Correct responses were given 1 point, and incorrect 0 point. The internal consistency of the construct was 0.754.

Comprehension
Reading comprehension was evaluated by two subtests. The first subtest included four groups of sentences and students were asked to find the two sentences in the group with the same meaning. The passages for the second reading comprehension exercise were one narrative and two expository texts ranging from 97 to 127 words and of ascending difficulty. Seven questions corresponded to each text and measured the three types of the reading comprehension question taxonomy of Pearson and Johnson (1978): textually explicit, textually implicit, and scriptually implicit. All right responses were scored with 1 point while all wrong responses were scored with 0. The stopping rule involved five errors in responding to questions. The internal consistency of reading comprehension was equal to 0.957 based on Cronbach's alpha.

Demographics of School
Schools were identified by the area in which they were located (rural, suburban, urban) based on data from the national statistics agency. There were 103 schools located in urban areas, 27 in suburban, and 37 in rural areas.

Statistical Analyses

Multilevel random coefficient modeling (MRCM) was implemented to aid diagnostic decision making (Bryk & Raudenbush, 1992; Choi, 2001; Kreft & de Leeuw, 1998; Roberts, 2004; Shin, Espin, Deno, & McConnell, 2004). We evaluated whether identification of a child as having an LD would relate to his/her achievement levels (e.g., in reading) or also on the characteristics of his/her school, such as the area in which the school was located. For that purpose we fitted the Bernoulli model with the dependent variable

(LD identification) being binary (Boomsma, 1986; Nezlek, 2001). In order for the resulting logistic coefficient to be transformed into percentage points, we employed the following formula (Nezlek, 2003; Raudenbush & Bryk, 2002):

$$\text{Probability of an outcome} = \frac{1}{1 + \exp\{-\varsigma_{ij}\}} \tag{1}$$

with η_{ij} being the logistic regression coefficient.

RESULTS OF STUDY 1

Unconditional Model of LD Identification

Initially an unconditional model (i.e., without predictors) was fit to the data in order to ascertain the prevalence rates of an LD, using a population-based model (Raudenbush & Bryk, 2002):

Level-1 Model

$$\text{Probability}_{\text{Diagnosis}} = \phi_{ij}$$

$$\text{Log}\left[\frac{\phi_{ij}}{(1-\phi_{ij})}\right] = \beta_{0j}$$

Level-2 Model

$$\beta_{0j} = \beta_{00} + u_{0j}$$

with the ϕ (phi) dichotomy representing the prevalence (mean) rates. This statistic is transformed into log units and is expressed with the term β_{0j}. Subsequently, prevalence rates are examined as a function of their intercept $\beta_{00,}$ the error u_{0j}, around that intercept, and any other predictor variables at Level-2 of the model. In this unconditional model the Level-1 variance is the reciprocal of the Bernoulli variance $\phi_{ij} = (1-\phi_{ij})$.

Results indicated that 10.84% of the students in the population were identified as having LD. However, in order to ascertain whether one type of school was predictive of LD identification, we bootstrapped the population mean (Chernick, 2007; Efron, 1982) to ensure that there were not substantial biases due to participant selection (Diaconis & Efron, 1983). These analyses were conducted using S+ and are described in the following section.

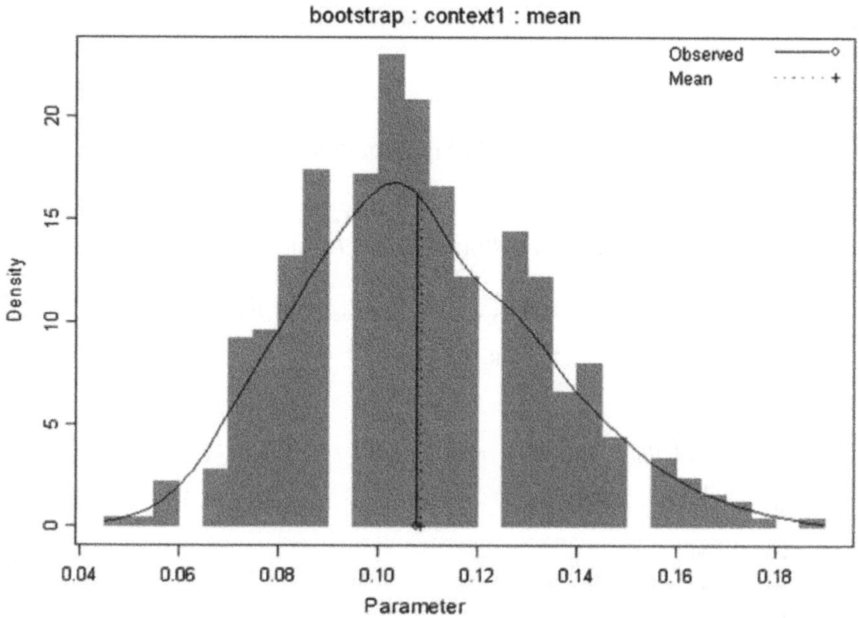

Fig. 4. Prevalence rates were bootstrapped in order to ensure stability of population estimates.

Bootstrapping the Mean Prevalence Rates of LD in the Population

In order to be confident that our sample estimates of the prevalence rates of LD were accurate, we bootstrapped the mean rate using the nonparametric bootstrap and 1,000 replications. The mean bias of the bootstrap distribution (see Fig. 4) was 0.00006707, which was miniscule. Furthermore the standard error of measurement was 0.025. Last, the empirical 95% confidence intervals were between 7.2% and 16.2%. Thus, these findings increase our confidence that our estimates of prevalence were close to population estimates.

Learning Disabilities as a Function of Reading Ability in the Absence of Context

The purpose of the present analysis was to test the hypothesis that students' reading achievement was predictive of an LD identification/diagnosis, in the absence of any other predictor. Thus, the following multilevel model was fit to the data:

Level-1 Model

$$\text{Probability}_{\text{Diagnosis}} = \phi_{ij}$$

$$\text{Log}\left[\frac{\phi_{ij}}{(1-\phi_{ij})}\right] = \beta_{0j} + \beta_{1j(\text{Decoding})} + \beta_{2j(\text{Grammar})} + \beta_{3j(\text{Syntax})} + \beta_{4j(\text{Fluency})} + \beta_{5j(\text{Comprehension})} + \beta_{6j(\text{Reading Rating})} + u_{0j}$$

Level-2 Model

$$\beta_{0j} = \gamma_{00} + u_{0j}$$
$$\beta_{1j} = \gamma_{10}$$
$$\beta_{2j} = \gamma_{20}$$
$$\beta_{3j} = \gamma_{30}$$
$$\beta_{4j} = \gamma_{40}$$
$$\beta_{5j} = \gamma_{50}$$
$$\beta_{6j} = \gamma_{60}$$

Results highlighted the presence of two significant findings (see Table 1). There was a significant slope linking fluency and teacher's ratings of reading with LD placement. Let us see what these significant slopes mean.

Table 1. Multilevel Random Coefficient Model Predicting Prevalence of Identification Rates Due to Student Level Variables.

Variables	Coefficient	SE	*t*-ratio	*p*	df
Intercept B_0					
Intercept γ_{00}	−1.762	0.403	−4.369	0.000**	66
Slopes of predictors					
Decoding β_1	0.006	0.054	0.118	0.907	115
Grammar β_2	0.656	0.498	1.318	0.190	115
Syntax β_3	−0.266	0.189	−1.044	0.163	115
Fluency β_4	−0.026	0.009	−2.893	0.005*	115
Comprehension β_5	−0.010	0.033	−0.301	0.764	115
Teacher ratings β_6	−0.189	0.094	−2.014	0.046*	115

Notes: The coefficients reflect the fixed effects part of the model; SE = standard error of measurement; $^{*}p<0.05$, $^{**}p<0.01$; as a probability level of zero cannot exist.

The intercept represents the log odds of LD identification for a student with average levels ($z = 0$) in decoding, grammar, syntax, fluency, comprehension, and teacher ratings of reading. When applying the formula 1/1{−Exp} the value of −1.76 is transformed into a probability and was 14.7%. This probability represents prevalence rates for students who are average across all independent variables. However, in order to evaluate the contribution of the significant predictors we need to apply predicted values.

Given that all independent variables, except area, were grand mean centered, then all partial regression coefficients become zero as we try to model an average student across all variables (with mean = $z = 0$ across predictors) except fluency for which we model the effect for 1 SD above and below the mean. Thus, before we apply the equation above to evaluate the effects of context we first need to evaluate the two significant effects in the absence of context. By applying predicted values at 1 SD above and below the mean in fluency and ratings of reading we obtain the following:

For Fluency levels at −1 SD[3]

$$\eta = \gamma_{00} + \gamma_{40\ \text{(Fluency)}} + u_0$$

which gives us:

$$\eta = -1.76 + (-0.026)(-1) = -1.734 \text{ (i.e., 15\% prevalence rates)}$$

For Fluency levels at +1 SD

$$\eta = \gamma_{00} + \gamma_{40\ \text{(Fluency)}} + u_0$$

which gives us:

$$\eta = -1.76 + (-0.026)(1) = -1.786 \text{ (i.e., 14.36\% prevalence rates)}$$

In other words, if a student had fluency levels 1 SD above the mean his/her probability to be identified as having LD is significantly less (14.4%) compared to having 1 SD below the mean in fluency (with the probability leveling up to 15%). This may seem like a small difference but it is evaluated as a function of the error of measurement and was nevertheless significant. The effects are more dramatic, however, when evaluating the effects of reading ability through teacher ratings (see below).

For reading ability ratings that place a student at 1 SD below the mean

$$\eta = \gamma_{00} + \gamma_{60} \text{ (Reading Ratings)} + u_0$$

which gives us:

$$\eta = -1.76 + (-0.189)(-1) = -1.571 \text{ (i.e., 17.2\% prevalence rates)}$$

For reading ability ratings that place a student at 1 SD above the mean

$$\eta = \gamma_{00} + \gamma_{60} \text{ (Reading Ratings) } + u_0$$

which gives us:

$$\eta = -1.76 + (-0.189)(1) = -1.786 \text{ (i.e., 12.47\% prevalence rates)}$$

Thus, for individuals who are rated as being 1 SD below the mean in reading ability as measured by teacher ratings, chances are that in approximately 17% of the time they will be identified as having LD. On the contrary, for students who are rated at reading ability levels above 1 SD from the mean chances for identification lie at approximately 12.5%. This finding substantiates the role of teacher ratings regarding overall reading ability. Subsequent modeling tested whether the relationship between fluency/reading ratings and LD placement is affected by the context in which students are educated (i.e., school area). In other words we attempted to test the stability of the slope coefficient as a function of the areas in which the school was located.

Cross-Level Interactions Between Context and Reading Ability for the Prediction of LD Identification

The above model suggested that students' actual fluency levels and their teachers ratings of their reading ability were significant predictors of LD identification. The purpose of the present modeling was to test the hypothesis that the above two significant relationships (slopes) would be *moderated* by school area/location (see Table 2). Thus, the following multilevel model was fit to the data:

Level-1 Model

$$\text{Probability}_{\text{Diagnosis}} = \phi_{ij}$$

$$\text{Log}\left[\frac{\phi_{ij}}{(1-\phi_{ij})}\right] = \beta_{0j} + \beta_{1j(\text{Decoding})} + \beta_{2j(\text{Grammar})} + \beta_{3j(\text{Syntax})} + \beta_{4j(\text{Fluency})} + \beta_{5j(\text{Comprehension})} + \beta_{6j(\text{Reading Rating})} + u_{0j}$$

Table 2. Multilevel Random Coefficient Model Predicting Prevalence of Identification Rates Due to the Moderating Role of School Location.

Variables	Coefficient	SE	t-ratio	p	df
Intercept B_0					
Intercept γ_{00}	−1.778	0.411	−4.321	0.000**	66
Slopes of predictors					
Decoding γ_{10}	0.001	0.053	0.019	0.985	113
Grammar γ_{20}	0.518	0.457	1.134	0.260	113
Syntax γ_{30}	−0.224	0.190	−1.176	0.243	113
Comprehension β_5	−0.005	0.031	−0.168	0.867	113
Slope for fluency					
Intercept γ_{40}	0.021	0.020	1.063	0.290	113
School location γ_{41}	−0.021	0.009	−2.498	0.014*	113
Slope for ratings of reading ability					
Intercept γ_{60}	−0.304	0.234	−1.298	0.197	113
Teacher ratings γ_{61}	0.046	0.089	0.517	0.605	113

Notes: The coefficients reflect the fixed effects part of the model; SE = standard error of measurement; $^{*}p<0.05$, $^{**}p<0.01$.

Level-2 Model

$$\beta_{0j} = \gamma_{00} + u_{0j}$$
$$\beta_{1j} = \gamma_{10}$$
$$\beta_{2j} = \gamma_{20}$$
$$\beta_{3j} = \gamma_{30}$$
$$\beta_{4j} = \gamma_{40} + \gamma_{41}\ \text{(School Area/Location)}$$
$$\beta_{5j} = \gamma_{50}$$
$$\beta_{6j} = \gamma_{60} + \gamma_{61}\ \text{(School Area/Location)}$$

In the "absence of context" model tested previously, when all independent variables were treated as predictors of LD prevalence rates, fluency emerged as a significant predictor. Specifically, for individuals 1 SD above the mean in fluency there was a significantly lowered probability of being diagnosed as having LD. However, when the relationship between fluency and LD identification was moderated by the area in which the school was located there was a significant moderating effect (cross-level interaction) of the area in which the school was located. This significant finding suggested that the relationship between fluency and LD identification was, in part, dependent upon the area in which the school was located. Similarly, with regard to teacher ratings, their relationship to LD identification "changed" as a function of school location, although the moderator by itself did not exceed conventional levels of significance. Let us see how area[4] affected the relationship between fluency and reading ability and LD identification by applying predicted values:

For Urban Area and the Relationship Between Fluency and LD Identification

$$\eta = \gamma_{00} + \gamma_{10}\,(\text{Decoding}) + \gamma_{20}\,(\text{Grammar}) + \gamma_{30}\,(\text{Syntax}) + \gamma_{40}\,(\text{Fluency}) + \gamma_{41}\,(\text{Fluency} \times \text{Area}) + \gamma_{50}\,(\text{Comprehension}) + \gamma_{60}\,(\text{Reading Ratings}) + u_0$$

Fig. 5 (upper and lower panels) displays predicted values for reading achievement ratings (upper panel) and fluency (lower panel). With regard to reading achievement ratings, the relationship between LD identification and reading is apparently moderated by the area in which the school is located. As shown in Fig. 5 (upper panel) the rates of identification are higher in urban schools compared to rural, for the same level of reading ability. In other words, students who possess the *same exact levels of reading achievement* (low) are more likely to be identified as having LD in an urban school compared to a rural school. These effects, even more pronounced, were observed with regard to fluency levels (see Fig. 5, lower panel). These findings confirmed the moderating role of context in the identification of students with LD.

BRIEF DISCUSSION OF STUDY 1

The purpose of Study 1 was to test the hypothesis that context would moderate the relationship between LD identification and achievement in reading. The first important finding of Study 1 was that students' reading ability (actual or through teacher ratings) was predictive of their LD. This finding was in the predictive direction and was a prerequisite of subsequent modeling. The second and most important finding was that the above relationship was moderated by the area in which the school was located. In urban schools, for a specific reading ability, the probability of being identified as having LD was significantly higher compared to the same-ability student who was located in a rural school. This finding, as disturbing as it can be seen, suggests that our identification criteria should take into account information from the schools in order for their estimates to be valid. Below we present a modified RAD model in order to aid identification in LD.

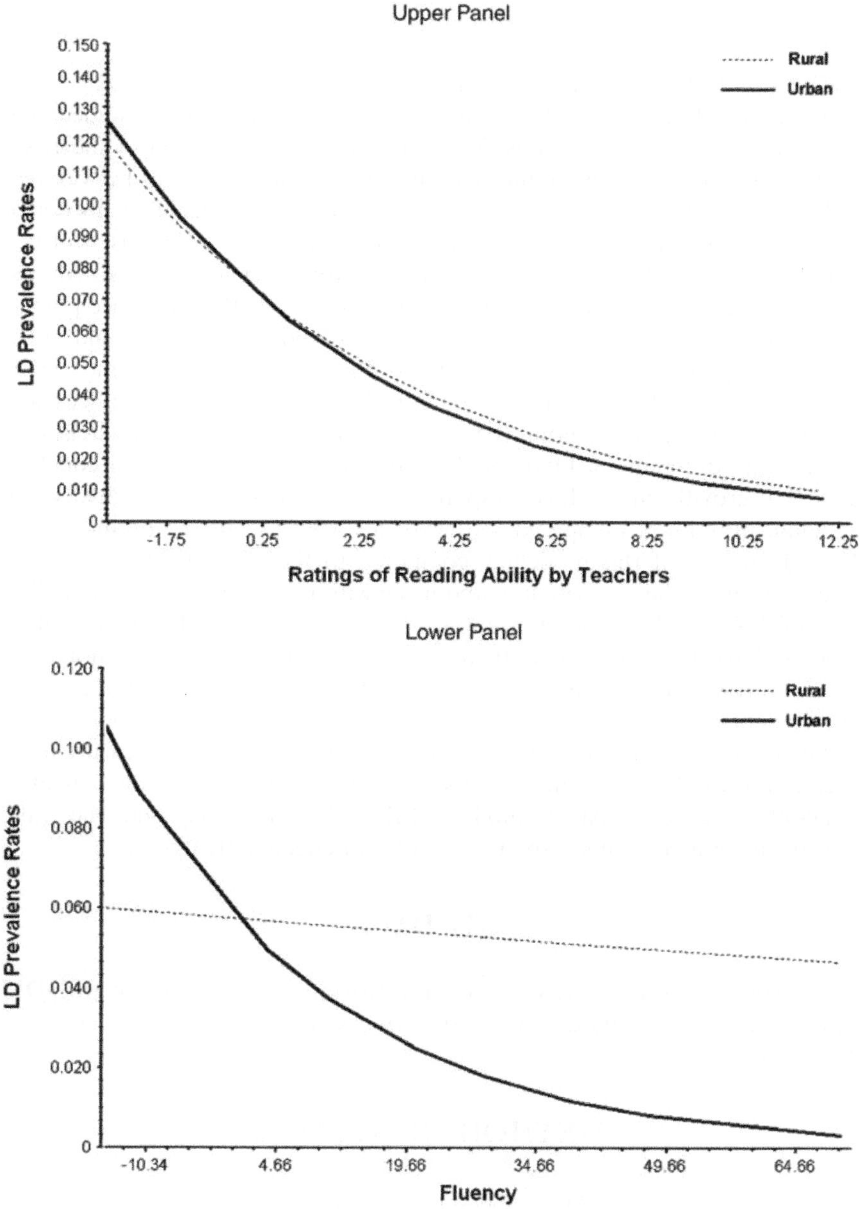

Fig. 5. Prevalence rates of LD identification as a function of reading ability level (teacher ratings) in urban versus rural school locations. Predictions are for reading achievement ratings (upper panel) and fluency (lower panel).

Proposed Model of LD Identification

The present authors see merit in the RAD model. We would like to extend this idea to a model that takes into account information from both the student and his/her context. We would, thus, like to propose a modification of the RAD model by taking into account information from the student and his/her variance and compare that to information about the mean of his/her class/district or other grouping[5]. In essence, the present model proposes a comparison of two slopes or two growth parameters: (a) the trajectory of a students' growth and (b) the trajectory of growth for his/her class/district or other reference point.

Let us assume that the individual slope of a student is positive and at 0.2 (i.e., within person slope). We can compare that slope that we assume reflects the performance of a student over time to the average slope of his/her class/district or other reference point (between-students slope). If the two slopes are significantly different (in favor of the group's slope), then we can conclude that the growth and, thus, responsiveness of a student to instruction is significantly lower compared to that of his/her class/district (grand slope). The advantages of this modeling, compared to the absolute[6] model of LD identification, is that information about the within-student variance as well as that of his/her class/district are taken into account in the identification process. Also, differences are estimated at the growth parameter and not at the mean level (which may reflect a "variable" and likely unreliable point estimate of a student's abilities). Thus, one has a better picture of the "responsiveness" attribute as it is established from multiple measurements (i.e., measurements over time). Study 2 presents a working example of the proposed "relative slope-difference discrepancy model (RSDDM)" that may aid the valid assessment of a student's responsiveness to an effective treatment.

STUDY 2

The purpose of Study 2 was to present a working example of the RSDDM within the multilevel data analysis framework. Data came from a study by Antoniou et al. (2009).

METHOD OF STUDY 2

Participants and Procedures

Participants were 29 students, whose writing ability was evaluated three times within a semester. All students came from one rural district, and included 19 boys and 10 girls. Also, two students were bilingual. Of these students 6 were 4th graders, 13 were 5th graders, and 10 were 6th graders. More information about the methodology of the study can be traced in Antoniou et al. (2009).

Measures

A standardized writing composition scale developed by Porpodas (2008) was implemented in the present study which involved measurements of structural parts of the produced composition such as coherence, relevance to the purpose, syntax, etc. The alpha reliability of the scale was 0.792.

Data Analyses

Multilevel modeling was again implemented in order to model the slopes of individual students compared to the mean of their district. Following this modeling, the two slopes were compared with each other using multivariate χ^2-tests[7].

RESULTS OF STUDY 2

Modeling Students' Growth in Writing Within a District

In order to evaluate the hypothesis that there was ample variability at the intercept and slope levels, the following multilevel model was fit to the data:

Level-1 Model

$$Y = \beta_0 + \beta_{1\ (\text{Growth})} + r_0$$

Level-2 Model

$$\beta_0 = \gamma_{00} + u_0$$
$$\beta_1 = \gamma_{10}$$

with β_0, γ_{00}, and γ_{10} representing intercepts and β_1 representing the growth parameter. The terms r_0 and u_0 represent error terms at levels one and two, respectively.

This model testified that means and slopes were nonzero. In the absence of, at least, a significant slope, further modeling would make no sense.

Results indicated that the grand slope was equal to 0.982, which was significantly different from zero [$t(82) = 3.329$, $p<0.01$]. Thus, this model acted as a baseline model in order to proceed with further testing. Subsequently, a student's growth was compared to a sample of students from his/her school district (we call him/her student 28) by creating a dummy term.

Growth in Writing Between Student 28 and a Sample of Students from His/Her District

In order to evaluate the hypothesis that student 28 was not responding equally well to effective instruction, compared to his/her peers, the following multilevel model was fit to the data:

Level-1 Model

$$Y = \beta_0 + \beta_1\,_{\text{(Growth)}} + r_0$$

Level-2 Model

$$\beta_0 = \gamma_{00} + u_0$$
$$\beta_1 = \gamma_{10} + \gamma_{11}\,_{\text{(Dummy)}}$$[8]

Results (see Fig. 6), indicated that there were significant differences between the slope of the students who came from District A ($b = 1.086$) [$t(81) = 2.718$, $p<0.01$] and the slope of student 28[9] who came from the same district ($b = -1.83$) [$t(81) = -2.082$, $p<0.05$]. This finding suggests that student 28 did not respond adequately to instruction in writing compared to the average growth produced by students of the same educational environment (district). These findings confirm the importance of moving into relative models of ability for the identification of LD as the respective finding would be saliently different if the reference criterion would involve the grand mean (i.e., through standardized assessments).

BRIEF DISCUSSION OF STUDY 2

The purpose of Study 2 was to present a working example of the proposed RSDDM within the multilevel data analysis framework. Study 2 demonstrated that it is possible to compare the "responsiveness" of a student to a treatment by comparing his/her growth parameter to that of a "relative" reference point (his/her class, district, random sample of the population

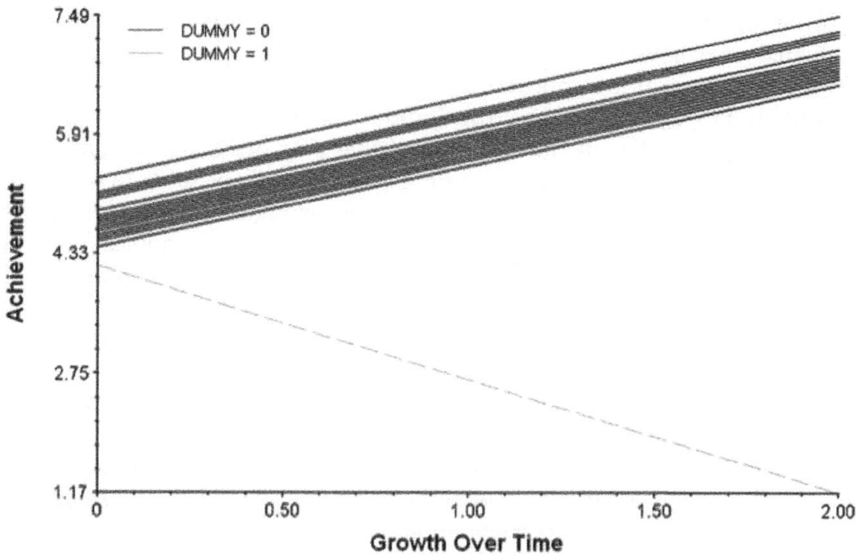

Fig. 6. Growth in reading (slopes) across individual students within a classroom. The Dummy = 0 level reflects the slopes of all students except student 28; the Dummy = 1 level represents student 28.

he/she belongs[10], etc.). The point to be made here is that the use of a relative, compared to absolute, criterion may prove to be a more appropriate reference point compared to federal norms. Furthermore, the application of the multilevel framework demonstrated the sensitivity of the model to estimate and compare growth parameters across different groups. Nevertheless, it is important to bear in mind that alternative "relative points of reference" exist and it may be worth exploring them. For example, one could select low-achieving students and evaluate hypotheses that a given low-ability student is significantly worst compared to low-achieving peers. Other alternative models could involve comparisons between pairs of students of low/average/high ability or the comparison of profiles for a given area of achievement.

GENERAL DISCUSSION

The purpose of the present studies was twofold: (a) to evaluate the role of context in the identification of LD within the RTI model and (b) to propose a model that would take into account context in the assessment of "unresponsiveness" within the RTI.

In Study 1, the potentially moderating role of school context was evaluated on whether it affects the relationship between achievement and LD identification. It is important to emphasize here that the purpose of the present studies was not to be critical about the RTI model. Nor was it to identify all parameters at the school level that may affect decision making. Instead, the primary purpose was to highlight the role of school context in order to aid decision making, as each decision regarding responsiveness should be (in our opinion) tied to the particular class/school/district in which the decision is made. Thus, the present findings aim to assist valid identification of students with LD, and suggest that the specifics of each school (meaning school achievement, school area) need to be taken into account in such diagnostic decisions.

The most important finding of Study 1 was the fact that the relationship between reading ability/achievement and LD identification was moderated by the area in which a school was located. Specifically in urban areas, compared to rural areas, the probability of being identified as having LD was significantly higher for a given ability student. In other words, in urban schools, low-achieving students had a much higher probability of being identified as having LD compared to rural and suburban schools. This finding highlights the moderating role of a school's characteristics in LD identification decision making and agrees with earlier concerns of leading researchers in the field on the salient role of context (Dean et al., 2006; Fuchs & Deshler, 2007; Johnson et al., 2005; Kavale et al., 2005; Mastropieri & Scruggs, 2005).

The above finding suggests that for a given student's low ability, the urban school's diagnostic teams and criteria of implementation are more likely to lead to a conclusion for identification compared to the decision made in rural schools. What factors contribute to this differentiation? We can only speculate what some of these factors maybe. For example, a schools efforts to increase its mean levels, to achieve excellence, to compete at the state level, maybe some relevant reasons. Nevertheless, we can only speculate why decision making at urban schools is much more strict, compared to the respective decision in rural and suburban schools.

Ecological Validity

The findings from Study 1 supported an ecological approach to decision making regarding identification in LD (Dean et al., 2006). The purpose of Study 2 was to present a working example of a modified RAD model in order to demonstrate how such a model works. The results of Study 2 suggested that multilevel modeling can aid our decision making as we can directly compare the growth parameters of individual students compared to a reference point (his/her group mean, grand mean, or other). Fig. 6 demonstrated that effect. Thus, the example of Study 2 strongly supported the premise and also use of an RAD model. This demonstration agrees with the recommendations of Fletcher, Francis, Morris, and Lyon (2005) who reported several psychometric problems of discrepancy models and concluded with a recommendation to apply hybrid models.

Limitations

It is important to acknowledge certain limitations of the present studies. With regard to Study 1, the findings are correlational in nature. Thus, conclusions about cause and effect relationships should not be drawn. Field studies in which school, teacher, assessment, and other environment characteristics are assessed are important in order to evaluate the validity of the responsiveness (compared to unresponsiveness) ratings (such as the Peterson & Shinn, 2002 study). Furthermore, the sample of the study was relatively small for estimating population parameters in means and relationships although we attempted to substantiate the effects by use of intensive simulations (i.e., the bootstrap).

With regard to Study 2, it is important to establish criteria pertaining to what constitutes a significant difference between a point/slope estimates of a student compared to his/her reference group[11] (class/district/norms/or other). The problem stems from the fact that such comparisons would be limited by the population of the class (anywhere between 15–25 students) or district (likely more than 25 students) and the time series representing responsiveness, thus low power will likely be an issue (Cohen, 1992). One potential solution would be the use of the bootstrap to estimate population parameters in growth based on (e.g., student 28) estimates (Chernick, 2007; Efron, 1979, 1982, 1985; Efron & Tibshirani, 1993). Another potential solution would be to use the standard error estimate of the reference population (i.e., class/district/other) as that of the individual low-achieving student. A third solution would be to "borrow" standard errors from the literature of the population of LD that are specific to the specific object under investigation. Following that decision regarding standard errors, one could use custom slope difference tests to assess differences between the two slopes (student's vs. his/her reference group). Other recommendations may involve the implementation of clinical means in assessing differentiation in growth (compared to statistical inferences that may likely reflect low power; see also Onwuegbuzie, Levin, & Leach, 2003), particularly if these means are defined by expert multidisciplinary teams (Fuchs & Deshler, 2007).

Conclusions and Recommendations

Fuchs and Deshler (2007) stated:

> It is untrue and misleading to claim that we currently have a necessary and sufficient knowledge base to guide the implementation of RTI as a process of early intervention and disability identification across all grades, for all academic skills, in all content areas, and for all children and youth. (p. 134)

Similar concerns have been raised by other leading researchers (e.g., Kavale et al., 2005). The intent of the present studies was to increase our knowledge base about how the RTI would be best implemented in order to deliver instruction to those who needed it the most (as well as diagnostic mean). Specifically, the present studies provided information on how "unresponsiveness" can be conceptualized using an ecological framework and the use of dual discrepancy criteria (evaluation of means and slopes) using a multilevel mathematical framework. We hope that the present work will stimulate more discussion regarding the determination of "responsiveness" for which, today, there is no consensus. Until this consensus is reached, different schools will be identifying different-ability students as those who need additional services and student identification would be tied to the specific school in which assessments are made.

Future Directions

In the future it is important to elaborate on the influential effects of school, family, and other contextual factors that may affect decision making within the RTI model. For example, Sideridis, Antoniou, and Padeliadu (2008) found a biasing factor related to the diagnosis made by male teachers compared to female teachers. This significant bias could be rooted to teacher's education, experience, personality, and other factors. Nevertheless, it is important to evaluate the contribution of personal and contextual factors that contribute error variance to our decision making regarding identification of students with LD. This systemic view of LD identification is particularly more important within the RTI model as responsiveness is likely a function of several influential factors involving the teacher, the school psychologist, the use of specific CBMs, and many more. Much more research work is needed in order to reach a valid model of LD identification.

NOTES

1. Fig. 1 will be discussed next within the multilevel modeling framework as a means to accommodate the variability due to classrooms/schools/districts and other means of differentiation.
2. As Good, Simmons, and Kame'enui (2001) stated those benchmarks would have to meet the criteria of empirical and theoretical soundness, and social validation.
3. Estimates are taken from Table 1.
4. "Area" and "school location" were used interchangeably.
5. This is the essence of the "relative" aspect of this model. To be able to compare the performance of a given student with the most appropriate reference point (point estimate) or rate of growth (slope). Whether that reference point is the mean of a student's class, or his/her district or other needs to be ascertained but nevertheless needs to be built in the model of LD identification. We certainly support a multiple measurement model that provides multiple points over time and provides a more consistent estimate of a student's ability.
6. Model in which the reference criteria involve the mean of a normative group.
7. These χ^2-tests run with 1 df.
8. The dummy variable represents student 28 with a 0 and the remaining students of the class with a 1.
9. Nevertheless, because the two slopes were evaluated against the absolute reference point of zero a χ^2-custom test was employed to test the hypothesis that the two coefficients were significantly different from each other. Results indicated that the null hypothesis of no differences was rejected [$\chi^2(1) = 7.085$, $p < 0.01$].
10. Certainly the most important element of "relative" models is definition of the relevant population to act as the reference point.
11. For Berninger and Abbott (1994), the criterion should be "within" the student and should be solely based on an intraindividual model, thus, comparisons between a student's performance at a given time from his/her common responding. In our RSDD model that would be equivalent to comparing the slope of the student to the absolute criterion of zero.

REFERENCES

Antoniou, F., Padeliadu, S., Papakonstantinou, K., Karagianni, A., Lisandrou, A., Anifantaki, G., Barbouni, A., Kalisperaki, P., Mpantra, A., Palierakis, N., Giotsis, N., Gavriilidou, A., & Xilouri, M. (2009). Increasing story quality, structure, and productivity through self-regulated strategy development: Short- and long-term effects on students with learning disabilities. Paper presented at the 18th Annual World Conference on Learning Disabilities, Learning Disabilities Worldwide, Boston.

Berninger, V. W., & Abbott, R. D. (1994). Redefining learning disabilities: Moving beyond aptitude-achievement discrepancies to failure to respond to validated treatment protocols. In: G. R. Lyon (Ed.), *Frames of reference for the assessment of learning disabilities : New views on measurement issues* (pp. 163–184). Baltimore, MD: Brookes.

Boomsma, A. (1986). On the use of bootstrap and jackknife in covariance structure analysis models. *Compstat, 7*, 205–210.

Bronfenbrenner, U. (1986). Ecology of the family as a context for human development: Research perspectives. *Developmental Psychology, 22*, 723–742.

Bryk, A. S., & Raudenbush, S. W. (1992). *Hierarchical linear models*. Newbury Park, CA. Sage.

Burns, M. K., Appleton, J. J., & Stehouwer, J. D. (2005). Meta-analytic review of responsiveness-to-intervention research: Examining field-based and research-implemented models. *Journal of Psychoeducational Assessment, 23*, 381–394.

Burns, M. K., & Senesac, B. V. (2005). Comparison of dual discrepancy criteria to assess response to intervention. *Journal of School Psychology, 43*, 393–406.

Carlisle, J. F. (2003). Morphology matters in learning to read: A commentary. *Reading Psychology, 24*, 291–322.

Castles, A., & Coltheart, M. (1993). Varieties of developmental dyslexia. *Cognition, 47*, 149–180.

Chernick, M. (2007). *Bootstrap methods: A guide for practitioners and researchers*. New York, NY: Wiley.

Choi, K. (2001). Latent variable modeling in the hierarchical modeling framework in longitudinal studies: A fully Bayesian approach. *Asia Pacific Education Review, 2*, 44–55.

Cohen, J. (1992). A power primer. *Psychological Bulletin, 118*, 155–159.

Compton, D. L. (2006). How should "unresponsiveness" to secondary intervention be operationalized? Is it all about the nudge. *Journal of Learning Disabilities, 39*, 170–173.

Dean, V. J., Burns, M. K., Grialou, T., & Varro, P. J. (2006). Comparison of ecological validity of learning disabilities diagnostic models. *Psychology in the Schools, 43*, 157–168.

Deno, S. L. (1989). *Curriculum based measurement and special education services: A fundamental and direct relationship*. New York, NY: Guilford.

Diaconis, P., & Efron, B. (1983). Computer intensive methods in statistics. *Scientific American, 248*, 116–130.

Efron, B. (1979). Bootstrap methods: Another look at the Jackknife. *Annals of Statistics, 7*, 1–26.

Efron, B. (1982). *The jackknife, bootstrap, and other resampling plans*. Philadelphia, PA: SIAM.

Efron, B. (1985). Bootsrap confidence intervals for a class of parametric problems. *Biometrica, 72*, 45–48.

Efron, B., & Tibshirani, R. (1993). *An introduction to the bootstrap*. New York, NY: Chapman & Hall.

Ehren, B. J., & Nelson, N. W. (2005). The responsiveness to intervention approach and language impairment. *Topics in Language Disorders, 25*, 120–131.

Elias, M. J. (2004). The connection between social-emotional learning and learning disabilities: Implications for intervention. *Learning Disability Quarterly, 27*, 53–63.

Elksnin, L. K., & Elksnin, N. (2004). The social-emotional side of learning disabilities. *Learning Disability Quarterly, 27*, 3–8.

Filippatou, D., Dimitropoulou, P., & Sideridis, G. (2009). Examining differences between students with specific learning disabilities and those with specific language disorders on cognition, emotions and psychopathology. *Learning Disabilities: A Contemporary Journal, 7*, 55–72.

Fletcher, J., Francis, D., Morris, R., & Lyon, R. (2005). Evidence-based assessment of learning disabilities in children and adolescents. *Journal of Clinical Child and Adolescent Psychology*, *34*, 506–522.

Fletcher, J., Francis, D., Shaywitz, S., Lyon, R., Foorman, B., Stuebing, K., & Shaywitz, B. (1998). Intelligence testing and the discrepancy model for children with learning disabilities. *Learning Disabilities Research and Practice*, *13*, 186–203.

Francis, D., Fletcher, J., Stuebing, K., Lyon, R., Shaywitz, B., & Shaywitz, S. (2005). Psychometric approaches to the identification of LD: IQ and achievement scores are not sufficient. *Journal of Learning Disabilities*, *38*, 98–108.

Fuchs, D., & Deshler, D. D. (2007). What we need to know about responsiveness to intervention (and shouldn't be afraid to ask). *Learning Disabilities Research and Practice*, *22*, 129–136.

Fuchs, D., Fuchs, L., & Compton, D. L. (2004). Identifying reading disabilities by responsiveness-to-intervention: Specifying measures and criteria. *Learning Disability Quarterly*, *27*, 216–227.

Fuchs, D., Mock, D., Morgan, P., & Young, C. (2003). Responsiveness-to-intervention: Definitions, evidence, and implications for the learning disabilities construct. *Learning Disabilities Research and Practice*, *18*, 157–171.

Fuchs, L., & Fuchs, D. (1998). Treatment validity: A unifying concept for reconceptualizing the identification of learning disabilities. *Learning Disabilities Research and Practice*, *13*, 204–219.

Fuchs, L. S., & Fuchs, D. (2006). A framework for building capacity for responsiveness to intervention. *School Psychology Review*, *35*, 621–626.

Fuchs, L. S., Fuchs, D., Compton, D., Bryant, J., Hamlett, C., & Seethaler, P. (2007). Mathematics screening and progress monitoring at first grade: Implications for responsiveness to intervention. *Exceptional Children*, *73*, 311–330.

Fuchs, L. S., Fuchs, D., & Hollenbeck, K. N. (2007). Extending responsiveness to intervention to mathematics at first and third grades. *Learning Disabilities Research and Practice*, *22*, 13–24.

Good, R. H., Simmons, D. C., & Kame'enui, E. J. (2001). The importance of decision-making utility of a continuum of fluency-based indicators of foundational reading skills for third-grade high-stakes outcomes. *Scientific Studies of Reading*, *5*, 257–288.

Greenway, P., & Milne, L. (1999). Relationship between psychopathology, learning disabilities, or both and WISC-III subtest scatter in adolescents. *Psychology in the Schools*, *36*, 103–108.

Griffiths, Y. M., & Snowling, M. J. (2002). Predictors of exception word and nonword reading in dyslexic children: The severity hypothesis. *Journal of Educational Psychology*, *94*, 34–43.

Grolnick, W. S., & Ryan, R. M. (1990). Self-perceptions, motivation, and adjustment in children with learning disabilities: A multiple group comparison study. *Journal of Learning Disabilities*, *23*, 177–184.

Hammill, D. D. (1990). On defining learning disabilities: An emerging consensus. *Journal of Learning Disabilities*, *23*, 74–84.

Heath, N. L., & Ross, S. (2000). Prevalence and expression of depressive symptomatology in students with and without learning disabilities. *Learning Disability Quarterly*, *23*, 24–36.

Hollenbeck, A. F. (2007). From IDEA to implementation: A discussion of foundational and future responsiveness-to-intervention research. *Learning Disabilities Research and Practice*, *22*, 137–146.

Individuals with Disabilities Education Improvement Act (IDEA). (2004). P.L. 108-446, 20 USC §§ 1400 et seq.

Johnson, E., Mellard, D. F., & Byrd, S. E. (2005). Alternative models of learning disabilities identification: Considerations and initial conclusions. *Journal of Learning Disabilities, 38*, 569–572.

Kavale, K. A., Holdnack, J. A., & Mostert, M. P. (2005). Responsiveness to intervention and the identification of specific learning disability: A critique and alternative proposal. *Learning Disability Quarterly, 28*, 2–16.

Kreft, I. G. G., & de Leeuw, J. (1998). *Introducing multilevel modeling*. London: Sage.

Labouvie, E. (1982). The concept of change and regression toward the mean. *Psychological Bulletin, 92*, 251–257.

Marston, D. (2005). Tiers of intervention in responsiveness to intervention: Prevention outcomes and learning disabilities identification patterns. *Journal of Learning Disabilities, 38*, 539–544.

Mastropieri, M. A., & Scruggs, T. E. (2005). Feasibility and consequences of response to intervention: Examination of the issues and scientific evidence as a model for the identification of individuals with learning disabilities. *Journal of Learning Disabilities, 38*, 525–531.

Mellard, D. F., Byrd, S. E., Johnson, E., Tollefson, J. M., & Boesche, L. (2004). Foundations and research on identifying model responsiveness-to-intervention sites. *Learning Disability Quarterly, 27*, 243–256.

Nesselorade, J., Stigler, S., & Baltes, P. (1980). Regression toward the mean and the study of change. *Psychological Bulletin, 88*, 622–637.

Nezlek, J. B. (2001). Multilevel random coefficient analyses of event and interval contingent data in social and personality psychology research. *Personality and Social Psychology Bulletin, 27*, 771–785.

Nezlek, J. B. (2003). Using multilevel random coefficient modeling to analyze social interaction diary data. *Journal of Social and Personal Relationships, 20*, 437–469.

Onwuegbuzie, A., Levin, J., & Leach, K. (2003). Do effect sizes measure up? A brief assessment. *Learning Disabilities: A Contemporary Journal, 1*, 37–40.

Padeliadu, S., & Sideridis, G. D. (2000). Discriminant Validation of the Test of Reading Performance (TORP) for identification of children with reading difficulties. *European Journal of Psychological Assessment, 16*, 139–146.

Padeliadu, S., & Sideridis, G. D. (2008). *Learning Disabilities Screening for Teachers*. YPEPTH, EPEAEK.

Pearson, P. D., & Johnson, D. D. (1978). *Teaching reading comprehension*. New York: Holt, Rinehart & Winston.

Perfetti, C. A., & Hart, L. (2001). The lexical bases of comprehension skill. In: D. S. Gorfien (Ed.), *On the consequences of meaning selection: Perspectives on resolving lexical ambiguity* (pp. 67–68). Washington, DC: American Psychological Association.

Peterson, K. M., & Shinn, M. R. (2002). Severe discrepancy models: Which best explains school identification practices for learning disabilities? *School Psychology Review, 31*, 459–476.

Porpodas, K. (2008). *Test of writing ability*. YPEPTH, EPEAEK.

Raudenbush, S. W., & Bryk, A. S. (2002). *Hierarchical linear models: Applications and data analysis methods* (2nd ed.). Thousand Oaks, CA: Sage.

Roberts, K. J. (2004). An introductory primer on multilevel and hierarchical linear modeling. *Learning Disabilities: A Contemporary Journal, 2*, 30–38.

Sampson, P., Faggella-Luby, M. N., & Fritschmann, N. S. (2005). An overview of responsiveness to intervention: What practitioners ought to know. *Topics in Language Disorders, 25*, 93–105.

Scruggs, T., & Mastropieri, M. (2002). On babies and bathwater: Addressing the problems of identification of learning disabilities. *Learning Disability Quarterly, 25*, 155–168.

Share, D. L., & Stanovich, K. E. (1995). Cognitive processes in early reading development: Accommodating individual differences into a model of acquisition. *Issues in Education: Contributions from Educational Psychology, 1*, 1–57.

Shin, J., Espin, C. A., Deno, S. L., & McConnell, S. (2004). Use of hierarchical linear modeling and curriculum-based measurement for assessing academic growth and instructional factors for students with learning difficulties. *Asia Pacific Education Review, 5*, 136–148.

Shinn, M. R. (2002). Best practices in curriculum based measurement. In: A. Thomas & J. Grimes (Eds), *Best practices in school psychology IV* (pp. 671–698). Bethesda, MD: National Association of School Psychologists.

Sideridis, G. D., Antoniou, F., & Padeliadu, S. (2008). Teacher biases in the identification of learning disabilities: An application of the logistic multilevel model. *Learning Disability Quarterly, 31*, 199–209.

Torgesen, J., Alexander, A., Wagner, R., Rashotte, C., Voeller, K., & Conway, T. (2001). Intensive remedial instruction for children with severe reading disabilities: Immediate and long-term outcomes form two instructional approaches. *Journal of Learning Disabilities, 34*, 33–58.

Vaughn, S., Linan-Thompson, S., & Hickman, P. (2003). Response to treatment as a means of identifying students with reading/learning disabilities. *Exceptional Children, 69*, 391–409.

Vellutino, F., Scanlon, D., Sipay, E., Small, S., Chen, R., Pratt, A., & Denckla, M. (1996). Cognitive profiles of difficult to remediate and readily remediated poor readers: Early intervention as a vehicle for distinguishing between cognitive and experiential deficits as basic causes of specific reading disability. *Journal of Educational Psychology, 88*, 601–638.

LITERACY SUPPORTS FOR ADOLESCENT STRUGGLING READERS: TAKING ACTION THROUGH COMPREHENSION INSTRUCTION

Michael Faggella-Luby and
Patricia Sampson Graner

ABSTRACT

In response to the urgent national need to implement evidence-based literacy supports for adolescent struggling readers (ASRs), this chapter provides a framework for addressing reading comprehension instruction. Schools face significant challenges in the education of ASRs including how to address the achievement gap that emerges between proficient readers and a variety of poor reader subgroups predicted by the Simple View of Reading. The authors present current research in the components of reading comprehension (e.g., text structures, vocabulary, prior knowledge, cognitive strategies, and motivation) and explicit pedagogical practices associated with improving outcomes for ASRs, including a school-wide framework called the Content Literacy Continuum. Two

Literacy and Learning
Advances in Learning and Behavioral Disabilities, Volume 23, 61–94

ISSN: 0735-004X/doi:10.1108/S0735-004X(2010)0000023005

specific interventions with supporting research are presented as model practices to improve outcomes for ASRs.

> We must not wait another moment. Our children, our communities, and our country's economic and social future depend upon our determination to put effective literacy programs for students in the fourth through twelfth grades into place in schools across America. (Frost, 2003, p. iv)

This quote from Susan Frost, former President of the Alliance for Excellent Education, speaks to the need for, and more recently the attention to, adolescent literacy. Education has taken an unprecedented front seat in the national conversation at the highest levels of the government with the advent of No Child Left Behind (NCLB). This renewed American emphasis on education makes sense given current reports of the staggering academic shortfall of students especially at the secondary level. Kamil (2003) estimated that almost eight million students in the fourth through twelfth grades are not reading at grade level, and this discrepancy is attributed to their inability to comprehend what they read. The most recent National Assessment of Educational Progress (NAEP) reading data reveal only a five-point improvement for 13 year olds and a single point improvement for 17 year olds over the past 30 years (Rampey, Dion, & Donahue, 2009). More than two-dozen documents addressing areas of literacy improvement for adolescents were published in the decade between 1999 and 2009; all provide definitions (see Table 1) with similar threads and recommendations for research-based interventions or instructional practices. While each document addresses the complexity of the issues surrounding adolescent literacy, few directly address the needs of students with learning disabilities (LDs), more often addressing the more general category of struggling readers. Within this chapter, the term adolescent struggling readers (ASRs) will be used to describe individuals in grades six through twelve, with LD, at-risk for LD identification, and/or reading at least two-years below grade level.

When the NCLB Act was signed into law in January of 2002, assessment of and accountability for all students, including students with disabilities (SWDs), became a fact of life in the American school. NCLB creates a new set of accountability challenges for general education teachers and their SWDs, because all students are expected to meet state standards in reading and other literacy areas by 2014.

In part, because of these requirements, SWDs in middle and high schools are increasingly enrolled in rigorous academic courses. These are general

Table 1. Competing Definitions of Adolescent Literacy.

An array of evolving and emerging definitions of literacy currently compete within the field of adolescent literacy. Deshler (2009) recently presented a sample of definitions in the literature that are played out in schools nationally.

- Adolescent *academic literacy* is defined by Torgesen and Miller (2009) as encompassing the ability to read for initial understanding of text and reading proficiency to construct meaning from content-area text.
- *Content literacy* is defined by Ehren (2005) as the listening, speaking, reading, writing, and thinking skills required to learn in each of the academic disciplines.
- Three types of literacy are defined by Shanahan and Shanahan (2008). *Basic literacy* includes basic decoding skills, recognition of high-frequency words, basic fluency and understanding of various print and literacy conventions. *Intermediate literacy* encompasses skills and strategies essential by the end of middle school including easy reading of multisyllabic words, automaticity with high-frequency vocabulary, and a variety of generic strategies useful for comprehension as well as cognitive endurance. *Disciplinary literacy* then is a combination of sophisticated and specialized routines and strategies that are applied in specific situations and may not be generalizable across disciplines.
- *Disciplinary Literacy Pedagogy* is addressed by a host of researchers (Collins, Brown, & Newman, 1989; Geisler, 1994; Tharp & Gallimore, 1988) as the integration of two dimensions, content knowledge and discipline-appropriate habits of thinking. In other words, students must develop both simultaneously, hence teachers must "teach on the diagonal" (Geisler, 1994) to achieve a balanced trajectory.
- *Cultural navigation* (Moje, 2007) values knowledge production with input from both students and teachers, and *new literacies* (digital vs. static) which are explored by a host of authors in the Handbook of Research on New Literacies (2008), edited by Coiro, Knobel, Lankshear, and Leu.

The importance of these often-competing definitions is that differences between them change what it means to comprehend text. Though not the focus of this chapter, by considering the importance of content knowledge, the role of the reader, and the broader components of literacy, there is great variability in measuring successful reading and designing instruction for meaningful learning.

education courses in which SWDs are expected to meet the same expectations as their peers without disabilities. For example, according to the second National Longitudinal Transition Study (Wagner, Newman, Cameto, & Levine, 2005) students with LDs are now enrolled in more core academic classes than ever before. Academic teachers hold reasonably high academic expectations that many students with LD struggle to meet (e.g., Deshler, Schumaker, Bui, & Vernon, 2005). Along with high academic expectations, the exponential increase in information and content being taught, and the demand for higher-order thinking, as demonstrated through the requirements of end-of-course and state competency tests, have made being a student with LD more challenging than ever. Such demands place a premium on a student's ability to read and comprehend independently, as well as to write, think, and function as complex communicators (Deshler et al., 2005).

CHALLENGES IN THE EDUCATION OF ADOLESCENT STRUGGLING READERS

While the literacy achievement of adolescents in fourth, eighth, and tenth grade has remained relatively constant over the past two decades (e.g., Rampey et al., 2009), the struggle to achieve adequate outcomes for all students centers on an achievement gap that results when the demands of the secondary curriculum are mismatched to individual learner characteristics. The resulting achievement gap is the byproduct of ASRs' inability to apply the literacy skills mastered by their typically developing peers to meet changing school demands as students progress from elementary to secondary school.

During the middle and high school years, all students simultaneously face structural, developmental, behavioral, and academic challenges that illustrate significant differences between the nature of elementary and secondary school contexts (Deshler & Schumaker, 2006). Perhaps most relevant to adolescent literacy is the secondary school focus on academic literacy.

High school's emphasis on discipline-specific knowledge is perhaps its most defining characteristic, placing a significant demand on students. Most states now have minimum graduation requirements based on numbers and types of core courses taken (US DOE, 2009). Given that approximately half of all SWDs spend at least 80% of their school day in the general education environment (US DOE, 2009), SWDs are exposed to the same rigorous content as their typically achieving peers. It is expected that this trend will continue as upcoming IDEA and ESEA reauthorizations will likely include commitments to further increase these students' access to the general education curriculum, high academic standards, goal oriented transition planning, and accountability for outcomes achieved (e.g., Wagner, Newman, Cameto, & Levine, 2005). Raising standards and increasing access may pose a significant challenge for SWDs as literacy becomes less and less a part of the core curriculum in secondary schools. Students who lack foundational skills and strategies may begin to fall further behind, or exhaust previously established accommodations without continued or additional supports.

To improve comprehension for struggling readers, the goal of literacy instruction is to engage students in processes equivalent to those that expert readers employ. In fact, the general thinking in comprehension instruction has been to identify the processes of proficient readers and then design instruction to address apparent gaps or inefficiencies in struggling reader knowledge and skills (Gersten, Fuchs, Williams, & Baker, 2001; National Reading Panel, 2000). In the section that follows, typical reading development is presented to demonstrate how efficient reading is conducted, thus providing a framework for instruction with ASRs.

TYPICAL READING DEVELOPMENT

Typically developing learners are able to meet the academic demands of the secondary curriculum because of their proficiency in skilled reading. Skilled reading, or the fluent execution and coordination of word recognition (WR) and text comprehension, is described in the reading framework the Simple View of Reading (Gough & Tumner, 1986). Understanding through text is the product of increasingly automatic WR and increasingly strategic language comprehension (LC). Typically expressed as an equation (e.g., $WR \times LC =$ Skilled Reading), the Simple View illustrates that skilled reading is a function of two independent but coordinated processes: WR and linguistic comprehension (Catts, Hogan, & Adlof, 2005). As in multiplication of any number by "0," if either WR or LC are absent or significantly impaired, then the product, or understanding is diminished. Consequently, proficient readers require successful development of both skilled reading components.

Learning to automatically recognize words is a multiphase developmental process that begins at the pre-alphabetic (or logographic) phase in which a reader "reads" words from memory or context but has no alphabetic knowledge. The process continues through partial and full alphabetic phases as letter–sound correspondence is learned via the alphabetic principle, phonemic awareness, and eventual decoding by associating sounds to letters in words. As larger units of grapheme–phoneme relations in different words are recognized, the consolidated alphabetic (or orthographic) phase begins as learners increase reading rate and learning of spelling patterns. Finally, proficient word reading becomes automatic with increasing speed in identifying familiar and even unfamiliar words as part of a growing sight vocabulary (e.g., Ehri & McCormick, 1998). The components of WR collectively translate print into linguistic form (Catts et al., 2005).

Simultaneously, typical learners begin developing LC abilities to create meaning from the linguistic form translated during WR. LC involves five component subskills: (a) background knowledge (facts, concepts, etc.),

(b) vocabulary (breadth, precision, links, etc.), (c) language structures (syntax, semantics, etc.), (d) verbal reasoning (inference, metaphor, etc.), and (e) literacy knowledge (print concepts, genres, etc.) (Gough & Tumner, 1986).

Empirical evidence reported by Catts and colleagues (2005) support not only the relatively independent nature of these two processes, but moreover the high correlation they share with reading comprehension (e.g., Hoover & Gough, 1990). When combined using multiple regression analyses, WR and listening comprehension can account for 65–85% of the variance in reading comprehension depending on the age and language level of the student (e.g., Catts et al., 2005). However, the individual components vary in relative contribution across grades. Drawing upon their longitudinal study, Catts and colleagues have been able to describe this trend using data collected from 527 students with complete data sets from kindergarten through eighth grade. Multiple regression analysis confirmed that composite measures of WR and listening comprehension at second, fourth, and eighth grades account for 76.6%, 71.8%, and 72.8% of the variance in reading comprehension ability, respectively. However, while the shared variance continued to account for approximately 40% of the variance across grade levels, unique variance for each of the processes significantly changed. Listening comprehension increased over time from 9% in the second grade to 21% and ultimately 36% variance accounted for in fourth and eighth grades, respectively. Conversely, the reverse trend was observed with unique variance related to WR as it dropped from 27% in the second grade, to 13% and ultimately only 2% accounted for in fourth and eighth grades, respectively (Catts et al., 2005). Moreover, several policy reports have indicated relatively small percentages of ASRs (<10%[1]) who have WR problems (e.g., Biancarosa & Snow, 2004; Kamil, 2003). These findings support the developmental predictions set forth in the Simple View indicating early literacy's substantial dependence on phonological awareness and decoding, while post fourth grade LC components like background knowledge and vocabulary become greater indicators of skilled reading.

How Proficient Readers Translate Language Comprehension into Efficient Reading

With acquisition of strong LC skills, proficient readers are able to meet the grade-appropriate academic literacy demands of the content-area classroom. A variety of sources report that proficient readers are able to engage in strategic practices before, during, and after reading (e.g., Barr, Blachowicz,

Katz, & Kaufman, 2002; Pressley & Afflerbach, 1995). For example, proficient readers are aware of the purpose or goal of reading, engaging in skimming to overview a text to see if it relates to the purpose. This allows for selective and focused reading on portions of the text related to accomplishing identified goals. Strong readers discover new meanings of words based on context, and problem-solve to support understanding. This often occurs through self-monitoring and self-questioning. Self-questioning involves making and revising hypotheses about textual content, drawing analogies from experience or prior knowledge, and making inferences to build understanding. Proficient readers also are sensitive to different text structures (e.g., narrative vs. expository), using the structure to organize comprehension and aid in inference making. When reading is complete, proficient readers typically respond thoughtfully and personally to what they have read, at times responding directly to the author. Additionally, knowledge from across texts is synthesized and integrated into memory with high degrees of critical and analytic thinking. Such skills are developed as LC increases, with academic literacy-related tasks in school serving as opportunities to practice and master such abilities. However, skill development is not universal and requires explicit instruction for some ASRs who can be lacking in language development.

PREDICTING POOR READER SUBGROUPS

While the Simple View of Reading certainly supports the importance of WR and its corresponding subskill component instruction, the emergence of a significant number of students beyond fourth grade (30.1% with specific comprehension disorders [SCD]) indicate the need for an instructional focus beyond just WR. Students with SCD, termed "late-emerging poor readers" (Leach, Scarborough, & Rescorla, 2003) or "late-emerging reading disability" (Compton, Fuchs, Fuchs, Elleman, & Gilbert, 2008), present an anomaly in current instructional practice, including Responsiveness to Intervention (RtI; see Fuchs, Mock, Morgan, & Young, 2003; Graner, Faggella-Luby, & Fritschmann, 2005). This is because students with SCD appear to respond to early literacy instruction (which typically focuses on an area of strength for students with SCD: WR) only to be identified as poor readers post third grade when listening comprehension skills become stronger predictors of reading success. However, these students have also not changed profiles over time. In fact, 77% of students with SCD in fourth/eighth grade had the same profile in the second grade but were not identified because of their response to instruction (Catts et al., 2005). Late-emerging poor readers are therefore characterized by reading problems related to listening comprehension deficits that become recognizable around the fourth grade including vocabulary knowledge that is moderately depressed and text-level comprehension that is substantially depressed (Catts et al., 2005).

Profile of Struggling Readers

Research is currently underway to identify late-emerging struggling readers as early as possible (e.g., Compton et al., 2008). However, the reading profile of ASRs is beginning to emerge, providing a framework for identifying areas of student need. For example, Hock and colleagues (2009) provide a descriptive analysis of the component reading skills of adolescent readers, including proficient readers in comparison to struggling adolescents with and without LDs in urban schools. The study characterized the reading of 345 adolescent readers across four domains of reading including word level, fluency, vocabulary, and comprehension using 11 standardized measures. Results confirm a significant gap of approximately one standard deviation across all four domains between the performance of proficient readers and readers who struggle. Moreover, 61% of the struggling reader population had significant deficits in all four areas (Hock et al., 2009). Results for students with reading-related LD indicated performance in all four domains significantly below that of the larger struggling reader subgroup in all areas except vocabulary where scores were approximately the same. While such results are in contrast to the shifting importance of WR to LC abilities, they underscore the continued importance of instruction to address areas commonly associated with LC ability.

The profile of struggling readers, especially students with LD, characterizes such students as inefficient in many of the areas that proficient readers excel. For example, Gersten et al. (2001) summarized student difficulties related to comprehension of text in the areas of (a) lack of knowledge of common text structures (e.g., narrative vs. expository), (b) limited vocabulary knowledge, (c) failure to appropriately use background knowledge while reading, (d) inactive reading and limited task persistence. Moreover, inefficient executive functions related to strategic processing and metacognition that help students to manage and self-regulate proficient reading behaviors negatively impact comprehension. Clearly, if the skills that aid proficient readers in meeting academic literacy demands are missing or inefficiently applied by struggling learners, an achievement gap emerges.

Resulting Achievement Gap

Less than desired academic outcomes for ASRs can be explained by a mismatch between curricular demands and learner characteristics. The resulting achievement gap occurs when students fail to acquire the necessary skills and strategies to meet grade-appropriate curriculum demands at the same rate as their typically achieving peers (Deshler & Schumaker, 2006). Stated differently, the impact of the widening gap is simple: students who lack appropriate academic strategies are unable to master the critical content necessary for adequate progress throughout school. As each school year passes, these students miss more and more of the knowledge they will be expected to apply later in school and life.

Failure to master critical content has an immediate impact on school performance and can result in disastrous long-term consequences. For example, students with at least five full-year course credits and no more than one F in a core class are four times more likely to graduate than those with additional failing grades (Allensworth & Easton, 2007). The same report indicates that freshman year GPA and ninth-grade failures, both directly impacted by instructional conditions, each predict which students will graduate with 80% accuracy. Surprisingly, Allensworth and Easton (2007) add that student background and prior achievement, both conditions beyond the scope of instructional influence, only contribute an additional half a percentage point to either prediction. Clearly, classroom preparation is essential. Finally, students with marginal performance, GPAs in the D+ or C− range, or those with just one failure in the first semester, are about as likely to graduate as to not. Students in the lowest 25% of achievement are twenty times more likely to drop out of secondary school than those in the highest 25% (Carnevale, 2001). Consequently, both groups of struggling students with and without identified disabilities require explicit instruction and alternative or supplementary supports beyond those they may already be receiving.

Instructional Focus

Given the prominent role that LC plays in skilled reading, and the large percentage of struggling adolescent readers who are inefficient in these areas (e.g., Catts et al., 2005; Gersten et al., 2001; Hock et al., 2009) direct and explicit instruction has proven effective to remediate learner skills. In the section that follows, the critical components of comprehension instruction are outlined to help close the achievement gap by providing struggling readers with the foundational skills and strategies to meet grade-level curriculum demands.

INSTRUCTIONAL COMPONENTS FOR ADOLESCENT STRUGGLING READERS

Components of Comprehension Instruction

The intent of each critical component of comprehension instruction is to support the potentially inefficient LC abilities of struggling readers. In fact, the general thinking in comprehension instruction has been to identify the behaviors of proficient readers and then design instruction to address apparent gaps or inefficiencies in struggling reader knowledge and skills. In a summary of the literature, Faggella-Luby and Deshler (2008) described five main components, or categories, of corresponding instruction: (a) knowledge of text structures (both narrative and expository), (b) vocabulary, (c) prior knowledge, (d) cognitive strategies, and (e) increased motivation/engagement. Each area is examined below including what the component is and how it helps improve comprehension for ASRs.

Knowledge of Text Structures

Text structure, or the organizational framework for a piece of prose writing, aids proficient readers by providing a lens through which to view the unique language features and conventions of discipline-specific texts, for example, science labs, historical documents, and novels (Heller & Greenleaf, 2007). Students with LDs have been shown to lack text structure awareness of both expository and narrative text types (Englert & Thomas, 1987; Montague, Maddux, & Dereshiwsky, 1990). Although students with LD are a heterogeneous group, in general they struggle with (a) poor recall of textual ideas, (b) identifying main ideas from extraneous details, (c) relating new information to prior knowledge, and (d) actively monitoring comprehension when reading expository texts (Gajria, Jitendra, Sood, & Sacks, 2007). Specifically, students with LD are challenged to both understand expository text structures and use them to promote acquisition and expression of content area information (Englert & Thomas, 1987). Consequently, struggling students have difficulty understanding and remembering important information (i.e., main ideas, central conflicts) when they cannot discern the author's organizational framework. Functionally, this means students may struggle to identify the essential from the nonessential information presented in the text (Ehren, 2005).

Instruction in the components of narrative text structure (e.g., main character, initiating event, central conflict, resolution) has demonstrated large effect sizes for students with LD and has been researched with greater frequency than expository text (Gersten et al., 2001; Edmonds et al., 2009). Recent research in this area has attempted to embed narrative text structure instruction into secondary English classes by incorporating elements as part of a package of self-questioning and summarization strategies with consistently positive results for ASRs (see Faggella-Luby, Schumaker, & Deshler, 2007).

Expository text structure, which is more commonly associated with the secondary curriculum, can be a considerable challenge for struggling readers. Research on the instruction of expository text structures has demonstrated substantially improved outcomes with both single strategies and packages of strategies. For example, Gajria and colleagues (2007) found effect sizes ranging from 1.64 to 2.38 among posttest scores for single strategies including text structure (2.38–2.27) and finding the main idea (1.64–2.55). When examining multiple strategies of identifying the main idea and self-monitoring, Graves (1986) demonstrated an effect size of 4.59. It should be noted however, that within the body of research on expository instruction, fewer than half (41%) included measures of treatment integrity and only 24% focused on high school students.

Vocabulary

Vocabulary instruction, especially related to increasing the depth understanding of word meaning, is central to secondary student academic success. In fact, an analysis of secondary textbooks demonstrated that more new vocabulary words were introduced in a single year of science than in the first year of a foreign language class (Yager, 1983). Fortunately, research has demonstrated generally enhanced vocabulary development for students with LD. In a review of research on vocabulary instruction across K-12 students with LD from 1978 to 2002, Jitendra, Edwards, Sacks, and Jacobson (2004) report improved outcomes related to mnemonic, cognitive strategy, direct instruction, activity-based, constant time delay, and computer-assisted methods of instruction. Results indicated effect sizes of 1.48 for middle school students and 1.79 for high school students, demonstrating promise for ASRs (Jitendra et al., 2004). Similarly, Kamil et al. (2008) summarized the evidence on explicit vocabulary instruction at all school levels and strongly recommend that content teachers engage in explicit vocabulary instruction routinely.

Prior Knowledge
Instruction in prior knowledge focuses on activating related background knowledge and life experiences that students bring to the content area classroom and help to support comprehension. In fact, Thoreau was more right than perhaps he knew when he said, "We hear and [comprehend] only what we already half know." For struggling readers, limited prior knowledge may also include the vocabulary and conceptual knowledge missed in previous elementary and middle school coursework as a result of their struggling reader profile (Ehren, 2005). Therefore, instruction around key vocabulary and critical concepts is essential. However, instruction cannot simply involve activating prior knowledge of a topic as a prereading activity.

While it has been shown that activation of prior knowledge can help students with LD integrate new information encountered in text with their existing knowledge as demonstrated through self-questioning strategies (Vaughn, Gersten, & Chard, 2000), emerging research in disciplinary specific literacy clarify this suggestion as follows. Disciplinary literacy, as engaged in by disciplinary experts within a field, involves application of specialized and robust routines and strategies for specific literacy tasks (Shanahan & Shanahan, 2008). Consequently, adolescents require instruction by content area teachers in the unique components of each discipline (e.g., science vs. English). However, at the core of disciplinary literacy is a deep reservoir of content-specific knowledge and experience maintained by experts, and not yet mastered by adolescents. Consider the critical challenge facing science teachers in teaching adolescents to engage in disciplinary literacy. Science teachers are challenged to help students shift understanding by changing what they believe intuitively, often based on misconceptions of prior knowledge or perceived experience (Shanahan & Shanahan, 2008). If students are taught solely to activate prior knowledge, they may read to confirm misconceptions, inhibiting comprehension, and blocking integration of new knowledge with old. Therefore, instruction around prior knowledge must address intuitive misunderstandings to prevent reader ignoring, discounting, and compartmentalizing accurate information. Such instruction seeks to clarify background knowledge and experiences prior to reading, not just activating it and leaving students to their own construction of knowledge. Research in disciplinary literacy is emerging and its full impact on struggling readers remains unknown.

Cognitive Strategies

Teaching students strategies, how a person thinks and acts when planning, executing, and evaluating performance on a task (Deshler & Schumaker, 2006), is perhaps the most robust instructional practice for ASRs. Functionally, readers must decide which strategies will be most helpful in supporting comprehension before, during, and after reading. Ehren (2005) describes three categories of strategies (a) goal-specific strategies including activating prior knowledge, text analysis, self-questioning, visual imagery, and paraphrasing/summarization, (b) monitoring and repair strategies, and (c) packaging multiple strategies. Concerning the acquisition of knowledge through reading, the largest effect sizes were found for strategies involving self-questioning, summarizing, and self-monitoring (Vaughn et al., 2000; Mastropieri, Scruggs, & Graetz, 2003; Edmonds et al., 2009). Additionally, many strategies (e.g., text analysis, self-questioning) tap into other critical components of comprehension instruction by supporting knowledge of text structures, vocabulary, and activation of prior knowledge by teaching students an independent and self-regulated problem-solving process.

In 2008, Faggella-Luby and Deshler provided a research summary identifying six consistent findings related to adolescent reading comprehension strategy instruction from across a combination of six literature reviews and meta-analyses written during the previous decade. Several findings are relevant here. First, moderate to large effect sizes were observed when struggling readers, including students with LD, received targeted instruction in components listed above (i.e., text structures, vocabulary, tapping prior knowledge, using cognitive strategies). These are the same components that parallel the reading behaviors of proficient readers. Second, strategy maintenance was highest for self-monitoring, summarizing, and story grammar self-questioning, indicating short-term (6–8 weeks) proficient use post instruction. Finally, reading comprehension strategy instruction resulted in improvements for both adolescents and elementary readers, providing evidence that remediation can be successful (Faggella-Luby & Deshler, 2008). The findings of moderate to large effect sizes for comprehension strategy instruction, especially when the instruction targets previously presented components of comprehension instruction is promising. Moreover, the maintenance of ability post instruction indicates the potential for meaningful change to student outcomes in classroom practice.

Increased Motivation/Engagement

The challenge of increasing student motivation is tied to helping students find material interesting and useful. Typically, engagement has been operationalized as task persistence (Gersten et al., 2001; Vaughn et al., 2000). For example, one study involving students with LD, as well as low- and average-achieving peers, examined task persistence and reading outcomes related to instruction in Peer-Assisted Learning Strategies (PALS). Students in the PALS condition demonstrated greater task persistence and reading progress on comprehension measures than the control group during 15 weeks of instruction (Fuchs, Fuchs, Mathes, & Simmons, 1997). While it is not possible to generalize this one study to all ASRs, the profile of struggling readers suggests instruction related to motivation and engagement is warranted. For example, instruction might focus on texts of multiple readability levels to ensure that students have access to ability level materials. Additionally, similar to PALS, collaborative reasoning might be taught, with individual student roles explicitly defined for cooperative learning. Finally, motivation is likely to be increased when readers have self-efficacy that comes from self-regulated application of problem-solving strategies when encountering reading difficulties.

Research to Practice

Finally, there have been several recent policy documents released to help guide practitioner implementation of the components of comprehension instruction at the state and local levels. Summarized in Faggella-Luby, Ware, and Capozzoli (2009) there is a great deal of consistency between the empirical literature on critical components of reading instruction (mentioned above) and the policy documents (see Table 2). Findings from across the reports found consensus recommendations around instructional components for core instruction and instruction for struggling adolescent readers. Core instruction consensus emerged around the need to teach all students: (a) essential content and vocabulary, (b) cognitive strategies and higher-level thinking skills, and (c) improving motivation and engagement. Core instructional practices are relevant to ASRs because the majority of their time is spent in core subject matter classes. Moreover, the initial consensus recommendation from across the policy documents for ASRs was for content area teachers to continue reinforcing previous core literacy practices. Additional specific recommendations for struggling readers included (a) providing multiple-tiers of increasingly intense instruction, (b) cuing students to activate prior knowledge and skills, and (c) teaching content-based language and literacy (Faggella-Luby et al., 2009). While a significant limitation across the majority of reports was the failure to

Table 2. Adolescent Literacy Reports in Chronological Order Included in Faggella-Luby et al. (2009).

Reading Next – A Vision for Action and Research in Middle and High School Literacy: A Report to Carnegie Corporation of New York (2004).
Reading to Achieve: A Governor's Guide to Adolescent Literacy (2005).
The Next Chapter: A School Board Guide to Improving Adolescent Literacy (2006).
The Secondary Literacy and Intervention Guide: Helping High School Districts Transform into Systems that Produce Life-Changing Results for all Children (2007).
Academic Literacy Instruction for Adolescents: A Guidance Document from the Center on Instruction (2007).
Double the Work: Challenges and Solutions to Acquiring Language and Academic Literacy for Adolescent English Language Learners – A Report to Carnegie Corporation of New York (2007).
Interventions for Adolescent Struggling Readers: A Meta-analysis with Implications for Practice (2007).
Literacy Instruction in the Content Areas: Getting to the Core of Middle and High School Improvement (2007).
Improving Adolescent Literacy: Effective Classroom and Intervention Practices: A Practice Guide (2008).
A Critical Mission: Making Adolescent Reading an Immediate Priority in SREB States (2009).
Assessments to Guide Adolescent Literacy Instruction (2009).

distinguish between levels of evidence supporting each recommendation (the IES Practice Guide [2008] being a notable exception), the considerable overlap between the empirical literature and policy recommendations provides practitioners with a solid foundation to guide instruction.

In the sections that follow, findings related to how teachers might teach the critical components of comprehension are presented. Two examples of evidence-based practices to illustrate both the content and pedagogy of adolescent literacy instruction for struggling readers are then described.

DELIVERING INSTRUCTION FOR ADOLESCENT STRUGGLING READERS

How does teachers teach matter? Are there practices or behaviors that a teacher should implement when teaching ASRs? How are these practices manifested in inclusive classrooms?

In order to ensure that students learn how to be effective learners and good readers, it is necessary for teachers to employ an instructional approach characterized by "certain regularities in the ways in which teachers and students interact with each other and with instructional materials that can be described, evaluated, and replicated" (Corcoran & Silander, 2009, p. 165). In short, it does matter how teachers teach. Older students require more support and effective instruction if they are to learn how to apply various reading comprehension strategies and coordinate the use of several strategies in school (Bean & Harper, 2004; Biancarosa & Snow, 2004; Torgesen et al., 2007).

Instructional Approaches for ASRs

As addressed earlier in this chapter, specific instructional approaches are necessary for ASRs to benefit from typical instructional practice. Ellis, Deshler, Lenz, Schumaker, and Clark (1991) describe educators' increasing awareness of the need for "instructional techniques and curricula" (p. 1) to promote academic success and lifelong independence for students with LD at the secondary level, a requirement that continues in 2009. Numerous studies conducted with students with LD have demonstrated their ability to master and generalize numerous strategies applicable to a variety of settings and academic tasks, particularly reading comprehension (Deshler & Schumaker, 2006; Edmonds et al., 2009; Gardill & Jitendra, 1999; Gersten et al., 2001; Jitendra, Hoppes, & Xin, 2000; Mastropieri, Scruggs, Bakken, & Whedon, 1996; Mastropieri et al., 2003; Pressley, Goodchild, Fleet, Zajchowski, & Evans, 1989).

Useful in the design of such strategies is Swanson's (1999) meta-analysis of reading research for students with LD which outlines six instructional components of reading comprehension instruction that have demonstrated treatment effectiveness:

1. Directed response/questioning in which the teacher asks the questions and/or a process of reciprocal engagement by the teacher and students.
2. Teacher control of task difficulty, through manipulation of the size of the task and level of difficulty, or through simplified demonstrations and sequencing of task steps.
3. Elaboration provided through clear descriptions, repetition, procedures, or steps.
4. Modeling by the teacher, accompanied by explanations.
5. Group instruction featuring interaction, generally in small student groups and sometimes with the teacher.
6. Strategy cues (think-alouds, verbal practice of steps, benefits of strategy use) that facilitate complex cognitive processes and act as reminders for independent use.

These six instructional components, representing a blend of direct instruction and strategy instruction can, when implemented as the structure of reading comprehension instruction, yield the most positive outcomes for students with LD. Indeed, these instructional approaches have been recommended and supported by empirical evidence (Kamil et al., 2008) as practices that should be used by content teachers, as outlined below.

Instruction for Adolescents

As stated earlier, a spate of reports from a variety of sources regarding adolescent literacy have been presented to the public and profession in the past decade. The reports have addressed how cognitive strategy instruction can improve literacy development and be used in a remedial fashion.

Some of the strongest recommendations about how to increase the reading ability of adolescents were presented by Kamil et al. (2008) in the form of an Institute for Education Sciences (IES) Practice Guide that presented five "specific and coherent evidence-based recommendations that educators can use" (p. 1). While the first four recommendations have been included in the components of instruction above, the fifth is addressed here. In recognition that some students need additional supports, the report specifically suggests making available intensive and individualized interventions for ASRs by trained specialists (Kamil et al., 2008). There is strong evidence to support the use of additional resources. However, it is also widely recognized that most secondary schools lack the structures to provide and support the necessary interventions and services for struggling readers who need more than the classroom teacher can provide. While the evidence suggests more supports be provided, few models have been constructed and tested at the secondary level to ensure such implementation.

School-Wide Structures that Can Help – The Content Literacy Continuum

Recently, secondary schools have been faced with the challenge of implementing less familiar practices in the form of RtI. Essentially, the goal of instruction is to ensure access to high-quality instruction to meet curriculum standards for *all* students including learners who struggle. Functionally, this means that high-quality, scientifically based instruction/intervention is matched to student needs, while using rate over time and level of performance so that important educational decisions can be made including disability determination (Ehren, Deshler, & Graner, in press; Kurns & Tilly, 2007). When implementing RtI, schools use a multitiered approach to provide the supports, academic and behavioral, to struggling learners at increasing levels of intensity.

There are several essential components to RtI (Kurns & Tilly, 2007; NJCLD, 2005):

- High quality scientifically based core instruction.
- Universal screening to identify struggling learners who need additional support.
- Increasingly intensive instruction in a multitiered approach for struggling students.
- Frequent progress monitoring to examine student achievement and monitor the effectiveness of instruction and intervention.
- Data-based decision-making regarding students' instructional needs based on multiple data points over time.

Currently, the majority of the development and research on the adoption of RtI has occurred at the elementary level although evidence for implementation at the secondary level is building (Burns, 2008; Canter, Klotz, & Cowan, 2008; Duffy, 2007; Ehren, 2008; Johnson & Smith, 2008).

One framework that secondary schools might consider as a way to engage in RtI is the Content Literacy Continuum (CLC) developed by the University of Kansas Center for Research on Learning (Lenz & Ehren, 1999; Lenz, Ehren, & Deshler, 2005). The CLC is comprised of five levels of literacy support that might be used in secondary schools. Implementation of all five levels of the CLC presents secondary schools with a structure to conceptualize and implement a comprehensive initiative to make literacy a priority, emphasizing the importance of infusing literacy instruction throughout the secondary school curriculum (Ehren et al., in press).

Level 1. Enhanced Content Instruction addresses the mastery of critical content required in academic subjects for all students. The purpose of Enhanced Content Instruction is focused delivery that ensures listening, speaking, reading, and writing access, skills students need to manipulate subject matter. Tools teachers utilize may include graphic organizers, prompted outlines, high-quality discussion of text meaning and interpretation, and the development of meaningful learning goals (Kamil et al., 2008) as well as tools such as Content Enhancement Routines (Bulgren, Deshler, & Lenz, 2007) to organize and enhance the curriculum content in ways that promote its understanding and mastery by all students.

Level 2. Embedded Strategy Instruction addresses how teachers can weave content literacy strategies into instruction so that students can acquire, manipulate, and demonstrate knowledge in specific subjects. Content teachers intentionally integrate instruction of appropriate literacy strategies into their classes, routinely modeling for students how particular strategies and techniques are useful for manipulation and learning of specific subjects. At this level, teachers (1) reflect before instruction to determine which strategies students will need, (2) engage students during explicit instruction that includes explanation and modeling using the class materials, (3) activate students' application of the strategy in class, and (4) determine student competence in application of the strategies or techniques across a variety of assignments (generalization).

Level 3. Intensive Strategy Instruction addresses the delivery of more intensive instruction of content literacy strategies so that students can master independent application and generalization across settings. The intensity of instruction at Level 3 is indicated for those students who do not benefit from the less explicit strategy instruction at Level 2, and who require smaller group instruction and conditions related to those suggested by Swanson's (1999) meta-analysis. In Level 3, generally delivered by a support teacher, Learning Strategies (Schumaker & Deshler, 2006) are taught within an explicit 8-stage instructional model (Ellis et al., 1991) designed for and validated with struggling learners.

Level 4. Intensive Basic Skill Instruction addresses the foundational language and literacy skills that students (usually below the fourth grade reading level) must acquire to be successful learners (Lenz & Ehren, 1999; Lenz et al., 2005). In this level, specialized, direct, and intensive instruction is provided to students who do not possess the fundamental literacy skills (decoding, fluency, and basic comprehension skills) necessary at this level.

Level 5. Therapeutic Intervention addresses intensive therapy in underlying language deficits for students with language impairments. In Level 5 interventions, students with underlying language disorders learn the linguistic, metalinguistic, and metacognitive underpinnings necessary to access and acquire the necessary content skills and strategies required in rigorous courses. In general, it is the speech-language pathologist (SLP) who will deliver small-group, curriculum-relevant language therapy (Ehren, 2002) in collaboration with both other support personnel teaching literacy and content teachers.

The CLC, implemented in secondary schools since 1999, fits within the essential structure, intent, and nature of the RtI framework and is elemental to ensuring the least restrictive environment for students with LD. When

CLC Levels 1 and 2 are well established in secondary schools, SWDs can be educated with nondisabled peers to the maximum extent possible in regular classes. Further articulation and development of Level 2 strategies, in particular, is an emerging area of work, and one that is critically important to ensuring a comprehensive approach to literacy within a school. Development of specific CLC Level 2 interventions provides content-area teachers with additional tools to enable students in the comprehension of subject matter, whether the interventions are used within the context of CLC implementation or not.

SPECIFIC INTERVENTIONS

In order to provide the reader with specific examples of CLC interventions, two literacy strategies for ASRs developed by the authors are described below. Each strategy presented was developed based on previously discussed research-based principles found to be effective for instruction of ASRs.

A Package of Reading Comprehension Strategies: The ESS Routine

A recent emphasis has been placed on the role of secondary E/LA teachers in improving literacy outcomes of secondary students (Biancarosa & Snow, 2004). Yet E/LA teachers are also held accountable on high-stakes AYP tests for teaching course content that might be sacrificed in place of reading instruction. Therefore, interventions are necessary to provide evidence-based instruction that is feasible and usable by emphasizing components of the E/LA teacher's curriculum, allowing teachers to use the intervention without sacrificing required content. To meet this challenge, Faggella-Luby and colleagues (2007) conducted an experimental study to investigate the effects of the Embedded Story Structure (ESS) Routine, an intervention informed by theory and research discussed above, and designed for use in general education E/LA classrooms serving heterogeneous populations of students.

The purpose of this experimental study was to investigate the effects of using the ESS Routine with 79 ninth-grade summer school students in an English class in order to improve student (a) use of reading comprehension strategies, (b) knowledge of strategy components and literary terms, (c) comprehension of stories, and (d) satisfaction with the routine. Study participants, including 14 students with LD, were randomly assigned to one of two conditions: ESS Routine (experimental) and Comprehension Skills

Instruction (CSI; control) with instruction occurring in groups of 12–14 students over nine days (total time in instruction was 17 h). ESS Routine instruction focused on: (a) student self-questioning of story grammar elements, (b) story-structure analysis in which students labeled plot diagrams, and (c) summarizing (see Fig. 1). CSI provided a package of three different research-based reading strategies focusing on (a) vocabulary, (b) self-questioning (nonstory grammar), and (c) semantic mapping. Both instructional conditions used a four phase mediated instruction framework that included (a) teacher demonstration and modeling, (b) guided practice, (c) cooperative learning, and (d) independent practice. Students in both conditions read eight authentic and unaltered short stories with discernable story structures drawn from renowned classics (e.g., Poe's *The Tell-Tale Heart*) as well as more contemporary stories (e.g., Myers' *The Treasure of Lemon Brown*).

Data were collected from four measures in this study: (a) Strategy-use Test, measuring actual strategy use with novel passages; (b) Knowledge Test, measuring student knowledge of ESS strategy components and related literary terms; (c) Unit Reading Comprehension Test, covering the eight short stories; and (d) two student satisfaction surveys related to personal beliefs about reading and instruction. The Unit Reading Comprehension Test used a mixture of story-structure (60%) and higher-order questions (40%) with 40 total questions. All measures were collected at pre- and posttest. The Strategy-use Test was also collected at progress (day five of instruction) and maintenance (8 weeks after instruction concluded).

Study results (see Table 3) support the use of the ESS Routine as an instructional intervention for improving reading comprehension of academically diverse learners in inclusive secondary classrooms for a variety of reasons. First, the Strategy-Use Test results indicated that students receiving the ESS Routine instruction not only outperformed control students [Wilks' $\Lambda = .330$, $F(3,73) = 49.5$, $p < .001$, multivariate $\eta^2 = .670$ (a large Effect Size, ES)], but gains were equivalent regardless of the disability/no disability category. Moreover, participation in the routine led to significant improvements in strategy use from pretest to posttest, and from pretest to maintenance [$t(38) = -18.3$, $p < .001$, $\Delta = 4.27$; and $t(38) = -10.84$, $p < .001$, $\Delta = 3.70$, respectively]. No such trend existed for control students, whose Strategy-Use Test scores remained linear and low. Similar results were also observed on the Knowledge Test [Wilks' $\Lambda = .376$, $F(1,75) = 124.4$, $p < .001$, multivariate $\eta^2 = .624$ (a large ES)]. Second, results from the Unit Reading Comprehension Test indicated once again that students, including those with disabilities, benefited equally from use of the ESS Routine (Wilks'

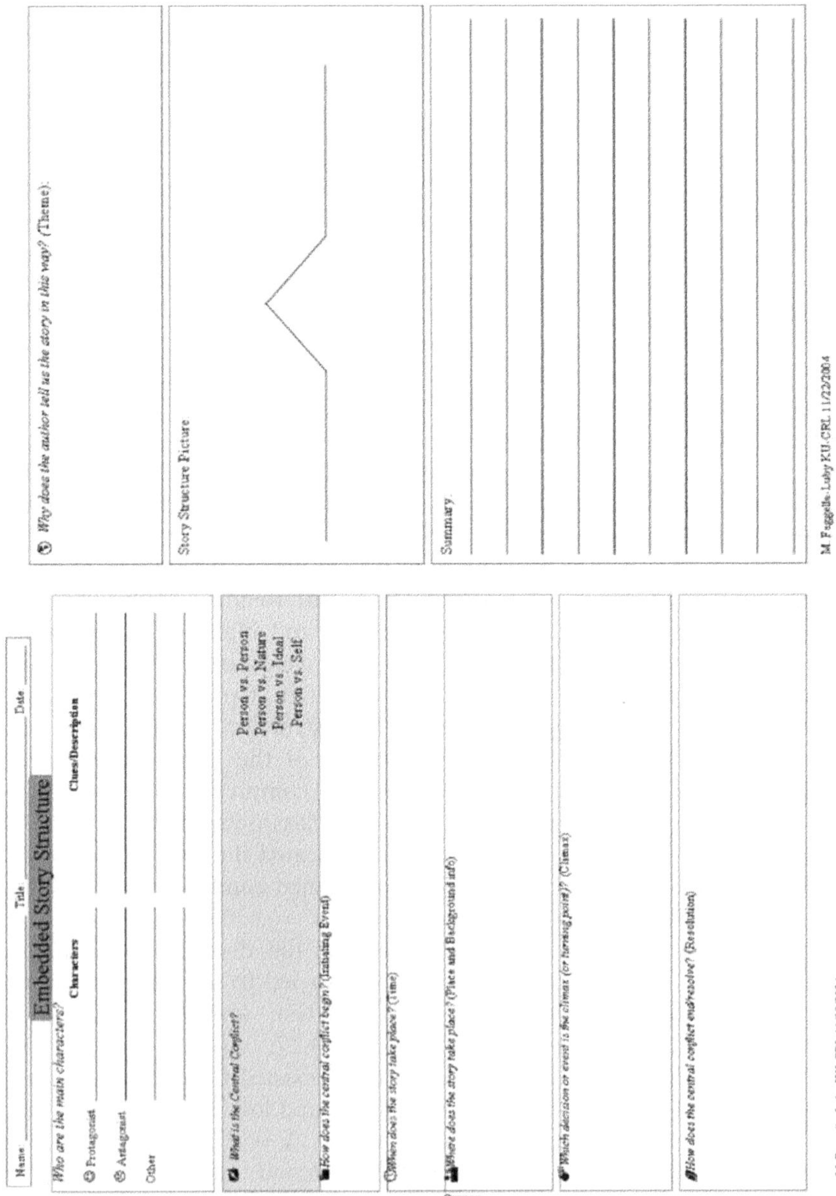

Fig. 1. Graphic Organizer for the ESS Routine.

Table 3. ESS Unit Reading Comprehension Test Results.

	N	Pretest		Posttest	
		Mean	SD	Mean	SD
Experimental					
Total	39	2.08	2.26	23.97	4.99
SwLD[a]	7	2.00	2.83	21.86	3.67
Other	32	2.09	2.18	24.44	5.17
Control					
Total	40	1.63	2.25	19.23	5.27
SwLD[a]	7	1.14	2.61	17.14	6.15
Other	33	1.72	2.2	19.67	5.06

[a]SwLD, students with learning disabilities.

$\Lambda = .908$, $F(1,75) = 7.61$, $p = .007$, multivariate $\eta^2 = .092$ (a medium ES)). Significant differences between students in the ESS experimental group and the control group on the reading comprehension measure and the Knowledge Test are particularly significant given their similar nature to criterion-referenced assessments common in language arts classrooms. These findings support the belief that instruction in the ESS Routine may bolster educational outcomes for individuals at-risk for failure in such classrooms.

Finally, socially significant findings across all survey measures (including a grand mean of 6.27/7 for ESS instructional satisfaction) are positive indicators of the palatability of the ESS Routine. More specifically, differences within both groups from pretest to posttest scores for the Reading Satisfaction Survey indicate that regardless of instruction type, students were more satisfied with their reading abilities after instruction. Student survey scores on the Satisfaction with Instruction Survey in both groups indicated not only overall satisfaction with the instruction, but also a feeling that this instruction: (a) helped them understand short stories, (b) was fun and interesting, and (c) would lead to likely independent use of the strategies. Again, these results are positive indicators to support the likelihood of instructional feasibility. For more information, see Faggella-Luby and colleagues (2007).

A Single Strategy: The Written Summarization Strategy (WSS)

Consistently, the ability to produce a summary is identified as an important reading tool (Kamil et al., 2008; Lee & Spratley, 2010; National Reading Panel, 2000; Reading Next, 2004) and is one indicator of higher-order thinking. Production of a summary benefits both the reading and writing processes. When readers summarize, they "clarify the meaning and significance of discourse" (Brown, Campione, & Day, 1981, p. 17) and apply a systematic decision-making process of reduction and organization to generate a unified, useful product for later review and study. Researchers have studied the production of summaries since the 1970s; however whether students with LD could learn how to apply a set of rules and steps to create a written summary was unknown. Hence, Graner (2007) conducted a quasi-experimental study to create and test the effects of an instructional program for teaching students with ($N = 4$) and without ($N = 38$) disabilities how to create written summaries of multiple paragraph passages. Three inclusive, intact tenth-grade English classes were randomly assigned to the experimental and comparison conditions.

The WSS designed for use by secondary teachers in general education classes over nine lessons, involves a set of steps that encompass what good summarizers do: (1) start reading with summarizing in mind, (2) underline main ideas and details, (3) make choices, (4) use a worksheet to guide writing, and (5) polish your product.

The instructional format for both conditions was similar. The control format instructional steps: (1) an advance organizer to outline the lesson purpose and student expectations; (2) a review and rationales for acquiring the new skills; (3) teacher modeling, guided paired practice, and independent practice; and (4) a post organizer to review the lesson and preview the next lesson. The comparison class was instructed in the Test-Taking Strategy (Hughes, Schumaker, Deshler, & Mercer, 1993) and the LINCS Vocabulary Strategy (Ellis, 2000) using the Strategic Instruction Model eight stages of acquisition and generalization from the Learning Strategy Curriculum.

Results (see Table 4) support the use of the WSS for teaching summarization skills; scores of SWDs were within the range of scores for the NSWDs, indicating that this instructional program seems appropriate for use in inclusive classes. The Strategy-Use Test revealed that students in the control group learned to follow the steps of the summarizing process and produce succinct written summaries. Control group posttest scores related to the skills were significantly higher than corresponding scores of students in the comparison group. ANCOVA results revealed a statistically significant difference between the posttest scores of the experimental general education students (NSWDs) and the comparison NSWDs in favor of the experimental group with regard to total posttest scores, [$F(1,53) = 401.105$, $p < .0005$, $\eta^2 = .883$, TMD posttest scores [$F(1,53) = 54.404$, $p < .0005$, $\eta^2 = .507$], and

Table 4. Written Summarization Strategy Mean Strategy – Use Pretest and Posttest Scores and Standard Deviations.

	N	Pretest		Posttest	
		Mean	SD	Mean	SD
Experimental Group					
NSwLD	38				
Total Reading Test Score		12.79	1.95	36.37	4.39
Procedure Score		0.0	0.0	14.84	.55
TMD Score		10.37	1.60	12.55	1.74
Summary Score		2.42	1.33	8.97	3.99
SwLD	4				
Total Reading Test Score		11.50	2.08	33.50	5.75
Procedure Score		0.0	0.0	15.00	.00
TMD Score		9.00	2.94	12.00	1.16
Summary Score		2.50	1.0	6.50	6.40
Comparison Group					
NSwLD					
Total Reading Test Score	18	13.33	2.14	11.67	4.33
Procedure Score		0.0	0.0	.00	.00
TMD Score		10.67	1.85	8.00	2.83
Summary Score		2.67	.97	3.67	2.50
SwLD					
Total Strategy-Use Score	4	11.25	2.06	10.25	2.75
Procedure Score		0.0	0.0	.00	.00
TMD Score		9.25	2.06	7.25	2.63
Summary Score		2.00	.00	3.00	1.16

summary posttest scores [$F(1,53) = 29.742$, $p < .0005$, $\eta^2 = .349$], representing large effect sizes in each case, according to Cohen (1988).

A *t* test was used to compare the procedure posttest scores for the NSWDs since all of the students earned a zero score on the pretest on this subtest, and an ANCOVA was not appropriate. The *t* test revealed a significant difference between the experimental NSWDs and the comparison NSWDs in favor of the experimental students on the procedure subtest (t [37] $= 167.4$, $p < .0005$, $d = 166.8$, representing a large effect size).

Two-tailed *t* tests revealed that there were no differences between the groups with regard to total test and subtest scores on the pretest. *t* tests also showed that the posttest scores of the SWDs in the experimental group were significantly higher than the posttest scores of the SWDs in the comparison group with regard to the total test ($t[6] = 7.299$, $p < .0005$, $d = 7.3$), the TMD subtest ($t[4.115] = 3.307$, $p = .028$, $d = 3.31$), and the summary subtest ($t[3.195] = 1.07$, $p = .356$, $d = 1.07$). All of these differences are very large, according to Cohen (1988).

ANCOVA results revealed no significant difference between the posttest scores of the GRADE total reading test. With regard to the SWDs, separate two-tailed *t* tests revealed that there was no difference between the experimental and comparison SWDs on the GRADE pretest and on the GRADE posttest.

Standard deviations range from .833 to 1.50 for NWSDs and from .000 to 1.91 for SWDs on the WSS Student Satisfaction Survey. All items were rated on a seven-point scale, indicating general satisfaction with the WSS and the instruction. The overall mean rating for the NSWDs was 5.9; the overall mean rating for the SWDs was 5.2.

Clearly, the two interventions presented here provide promising evidence that such reading comprehension interventions, CLC Level 2 interventions, can be learned by students with and without disabilities and that they do not require undue amounts of time to teach and implement. Class activities and assignments can be structured by content teachers to require students to identify key narrative components by using self-questioning related to text structure or summarize text and use that summarized information to demonstrate their ability to synthesize content information.

CONCLUSION

The practices surrounding components of literacy, explicit instruction, and school-wide frameworks to improve outcomes for struggling adolescent readers presented in this chapter outline steps for action. In response to the call to action underscored at the beginning of the chapter, researchers have begun to outline promising practices to address learner needs that can be implemented by practitioners at once. The climate of accountability emphasized by NCLB and IDEA and the increasing demands of the secondary school curriculum necessitate such action for all adolescents, but especially for those who struggle to meet grade-level goals. Literacy is no longer solely the purview of the elementary school. Secondary school teachers, attempting to increase disciplinary knowledge and expertise of their academically diverse students, must see the direct connection between mastery of critical content and addressing the literacy needs and characteristics of struggling readers.

While ASRs clearly have not developed skills similar to their typically achieving peers, research indicates that teachers can begin to address the achievement gap through critically important components of instruction emphasizing: (a) knowledge of text structures (both narrative and expository), (b) vocabulary, (c) prior knowledge, (d) cognitive strategies, and (e) increased motivation/engagement. Moreover, for this instruction to truly make an impact for students with LDs, it must be characterized by the equally critical components of explicit instruction including: (a) direct response/questioning, (b) controlling task difficulty, (c) elaboration, (d) teacher modeling, (e) interactive, small group instruction, and (f) strategy cueing. One way that schools can support such comprehensive reading goals is through equally comprehensive school-wide efforts including RtI and the CLC that provide systemic support for the use of interventions like the ESS Routine and the WSS.

However, despite the promise of existing research, it is clear that more work is necessary to achieve grade-level outcomes for all students. For all students, including students with LD and those who struggle, success in rigorous coursework is more important than ever in today's knowledge-based economy. How teachers approach helping students to reach such success is the most important factor in their achievement (Weisberg, Sexton, Mulhern, & Keeling, 2009).

KEY RESOURCES

Work related to adolescent literacy is currently experiencing an explosion of interest. New publications related to adolescents and literacy in peer-reviewed journals and more widely disseminated reports, policy documents, and books appear each year. Information is available to researchers and practitioners in a variety of media, including collections of research reports, policy documents, and practitioner-ready materials hosted on websites, as well as the more classical edited books with chapters from a wide range of authors. While the explosion of knowledge will hopefully continue, several resources have been central to our current thinking and are worthy of mention and exploration by the reader. Table 5 includes a brief list of websites and Table 6 a list of books presenting ideas and research around adolescent literacy or topics related to adolescents, literacy, and schools. The following list, although far from exhaustive, was chosen based on each resource's commitment to research-based practices.

Table 5. Suggested Websites for Further Examination.

Websites
www.all4ed.org: *The Alliance for Excellent Education* is a national policy organization focused on how to help all at-risk secondary students graduate from high school. The Alliance's landmark publication *Reading Next*, has been a catalyst for conceptualizing issues in adolescent literacy. Additional reports and resources can be found here as well. Search: Publications, Adolescent Literacy.
www.carnegie.org: *The Carnegie Corporation of New York* has become a major player in funding and research related to adolescent literacy, including *Reading Next,* through their ongoing Adolescent Literacy Project. Most recently, Carnegie has published *Time to Act*, reflecting 5 years of research on adolescent literacy. Search: Advancing Literacy.
www.centeroninstruction.org: *The Center on Instruction* supports regional Comprehensive Centers goals to close the achievement gap and improve teaching and learning for all students. The Center has provides a variety of documents related to reading instruction in grades 4–12. Search: Reading, Resources, 4–12.
www.fcrr.org: *The Florida Center for Reading Research*, established at the Florida State University conducts and disseminates research on reading, reading growth, reading assessment and reading instruction. FCRR provides information for teachers, literacy coaches, administrators, parents, and researchers mainly related to elementary and upper-elementary students. Search: Struggling readers, Curriculum and Instruction.
www.ies.ed.gov/ncee/wwc: Housed within the *Institute for Educational Sciences* (IES) under the US Federal Government, the *What Works Clearinghouse* evaluates scientific evidence related to education. Research on interventions and strategies in the areas of alphabetics, reading fluency, comprehension and general literacy achievement are available for adolescents. Search: Adolescent Literacy.
www.ku-crl.org: For more than 35 years the *Center for Research on Learning* at the University of Kansas has been conducting research related to adolescents with learning disabilities. Initiatives such as the Content Literacy Continuum and evidence-based interventions for literacy instruction are available. Search: Adolescent Literacy, Whole School Reform.
www.nifl.gov: *The National Institute for Literacy*, created in 1991, seeks to develop literacy by disseminating high-quality information and resources ground in research. Specific information is available on adolescents, including key issues, reading components, teaching approaches and research. Search: Adolescence.
www.rti4success.org: The *National Center on Response to Intervention* was established through finding from the US Department of Educations' Office of Special Education Programs to respond to challenges in the development and implementation of RtI in K-12 schools. While not a significant source of information on RtI for secondary schools, as this research is ongoing, information is continually updated. Search: Secondary Schools, Secondary Level, Older Students.

In reviewing these resources, the reader is encouraged to think critically about the direction of research and practice by adding some of the following questions to their own:

- How does this resource define adolescent literacy?
- How does the author define terms such as adolescent, struggling reader, or explicit instruction?

Table 6. Suggested Books for Further Examination.

Books
Deshler, D., Palincsar, A., Biancarosa, G., & Nair, M. (2007). *Informed choices for struggling adolescent readers: A research-based guide to instructional programs and practices.* Newark, DE: International Reading Association.
Jetton, Tamara L. & Dole, J. A. (Eds). (2004). *Adolescent literacy research and practice.* New York: The Guilford Press.
Reid, R. & Lienemann, T. (2009). *Strategy instruction for students with learning disabilities.* New York: The Guilford Press.
Sweet, A. & Snow, C. (Eds). (2003). *Rethinking reading comprehension.* New York: The Guilford Press.
Wood, K. D., & Blanton, W. (Eds). (2009). *Literacy instruction for adolescents: Research-based practice.* New York: The Guilford Press.

- Does the resource consider students with LDs, students at-risk for learning disability identification, or students reading at least two-years below grade level?
- How does the resource present the components or content of instruction for adolescent learners? Does the resource explain why these components might improve comprehension?
- How does the resource present the instructional sequence or pedagogy of instruction for adolescent learners? How might these practices meet the needs of academically diverse groups of students?

Finally, the purpose of literacy must always be at the heart of discussions around adolescent literacy and how to meet the instructional needs of students with LDs or students at-risk for failure. Academic outcomes for struggling students serve as a proxy for preparation for participation in society. The literacy tasks of the "real world" including, reading the newspaper, critiquing information presented via the web, or job-related paperwork are essential to life in the 21st century. Even the more mundane tasks such as paying bills, following a recipe, or making a grocery list require such skills. Susan Frost is correct to instill in practitioners a sense of urgency about the needs of adolescents. While the field has yet to supply complete or definitive answers related to the scope of instruction for adolescents, clearly a direction has been provided, and researchers and practitioners alike must embark together on this path, collectively working to improve outcomes for students who struggle.

NOTE

1. There is disagreement in the field around number of students who continue to struggle with word recognition (see also Hock et al., 2009), however the focus of this chapter is on improving reading comprehension and therefore focused on components of instruction associated with language comprehension. Clearly, instructions in the components of early literacy are necessary for students who struggle with word recognition. For additional discussion see Compton et al. (2008).

REFERENCES

Allensworth, E. M., & Easton, J. Q. (2005). The on track indicator as a predictor of high school graduation. Chicago, IL: Consortium on Chicago school research. Retrieved October 10, 2007, from http://ccsr.uchicago.edu/publications/p78.pdf

Barr, R., Blachowicz, C., Katz, C., & Kaufman, B. (2002). *Reading diagnosis for teachers, an instructional approach* (4th ed.). Boston, MA: Pearson.

Bean, T. W., & Harper, H. J. (2004). Teacher education and adolescent literacy. In: T. L. Jetton & J. A. Dole (Eds), *Adolescent literacy research and practice* (pp. 392–411). New York: Guilford.

Biancarosa, G., & Snow, C. E. (2004). *Reading next – a vision for action and research in middle and high school literacy: A report from Carnegie Corporation of New York*. Washington, DC: Alliance for Excellent Education.

Brown, A. L., Campione, J. D., & Day, J. D. (1981). Learning to learn: On training student to learn from texts. *Educational Researcher*, *10*(2), 14–21.

Bulgren, J., Deshler, D. D., & Lenz, B. K. (2007). Engaging adolescents with LD in higher order thinking about history concepts using integrated content enhancement routines. *Journal of Learning Disabilities*, *40*, 121–133.

Burns, M. (2008). Response to intervention at the secondary level. *Principal Leadership (Middle School Edition)*, *8*(7), 12–15.

Canter, A., Klotz, M., & Cowan, K. (2008). Response to intervention: The future for secondary schools. *Principal Leadership (Middle School Edition)*, *8*(6), 12–15.

Carnevale, A. P. (2001). *Help wanted ...college required.* Washington, DC: Educational Testing Service, Office for Public Leadership.

Catts, H. W., Hogan, T. P., & Adlof, S. M. (2005). Developmental changes in reading and reading disabilities. In: H. W. Catts & A. G. Kahmi (Eds), *The connections between language and reading disabilities* (pp. 50–71). Mahwah, NJ: Lawrence Erlbaum Associates.

Cohen, J. (1988). *Statistical power analysis for the behavioral sciences* (2nd ed.). Hillsdale, NJ: Erlbaum.

Coiro, J., Knobel, M., Lankshear, C., & Leu, D. J. (2008). *Handbook of research on new literacies.* New York: Routledge.

Collins, A., Brown, J. S., & Newman, S. E. (1989). Cognitive apprenticeship: Teaching the crafts of reading, writing, and mathematics. In: L. B. Resnick (Ed.), *Knowing, learning, and instruction: Essays in honor of Robert Glaser* (pp. 453–494). Hillsdale, NJ: Erlbaum.

Compton, D. L., Fuchs, D., Fuchs, L. S., Elleman, A. M., & Gilbert, J. K. (2008). Tracking children who fly below the radar: Latent transition modeling of students with late-emerging reading disability. *Learning and Individual Differences, 18*, 329–337.

Corcoran, T., & Silander, M. (2009). Instruction in high school: The evidence and the challenge. *The Future of Children, 19*(1), 157–183.

Deshler, D. D. (2009). Keynote: Rethinking SIM, literacy, and professional development. Paper presented at the International SIM Conference, Lawrence, KS.

Deshler, D. D., & Schumaker, J. (Eds). (2006). *Teaching adolescents with disabilities: Accessing the general education curriculum*. Thousand Oaks, CA: Corwin Press.

Deshler, D. D., Schumaker, J. B., Bui, Y., & Vernon, S. (2005). High schools and adolescents with disabilities: Challenges at every turn. In: D. D. Deshler & J. B. Schumaker (Eds), *Teaching adolescents with disabilities: Accessing the general curriculum* (pp. 1–34). Thousand Oaks, CA: Corwin.

Duffy, H. (2007). *Meeting the needs of significantly struggling learners in high school: A look at approaches to tiered intervention*. Washington, DC: National High School Center.

Edmonds, M., Vaughn, S., Hjelm, J., Reutebuch, C., Cable, A., Tackett, K., et al. (2009). A synthesis of reading interventions and effects on reading outcomes for older struggling readers. *Review of Educational Research, 79*, 262–300.

Ehren, B. J. (2002). Speech-language pathologists contributing significantly to the academic success of high school students: A vision for professional growth. *Topics in Language Disorders, 22*, 60–80.

Ehren, B. J. (2005). Looking for evidence-based practice in reading comprehension instruction. *Topics in Language Disorders, 25*, 310–321.

Ehren, B. J. (2008). *Response to intervention in secondary schools: Is it on your radar screen*. Retrieved October 2, 2008, from http://www.rtinetwork.org/Learn/Why/ar/RadarScreen

Ehren, B. J., Deshler, D. D., & Graner, P. S. (in press). Using the Content Literacy Continuum as a framework for implementing RTI in secondary schools. *Theory into Practice*.

Ehri, L. C., & McCormick, S. (1998). Phases of word learning: Implications for instruction with delayed and disabled readers. *Reading and Writing Quarterly: Overcoming Learning Difficulties, 14*, 135–164.

Ellis, E. S. (2000). *The LINCS vocabulary strategy* (2nd ed.). Lawrence, KS: Edge Enterprises.

Ellis, E. S., Deshler, D. D., Lenz, B. K., Schumaker, J. B., & Clark, F. L. (1991). An instructional model for teaching learning strategies. *Focus on Exceptional Children, 24*(1), 1–14.

Englert, C. S., & Thomas, C. C. (1987). Sensitivity to text structure in reading and writing: A comparison between learning disabled and non-learning disabled students. *Learning Disability Quarterly, 10*, 93–105.

Faggella-Luby, M., & Deshler, D. (2008). Reading comprehension in adolescents with LD: What we know; what we need to learn. *Learning Disabilities Research & Practice, 23*(2), 70.

Faggella-Luby, M., Ware, S., & Capozzoli, A. (2009). Adolescent literacy – Reviewing adolescent literacy reports: Key components and critical questions. *Journal of Literacy Research, 41*, 453–475.

Faggella-Luby, M. N., Schumaker, J. S., & Deshler, D. D. (2007). Embedded learning strategy instruction: Story-structure pedagogy in heterogeneous secondary literature classes. *Learning Disability Quarterly, 30*, 131–147.

Frost, S. (2003). Forward. In: M. Kamil (Ed.), *Adolescents and literacy: Reading for the 21st century* (p. iv). Washington, DC: Alliance for Excellent Education.

Fuchs, D., Fuchs, L. S., Mathes, P. H., & Simmons, D. C. (1997). Peer-assisted strategies: Making classrooms more responsive to diversity. *American Educational Research Journal, 34*, 174–206.

Fuchs, D., Mock, D., Morgan, P. L., & Young, C. L. (2003). Responsiveness-to-intervention: Definitions, evidence, and implications for the learning disabilities construct. *Learning Disabilities Research & Practice, 18*, 157–171.

Gardill, M. C., & Jitendra, A. K. (1999). Advanced story map instruction: Effects on the reading comprehension of students with learning disabilities. *Journal of Special Education, 33*, 2–17.

Gajria, M., Jitendra, A., Sood, S., & Sacks, G. (2007). Improving comprehension of expository text in students with LD: A research synthesis. *Journal of Learning Disabilities, 40*, 210–225.

Geisler, C. (1994). *Academic literacy and the nature of expertise: Reading, writing, and knowing in academic philosophy*. Hillsdale, NJ: Erlbaum.

Gersten, R., Fuchs, L., Williams, J., & Baker, S. (2001). Teaching reading comprehension strategies to students with learning disabilities: A review of research. *Review of Educational Research, 71*, 279–320.

Gough, P. B., & Tumner, W. E. (1986). Decoding, reading, and reading disability. *Remedial and Special Education, 7*, 6–10.

Graner, P. S. (2007). *The effects of strategic summarization instruction on the performance of students with and without disabilities in secondary inclusive classes*. Unpublished doctoral dissertation, University of Kansas, Lawrence, KS.

Graner, P. S., Faggella-Luby, M. N., & Fritschmann, N. S. (2005). An overview of responsiveness to intervention: What practitioners ought to know. *Topics in Language Disorders, 25*, 93–105.

Graves, A. W. (1986). Effects of direct instruction and metacomprehension training on finding main ideas. *Learning Disabilities Research, 1*, 90–100.

Heller, R., & Greenleaf, C. (2007). *Literacy instruction in the content areas: Getting to the core of middle and high school improvement*. Washington, DC: Alliance for Excellent Education.

Hock, M. F., Brasseur, I. F., Deshler, D. D., Catts, H. W., Marquis, J. G., Mark, C. A., & Stribling, J. W. (2009). What is the reading component skill profile of adolescent struggling readers in urban schools? *Learning Disability Quarterly, 32*, 21–38.

Hoover, W. A., & Gough, P. B. (1990). The simple view of reading. *Reading and Writing: An Interdisciplinary Journal, 2*, 127–160.

Hughes, C. A., Schumaker, J. B., Deshler, D. D., & Mercer, C. D. (1993). *The test-taking strategy*. Lawrence, KS: Edge.

Jitendra, A., Hoppes, M., & Xin, Y. (2000). Enhancing main idea comprehension for students with learning problems: The role of a summarization strategy and self-monitoring instruction. *Journal of Special Education, 34*(3), 127–139.

Jitendra, A. K., Edwards, L. L., Sacks, G., & Jacobson, L. A. (2004). What research says about vocabulary instruction for students with learning disabilities. *Exceptional Children, 70*, 299–322.

Johnson, E., & Smith, L. (2008). Implementation of response to intervention at middle school: Challenges and potential benefits. *Exceptional Children, 40*, 46–52.

Kamil, M. (2003). *Adolescents and literacy: Reading for the 21st century*. Washington, DC: Alliance for Excellent Education.

Kamil, M. L., Borman, G. D., Dole, J., Kral, C. C., Salinger, T., & Torgesen, J. (2008). *Improving adolescent literacy: Effective classroom and intervention practices: A practice guide* (NCEE #2008–4027). Washington, DC: National Center for Education Evaluation and Regional Assistance, Institute of Education Sciences, U.S. Department of Education. Retrieved from http://ies.ed.gov/ncee/wwc

Kurns, S., & Tilly, W. D. (2007). *Response to intervention blueprints: School building level edition*. Alexandria, VA: The National Association of State Directors of Special Education (NASDSE). Retrieved July 7, 2007, from http://www.nasdse.org/Portals/0/SCHOOL.pdf

Leach, J., Scarborough, H., & Rescorla, L. (2003). Late-emerging reading disabilities. *Journal of Educational Psychology, 95*, 211–224.

Lee, C. D., & Spratley, A. (2010). *Reading in the disciplines: The challenges of adolescent literacy*. New York, NY: Carnegie.

Lenz, B. K., & Ehren, B. (1999). Strategic content literacy initiative: Focusing on reading in secondary schools. *Stratenotes, 8*, 1–6.

Lenz, B. K., Ehren, B. J., & Deshler, D. D. (2005). The content literacy continuum: A school reform framework for improving adolescent literacy for all students. *Teaching Exceptional Children, 37*(6), 60–63.

Mastropieri, M., Scruggs, T., & Graetz, J. (2003). Reading comprehension instruction for secondary students: Challenges for struggling students and teachers. *Learning Disability Quarterly, 26*, 103–116.

Mastropieri, M. A., Scruggs, T. E., Bakken, J. P., & Whedon, C. (1996). Reading comprehension: A synthesis of research in learning disabilities. In: T. E. Scruggs & M. A. Mastropieri (Eds), *Advances in learning and behavioral disabilities: Intervention research* (Vol. 10, Part B, pp. 201–227). Greenwich, CT: JAI Press.

Moje, E. B. (2007). Developing socially just subject-matter instruction: A review of the literature on disciplinary literacy teaching. *Review of Research in Education, 31*, 1–44.

Montague, M., Maddux, C. D., & Dereshiwsky, M. I. (1990). Story grammar and comprehension and production of narrative prose by students with learning disabilities. *Journal of Learning Disabilities, 23*, 190–197.

National Joint Committee on Learning Disabilities. (2005). *Responsiveness to intervention and learning disabilities*. Retrieved December 27, 2008, from http://www.ldonline.org/njcld

National Reading Panel. (2000). Teaching children to read: An evidence-based assessment of the scientific research literature on reading and its implications for reading instruction. Retrieved August 15, 2005 from http://www.nationalreadingpanel.org/Publications/summary.htm

Pressley, M., & Afflerbach, P. (1995). *Verbal protocols of reading: The nature of constructively responsive reading*. Hillsdale, NJ: Erlbaum.

Pressley, M., Goodchild, F., Fleet, J., Zajchowski, R., & Evans, E. D. (1989). The challenges of classroom strategy instruction. *Elementary School Journal, 89*, 301–342.

Rampey, B.D., Dion, G.S., & Donahue, P.L. (2009). *NAEP 2008 Trends in Academic Progress in Reading and Mathematics* (NCES 2009-479). Washington, DC: National Center for Education Statistics, Institute of Education Sciences, U.S. Department of Education.

Schumaker, J. B., & Deshler, D. D. (2006). Teaching adolescents to be strategic learners. In: J. B. Schumaker & D. D. Deshler (Eds), *Teaching adolescents with disabilities: Accessing the general education curriculum* (pp. 121–156). Thousand Oaks, CA: Corwin.

Shanahan, T., & Shanahan, C. (2008). Teaching disciplinary literacy to adolescents: Rethinking content-area literacy. *Harvard Educational Review*, *78*, 40–59.

Swanson, H. L. (1999). Reading research for students with LD: A metaanalysis of intervention outcomes. *Journal of Learning Disabilities*, *32*, 504–532.

Tharp, R. G., & Gallimore, R. (1988). *Rousing minds to life: Teaching, learning, and schooling in social context*. Cambridge: Cambridge University Press.

Torgesen, J. K., Houston, D. D., Rissman, L. M., Decker, S. M., Roberts, G., Vaughn, S., Wexler, J., Francis, D. J., Rivera, M. O., & Lesaux, N. (2007). *Academic literacy instruction for adolescents: A guidance document from the Center on Instruction*. Portsmouth, NH: RMC Research Corporation, Center on Instruction.

Torgesen, J. K., & Miller, D. H. (2009). *Assessments to guide adolescent literacy instruction*. Portsmouth, NH: RMC Research Corporation, Center on Instruction.

United States Department of Education (US DOE). (2009). *28th annual report to congress on the implementation of the Individuals with Disabilities Education Act, 2006* Vol. 2). Washington, DC: Office of Special Education and Rehabilitative Services.

Vaughn, S., Gersten, R., & Chard, D. J. (2000). The underlying message in LD intervention research: Findings from research synthesis. *Exceptional Children*, *67*, 99–114.

Wagner, M., Newman, L., Cameto, R., & Levine, P. (2005). *Changes over time in the early postschool outcomes of youth with disabilities*. A report of findings from the National Longitudinal Transition Study (NLTS) and the National Longitudinal Transition Study-2 (NLTS2).

Weisberg, D., Sexton, S., Mulhern, J., & Keeling, D. (2009). *The widget effect: Our failure to acknowledge and act on differences in teacher effectiveness*. Brooklyn, NY: The New Teacher Project. Retrieved from http://widgeteffect.org/downloads/TheWidgetEffect.pdf

Yager, R. E. (1983). The importance of terminology in teaching K-12 science. *Journal of Research in Science Teaching*, *20*, 577–578.

DEVELOPMENTAL DYSLEXIA IN A TRANSPARENT ORTHOGRAPHY: A STUDY OF SPANISH DYSLEXIC CHILDREN

Manuel Soriano and Ana Miranda

ABSTRACT

Spanish-speaking children learn to read words written in a relatively transparent orthography. Variations in orthographic transparency may shape the manifestation of reading difficulties. This study was intended to help clarify the nature of developmental dyslexia in Spanish. Developmental dyslexic group (DD) were compared to two control groups, a chronological age-matched control group (CA) and a reading level-matched control group (RL). Measures included naming speed, verbal working memory (WM), phonological short-term memory (STM), phonemic awareness, and different reading subtests (letter, word and pseudoword reading, punctuation mark, reading skills). On the reading subtests, accuracy and reading speed were measured. Results demonstrated that developmental dyslexics show a severe deficit in lexical access on accuracy and speed measures, in addition to reading-related cognitive deficits in areas such as naming speed, verbal WM, phonological STM, and phonemic awareness. Hierarchical cluster analysis demonstrated that a subgroup of children with DD showed lower IQs and more

Literacy and Learning
Advances in Learning and Behavioral Disabilities, Volume 23, 95–114

ISSN: 0735-004X/doi:10.1108/S0735-004X(2010)0000023006

severe reading-related cognitive deficits in naming speed, verbal WM, and phonological STM. Our results are consistent with studies conducted in the Spanish language and in other transparent orthographies.

Developmental dyslexia has been characterized by nonfluent and inaccurate reading. Individuals with developmental dyslexia typically exhibit important difficulties in single word recognition. Thus, developmental dyslexia occurs in the context of adequate intelligence and educational opportunity, with an absence of known sensory, neurological, or behavioral problems that would otherwise account for the deficiency (American Psychological Association [APA], 2000). The International Dyslexia Association's definition (see Lyon, Shaywitz, & Shaywitz, 2003) clarifies that:

> [Dyslexia] is a specific learning disability that is neurobiological in origin. It is characterized by difficulties with accurate and/or fluent word recognition and by poor spelling and decoding abilities. These difficulties typically result from a deficit in the phonological component of language that is often unexpected in relation to other cognitive abilities and the effective classroom instruction (p. 2).

However, emerging data indicate that dyslexia is manifested in distinctly varied ways in different orthographies (Joshi & Aaron, 2006; Katzir, Shaul, Breznitz, & Wolf, 2004; Miles, 2000). The alphabetic writing systems are situated along a continuum of opacity–transparency, depending on their code consistency. Transparent orthographies are those in which grapheme–phoneme correspondences are mainly one-to-one (e.g. Finnish, Greek, Italian, and Spanish), whereas in opaque orthographies several graphemes may correspond to the same phoneme and, conversely, several phonemes may be represented by the same grapheme (e.g., English, French, Danish, and Portuguese). Specifically, the Spanish orthography has 24 graphemes (5 vowels and 19 consonants), each of which represents a unique sound. Therefore, the process of translating print to sound is never ambiguous because each letter of the alphabet has a unique pronunciation, except the letters c, g, and r. However, phonological errors can result from a misapplication of accent rules (e.g., melón as mélon).

According to crosslinguistic studies, reading acquisition takes place differently depending on the orthographic system (Defior, 2004; Seymour, Aro, & Erskine, 2003; Ziegler & Goswami, 2005). Thus, children whose languages have transparent orthographies, like Spanish, learn to read more easily than children whose languages have deeper orthographies, like English. Manifestations of dyslexia may also vary depending on the writing system under consideration. Dyslexia in less consistent orthographies becomes apparent when there are problems in reading accuracy, although speed problems are also characteristic of dyslexia. For example, whereas German children are faster and more accurate than English children, in both languages dyslexic children are no less accurate but significantly slower than a reading-level control group (Ziegler, Perry, Ma-Wyatt, Ladner, & Körne, 2003). Various studies have confirmed that in more transparent orthographies, slower reading speed appears to be a critical factor in dyslexia (Jiménez & Hernández, 2000; López-Escribano, 2007; Müller & Brady, 2001; Tressoldi, Stella, & Faggella, 2001; Wimmer, Mayringer, & Landerl, 1998). Specifically in the Spanish language, a recent study (Davis, Cuetos, & González-Seijas, 2007) showed that the dyslexic group was not significantly different from the reading-level-matched group on reading times. Thus, the reading development of dyslexic children seemed delayed rather than deviant. However, other studies (Jiménez et al., 2009; Serrano & Defior, 2008) showed that dyslexics performed worse than reading-level-matched groups on both accuracy measures and speed measures, suggesting that developmental dyslexia in Spanish represents a severe deficit in lexical access.

COGNITIVE DEFICITS INVOLVED IN DEVELOPMENTAL DYSLEXIA

Students with developmental dyslexia can show a range of reading-related cognitive deficits (Vellutino, Fletcher, Snowling, & Scanlon, 2004). For this reason, it is important to understand which reading-related cognitive skills are relevant to reading success. One frequently debated issue is whether the reading-related cognitive abilities of dyslexics are in all respects identical to those of younger average readers. Next, we will discuss those skills that have more consistently been shown to be related to reading and its difficulties: phonological awareness, naming speed, and WM.

Reading level-matched design studies have provided an abundance of evidence on phonological deficits in alphabetic languages. In other words, children with developmental dyslexia commonly manifest difficulties in acquiring phonological awareness (e.g., phonemic awareness). They show deficient phonological decoding skills during their childhood years, and continue to be deficient in phonological analysis during their adult years, as at least three literature reviews have shown (Herman, Matyas, & Pratt, 2006; Ijzendoorm & Bus, 1994; Rack, Snowling, & Olson, 1992). Because reading acquisition requires the child to learn the mapping between phonology (e.g., phonemes) and orthography (e.g., graphemes), problems in the representation and use of phonological information inevitably lead to problems in reading acquisition.

However, studies carried out on phonological deficits in transparent languages (consistent orthography) have shown contradictory results. One study in Italian (Brizzolara et al., 2006) confirmed that only the children with reading problems and a history of language disorder presented a phonological deficit, while all the children with reading problems presented problems with naming speed. On the other hand, various studies carried out in Spanish with dyslexic children have found a deficit in phonological awareness (Jiménez, 1997; Jiménez & Ramírez, 2002; Jiménez et al., 2009; Serrano & Defior, 2008).

Naming speed, defined as the ability to name highly familiar visual stimuli as fast as possible, has been shown to be a strong concurrent and longitudinal predictor of reading ability in both consistent and inconsistent orthographies (see Georgiou, Parrilla, & Liao, 2008). In addition, many studies have indicated that reading disabilities appear to be accompanied by impairments in naming speed, and these impairments are found regardless of the orthography of the language in which children learn to read (Denckla & Rudel, 1976; de Jong & van der Leij, 2003; Wolf & Bowers, 2000). Naming speed deficits are caused by disruption of a "precise timing mechanism" that normally influences temporal integration of the phonological and visual counterparts of printed words, thereby impairing the child's ability to detect and represent orthographic patterns (Vellutino et al., 2004).

Processes related to memory, specifically verbal WM and phonological STM, have been some of the most extensively researched cognitive processes in children with reading disabilities for the past 30 years. Both STM and WM tasks involve controlled processes such as rehearsal. However, controlled processing on WM tasks emerges in the context of high demands on attention, drawing on resources from the executive system. In contrast, controlled processing on STM tasks attempts to maintain memory traces above some critical threshold, and this maintenance does not directly require resources from the central executive system. The recent meta-analysis carried out by Swanson, Zheng, and Jerman (2009) indicated that children with reading disabilities were disadvantaged on: (a) short-term measures requiring the recall of phonemes and digit sequences; and (b) WM measures requiring the simultaneous processing and storage of digits within sequences and final words from unrelated sentences.

THE QUESTION OF THE DYSLEXIC SUBGROUPS

The heterogeneous manifestations of dyslexia may represent different patterns of performance on reading and/or reading-related cognitive tasks, so that it would be possible to identify subgroups within the population of developmental dyslexics. Numerous attempts have been made in the past to classify dyslexics, some of them based on theoretical models of word recognition (Castles & Coltheart, 1993; Jiménez & Ramírez, 2002; Stanovich, Siegel, & Gottardo, 1997), while others looked for profiles using neuropsychological tests, reading-related cognitive tests, and educational test scores.

Morris et al. (1998) used cluster analysis techniques with large reading disabled populations. They provided documentation for seven natural subgroups of disabled readers: two were globally deficient in language skills; four displayed a relative weakness in phonological awareness and variations in naming speed and verbal STM; and the remaining disabled subgroup was impaired on verbal and nonverbal measures of rate of processing, including rate and accuracy of oral reading. This study provided support not only for the double deficit hypothesis of dyslexia – phonological impairment plus deficit in naming speed – but also for the models that separate specific reading difficulties from garden variety reading delays. On the other hand, Catts, Hogan, and Fey (2003) formed subgroups in a large sample of poor readers on the basis of relative strengths and weaknesses in word recognition and listening comprehension. Although homogeneous subgroups were not identified, poor readers could be classified into four subgroups that differed significantly in reading-related abilities. However, all of the classification studies carried out in Spanish have been based on theoretical models of word recognition (Jiménez & Ramírez, 2002; Jiménez et al., 2009), and no study has tried to find subgroups based on reading performance measures and reading-related abilities.

Objectives

This research had three purposes: (1) to study the characteristics of dyslexic children in Spanish and contribute to clarifying the nature of this problem in the context of a transparent writing system; (2) to investigate the existence of reading-related cognitive deficits associated with developmental dyslexia in Spanish; and (3) to investigate whether forming subgroups of developmental dyslexics using hierarchical cluster analysis revealed differences in reading-related cognitive abilities.

METHOD

Participants

In this study, participants were 82 primary grade students from different schools in Valencia, Spain. All the children were of lower-middle socioeconomic status, but had no cultural or environmental disadvantages. All of the subjects were Caucasian and spoke Spanish as their primary language. They ranged in age from 6 to 12 years (mean age = 9 years 9 months, SD = 1 year 5 months). Of the entire sample, 49 were boys and 33 girls. These children were classified into three groups: (a) the DD, which was made up of 36 students (mean age = 10 years 5 months, SD = .50; 23 males and 13 females); (b) the reading level-matched control group (RL), which was composed of 19 younger children with the same reading level as the developmental dyslexic group (mean age = 7 years 3 months, SD = .59; 12 males and 7 females); and (c) the chronological age-matched control group (CA), which consisted of 27 normal readers matched in age with the DD (mean age = 10 years 9 months, SD = .78; 14 males and 13 females).

The presence of developmental dyslexia was determined by using an adaptation of the multifaceted approach developed by Pereira-Laird, Deane, and Bunnell (1999). The requirements followed in the assessment were: (a) poor academic performance in reading using a teacher's rating report, and average achievement in other academic areas (e.g., arithmetic); (b) scores of 80 or higher on an intelligence test (Cattell & Cattell, 1950/1989), in order to exclude students with intellectual deficits; (c) no evidence or history of neurological damage, environmental disadvantage, emotional disturbance, hearing and vision abnormalities, or any other major handicapping condition, in accordance with the conventional exclusion criteria for the learning disabilities (LD) field; and (d) a score on the standardized subtest of word and pseudoword reading from the Battery of Reading Evaluation (BEL) (López-Higes, Mayoral, & Villoria, 2002) corresponding to the 15th percentile or less. This achievement criteria in reading has been commonly used in the LD literature.

Results of analysis of variance (ANOVAs) and post hoc comparisons using the Scheffé test showed that the developmentally dyslexic group performed significantly worse than the CA control group, and similarly to the RL control group, on word and pseudoword reading, $F(2, 79) = 63.87$, $p < .000$, $\eta^2 = .61$. Consequently, both DD and younger normal readers were matched on word and pseudoword reading using the Spanish standardized reading battery (BEL; López-Higes et al., 2002).

There were significant differences among the groups in age, $F(2, 79) = 178.71$, $p<.000$, $\eta^2 = .81$. Post hoc comparisons revealed that the DD and CA groups were matched in age, and both groups were older than the RL control group. However, there were no significant differences in the distribution of the participants as a function of IQ, $F(2, 79) = 1.64$, $p<.199$, $\eta^2 = .04$. The means and standard deviations for age, IQ, and word and pseudoword reading measures by group are presented in Table 1.

Children in the study learned to read with a focus on spelling-sound mapping at the syllable level. The children were taught to pronounce consonants associated with vowels in simple consonant–vowel syllables (e.g., ma, me, mi, mo, and mu). The teaching builds on the pronunciation of these simple syllables by showing the children how the syllables can be combined to constructs words (e.g., mama [mother]). These lessons are then extended to wider sets of syllables through the association of different consonants with the same vowels (e.g., pa, pe, pi, po, and pu). Further teaching extends to more complex syllables (e.g., cos, a consonant–vowel–consonant syllable) and later to the construction of words from these syllables.

Table 1. Descriptive Data for the Sample Groups.

	Group			F	p	η^2	Post hoc Comparisons
	DD ($N = 36$)	RL ($N = 19$)	CA ($N = 27$)				
Word and pseudoword reading (BEL)							
Mean	48.86	48.15	58.18	63.87	.000	.61	DD, RL<CA
SD	4.3	3.0	2.7				DD = RL
Age							
Mean	10.54	7.39	10.94	178.71	.000	.81	DD, CA>RL
SD	.50	.59	.78				DD = CA
IQ							
Mean	107.08	106.79	110.81	1.64	.199	.040	n.s.
SD	9.53	6.9	9.5				
Sex							
Male	19	12	14				
Female	17	7	13				

Note: DD = developmental dyslexic group; RL = reading level-matched control group; CA = chronological age-matched control group.

Measures and Procedure

Various reading and reading-related cognitive tests were used to compare the three groups. All the tests were carried out individually in a quiet room, and the same experimenter administered all of them. The presentation order of the tests was randomized. Several sessions were used to avoid fatigue effects in the children.

Culture Fair (or Free) Intelligence Test (Scales 1 and 2, Form A)
This test (Cattell & Cattell, 1950/1989) allows the measurement of general mental capacity without the interference of cultural basis. The authors used the "two halves" method to calculate reliability, and they reported a correlation coefficient of .86. For validity, they used criteria scores on the TEA test (Seisdedos, De la Cruz, Cordero, & González, 1991). A correlation coefficient of .68 was found between the *g* factor measure and results on the TEA test, which measured verbal, reasoning, and numerical aptitudes.

Word and Pseudoword Reading
We administered the word and pseudoword reading subtest from The BEL (López-Higes et al., 2002). This subtest requires the correct identification of 30 words and 30 pseudowords with different lengths, linguistic structures, and frequencies. The subtest measures the accuracy of the responses. This reading subtest has been found to have a Cronbach's *alpha* of .71 for level 1 and .77 for level 2.

Standardized Reading Skills Battery (PROLEC-R, Cuetos, Rodríguez, Ruano, & Arribas, 2002)
This battery includes several reading subtests administered individually. We administered the following: (a) *Letter reading*. This test requires the child to read 20 lowercase letters as quickly and accurately as possible. (b) *Word reading*. This test requires the correct identification of 40 words that vary greatly in frequency, length, and linguistic structure (CCV, CVV, CVC, CCVC, CVVC, and VC, where C = consonant and V = vowel). (c) *Pseudoword reading*. This test consists of 40 pseudowords (e.g., erpisa), which were constructed by changing or adding one or two letters of each of the 40 words on the reading test. (d) *Punctuation mark*. On this task the child has to read a short story, paying attention to the main punctuation marks. Specifically, the correct reading intonation of 11 punctuation marks is rated (4 periods, 2 commas, 3 question marks, and 2 exclamation marks). On all the tests, the children's scores consisted of an accuracy score and a score for

reading speed, measured as the time taken to complete the task; (e) *Reading skills*. Two combined scores of reading skills were taken, one based on word reading skill and the other on pseudoword reading skill. In both cases, accuracy is divided by the reading speed, and then multiplied by 100. The reading battery has been found to have an internal consistency of Cronbach's *alpha* = .74. The teachers' ratings of reading ability were used as validity criteria. Teachers were asked to rate reading ability on a 10-point scale ranging from low (1) to high (10) ability. Correlations between reading measures and teachers' ratings were statistically significant ($p < .001$).

Phonemic Awareness

We administered the Test of Phonemic Awareness (Jiménez, 1995). This test evaluates the participant's ability to manipulate the sounds or phonemes of spoken words, and it consists of four tasks containing 15 items each. On the isolation task, the child listened to a word (e.g., lana [wool]) and had to say its beginning sound, /l/. On the segmentation task, the child listened to a word (e.g., rana [frog]) and then had to say its constituent sounds, phoneme by phoneme (e.g., /r//a//n//a/). Pronouncing the sounds or saying the names of the letters constituted a correct response. On the deletion task, the child listened to a word (e.g., blusa [blouse]) and then had to delete its initial sound and say the remaining sounds (e.g., lusa). On the blending task, the child listened to a sequence of phonemes (e.g., /m//e//s//a/) and had to say the whole word (e.g., mesa [table]). The total score was calculated by adding the correct responses on the four tasks. Each task had a Cronbach's *alpha* ranging from .75 to .86.

Naming Speed

The subtest of color naming from the Stroop test (Golden, 1994) was administered. The child was required to name the color, as rapidly as possible, of five rows of "xxxx" written in three basic colors (red, green, and blue). The test–retest reliability of this test was .85.

Verbal Working Memory

To assess the child's WM, we administered the task used by Siegel and Ryan (1989). The child heard sentences that had the final word missing. The task was to supply the missing word and then repeat all the missing words from the set. There were three trials at each level or set size (two, three, four, or five words). For each trial, the score was 1 point (3 for the set) when the child performed the task successfully, and the score was 0 when the child failed to complete the task. Task administration was stopped when the child failed all the trials at one level.

Phonological Short-Term Memory
To assess STM, we used a phonological memory task adapted from a task developed by Geva, Yaghoub-Zadeh, and Schuster (2000). On this task, the child needed to repeat 20 Latin words not related to the Spanish lexicon (e.g., umbrifer). The rationale for using a Latin-based phonological memory task is that it requires children to repeat phonological strings. Children's repetition abilities are highly associated with the speed of learning the phonological forms of new words. In the construction of this task, we took the precaution that the Latin words were not similar to Spanish morphology. The total number of correctly repeated Latin words was calculated for each child. The Cronbach's *alpha* was .74.

DATA ANALYSIS

With regard to our first and second objectives, multivariant analysis of variance (MANOVA) was performed, based on the dependent variables, with the group of origin as the grouping factor. Next, an ANOVAs for one factor (developmental dyslexics vs. normal readers matched in age vs. younger normal readers) was conducted. Post hoc planned contrasts (Scheffé test) were performed to determine between which pairs of groups differences appeared. We report effect size using the partial eta squared statistic (η^2), which estimates the proportion of the total variance accounted for by the independent variables. For this statistic, values between .01 and .10 are considered a small effect size, values between .10 and .30 are considered a medium effect size, and those above .30 are considered a large effect size. To achieve our third objective, hierarchical cluster analysis was performed to identify subgroups of developmental dyslexics.

RESULTS

Comparison of Groups on Reading Measures

The MANOVA performed with the reading measures revealed that there were significant main group effects (Wilks' Lambda (Λ) = .013, F(20, 140) = 59.63, p = .000, η^2 = .88) with a large effect size. The ANOVAs carried out later to compare the groups (see Table 2) indicate differences in

Table 2. Means, Standard Deviation, and *F*-Values on Reading Measures.

	Group			F	p	η^2	Post hoc Comparisons
	DD ($N = 36$)	RL ($N = 19$)	CA ($N = 27$)				
Letter reading speed							
Mean	32.11	22.68	13.22	67.46	.000	.63	DD > CA, RL
SD	7.2	6.9	4.56				RL > CA
Letter reading accuracy							
Mean	19.5	18.68	19.85	10.86	.000	.21	DD = CA
SD	.73	1.37	.36				RL < DD, CA
Word reading speed							
Mean	98.53	54.84	31.03	284.31	.000	.87	DD > CA, RL
SD	12.78	13.38	6.97				RL > CA
Word reading accuracy							
Mean	30.05	38.42	39.85	283.13	.000	.88	DD < CA, RL
SD	2.37	1.50	.36				RL < CA
Pseudoword reading speed							
Mean	121.77	79.21	50.77	228.59	.000	.85	DD > CA, RL
SD	10.93	16.38	13.57				RL > CA
Pseudoword reading accuracy							
Mean	26.22	35.15	38.92	206.38	.000	.83	DD < CA, RL
SD	3.00	2.85	1.35				RL < CA
Punctuation mark speed							
Mean	96.88	72	40.66	44.53	.000	.53	DD > CA, RL
SD	33.15	12.35	8.85				RL > CA
Punctuation mark accuracy							
Mean	4.52	8.94	10.48	195.70	.000	.83	DD < CA, RL
SD	1.02	1.89	.84				RL < CA
Word Reading skill (accuracy/speed) × 100							
Mean	30.80	74.85	133.95	240.90	.000	.85	DD < CA, RL
SD	3.07	21.56	26.46				RL < CA
Pseudoword reading skill (accuracy/speed) × 100							
Mean	21.60	46.43	81.53	168.95	.000	.81	DD < CA, RL
SD	2.19	11.47	20.01				RL < CA

Note: DD = developmental dyslexic group; RL = reading level-matched control group; CA = chronological age-matched control group.

letter reading speed, $F(2, 79) = 67.46$, $p < .000$, $\eta^2 = .63$. The Scheffé comparison test showed that the group of children with developmental dyslexia took more time to read the letters than the two comparisons groups, the reading level-matched control group (RL) and the chronological age-matched control group (CA). Moreover, the reading level-matched control group took longer to read the letters than the chronological age-matched control group.

With regard to letter reading accuracy, the ANOVA showed significant differences among the groups, $F(2, 79) = 10.86$, $p < .000$, $\eta^2 = .21$, with the Scheffé test indicating that the reading level-matched control group was less accurate (had fewer correct answers) than the DD and CA groups, which showed no differences between them.

There were significant differences among all the groups on word reading speed, $F(2, 79) = 284.31$, $p < .000$, $\eta^2 = .87$, word reading accuracy, $F(2, 79) = 283.13$, $p < .000$, $\eta^2 = .88$, pseudoword reading speed, $F(2, 79) = 228.59$, $p < .000$, $\eta^2 = .85$, pseudoword reading accuracy, $F(2, 79) = 206.38$, $p < .000$, $\eta^2 = .83$, punctuation mark speed, $F(2, 79) = 44.53$, $p < .000$, $\eta^2 = .53$, punctuation mark accuracy, $F(2, 79) = 195.70$, $p < .000$, $\eta^2 = .83$, word reading skill [(accuracy/speed) $\times$ 100], $F(2, 79) = 240.90$, $p < .000$, $\eta^2 = .85$, and pseudoword reading skill [(accuracy/speed) $\times$ 100], $F(2, 79) = 168.95$, $p < .000$, $\eta^2 = .81$, with large effect sizes in all cases. Planned contrast revealed that the DD performed more poorly than the CA and RL control groups on word reading speed, word reading accuracy, pseudoword reading speed, pseudoword reading accuracy, punctuation mark speed, punctuation mark accuracy, word reading skill, and pseudoword reading skill. Finally, the RL group performed worse than the CA group on these variables.

Between-Groups Comparison on Reading-Related Cognitive Measures

The MANOVA performed with the reading-related cognitive measures showed that there were significant main group effects (Wilks' Lambda (Λ) = .164, $F(4, 76) = 27.892$, $p = .000$, $\eta^2 = .59$) with large effect sizes. The results obtained from comparing the three groups of children (see Table 3) on their cognitive characteristics point out differences in phonemic awareness, $F(2, 79) = 84.613$, $p < .000$, $\eta^2 = .68$, naming speed, $F(2, 79) = 79.987$, $p < .000$, $\eta^2 = .66$, verbal WM, $F(2, 79) = 42.02$, $p < .000$, $\eta^2 = .51$, and phonological STM, $F(2, 79) = 36.758$, $p < .000$, $\eta^2 = .48$. For these four variables, the Scheffé test indicated that the group of children with developmental dyslexia

Table 3. Means, Standard Deviation, and *F*-Values on Cognitive Measures.

	Group			*F*	*p*	η^2	Post hoc Comparisons
	DD ($N = 36$)	RL ($N = 19$)	CA ($N = 27$)				
Naming speed							
Mean	38	44.84	59.29	103.40	.000	.74	DD<CA, RL
SD	3.57	7.01	7.25				RL<CA
Verbal working memory							
Mean	3.66	4.52	6.44	42.02	.000	.51	DD<CA, RL
SD	.98	1.07	1.50				RL<CA
Phonological short-term memory							
Mean	10.38	18.05	19.92	218.56	.000	.84	DD<CA, RL
SD	2.47	1.98	.26				RL<CA
Phonemic awareness							
Mean	38.11	55.36	59.18	510.96	.000	.92	DD<CA, RL
SD	2.93	3.65	1.56				RL<CA

Note: DD = developmental dyslexic group; RL = reading level-matched control group; CA = chronological age-matched control group.

performed significantly worse than the two comparison groups, the reading level-matched control group (RL) and the chronological age-matched control group (CA). Furthermore, the reading level-matched control group performed worse than the chronological age-matched control group.

Hierarchical Cluster Analysis for the Classification of Dyslexic Children

In the current study, the hierarchical cluster was used to identify and characterize different subgroups of developmental dyslexics based on their cognitive and reading characteristics. Due to the number of subjects with developmental dyslexia ($N = 36$) who participated in this study, the seven most clinically relevant variables were chosen to perform the cluster analysis: IQ, naming speed, verbal WM, phonological STM, phonemic awareness, word reading skill, and pseudoword reading skill.

In order to minimize variance and produce more homogeneous groups, we used the *k*-means algorithm, which assigns each point to the cluster whose centroid is nearest. The results of the application of this clustering technique are described in the form of a dendrogram, which is a tree for the visual classification of similarity. As Fig. 1 shows, the participants appear grouped in two clusters with similar weights. The first cluster contains

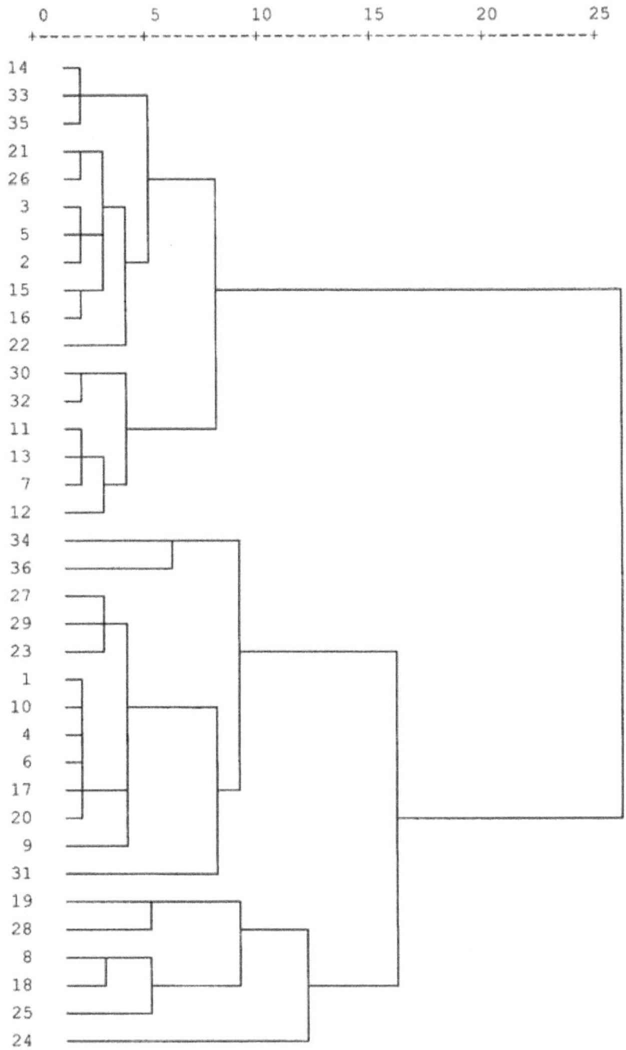

Fig. 1. Dendrogram.

17 participants, and the second cluster includes 19. Furthermore, the two clusters have sufficient compactness and distinctness. In sum, the two-cluster solution is the one that had the most clinical relevance, showing the existence of two differentiated cognitive-reading clusters of patterns.

Table 4. Means, Standard Deviation, and *F*-Values on Cognitive and Reading Measures.

	Cluster 1 ($N = 17$)	Cluster 2 ($N = 19$)	F	p	η^2
	Mean (SD)	Mean (SD)			
IQ	115.47 (3.9)	99.58 (6.07)	84.39	.000	.71
Naming speed	40.11 (2.89)	36.10 (3.07)	16.17	.000	.32
Verbal working memory	4 (.79)	3.36 (1.06)	4	.054	.10
Phonological short-term memory	11.76 (1.71)	9.15 (2.43)	13.49	.001	.28
Phonemic awareness	39 (1.7)	37.31 (3.5)	3.134	.086	.08
Word reading skill	30.59 (2.89)	30.99 (3.2)	.148	.703	.004
Pseudoword reading skill	21.72 (2.31)	21.49 (2.14)	.099	.755	.003

In order to provide a more accurate profile of the characteristics of the clusters, MANOVA was then performed based on the dependent variables, with the cluster of origin as the grouping factor. Next, a between-groups ANOVA was performed for each of the measures (see Table 4).

The MANOVA performed with the seven measures included in the Cluster analysis revealed significant main group effects (Wilks' Lambda (Λ) = .148, $F(7, 28) = 22.952$, $p = .000$, $\eta^2 = .85$) with large effect sizes. The results of the ANOVAs indicate that there were no significant differences between the clusters of developmental dyslexics on phonemic awareness, $F(1, 34) = .985$, $p = .328$, $\eta^2 = .02$, word reading skill, $F(1, 34) = .148$, $p = .703$, $\eta^2 = .004$, or pseudoword reading skill, $F(1, 34) = .099$, $p = .755$, $\eta^2 = .003$. However, the ANOVA revealed significant differences in IQ, $F(1, 34) = 84.39$, $p = .000$, $\eta^2 = .71$, naming speed, $F(1, 34) = 24.941$, $p = .000$, $\eta^2 = .42$, verbal WM, $F(1, 34) = 4.00$, $p = .054$, $\eta^2 = .10$, and phonological STM, $F(1, 34) = 57.676$, $p = .000$, $\eta^2 = .62$, with the developmental dyslexics grouped in Cluster 1 performing worse.

DISCUSSION

Our first purpose was to study the characteristics of dyslexic children in Spanish and contribute to clarifying the nature of dyslexia in the context of a transparent writing system, using both chronological age-matched and reading level-matched control groups.

Results show that, compared to typical readers of the same age, the dyslexic children clearly had lower reading competence on all the measures, as was expected. Indeed, DD showed a severe deficit in lexical access, as they were slower and less accurate in performing reading tasks than the RL control group. These results agree with findings from other studies conducted in the Spanish language (Jiménez, Rodríguez, & Ramirez, 2009; Serrano & Defior, 2008). Specifically, on the standardized accuracy reading tests, the dyslexic children's performance was significantly lower than that of the younger children. This result on accuracy measures suggests that a phonological deficit exists in dyslexic children who learn in a transparent orthography. However, the fact that the dyslexic children had problems on pseudoword reading accuracy is a finding that contradicts results from other studies carried out with transparent languages (e.g., Wimmer et al., 1998; Tressoldi et al., 2001), where differences were found in speed but not in accuracy. Moreover, the dyslexic children were significantly slower than the younger children on speed measures. We consider the dyslexic children's lower performance to be an indication that phonological processing is not automated, as proposed by the automatization deficit in dyslexia (Nicholson & Fawcett, 1990; Savage, 2004). This finding suggests that besides the phonological deficit, which is widely accepted, children with dyslexia also have deficits in automatization. The existence of an automatization deficit in dyslexics is consistent with results from studies involving Spanish (Jiménez et al., 2009; Jiménez & Hernández, 2000; Rodrigo & Jiménez, 1999; Serrano & Defior, 2008) and other transparent orthographies (Tressoldi et al., 2001; Wimmer & Mayringer, 2001; Wimmer et al., 1998). In transparent writing systems, it is easier to learn the grapheme–phoneme correspondences than in an opaque orthography because the application of grapheme–phoneme correspondences consistently confirms and strengthens the association, which is not necessarily the case in opaque systems, due to the numerous exceptions and irregularities.

Our second purpose was to investigate the existence of reading-related cognitive deficits associated with developmental dyslexia in Spanish.

In the current study, a deficit in phonological awareness was confirmed by comparing DD and younger children. This result is interesting because the effect of reading skill is controlled. Thus, as in other studies carried out in the Spanish language (Jiménez, 1997; Jiménez et al., 2009; Serrano & Defior, 2008), the findings suggest that a phonological deficit exists in dyslexic children who learn to read in a transparent orthography.

Furthermore, our findings support the hypothesis that, in a transparent orthography, naming speed is one of the most reading-related deficits, which is consistent with the results from studies carried out in Italian (Brizzolara et al., 2006) and in Spanish (Jiménez et al., 2009; López-Escribano, 2007).

The DD also showed lower verbal WM and lower phonological STM than the chronological age and reading-level control groups. This finding suggests that WM and STM deficits can co-occur in Spanish DD, as was also shown in the recent selective meta-analysis carried out by Swanson et al. (2009). Thus, deficiencies in memory can be due to both phonological and executive processing demands.

Our third purpose was to investigate whether subgrouping DD by means of hierarchical cluster analysis showed differences in reading performance and reading-related cognitive abilities. Through hierarchical clustering, two homogeneous subgroups of children with dyslexia were identified. As expected, both subgroups of dyslexics presented deficiencies in phonemic awareness, as well as in word and pseudoword skills. However, the two subgroups differed with regard to their cognitive profiles. One of the subgroups showed a significantly more severe impairment in naming speed, verbal WM, and phonological STM, along with lower intelligence. These results lend support to the subgroup of dyslexics who experience the double deficit – phonological impairment plus impairment in naming speed – which is the most serious dyslexic subgroup (Wolf & Bowers, 2000). Moreover, the more severe reading-related cognitive deficits associated with this subgroup of dyslexics are similar to those manifested by the lower responders to intervention (Vaughn et al., 2009), or those described as treatment resistant or nonresponders (Al Otaiba & Fuchs, 2006; Nelson, Benner, & Gonzalez, 2003).

In summary, results from this study help to clarify the manifestations of dyslexia in transparent languages like Spanish. Our results show that developmental dyslexics were slower and less accurate on reading tasks than the RL control group, thus demonstrating a severe deficit in lexical access. Developmental dyslexia in Spanish seems to be associated with reading-related cognitive deficits that involve verbal WM, naming speed, and impairments in two main phonological skills related to learning to read, phonemic awareness, and phonological STM. One major implication of these results is that there may be multiple pathways to developmental dyslexia in the Spanish language. Nevertheless, the findings suggest that measures of these impairments are needed to identify the nature of children's difficulties and effectively determine the appropriate support.

ACKNOWLEDGMENT

This research was supported by a grant from the Plan Nacional I+D+I (Ministerio de Ciencia e Innovación), number EDU2009-08082, awarded to Manuel Soriano.

REFERENCES

Al Otaiba, S., & Fuchs, D. (2006). Who are the young children for whom best practices in reading are ineffective? An experimental and longitudinal study. *Journal of Learning Disabilities*, *39*, 414–431.

American Psychological Association. (2000). *Diagnostic and statistical manual of mental disorders, 4th ed., text revision* (Trad. cast. Manual Diagnóstico y Estadístico de los Trastornos Mentales. Texto Revisado. DSM-IV-TR. Barcelona: Masson. 2002). Washington, DC: Author.

Brizzolara, D., Pecini, C., Chilosi, A., Cipriani, P., Gasperini, F., Mazzotti, M., & Zoccolotti, P. (2006). Do phonological and rapid automatized naming deficits differentially affect dyslexic children with and without a history of language delay? A study on Italian dyslexic children. *Cognitive and Behavioral Neurology*, *19*, 141–149.

Castles, A., & Coltheart, M. (1993). Varieties of developmental dyslexia. *Cognition*, *47*, 149–180.

Cattell, R. B., & Cattell, A. K. S. (1950/1989). *Test de Factor "g". Escala 2.* (Cordero, de la Cruz y Seisdedos, Trans.). Madrid: TEA (Original publicado en 1950).

Catts, H. W., Hogan, T. P., & Fey, M. E. (2003). Subgrouping poor readers on the basis of individual differences in reading-related abilities. *Journal of Learning Disabilities*, *36*, 151–164.

Cuetos, F., Rodríguez, B., Ruano, E., & Arribas, D. (2002). *Batería de evaluación de los procesos lectores. PROLEC-R.* Madrid: TEA.

Davis, R., Cuetos, F., & González-Seijas, R. M. (2007). Reading development and dyslexia in a transparent orthography: A survey of Spanish children. *Annals of Dyslexia*, *57*, 179–198.

de Jong, P. F., & van der Leij, A. (2003). Developmental changes in the manifestation of a phonological deficit in dyslexic children learning to read a regular orthography. *Journal of Educational Psychology*, *95*, 22–40.

Defior, S. (2004). Phonological awareness and learning to read: A crosslinguistic perspective. In: P. Bryant & T. Nunes (Eds), *Handbook on children's literacy* (pp. 163–174). Dordrecht: Kluwer.

Denckla, M., & Rudel, R. (1976). Naming of object-drawings by dyslexic and other learning disabled children. *Brain and Language*, *3*, 1–15.

Georgiou, G. K., Parrilla, R., & Liao, Ch.-H. (2008). Rapid naming speed and reading across languages that vary in orthographic consistency. *Reading and Writing: An Interdisciplinary Journal*, *21*, 885–903.

Geva, E., Yaghoub-Zadeh, Z., & Schuster, B. (2000). Understanding individual differences in Word recognition skills of ESL children. *Annals of Dyslexia*, *50*, 123–154.

Golden, C. J. (1994). *STROOP. Test de Colores y Palabras.* Madrid: TEA.

Herman, J. A., Matyas, T., & Pratt, C. (2006). Meta-analysis of the nonword reading deficit in specific reading disorder. *Dyslexia*, *12*, 195–221.

Ijzendoorm, M. H. V., & Bus, A. G. (1994). Meta-analytic confirmation of the nonword reading deficit in developmental dyslexia. *Reading Research Quarterly*, *29*, 266–275.

Jiménez, J. E. (1995). Prueba de consciencia fonémica. In: J. E. Jiménez & M. R. Ortíz (Eds), *Consciencia fonológica y aprendizaje de la lectura. Teoría, evaluación e intervención* (pp. 74–78). Madrid: Síntesis.

Jiménez, J. E. (1997). A reading-level match study of phonemic processes underlying reading disabilities in a transparent orthography. *Reading and Writing: An Interdisciplinary Journal*, *9*, 23–40.

Jiménez, J. E., & Hernández, I. (2000). Word identification and reading disorders in the Spanish language. *Journal of Learning Disabilities, 33*, 44–60.

Jiménez, J. E., & Ramírez, G. (2002). Identifying subtypes of reading disability in the Spanish language. *The Spanish Journal of Psychology, 5*, 3–19.

Jiménez, J. E., Rodríguez, C., & Ramirez, G. (2009). Spanish developmental dyslexia: Prevalence, cognitive profile and home literacy experiences. *Journal of Experimental Child Psychology, 103*, 167–185.

Joshi, M., & Aaron, P. G. (2006). *Handbook of orthography and literacy*. Mahwah: LEA.

Katzir, T., Shaul, S., Breznitz, Z., & Wolf, M. (2004). The universal and the unique in dyslexia: A cross-linguistic investigation of reading fluency in Hebrew and English-speaking children with reading disorders. *Reading and Writing: An Interdisciplinary Journal, 17*, 739–768.

López-Escribano, C. (2007). Evaluation of the double-deficit hypothesis subtype classification of readers in Spanish. *Journal of Learning Disabilities, 40*, 319–330.

López-Higes, R., Mayoral, J. A., & Villoria, C. (2002). *Batería de Evaluación de la Lectura – BEL*. Madrid: Psymtec.

Lyon, G. R., Shaywitz, S. E., & Shaywitz, B. E. (2003). Defining dyslexia, comorbidity, teacher's knowledge of language and reading. A definition of dyslexia. *Annals of Dyslexia, 53*, 1–14.

Miles, E. (2000). Dyslexia may show a different face in different languages. *Dyslexia, 6*, 193–201.

Morris, R., Stuebing, K., Fletcher, J., Shaywitz, S., Lyon, G., Shankweiler, D. P., Katz, L., Francis, D. J., & Shaywitz, B. A. (1998). Subtypes of reading disability: Variability around a phonological core. *Journal of Educational Psychology, 90*, 347–373.

Müller, K., & Brady, S. (2001). Correlates of early reading performance in a transparent orthography. *Reading and Writing: An Interdisciplinary Journal, 14*, 757–799.

Nelson, J. R., Benner, G. R., & Gonzalez, J. (2003). Learner characteristics that influence the treatment effectiveness of early literacy interventions: A meta-analytic review. *Learning Disabilities Research and Practice, 18*, 255–267.

Nicholson, R., & Fawcett, A. (1990). Automaticity: A new framework for dyslexia research. *Cognition, 35*, 159–182.

Pereira-Laird, J., Deane, F. P., & Bunnell, J. (1999). Defining reading disability using a multifaceted approach. *Learning Disability Quarterly, 22*, 59–71.

Rack, J. P., Snowling, M., & Olson, R. K. (1992). The nonword reading deficit in developmental dyslexia: A review. *Reading Research Quarterly, 27*, 29–53.

Rodrigo, M., & Jiménez, J. E. (1999). An analysis of the word naming errors of normal readers and reading disabled children in Spanish. *Journal of Research in Reading, 22*, 180–197.

Savage, R. (2004). Motor skills, automaticity and developmental dyslexia: A review of the research literature. *Reading and Writing: An Interdisciplinary Journal, 17*, 301–324.

Seisdedos, N., De la Cruz, V., Cordero, A., & González, M. (1991). *Test de Aptitudes Escolares (TEA)*. Madrid: TEA.

Serrano, F., & Defior, S. (2008). Dyslexia speed problems in a transparent orthography. *Annals of Dyslexia, 58*, 81–95.

Seymour, P. H. K., Aro, M., & Erskine, J. M. (2003). Foundation literacy acquisition in European orthographies. *British Journal of Psychology, 94*, 143–174.

Siegel, L. S., & Ryan, E. B. (1989). The development of working memory in normally achieving and subtypes of learning disabled children. *Child Development, 60*, 973–980.

Stanovich, K. E., Siegel, L., & Gottardo, A. (1997). Converging evidence for phonological and surface subtypes of reading disability. *Journal of Educational Psychology*, *89*, 114–127.

Swanson, H. L., Zheng, X., & Jerman, O. (2009). Working memory, short-term memory and reading difficulties. A selective meta-analysis of the literature. *Journal of Learning Disabilities*, *42*, 260–287.

Tressoldi, P. E., Stella, G., & Faggella, M. (2001). The development of reading speed in Italians with dyslexia: A longitudinal study. *Journal of Learning Disabilities*, *34*, 414–417.

Vaughn, S., Wanzek, J., Murray, C. S., Scammacca, N., Linan-Thomson, S., & Woodruff, A. L. (2009). Response to early reading intervention: Examining higher and lower responders. *Exceptional Children*, *75*, 165–183.

Vellutino, F., Fletcher, J. M., Snowling, M. J., & Scanlon, D. M. (2004). Specific reading disability (dyslexia): What have we learned in the past four decades? *Journal of Child Psychology and Psychiatry*, *45*, 2–40.

Wimmer, H., & Mayringer, H. (2001). Is the reading-rate problem of German dyslexic children caused by slow visual processes? In: M. Wolf (Ed.), *Dyslexia, fluency and the brain* (pp. 116–133). New York: York.

Wimmer, H., Mayringer, H., & Landerl, K. (1998). Poor reading: A deficit in skill-automatization or a phonological deficit? *Scientific Studies of Reading*, *2*, 321–340.

Wolf, M., & Bowers, P. G. (2000). Namings processes and developmental reading disabilities: An introduction to the special issue on the double-deficit hypothesis. *Journal of Learning Disabilities*, *33*, 322–324.

Ziegler, J., & Goswami, U. (2005). Reading acquisition, developmental dyslexia, and skilled reading across languages: A psycholinguistic grain size theory. *Psycholinguistic Bulletin*, *131*, 3–29.

Ziegler, J., Perry, C., Ma-Wyatt, A., Ladner, D., & Körne, G. (2003). Developmental dyslexia in different languages: Language-specific or universal? *Journal of Experimental Child Psychology*, *86*, 169–193.

READING COMPREHENSION: UNANSWERED QUESTIONS AND READING INSTRUCTION CHALLENGES

Solveig-Alma Halaas Lyster

ABSTRACT

Literacy demands have changed over the years and for success in society it is necessary to handle a wide range of texts and written information. The school has been criticized for not giving their pupils the necessary abilities to handle the kind of information they are faced with in society. One important dimension of literacy is reading comprehension, but even though much written information has the form of tables, drawings, graphs, etc. such presentations are most often accompanied by written text. This chapter focuses the comprehension of different kinds of written information, and data from different tasks are evaluated in light of the simple view of reading. A total of 132 grade 6 readers were given four reading comprehension tasks concurrently with a decoding task and a listening comprehension task. It was found that the sum of decoding and listening comprehension accounted for a larger part of the variance in all the reading comprehension tasks than the product of decoding and listening comprehension. The pupils' results on a naming task and morphological tasks from preschool accounted for significant parts of the

Literacy and Learning
Advances in Learning and Behavioral Disabilities, Volume 23, 115–153

ISSN: 0735-004X/doi:10.1108/S0735-004X(2010)0000023007

variance in the comprehension of both plain text and text combined with tables and graphs over and above the concurrent decoding and listening comprehension results. Speed of orthographic identification in 2nd grade accounted for an additional, significant part of the variance in the plain text reading tasks. These results show that processing speed and linguistic knowledge, such as morphological knowledge, are important contributors to the comprehension of different kinds of written information. Even if speed of orthographic identification is especially important for comprehending plain texts, a broad linguistic and cognitive perspective seems to be important when preparing pupils to comprehend different kinds of written material.

Literacy demands have changed drastically over the past years. Even if the complexity of the written language has not changed, the quantity of print has increased. More written information is distributed, more material has to be read and it has to be read faster than before (Blake & Blake, 2002). There have been changes in the literacy demands for various kinds of work and in the labour market. New literacy concepts such as digital literacy, media literacy, visual literacy, etc. have been developed in society, placing overwhelming demands on the educational system. Literacy is most often defined as using printed and written information to function in society and to achieve one's goal and to develop one's knowledge and potential (OECD/Statistics Canada, 1995). This definition can be seen as broad enough to include the broader perspective we need to have on literacy in today's society. Reading cannot be taught without focusing on the literacy abilities required in society. Having poor literacy abilities in today's society is not only an educational issue, but also a public health issue. The report *Literacy in the Information Age* shows that there is a clear connection between reading ability and unemployment (OECD/Statistics Canada, 2000). Low reading ability places the individual at a particular disadvantage in the labour market. Unemployment is, for many reasons, a risk factor for both failure to succeed in society and for the individual's lack of well-being.

Many definitions of literacy have been put forward through the years, with the later definitions, as the one given by OECD/Statistics Canada (1995), defining literacy as a relatively broad concept. The Workforce Investment Act of 1998 defines literacy as "an individual's ability to read, write, speak, compute and solve problems at levels of proficiency necessary to function on the job, in the family of the individual and in society" (US Department of Labor Employment and Training Administration, 1998).

This is a broader view of literacy than just the individual's ability to read, the more traditional concept of literacy. National Institute for Literacy is supporting this definition in writing that "As information and technology have increasingly shaped our society, the skills we need to function successfully have gone beyond reading, and literacy has come to include the skills listed in the current definition." (National Institute for Literacy, 2009, "What is literacy," para. 1). This definition is important as it views literacy, at least to some extent, from a more contextualized perspective. So, the definition of "literate" depends on the skills required within a particular environment.

Venezky (1990) emphasized that it is reasonable to define literacy as a referent for adult reading or close to adult reading and introduced the term "functional literacy" to mean "an acceptable grasp of the skills of reading and writing for functioning in society as a young adult." (Blake et al., 2002, p. 13). There is disagreement, however, as to the levels or types of reading necessary for functional literacy (Blake et al., 2002). In school, reading is usually assessed by using a selection of texts, but whether the selected text(s) assess all aspects of functional literacy remains a question. The literacy level required in a given social context will change over time, place and social condition, according to Venezky (1990).

Other authors have also pondered the complexity of applying definitions of literacy, whether traditional or evolving, to individuals with disabilities. While most authors in this field have recognized literacy as "interactive, constructive, strategic, and meaning-based" (Steelman, Pierce, & Koppenhaver, 1994, p. 201), they also typically maintain the notion that comprehension and use of *written* text is central to literacy. Steelman, Pierce and Koppenhaver's definition is a good example: "To be literate is to be able to gather and to construct meaning using written language" (p. 201).

Categories such as reading, writing, numeracy and document processing are most often included in the term literacy. Multimedia literacy is also often included in the current concept of literacy. Texts usually read in schools, however, seem to differ considerably from the texts and written information faced by adults in the society (Venezky, 2000). Venezky points out that adults need a certain set of literacy skills for success in everyday life: for work, for citizenship and for recreation. More document knowledge, for example, is needed at the adult level. Many adults will not be able to cope with document formats, such as job application forms, if they have not learned how to cope with such formats in school.

Even though non-fiction texts (e.g., information pamphlets, instruction manuals and application forms) have been lately more in focus in international assessments and surveys, there is still an open question as to for how much time the schools teach reading of various kinds of written texts and materials and how well they do this. According to Venezky (2000) the schools are not teaching the non-fiction literacy needed for success in society. He says they are teaching something that does not provide the skills needed by adults. It is necessary to ask what the necessary skills for reading competence in society are. What abilities does the school need to provide their pupils? It seems as if the school primarily focuses on fiction and less often on abilities required for understanding non-fiction materials. Outside of school, the individual needs to read texts containing many graphs and charts, and operating manuals for household appliances and gadgets. The individual needs document knowledge in order to cope with job application forms or obtain information from the Internet to book a flight, etc. Many adults will not be able to handle these types of non-fiction texts if they have not learned how to cope with such formats in school. Pupils with learning disabilities are especially vulnerable if the school's focus does not cover these abilities to cope with various kinds of written information.

Since comprehension is the ultimate goal of getting information from written materials, and since written information is often presented in the form of a lot of written text, even though they may include tables, charts and graphs, it can be argued that the simple view of reading (SVR; Gough & Tunmer, 1986) is a model that works with most of the non-fiction written materials in society, as well as for the fiction or non-fiction plain-text materials used in the school. Tables, graphs and charts usually have some text attached to them, or explanatory texts following the graphic representations. The individual needs to decode and understand the language in the texts in the surrounding society, even if the majority of these texts are accompanied with other, more graphic kinds of information. New words have to be decoded with the reader's language ability, as measured by listening comprehension tasks, determining what information the reader can get from the words and sentences provided by the written text. The ability to understand the words and sentences and the ability to draw inferences are the basic skills needed to understand written information. Still, discontinuous texts, that is, texts that require the reader to shift attention from the text to tables, charts or drawings (such as the assembly instructions for IKEA flat-packed furniture) place different demands on a reader's language and cognitive abilities.

The skills needed to understand written material are complex skills; different skills may be needed for different types of written material. Word reading and various listening comprehension abilities will interact in different ways with cognitive abilities, experiences and motivation when different written information is interpreted. This chapter will focus on the complexity of reading comprehension and the SVR. One of the questions is to what extent the SVR model can explain the variance in comprehension across different types of texts. Another question focuses on the unexplained variance in reading comprehension. To what extent can variables other than decoding and listening comprehension explain the variance in reading comprehension?

MODELS OF READING COMPREHENSION

Reading is usually defined as being the product of decoding and listening comprehension (Gough & Tunmer, 1986; Hoover & Gough, 1990). This model has, however, been challenged in several studies by replacing the product of decoding and listening comprehension with the sum of these two variables, or by including both an additive model and a multiplicative model in various analyses of reading comprehension. Various studies have tested the uniqueness of the additive model and the multiplicative model (Chen & Vellutino, 1997; Conners, 2009; Hoover & Gough, 1990; Georgiou, Das, & Hayward, 2009; Savage & Wolforth, 2007), but whether using one of the models or a combination of them, all of these studies have documented that decoding and listening comprehension account for a relatively similar but substantial amount of the variance in reading comprehension. The variance explained by the product of decoding and listening comprehension varies a lot from study to study (Adlof, Catts, & Little, 2006; Aaron, Joshi, & Williams, 1999; Conners, 2009; Johnston & Kirby, 2006). In some studies only 45% of the variance in reading comprehension is explained by the multiplicative model (Georgiou et al., 2009), while in other studies up to 85% of the variance is explained (Hoover & Gough, 1990), with the explained variance often closer to 50% than to 70%. The explained variance also changes from age level to age level, but not necessarily in the same direction. Johnston and Kirby (2006) found the explained variance in reading comprehension in grade 5 to be less than that in grade 3, while Hoover and Gough (1990) found that the explained variance increased somewhat with age. The amount of explained variance also appears to be dependent on the kind of decoding or word reading that is in focus. More of the variance is usually explained if word reading, but not non-word reading, is one of the multiplicative factors (Conners, 2009; Johnston & Kirby, 2006; Savage, 2006).

As mentioned previously and in a range of studies of reading comprehension, understanding written text is a complex task that is still not fully understood. Even though we know the importance of word identification and listening comprehension we know less about other contributors to reading comprehension. Some other factors have been connected to reading comprehension. Various kinds of reading strategies, such as using "fixing up strategies" when there is a consciousness about failing comprehension, and the adding of new information to what is previously known by the reader, help support the comprehension process (Alexander & Jetton, 2000). Theories and models connecting background knowledge and reading comprehension have been supported (Anderson, 1994; Kintsch, 1988; Bråten, 1993). Several studies have focused on the interaction between reading comprehension strategies and background knowledge (Alexander & Jetton, 2000). In Norway, Bråten and colleagues (Anmarkrud & Bråten, 2009; Bråten, 1993; Samuelstuen & Bråten, 2005) have recently looked at the role played by topic knowledge and motivation in reading comprehension. Samuelstuen and Bråten (2005) examined the relative contribution of decoding, topic knowledge and strategic processing to the comprehension of a social studies text by grade 10 readers. Their findings suggest that good comprehension may be associated with the use of good strategies, good topic knowledge or both. Even though both decoding and the use of strategies explained significant parts of the variance in reading comprehension, the single best predictor was topic knowledge. Some of the participants in the study, however, had poor decoding skills but good comprehension that could not fully be explained by examining the relative contribution of topic knowledge and strategies to their reading comprehension. The researchers suggest that other factors than strategy use and topic knowledge may compensate for poor decoding skills in pupils showing good comprehension performance. They suggest that the manner in which information is stored and accessed, good memory skills and ability to comprehend spoken language may be examples of such compensatory factors.

In addition to the factors already mentioned, there are also motivational factors influencing reading comprehension. Guthrie and Wigfield (2000) found that motivation appears to be an important factor in explaining variance in reading comprehension, and Guthrie et al. (2007) showed that reading motivation constructs based on interviews predicted reading comprehension. Also, Anmarkrud and Bråten (2009) focused on the role of motivation for reading comprehension. They gave 9th graders the Motivation for Reading questionnaire (Wigfield & Guthrie, 1997), with items focusing on reading comprehension rather than on reading in general.

From their findings they concluded that prior knowledge or topic knowledge, as well as the use of deeper-level strategies are important for reading comprehension and reading instruction, but there should also be a focus in reading comprehension instruction on motivation for comprehension (the pupil's belief in the importance of comprehension) since that contributes significantly in explaining variance in reading comprehension. Thus, reading comprehension concerns knowledge that is dependent on the teacher's ability to support the pupils in developing the knowledge, strategies and motivation for understanding what is read. It also depends on the parents' ability to create an environment that supports the child in developing the knowledge and motivation for comprehending written text.

Other than the elements or factors mentioned previously, there are individual differences among children in their approach to the task of reading. Processing speed, phonological awareness, syntactic abilities, etc. are linguistic and cognitive measures which can be supported by the child's environment, but which may also be influenced by biological or genetic factors. Even though factors such as motivation, processing speed, etc. have been considered in addition to decoding and listening comprehension in explaining reading comprehension, much of the variance in reading remains unexplained. Anmarkrud and Bråten (2009) found that school achievement, gender, topic knowledge, two kinds of strategy measures and two kinds of reading motivation measures accounted for 48% of the variance in reading comprehension in the reading of a social studies text. Even though the variables of word decoding or speed of word decoding might have explained a little more of the variance, if they had been included in the analysis, so far less than 50% of the variance is explained in this study, a result much in line with results from other studies.

Topic knowledge, as focused on by Bråten and his colleagues, is to some extent connected to words that are central to a topic. It is known that vocabulary plays an important role in reading comprehension (Anderson & Nagy, 1992; Biemiller, 2003; National Reading Panel, 2000). If a listening task is matched well with a reading comprehension task, topic knowledge and words central to the topic are probably accounted for by the listening task. In other circumstances, vocabulary might account for an additional part of the variance in reading comprehension than what is explained by the listening task. In a Norwegian study, Lervåg and Aukrust (2009) found that reading comprehension differences between language 1 and language 2 learners could be fully attributed to initial differences in vocabulary skills. Even though language 2 learners with a poorly developed vocabulary will especially be at risk for developing poor reading comprehension, variation in language 1 language learners will also become evident as variation in their reading comprehension. Written language uses many more words than oral language. Also, written words used intend to be more academic words (Corson, 1997). These are words used much more in school than in daily life. Even if they are less frequently used than many words that are used on a daily basis, they may appear frequently in school books or in other school texts. Knowledge of academic words is the key to understanding texts used in school and for understanding various subjects.

CHALLENGES TO THE SIMPLE VIEW OF READING

As mentioned above in the discussion about the SVR model, there have been several challenges to the model. The study by Keenan, Betjemann and Olson (2008) along with other studies have challenged SVR (Gough & Tunmer, 1986). Even though a large amount of evidence has emerged to support SVR (e.g., Aaron et al., 1999; Catts, Hogan, Adlof, & Barth, 2003; Adlof et al., 2006) it is a fact that in some studies decoding multiplied by listening comprehension (the multiplicative model), whereas in other studies the sum of decoding and listening comprehension (the additive model) often have explained less than half of the variance in reading comprehension (see Conners, 2009; Georgiou et al., 2009). In many of the studies it seems to matter little whether the product of decoding and listening comprehension, the linear combination or both are used to predict reading comprehension. Georgiou et al. (2009) found that the product of the two factors (decoding and listening comprehension) and the sum of those factors explained nearly the same amount of the variance in reading comprehension, 45 and 47%, respectively. They found the very same results in a group of poor reading comprehenders, the multiplicative model accounting for 45% of the variance in reading comprehension and the additive model accounting for the same amount of variance. In addition to decoding and listening comprehension, they added two additional factors to the model: naming speed and phonological awareness as tested by phoneme elision. These two additional factors explained no significant additional part of the variance whether they were entered after the multiplicative factors or after the additive factors, neither in the full sample of readers nor in the sample of poor reading comprehenders. However, since the subjects performed within the average range in both decoding and listening comprehension, the researchers suggest that the SRV cannot be the product of decoding and listening comprehension. The results also support findings of

Savage and Wolforth that both the multiplicative model and the additive model have equal explanatory power. However, the findings that naming speed and phonological awareness had no additional explanatory power contradicted findings of Johnston and Kirby that both naming speed and phonological awareness accounted for a significant portion of the variance when entered after the multiplicative model.

The SVR model only partly explains reading comprehension. The part of the variance in reading comprehension that is explained by decoding and listening comprehension varies in different studies. If different text reading tasks also vary in the competencies they measure, the part of reading comprehension that is explained by the decoding times listening comprehension or decoding plus listening comprehension may vary from task to task and other, different variables may in different ways and in different degrees explain additional variance in reading comprehension. The more that is known about the variables influencing reading comprehension, the more is known about what to focus on in reading comprehension instruction and about the factors that may cause reading comprehension disabilities. The aim of the analyses that follows in this chapter is to get a broader view and understanding of components, in addition to decoding and listening comprehension, that contribute to reading comprehension.

WHAT INFORMATION CAN READING COMPREHENSION TESTS PROVIDE?

In addition to the awareness of the broad definition of literacy and to the need for providing support for children with many kinds of literacy experience in order to ensure success in society, it is also necessary to broaden our understanding of reading comprehension in its own right. The ability to comprehend narrative and especially expository, non-fiction texts is the most important requirement, not only for success in school but also for success in society and in the labour market. How should reading comprehension tests be interpreted? Low correlations among results from different reading comprehension tasks tell us that different kinds of texts require different kinds of knowledge or abilities (Keenan et al., 2008). Keenan et al. not only found moderate correlations among the reading comprehension tests commonly used in the United States, but also they ran an exploratory factor analysis and found that the tests loaded on two factors. Even though there was a decoding factor and a comprehension factor, the Reading Comprehension Test from the Peabody Individual Achievement Test (PIAT; Dunn & Markwardt, 1970), and the Woodcock–Johnson Passage Comprehension subtest (WJPC; Woodcock, McGrew, & Mather, 2001) had higher loadings on the decoding factor than on the comprehension factor. These results were supported by results from regression analyses showing that decoding and not listening comprehension accounted for most of the variance in PIAT and WJPC. For the two other reading comprehension measures, the Qualitative Reading Inventory (QRI; Leslie & Caldwell, 2001) and the Gray Oral Reading Test (GORT; Wiederholt & Bryant, 1992), listening comprehension accounted for most of the variance.

If reading comprehension tests, to a large extent, measure different abilities, this is not only a challenge from an assessment perspective, it is a specific challenge from a special needs perspective. These findings make it necessary to evaluate more closely the texts that are presented to students within the field of special needs education. In the assessment of pupils' reading comprehension, why does a pupil do better on one reading comprehension task compared to another? What abilities should be focused on to develop the kind of comprehension strategies and knowledge required by various texts or tasks? Do pupils read some texts better because their topic knowledge differs from text to text, are some tests or tasks more cognitively loaded than others or are the differences between mastery of texts caused by the words used and other linguistic elements? What compensatory strategies and knowledge should a pupil with poor decoding abilities develop in order to master various kinds of texts? What kind of reading comprehension programme should be developed for a pupil that only has a reading comprehension problem? Is it better for a dyslexic pupil to read texts that are primarily dependent on decoding abilities to strengthen this important ability? Is it better for dyslexic pupils to read texts that rely more on listening comprehension than on decoding ability or would that lead to more guessing about words based on the context so that little progress in decoding takes place? It might be easy to say that reading instruction needs to focus on all kind of texts that are important for academic success and for success in society, but still these questions represent challenges that need to be met concerning students with various kinds of reading disabilities, especially dyslexic pupils. Even though there is a lot known about how to support a child with reading difficulties, understanding what is required by various types of texts as well as how these demands can best be met may provide an even better platform for building good teaching programmes.

There are many unanswered questions as to what information reading tests and listening tests can provide. Inferences about reading comprehension are made partly "by the material presented for comprehending and the format that is used for assessing comprehension of the material" (Fletcher, 2006, p. 323). The measurement issues are complicated.

HOW TEXTS ARE BUILT

Narrative and expository texts represent different ways of knowing, which means that they differ in content and overall organization (Westby, 2005). Narrative texts usually have an event chain or story grammar. The story grammar describes the typical elements frequently found in stories and pupils use these elements when retelling stories. These texts usually begin with a setting that presents the characters, followed by an event where the characters respond to various happenings. These texts then have an ending to the happening or activity or story, sometimes with some kind of a conclusion or moral. Pupils with reading disabilities are reported to have difficulties with narrative texts because the pupils are less efficient in using content schemata and text grammar (see Westby, 2005). Fairy tales are good examples of narrative texts. Expository texts are described using other concepts. They are more descriptive; they make comparisons and present problems and solutions; they can be argumentative. Because of these differences, different strategies are needed to comprehend the different types of texts. Narratives are reported to be easier to comprehend than expository texts (Graesser & Goodman, 1985; Saenz & Fuchs, 2002; Vacca, Vacca, & Grove, 2003). However, little research has been conducted to understand the challenges pupils with learning disabilities face when reading expository texts. Expository texts often carry much more new information than narratives, so comprehension depends much more on the individual reader's previously acquired topic knowledge. Even if there are patterns in expository texts, they are different from the narrative text patterns. The comprehension of expository texts, and also narrative texts, depends heavily, as mentioned previously, on vocabulary knowledge. Vocabulary instruction is therefore important in supporting the pupils' abilities to read different kind of texts. If Vygotsky's (1962) statement that "language is the tool for our thoughts" is true, language competence more than non-verbal abilities should be important in the interpretation of all kinds of texts and written material. It remains to be discovered, however, what other linguistic abilities than those measured from listening comprehension, vocabulary and decoding tasks can explain additional variance in reading. How do various linguistic abilities interact with cognitive abilities that are important for reading comprehension? The question has been posed if a fluency component, naming speed, attention control or phonemic awareness should be added to modify the SVR model (Adlof et al., 2006; Conners, 2009; Johnston & Kirby, 2006). However, no clear-cut answers have been found even though some studies have uncovered evidence that several variables can explain variance in reading comprehension beyond decoding and listening comprehension.

So far the focus has been on the use of continuous texts in predicting students' reading comprehension. The texts students face today, however, are often discontinuous. Information presented in tables, pictures, histograms, etc. need to be combined with information found in running texts. A better understanding of the factors that contribute to the understanding of various kinds of written material faced by pupils is important. The more that is known about the challenges presented to the reader by various texts, the more can be done to provide the reader with the support he/she needs.

In a special issue of *Scientific Studies of Reading,* Fletcher (2006) concludes that "... the material that participants in studies are asked to read is a major determinant of the inferences made about the quality of comprehension" (p. 326). He further states that "... different inferences will be made depending not only on the difficulty of the text but also on the semantic, syntactic, and related characteristics of the text" (p. 326). This underlines the importance of understanding text variability when assessing pupils reading comprehension and when teaching reading comprehension.

VOCABULARY KNOWLEDGE AND LEXICAL QUALITY

If reading comprehension is the product of decoding and listening comprehension, it is natural to ask what role decoding alone plays in reading comprehension. As seen from the results in Keenan et al. study (2008), decoding plays a more important role than listening comprehension for some reading comprehension tests. Decoding is not necessarily only a result of decoding graphemes into sounds to get "a sound package" which can be linked to meaning or be understood from the context in which it appears. Decoding is also driven by meaning. When enough sound information is available, the word can be retrieved from the lexicon.

On several occasions, Perfetti and his colleagues (Perfetti, 1985, 1992; Perfetti & Hart, 2002; Landi, 2005; Landi & Perfetti, 2007) have shown how lexical quality determines the accuracy and fluency of word identification and that lexical quality also determines comprehension. Rapid retrieval of a word's phonology and meaning is the most important part of the reading comprehension process (Perfetti, 1992). Automatic word identification has been looked upon as an automatic process that could preserve processing resources for higher level comprehension (LaBerge & Samuels, 1974). This is also the theoretical ground for different repeated reading programmes developed over the past decades (Klinkenberg, 2005). The effects of these programmes have been incontestable; repeated reading is the best method for helping children to identify words effortlessly and immediately. Perfetti (2007) underlines that the relationship between word identification and reading comprehension is present in both young and older readers. However, he criticizes that

> emphasis on completely general processes – decoding, phonological processes, retrieval, memory, automaticity – although theoretically consistent, seemed to leave knowledge out of the picture. Skilled reading was about efficient processing mechanisms and less skilled reading was about the same mechanisms executed inefficiently. (Perfetti, 2007, p. 358)

Perfetti emphasizes that efficiency in word decoding is not the same as identifying words at a high speed. According to Perfetti, rather than seeking to understand the effect word identification speed has on reading comprehension, efforts should be made to understand the ability to "retrieve word identities that provide the meanings the reader needs in a given context" (2007, p. 359). According to Perfetti, what lies behind such efficient processes are knowledge components, that is, knowledge about word forms and meanings. Lexical quality is defined as "… the extent to which a word specifies its form and meaning components in a way that is both precise and flexible." (2007, p. 359). He emphasizes that precision is necessary when the reader has to differentiate between words such as "pretty" and "petty" and that flexibility is important when confronted with homophones and decisions have to be taken about which meaning is correct.

In reviewing studies of reading concerning lexical quality, Perfetti and colleagues (Haenggi & Perfetti, 1994; Perfetti & Hart, 2002) show that children can have semantic problems at the word level even if they have adequate decoding and phonological skills. Skilled comprehenders take faster decisions about meaning; they exhibit faster semantic processing. They also learn new words more effectively than less skilled comprehenders and easily integrate a word with previous text through paraphrase.

If they read "explosion", as in one example from Perfetti (2007), they easily link the word to "blew up" in the preceding sentence.

Based on the above, it can be concluded that phonology and semantics must be integrated in the teaching of reading. Word forms and word meanings have to be integrated if comprehension is to be effortless.

One important connection between phonology and semantics is the morpheme. A morpheme has a phonological form and it has a meaning. More facts about the relationship between reading and morphological knowledge and awareness have been uncovered during the past years. There is now strong evidence that morphological awareness makes a unique contribution to reading abilities, after controlling for cognitive and linguistic factors such as IQ and phonological awareness (Bryant, Nunes, & Bindman, 1998; Carlisle & Stone, 2003; Kirby, Desrochers, Roth, & Lai, 2008).

Lyster (1998, 2002) conducted a training study following the effects of both phonological awareness training and morphological awareness training on reading development. The two experimental groups were trained for 17 weeks at the end of their preschool years and then followed until the end of grade 3. Both the phonological group and the morphological group developed their linguistic awareness during the training period. Even if the content of the morphological training focused the morphemes in words, the training had an effect on the children's phonological development as well as on their morphological development. This also worked the other way around for the children in the phonological group who developed their morphological awareness to a significantly higher level than the control group, although not to the same extent as the morphological group. A 1-year follow-up showed that the effect of training on reading development varied according to mother's education. At the end of grade 1, there was found a significant interaction effect between group and the maternal educational level for most of the reading measures. Children of relatively highly educated mothers started preschool with better-developed metalinguistic awareness than children of less-educated mothers. The children with more highly educated mothers profited greatly from morphological awareness training. Children of less-educated mothers profited the most from phonological awareness training that focused on both larger and smaller phonological units. Since morphological development had an effect on reading development for children with a certain level of phonological awareness, it means that morphological awareness training should build on some basic phonological awareness in order for it to be most effective.

READING COMPREHENSION AND INSTRUCTIONAL CHALLENGES

Valid assessments are necessary to meet each child's needs. In order to conduct purposeful and systematic assessments, it is necessary to decide what needs to be assessed (National Research Council of the National Academies, 2008). The low correlations among different reading tests and, in many studies, the failure to explain more than approximately 50% of the variance in reading comprehension make reading comprehension assessment challenging. Different texts measure different abilities, and different texts rely differently on cognitive and linguistic abilities. A closure task may rely less on verbal memory than a task with multiple-choice questions based on the reading of a paragraph. Such differences in test design must be taken into account in the interpretation of test results.

A child's experience outside school may provide support in the comprehension of a wide range of texts while vocabulary knowledge within a specific area may explain the comprehension of other texts. For example, a child who plays soccer may be able to read a text about a soccer player much better than a text about flowers. A European child who has visited Washington DC, but not Sydney, may be more motivated to read a text about Washington DC than a text about Sydney. Since the child has experienced Washington DC, he/she probably has knowledge about Washington DC that supports the comprehension of the text about Washington DC. The situation might be different for a text about Sydney.

There has been considerable focus on text reading in recent years. One reason for this is the international assessment programmes Progress in International Literacy Study (PIRLS) and Program for International Student Assessment (PISA). Norwegian students, in particular, perform less well on expository texts than they do on fiction. The reason for this is unknown, but Rasmussen (2003) has found that Norwegian teachers do not teach reading comprehension in a systematic way. He interviewed academics, school administrators, and teachers to investigate factors associated with literacy performance and to gather recommendations for improvement. A central theme in these recommendations was the necessity to teach reading strategies in a far more systematic way.

For expository texts, it is important to focus on headings, subheadings and specific words. Narratives and expository texts not only rely on various kinds of knowledge, schemata or text grammar used by the reader, but also on metacognitive processes in different ways. Even if different metacognitive processes play different roles in different types of texts, strategic reading and comprehension monitoring are important for all kinds of reading (Dunlosky, Rawson, & Hacker, 2002). Metacognitive strategies are conscious, controllable processes (Alexander & Jetton, 2000). Mastropieri and Scruggs (1997) identified self-questioning as among the best practices for supporting reading comprehension of students with learning disabilities. Also, the dialogue between teachers and students has been focused as an important factor in facilitating reading comprehension. This dialogue is the means whereby support is provided and adjusted to jointly develop such strategies and construct the meaning of a text. Children's unfamiliarity with different types of text structure will impede their comprehension of different kinds of texts (Bakken, Mastropieri, & Scruggs, 1997). They need to learn strategies that help them solve the different challenges different texts present. Palincsar & Brown (1987) focus on four strategies that seem to be used by successful readers: question generating, summarizing, clarifying and predicting. Other strategies and concepts (e.g., understanding the purpose of the reading assignment) have also been focused on (Bruce, 1980), but the important message is that different strategies can be supported through teaching and through teacher–pupil dialogue. Even if language knowledge or listening comprehension is the most important factor for reading comprehension along with decoding abilities, lack of metalinguistic strategies may hinder the development of good reading comprehension despite the presence of well-developed listening comprehension. Metacognitive abilities may be one factor that can explain additional variance in reading comprehension, as was shown by Samuelstuen and Bråten (2005).

When Venezky (2000) accused the American school system of having a literacy programme that did not take into account the competency needs of society, he used the concept "chasm" to explain the difference between literacy abilities focused in the school and the literacy abilities needed in society. Venezky (2000) explained the term"chasm" in the following way:

> What I mean by chasm in this context is simply a big, yawning hollow that exists between the form of literacy that is promulgated by the schools under the curricular title of reading instruction, and what adults need to survive as good citizens, as multiplicative contributors to the national good, as realizers of their own potential." (p. 20).

He points to the fact that while the literacy programs focus on fiction and narrative texts, 75% or more of what a child reads in school by 6th grade consists of non-narrative and non-fictional materials. In the upper grades this percentage is even greater.

Adults need a certain set of literacy skills to be successful in daily life. The schools are teaching something else. Venezky (2000) also focuses on the need for better comprehension instruction. Comprehension has been neglected and he stresses that high literature has been given too much emphasis in relation to its real importance:

> The skills required for reading graphs and charts, for deriving time lines, and for diagramming math story problems (among others) are as complex and as sophisticated as those required for deciding on main idea and characterization, yet somehow the former set, because they apply primarily to utilitarian materials, have been relegated to a low status in the school curriculum while the latter, since they involve the student in "high" literature, have been elevated far beyond their importance. (p. 29)

If this is still true, if schools primarily focus on high literature, fiction and, to a great extent, narrative texts in literacy instruction, this is especially serious for children with learning disabilities. Many of these children will never read books by Ibsen, Shakespeare or other famous authors of the world. They will not even read fiction by modern authors. However they will find it more helpful to be able to read the brochures from their cell phone provider when they get a new cell phone, or advertising flyers from local grocery shops with offers that will help them save money when the economy is bad.

It is not a question of choosing non-fiction texts over fiction. Literature should definitely be part of the curriculum. Literature is an important part of culture, both historically and for the future. Many students will continue to read literature outside school, reading which will enrich their lives. However, others will stop reading literature when they leave school. They will still need to read brochures, advertisements, papers and documents that are important for them. Some will never manage to read these materials because they never learned how to do so. While many adults can just book a hotel room or an airline ticket on the Internet, some people are unable to do so because they were never taught the necessary skills. So, to cite Venezky once more, "Schools must and can teach those literacy skills that adults desperately need to survive in society" (p. 29).

Vygotsky (1962) claims that development follows learning. Reading comprehension is dependent on knowledge. Helping children to understand words, to develop strategies and motivation is important, but perhaps the very best element of instruction is the teacher acting as a model reader. In reading both narratives and expository texts, the reader needs to be in dialogue with the author. Even if the author is not present except through words and sentences, he/she is sending a message for the reader to interpret.

It is more difficult to understand written text than spoken language, not just because there are more words in the written text but also because in the interpretation of written text, the signs and body language that support the interpretation of the spoken language are lacking. Dialogue with a more competent person may help a child to see new connections and to discover new meanings. This is exactly what teachers should do when helping children to comprehend various texts. The child, the teacher and the text should enter into a dialogue. The teacher can put forward questions, focus on issues such as: Why were atom bombs dropped over Hiroshima and Nagasaki during World War II? Was it not very unfair to use a weapon that destroyed so many lives and handicapped thousands for the rest of their lives? Did it stop the war? Would it otherwise have gone on for many more years? What were the reasons for the World War II? Discussions "with the text" are an important part of the comprehension construct. It is the responsibility of the school to help pupils to become active readers, readers that enter into dialogue with the texts they are reading, to read critically and to be cognitively alert. It is important to recognize when comprehension fails, when happenings or facts are not understood, when words are not understood or conclusions are not consistent. This is metacognition. Within the field of special needs education, it is important to select texts that are within the range of the child's knowledge, experience and cognitive abilities, while still at a level that can support new learning and development. When a child has developed metacognitive awareness and has become an active reader that enters into dialogue with the text that is being read, this knowledge will be successfully used on more advanced texts.

READING COMPREHENSION IN A NORWEGIAN CONTEXT

As discussed by Lyster (2007), the Norwegian results from PIRLS and PISA have been disappointing from the Norwegian point of view. For Norwegian pupils, the decline from the 2000 and 2003 PISA results to the 2006 PISA results was of such an extent that it drew considerable attention from the Norwegian Government. In comparison with other countries (especially the Nordic countries), the poorest results were in reading expository texts. According to the 2006 PISA results, reading comprehension of Norwegian 15-year olds is below the OECD average, even worse than the 2000 and 2003 results (Kjærnsli, Lie, Olsen, & Roe, 2007) despite efforts that were made to strengthen the earlier, slightly more negative trends concerning reading levels in Norway. Together with Iceland, Norway performed lower than the other Nordic countries. The variability is higher in Norway than in any other Nordic country. The number of pupils scoring at the lowest level has increased.

The results show that Norway has great challenges in meeting the needs of poor readers. Both Klette (2007) and Kjærnsli et al. (2007) discuss reasons for the disappointing results from PISA 2006. The many changes in the national curriculum over the past years and the methods and elements focused on in the curriculum have been questioned (Klette, 2007). According to Klette, the extensive use of individual work plans might be detrimental to the class and pupils collectively by making the pupil less motivated to participate in collective discussions and dialogues. Learning does not take place in a vacuum. Even though reading and individual work may support both vocabulary learning and language development which is important for comprehension, other activities might be more effective (Kjærnsli et al., 2007). Self-regulated pupils may be much less effective in their learning than other-regulated pupils. At least pupils with learning disabilities will have great challenges working on their own for a large part of the school day. In addition, the concept of class is no longer relevant. Teams of teachers are responsible for groups of pupils that may vary in size. This flexibility in organization may not have created the safe learning environment that pupils with learning disabilities especially need, even though it has given the school the possibility of creating smaller groups that may have benefited children with special needs. However, there is little research in Norway that has focused on the working environment in the school and on the class as a social unit. Another question raised is to what degree class time is actually spent on teaching. There appears to be relatively many things going on in the Norwegian classroom that have little to do with the subjects being taught (Kjærnsli et al., 2007). In Norway, there are large individual differences and differences between classrooms concerning the PISA and PIRLS results and there is a tendency for larger differences among the schools in the 2006 PISA results than was found earlier (Kjærnsli et al., 2007; Van Daal, Solheim, Gabrielsen, & Begnum, 2007). Therefore, the Norwegian school authorities, in the past years, had a clear focus on both school administration and the teachers' knowledge about how to teach reading, especially reading comprehension. Good schools and teachers focus on academics; they have high expectations for their pupils. Time is spent on teaching and learning. However, Norway is still waiting for the results of the efforts taken to strengthen the teaching of reading and to foster reading development for various groups of children. So far there has clearly been success in the capital, Oslo. Even though there are greater challenges in Oslo than in other Norwegian communities due to the large number of minority-language pupils, there has been faster progression in primary-school reading results than in any other community in the country. Even the inner-city schools in Oslo are doing well. Even though there may be various reasons for these results, this positive development may be partly due to the training given to the teachers about the reading process, as well as the responsibility taken by school administrators for the teaching of reading.

COMPREHENSION OF WRITTEN MATERIAL IN GRADE 6 – A 6-YEAR FOLLOW-UP STUDY

The following is a presentation of a follow-up study of 132 children, based on a study reported previously (Lyster, 1998, 2002). The primary aim of this follow-up study was to search for lasting effects of two metalinguistic approaches, a phonological and a morphological approach (Lyster, 1998, 2002, 2003). Some results from this follow-up study have been published previously (Lyster, 2007). With the general question "how do pupils' understanding of written material vary from text to text?", the present substudy aims at (a) evaluating SVR and the role it plays for different kinds of written texts in a Norwegian context and (b) examining what role memory, naming speed, vocabulary, morphological knowledge and awareness, phoneme awareness, early orthographic identification and non-verbal abilities play, in addition to the role of decoding and listening comprehension, in explaining variability in reading comprehension

Sample

The sample included 132 randomly selected children (from a group of 273 children assessed in preschool) who were tested again approximately 6 years later in grade 6 (see Lyster, 2007). The children came from one community outside Oslo. At this time Norwegian children started school the year they turned 7 years old, as in other Scandinavian countries. The children ranged in age from 6 years 4 months to 7 years 3 months at the time of assessment prior to the start of school.

Measures

The measures used in this substudy were selected from a large battery of tests used by Lyster in earlier previously reported study and a follow-up study (2002, 2007).

Measures Prior to Starting School

All tasks were given in small groups of children. When answering the various items in the different tasks, the children marked drawings on sheets they were given.

Word Compounds. The children were asked to blend two words together to get the target word. For each item, the correct word had to be identified among the four given drawings. When the words *brann* [fire] and *bil* [car] were to be blended to make *brannbil* [fire engine] a drawing presenting *bilbrann* [car fire] was among the distractors. Reliability (alpha) was .64.

Analyses of Compound Words. Given a compound word, the children were asked to find the word that remained when one of the component words was deleted. For each item the target word was presented in a row of four pictures. Among the distractors there was a picture representing the compound word as well as one representing the part that was deleted. Reliability (alpha) was .72.

Homophones. This task was a naming task. The children had to identify two drawings (mark two out of four drawings) representing items with the same name (homophones such as the Norwegian words for Christmas and wheel which are homophones in Norwegian). There was a time limit of 5 min for this task. The test consisted of one practice item and 16 test items. Reliability (alpha) was .85.

Grade 1 Measure – IQ

Raven's Progressive Matrices (Raven, 1976; Raven, Court, & Raven, 1983) and vocabulary from WISC-R (Undheim, 1978).

Grade 2 Measure – Orthographic Coding

The children were presented with 20 word/pseudo-homophone pairs. The task was to underline the word in each pair (Lyster, 1994). In the pair *skole/sgole*, both the non-word and the word sound like the Norwegian word for "school" Only *skole*, however, has the correct spelling.

The task is similar to the task described by Olson, Kliegel, Davidson, and Foltz (1985) and to the one used by Baron and Strawson (1976). There was a time limit of 120 s to underline the correctly spelled word in each pair for as many items as possible. The score equalled the number of correct choices minus the number of incorrect choices. Reliability (alpha) was .91.

Grade 6 Measures

The grade 6 tests are part of a Norwegian standardized reading assessment battery (Nasjonalt Læremiddelsenter, 1995). Reliability scores (alpha) range from .89 to .97.

Word–Picture Matching. This test was a word-decoding/word-reading task. Presented with a word, the pupil was asked to pick the one drawing out of four that represented the word. The test included 40 items and was time limited.

Listening Comprehension. The listening comprehension task consisted of a text that was read to the pupils and that was followed by seven multiple-choice questions each with three alternatives.

Continuous, Narrative Text Reading 1 (CTR 1). This task consisted of four short prose texts, each followed by a multiple-choice question with four alternatives. There was a time limit for the task. Altogether there were 21 questions.

Continuous, Narrative Text Reading 2 (CTR 2). This was a relatively challenging text of 1,099 words. It was followed by 16 multiple-choice questions, each with four alternatives. The task was time limited.

Discontinuous, Expository Text Reading1 (DTR 1). This task consisted of a relatively short text and a table with information about proteins, fat and carbohydrates in various foods. Seven multiple-choice questions each with three alternatives were presented. The task was timed. Answers to the questions were mostly found in the table presented, but the text also included information about the task.

Discontinuous, Expository text Reading 2 (DTR 2). This task also had a short text introduction and was accompanied by a map of the world. Bars were placed different places around the world map to show how much oil and gas there is in different places in the world. Part of the bar was grey, (showing the amount of oil) and part was white (showing the amount of gas). The answers to the questions were found primarily in the map and the bars, but were supported by the text. Reliability (alpha) was .92.

RESULTS

Descriptive Statistics and Correlations between Measures

Table 1 shows the means, the maximum and minimum scores and the standard deviations for the different measures that were in focus in the substudy.

There was a tendency for ceiling effect for the reading measures as well as for some of the preschool measures, which must be taken into account when interpreting the data. The skewness for word decoding was −1.943 and for listening comprehension −1.257. Such results mean that there is a possibility for type I error inflation to occur if using linear regression analyses (see Austin & Brunner, 2003). The skewness, however, is not substantial and the variations among pupils seem to be large enough not to present too great a challenge concerning the distribution of scores and the choice of an ordinary least-square regression approach.

Table 1. Minimum and Maximum Scores, Means and Standard Deviations for the Preschool, Grades 1 and 2 and Grade 6 Measures.

Measure	Minimum score	Maximum Score	Mean	SD
Word compounds	0	7	5.96	1.58
Analyses of compound words	1	8	5.46	2.01
Homophones	0	16	8.80	4.08
Memory for word sequences	1	8	6.18	1.97
Sound deletion	1	9	6.14	2.12
Raven's progressive matrices	11	43	23.20	7.29
Vocabulary (WISC-R)	4	19	9.44	2.61
Orthographic coding	1	20	16.81	5.09
Word decoding	18	40	37.14	4.66
Simple texts (CTR1)	2	21	17.54	4.46
Advanced text (CTR2)	0	16	11.71	5.45
Text with table (DTR1)	0	9	7.60	1.77
Text with bars/histograms (DTR2)	0	8	6.34	1.90
Listening comp.	0	7	5.46	1.86

Table 2. Correlations Among the Reading Comprehension Tasks, Word Reading and Listening Comprehension Grade 6.

	1	2	3	4	5
1. CTR 1	–				
2. CTR 2	.67*	–			
3. DTR 1	.49*	.49*	–		
4. DTR 2	.41*	.50*	.56*	–	
5. Listening comp.	.62*	.46*	.50*	.45*	–
6. Word reading	.65*	.51*	.46*	.38*	.43*

Note: CTR = continuous text reading, DTR = discontinuous reading.
$^{*}p<.001$.

Table 2 presents the correlations among the grade 6 measures. From Table 2, it is apparent that most of the correlations are moderate.

The highest correlation is between the two continuous text-reading tasks. The other correlations are somewhat lower. The listening comprehension task has its highest correlation with CTR1, the first continuous text task with four short texts. This would also have been expected because the listening comprehension was composed in a similar manner as the continuous text reading tasks, with fewer low-frequency words and complex words than in the case of the long text reading task and the two discontinuous texts reading tasks.

However, the relatively low correlations among tasks that were supposed to uncover understanding of written texts show that different texts assess different competencies. The findings are in line with the findings of Keenan et al. (2008). As could have been expected, tasks that required most of the information to be collected from tables and graphs appear to be less dependent on word decoding and listening comprehension in comparison to the correlations between decoding and listening comprehension and the different reading measures. However, these differences were only found for CTR1 (reading short paragraphs). The correlations between decoding and listening comprehension is just as high (or low) between these two measures and CTR2 (reading a lengthy text) as between these two measures and the two discontinuous text reading tasks. The correlations indicate that decoding and listening comprehension possibly play the same role in collecting information from plain texts as from texts that are combined with tables and graphs. Since the correlations are moderate, a wide spectre of abilities, such as oral vocabulary, word-decoding speed, experience with various kinds of reading tasks/texts, cognitive capacity, prior knowledge of the main topics in the texts, reading comprehension strategies, etc., may have had an influence on various levels of pupil comprehension for the different tasks. Other than decoding and listening comprehension, some possible contributors to comprehension of different kinds of written texts that may explain variance in reading comprehension are discussed in the introduction to this chapter and in the following section. Preliminary analyses showed that both of these morphological measures correlated equally with all the reading measures and highly with each other. Therefore, an explanatory principal component factor analysis using oblique rotation was run. This resulted in the two morphological tasks loading highly on one factor. It was therefore decided to use the factor score in the analyses.

The correlations among the different cognitive and linguistic tasks from preschool, grade 1 and grade 2 and the reading comprehension measures are shown in Table 3. The morphology variable is based on the factor score.

As Table 3 shows orthographic coding in grade 2 has its highest correlations with both the simple text and the more advanced text, .70 and .62, respectively. The correlations with the two discontinuous texts are somewhat lower.

Raven has lower correlations with all the reading texts than homophones (naming) and morphology, telling us that language measures and the

Table 3. Correlations Among the Four Reading Comprehension Tasks in Grade 6 and the Preschool, Grade 1 and Grade 2 Measures.

	1	2	3	4	5	6	7	8
CTR 1 (G6)	–							
CTR 2 (G6)	.67**	–						
DTR 1 (G6)	.49**	.49**	–					
DTR 2 (G6)	.41**	.50**	.56**	–				
Ortogr (G2)	.70**	.62**	.40**	.36**	–			
Voc (G1)	.44**	.28*	.27**	.14	.29**	–		
Raven (G1)	.27**	.21*	.31**	.30**	.31**	.28**	–	
Hom (Pre)	.49**	.50**	.48**	.47**	.46**	.43**	.42**	–
Morph (Pre)	.43**	.46**	.45**	.44**	.43**	.30**	.35**	.55*

Note: CTR = continuous text reading, DTR = discontinuous reading, G = grade, Ortogr = orthographic coding, Voc = vocabulary, Hom = homophones (naming), Morph = morphological awareness, Pre = preschool.
$^{*}p<.05$; $^{**}p<.01$.

phonological speed measure included in the homophone measure are better predictors of reading comprehension than the non-verbal abilities measured by Raven – even though for the tasks with little text and most information to be collected from a table or from a map with bars representing the amount of oil and gas in oil and gas fields.

The Contribution of Naming Speed, Speed of Orthographic Identification, Vocabulary, Morphemic Knowledge and Non-Verbal IQ to SVR

As a first step in the data analyses presented below, regression analyses were run to see which of the additive or multiplicative models of reading comprehension that best fitted the current Norwegian data from grade 6. The suggestion from Johnston and Kirby concerning the problem of negative *z* scores was followed. The *z* scores for decoding and listening comprehension was added the constant 10. The product term in the regression analyses was based on these transformed *z* scores by multiplying the decoding *z* score by the listening comprehension *z* score. The results for the additive and the multiplicative model is presented in Table 4.

As shown in Table 4, the decoding plus the listening model with concurrent measures of decoding and listening comprehension explains more of the variance in all grade 6 reading comprehension tasks than the multiplicative model. The multiplicative model explains a small, significant

Table 4. Proportion of Variance in Reading Comprehension Accounted for by the Additive and Multiplicative Model of SVR.

Step, Predictor	Outcome Variable							
	CTR1		CTR2		DTR1		DTR2	
	R^2	ΔR^2	R^2	ΔR^2	R^2	ΔR^2	R^2	ΔR^2
Model 1								
Decoding + listening comp	.559***		.329***		.322***		.245***	
Decoding × listening comp	.583	.024**	.334	.005	.345	.024*	.246	.002
Model 2								
Decoding × listening comp	.462***		.267**		.278**		.229**	
Decoding + listening comp	.583	.121***	.334	.068**	.345	.067**	.246	.017

Note: CTR = continous text reading; DCT = discontinous text reading, comp = comprehension. *$p<.05$; **$p<.01$; ***$p<.001$.

part of the variance in the simple text reading task (CTR1) and in one of the discontinuous text reading tasks (DTR1) when entered into the regression analysis as a second step. When entered as a second step, the additive model explains relatively large additional parts of the variance for three of the four tests, 12.1, 6.8 and 6.7%, respectively. These results are in line with results presented by Conners (2009) although he used different word and non-word measures as dependent variables. He found that the multiplicative model added no significant variance to the additive combination. Even though Hoover and Gough (1990) conclude from an earlier study that neither the additive nor the multiplicative model is adequate alone, the present results show that the multiplicative model adds only a small unique part to the variance in only two of the reading comprehension tasks when entered after the additive model. For this reason, and the fact that the additive model explains a larger part of the variance in all the reading tasks than the multiplicative model, the additive model was adopted for further analyses.

Before looking more closely at various cognitive and language variables expected to explain some variance in reading comprehension, however, the role of non-verbal IQ as tested by Raven's Progressive Matrices (Raven et al., 1983) in grade 1 was entered as a second step after the additive model. The analyses showed that Raven explained no additional, significant part of the variance in any of the four reading tasks. For one of the discontinuous texts (DTR2) where just a few lines had to be read and the primary task was to understand the map with its bars telling about the amount of oil and gas throughout the world, the results approached a significant level. Raven explained 2.2% of the variance in this reading task, but failed to reach the .05 level ($p = .053$). Because of these results, Raven was not included in the other analyses.

It is known that vocabulary is an important and strong predictor of reading comprehension. However, both word reading and listening comprehension may in a first step in a regression analysis account for vocabulary as well as for other linguistic elements. This was also uncovered by the regression analyses entering vocabulary in the second step after the additive model. Vocabulary did explain an additional part of the variance in only one of the reading comprehension tests, the simplest text-reading task (CTR1). An additional 2% of the variance was explained by the vocabulary task ($p = .014$). Therefore, vocabulary was not included in the analyses that were run after that.

It is apparent that the different tasks may depend on a range of abilities. Even though there are many similarities in how results from Raven and vocabulary explain variance in the different texts, they hardly explain any variance when entered at a second step, there are differences in the additional explained variance. Raven came close to explain a significant part of the variance in one of the discontinuous text reading tasks while vocabulary explained a small, additional part of the variance in one of the continuous text reading tasks. Since the different tasks have different demands, it would be advisable to look for variables unique in the prediction of variance in the different reading comprehension tasks. However, before looking for these unique variables, it is important to uncover variables that are important in various kinds of reading tasks as well. The next analyses included homophones in the second step to uncover a possible effect of naming. In the third step, the morphological awareness factor, morphology, was entered. In the fourth step, orthographic identification, the speed by which orthographic identities were identified, was entered.

Table 5 shows the results from these hierarchical regression analyses. Even though multiple regression analyses could have shown the unique contributions of these variables when entered simultaneously, a step-wise procedure was utilized.

Table 5 shows that homophones or speed of naming contribute significantly to the variance in reading comprehension for three of the tests. This test explains 4.3–6.5% of variance beyond the variance explained by decoding and listening comprehension. Morphology or morphological

Table 5. Proportion of Unique Variance in Reading Comprehension Accounted for by Naming Speed, Morphological Knowledge and Orthographic Identification.

Step, Predictor	Outcome Variable							
	CTR1		CTR2		DTR1		DTR2	
	R^2	ΔR^2	R^2	ΔR^2	R^2	ΔR^2	R^2	ΔR^2
Decoding + listening comprehension	.576**	–	.356**	–	.370*	–	.235**	–
Homophones	.582	.006	.400	.044*	.413	.043**	.299	.065**
Morphology	.599	.017	447	.047**	491	.078***	.338	.038*
Orthographic id.	.671	.072**	543	.096***	.491	.000	.338	.000

Note: Morphology = morphological knowledge, orthographic id. = orthographic identification.
$^*p<.05$; $^{**}p<.01$; $^{***}p<.001$.

knowledge also contributed significantly in explaining variance for three of the tests when entered in a third step. In line with homophones, morphology did not explain any significant part of the variance in the simplest text reading task when entered after decoding and listening comprehension. However, comprehension of the more advanced prose text and the two discontinuous texts was explained by an additional 4.7, 7.8, and 3.8%, respectively. Orthographic identification also explained a large and significant part of the variance in the two continuous text reading tasks when entered in a fourth step after the additive model, homophones and morphology. However, this variable did not account for any additional part of the variances in the discontinuous text reading tasks. This result was expected since most of the information had to be collected from the table or the bars in these tasks, not from the texts which were also very short.

DISCUSSION

Reading comprehension tests measure different skills. The findings from the present substudy are in line with finding from Keenan et al. (2008). As long as the developers of reading comprehension tests aim at constructing texts in a manner that can measure a broad range of abilities and as long as the users (i.e., teachers) are aware of the differences in what the different tests measure, then different tests may provide the opportunity to obtain a broad knowledge of how pupils develop reading comprehension. However, it is not easy to compare results from different tests if the different tests measure different abilities. If it is possible to uncover the specific variables important in all the different kinds of reading comprehension tests, this will provide information about critical factors that could prevent reading comprehension problems and information about what factors to focus on when teaching reading comprehension.

As shown in this study, as in a range of other studies (Gough & Tunmer, 1986; Hoover & Gough, 1990; Johnston & Kirby, 2006; Savage, 2006) decoding and listening comprehension are important for all reading comprehension tests. Since vocabulary knowledge is central to listening comprehension, it will be a very important variable to focus on in school in a more systematic way than is often done (Anderson & Nagy, 1992; Biemiller, 2003). Vocabulary has had a strong focus lately, but how schools best can develop systematic approaches to vocabulary requires further study. Even though listening comprehension may depend on factors or variables other than vocabulary, the relationship between listening comprehension and reading indicates that there must be a focus on pupil language development starting in the early years and throughout school.

Since the results, as in other studies, only partially support SVR, it is important to continue the search for other variables covering the variance in reading comprehension. Before other variables than decoding and listening comprehension that predict reading comprehension are known, there is less possibility of designing the optimum teaching programme for reading instruction.

Homophones, morphology and orthographic identification stand out as variables with specific connections to reading comprehension in the present substudy, and these variables are important explaining significant parts of the variance in all the different kinds of texts/tasks. These variables explain significant parts of the variance in the different reading tasks when both decoding and listening comprehension in the first step in the regression analyses have accounted for large parts of the variances. Homophone draws on vocabulary, naming speed and ability to compare phonological identities and is therefore difficult to evaluate as a pure naming speed measure. Still, it can be assumed that this task measures what Perfetti (2007) calls lexical quality, a factor important for reading comprehension, and this quality is not fully accounted for by the listening comprehension task. The task requires the comparison of semantic and phonological word identities. In some ways, the task is similar to the morphological tasks that make up the morphology factor. Working on morphological tasks, the children had to blend words with a semantic and phonological identity to create a new word with a different semantic and phonological identity, or they had to delete one part of a compound word to identify the phonological remainder of the compound word and its meaning.

The quality of words in lexicon may depend on other kinds of knowledge about words, not just phonological and semantic quality. Morphemes are used to make new words, to change existing words, to make plural out of singular and to change a verb that describes something that happened yesterday into a verb that describes a present happening, etc. If lexical quality supports identification of words and if lexical quality, as it is described by Perfetti (2007), also depends on morphological knowledge and awareness, this knowledge and awareness might be important not only in word comprehension but also in reading comprehension per se. Lyster (2003) shows that morphological awareness training in preschool affects reading comprehension more than phonological awareness training when the effects on reading comprehension are evaluated after 6 years. The present results, showing that morphology can explain additional and significant parts of the variances in comprehending both continuous and discontinuous texts and the long term effect of morphological training, underline what an important factor morphological knowledge and awareness is for reading comprehension.

Other than decoding, listening comprehension, homophones and morphology, another variable contributing to reading comprehension in the present substudy is orthographic identification, at least concerning pure text reading tasks. The speed of orthographic identification is probably not just driven by phonological decoding or orthographic identification isolated from the words' semantic; the knowledge of a word's meaning may also speed up the word identification process (see Perfetti, 2007). In the orthographic identification task, pairs of homophones were presented and the child had to identify the string of graphemes that represented a real word. Since the effect of naming is accounted for by homophones in an earlier step in the analyses, it might first of all be the speed of identifying of the letter string itself that is important at the fourth step. In Norwegian *sgo* and *sko* sound the same, but only *sko* [shoe] represents a real word. The speed by which phonology and semantics can be matched makes a difference.

Listening comprehension, as it is measured in the present study, might not uncover the differences in children's vocabulary. For example, the Norwegian language contains many compound words and knowledge of compound words and awareness about how they are composed may speed up the word identification process and be important to reading comprehension over and above the contribution of listening comprehension tasks. It could be expected that the comprehension of texts that are discontinuous and include tables, maps, histograms, etc. relies more heavily on non-verbal IQ than texts that are purely written text. This was not the case in the present this substudy. Even for tasks with little text and more dependency on other information sources than running text, non-verbal IQ explained no or little part of the variance while homophones and morphology could explain significant parts of the variances. It is also important to bear in mind that both homophones and morphology were variables from preschool. Their impact on reading comprehension 6 years later indicate that they represent areas important to reading comprehension. Even though there is a speed factor connected to the homophone task, the results highlight the importance of verbal abilities for comprehending written or printed information and underline the necessity of working systematically with children's language development throughout school. Since both the homophone and morphology tasks possibly measure vocabulary in a way that is not accounted for by listening comprehension, the results may underline how important vocabulary actually is for reading comprehension (Biemiller, 2003).

CONCLUSION

This chapter has concentrated on several dilemmas within the field of literacy and reading comprehension. The definition of literacy has changed over the years and now covers a broad range of abilities. Most definitions focus on interpretation and understanding of written or printed text. Reading comprehension overlaps a great deal with what is defined as literacy. Understanding written information also depends on how the reader or rather the interpreter is able to draw inferences from both text and other information sources that are presented together to give information about the same topic. Even though it is important to bear in mind the clear tendency for ceiling effects for several variables in the presented substudy, there are clear tendencies in the results that may be important to follow up. The study shows that both the additive model and the multiplicative model of SVR account for large parts of the variance in text reading tasks as well as for tasks with little text and much information provided in tables, graphs or charts. Even though decoding and listening comprehension accounted for more of the variance in plain-text reading tasks than in reading discontinuous texts (where information also has to be collected from other sources than the text itself), the decoding and listening comprehension sum or product explained variances in all the tasks. Until now, knowledge about reading comprehension has been incomplete. In his article "Measuring Reading Comprehension", Fletcher (2006) concludes his discussion about the complexity of reading comprehension by stating that research is needed to isolate specific factors in reading comprehension, but there is also a need for research that "integrates across methods and specific attempts to identify constructs that are specific to reading comprehension and their relation to other constructs that make up reading and other cognitive skills" (pp. 328–329). In this chapter, the attempt to uncover variables that can account for variance in reading comprehension across different reading tasks shows that both decoding and listening comprehension abilities are important variables in explaining very different types of written texts. The quality and speed of orthographic identification, however, only explained variance in tasks with relatively large amount of text to be read. In tasks with relatively little text and additional information sources, comprehension relies on other abilities in addition to speeded orthographic identification as long as word decoding is accounted for. Since both morphology and the search for homophones in the lexicon accounted for significant parts of the variance in three of the reading tasks, both in the advanced long text and in the two tasks with discontinuous texts, there should be more focus on abilities that are measured by these tests when working with children's reading comprehension. The naming task, Homophones and the two morphological tasks included in the morphological factor, morphology, may all be possible parts of the constructs that Perfetti (2007) terms lexical quality. Still, to capture the complexity of reading comprehension (Blake et al., 2002; Georgiou et al., 2009; Johnston & Kirby, 2006) we need to focus different texts reading tasks or focus different kinds of listening comprehension tasks or decoding tasks. We need to identify different constructs that are specific to reading comprehension and we need to take approaches that will "move beyond mono-operation bias and lead to assessment that capture the richness of reading comprehension (Fletcher, 2006, p. 329). The present substudy shows, in line with other studies (Chen & Vellutino, 1997; Conners, 2009; Georgiou et al., 2009; Hoover & Gough, 1990; Johnston & Kirby, 2006; Savage & Wolforth, 2007), that much variance is unexplained in different reading tests when decoding and listening comprehension has accounted for their part of the variance. The results also show, in line with findings from several other studies, that other cognitive and linguistic variables account for additional variance in reading comprehension (Aaron et al., 1999; Johnston & Kirby, 2006). More complex models where both cognitive and linguistic variables as well as motivational and strategic variables are included may help us capture the "richness of reading comprehension" focused by Fletcher (2006). The SVR model has been of great support until now to understand at least part of what is defined as reading comprehension. The model does not capture, however, the complexity of the concept reading comprehension. To develop teaching methods for reading comprehension and to support abilities important for developing good reading comprehension, we need to uncover the different variables predicting reading comprehension over and above decoding and listening comprehension and we need to understand how these variables interact.

So far, our knowledge about the impact of decoding and listening comprehension (Aaron et al., 1999; Adlof et al., 2006; Conners, 2009; Gough & Tunmer, 1986; Hoover & Gough, 1990; Johnston & Kirby, 2006) shows that these two factors are important to focus in the teaching of reading. As discussed above, we also have knowledge about how different kinds of strategy use, background knowledge and more specific topic knowledge support reading comprehension (Anmarkrud & Bråten, 2009; Alexander & Jetton, 2000; Bråten, 1993; Guthrie & Wigfield, 2000; Mastropieri & Scruggs, 1997; Samuelstuen & Bråten, 2005). From one of the studies discussed above we have also seen that naming speed and phonological awareness explained additional variance in reading comprehension (Johnston & Kirby, 2006). The effect of the homophone variable in the substudy presented in this chapter, also give support to the findings of Johnston and Kirby. There seem to be a speed construct that can explain variance in reading comprehension. The additional finding presented her is the effect of morphological knowledge (or awareness), suggesting that it is important to take a much broader language perspective when assessing and teaching reading comprehension and when remediating reading comprehension difficulties. So even though we still have not answered fully how a range of linguistic and cognitive variables interact with reading comprehension and with each other during the comprehension process, we have a solid basis for developing effective reading comprehension methods and programs.

The National Reading Panel found that reading comprehension of texts is best facilitated by teaching pupils a variety of techniques and systematic strategies to assist in recall of information, question generation, and summarizing of information. The panel found that teachers must be provided with appropriate and intensive training to ensure that they know when and how to teach specific strategies.

More quality research on teacher training is one of the major research needs identified by the National Reading Panel. The teacher education in Norway has been criticized for not giving the teacher students enough knowledge about reading development and about the teaching of reading. The school reforms of 1997 and 2006 have to some extent taken the critique into account. The Government is now proposing a new teacher education programme for primary and lower secondary education with a stronger emphasis on subject knowledge and teaching skills, quality of studies and research orientation (Ministry of Education and Research, 2009).

REFERENCES

Aaron, P. G., Joshi, M., & Williams, K. A. (1999). Not all reading disabilities are alike. *Journal of Learning Disabilities*, *32*, 120–127.

Adlof, S. M., Catts, H., & Little, T. D. (2006). Should the simple view of reading include a fluency component? *Reading and Writing*, *19*, 933–958.

Alexander, P. A., & Jetton, T. L. (2000). Learning from text: A multidimensional perspective. In: M. L. Kamil, P. B. Mosentahl, P. D. Pearson & R. Barr (Eds), *Handbook of reading research* (Vol. 3, pp. 285–310). Mahwah, NJ: Erlbaum.

Anderson, R. C. (1994). Role of the reader's schema in comprehension, learning and, memory. In: R. B. Ruddell, R. Ruddell & H. Singer (Eds), *Theoretical models and processes of reading* (pp. 469–482). Newark, DE: International Reading Association.

Anderson, R. C., & Nagy, W. E. (1992). The vocabulary conundrum. *American Educator, 16*(4), 14–18, 44–47.

Anmarkrud, Ø., & Bråten, I. (2009). Motivation for reading comprehension. *Learning and Individual Differences, 19*, 252–256.

Austin, P. C., & Brunner, L. J. (2003). Type I error inflation in the presence of a ceiling effect. *The American Statistician, 57*, 97–104.

Bakken, J. P., Mastropieri, M. A., & Scruggs, T. E. (1997). Reading comprehension of expository science material and children with learning disabilities: A comparison of strategies. *The Journal of Special Education, 31*, 300–324.

Baron, B. A., & Strawson, C. (1976). Orthographic and word-specific mechanisms in reading words aloud. *Journal of Experimental Psychology: Human Perception and Performance, 2*, 386–393.

Biemiller, A. (2003). Oral comprehension sets the ceiling on reading comprehension. *American Educator, 27*(1), 1–17.

Blake, B. E., Blake, R. W., & Blake, R. W. (2002). *Literacy and learning: A reference handbook*. Santa Barbara, CA: ABC–CLIO.

Bråten, I. (1993). Cognitive strategies: A multi-componential conception of strategy use and strategy instruction. *Scandinavian Journal of Educational Research, 37*, 217–242.

Bruce, B. (1980). Plans and social action. In: R. Spiro, B. Bruce & W. Brewer (Eds), *Theoretical issues in reading comprehension* (pp. 367–384). Hillsdale, NJ: Erlbaum.

Bryant, P., Nunes, T., & Bindman, M. (1998). Awareness of language in children who have reading difficulties. Historical comparisons in a longitudinal study. *Journal of Child Psychology and Psychiatry, and Allied Disciplines, 39*(4), 501–510.

Carlisle, J. F., & Stone, C. A. (2003). The effects of morphological structure on children's reading of derived words. In: E. Assink & D. Santa (Eds), *Reading complex words: Cross-language studies* (pp. 27–52). New York, NY: Kluwer Academic.

Catts, H. W., Hogan, T. P., Adlof, S. M., & Barth, A. E. (2003). *The simple view of reading changes over time*. Boulder, CO: Society for Scientific Study of Reading.

Chen, R., & Vellutino, F. R. (1997). Prediction of reading ability: A cross-validation study of the simple view of reading. *Journal of Literacy Research, 29*, 1–24.

Conners, F. A. (2009). Attentional control and the simple view of reading. *Reading and Writing, 22*, 591–613.

Corson, D. (1997). The learning and use of academic English words. *Language Learning, 47*, 671–718.

Dunlosky, J., Rawson, K. A., & Hacker, D. J. (2002). Metacomprehension of science texts: Investigating the levels-of-disruption hypothesis. In: J. Otero, J. A. León & A. C. Graesser (Eds), *The psychology of science text comprehension* (pp. 255–279). Mahwah, NJ: Lawrence Erlbaum.

Dunn, L. M., & Markwardt, F. C. (1970). *Examiner's manual: Peabody individual achievement test*. Circle Pines, MN: American Guidance Service.

Fletcher, J. M. (2006). Measuring reading comprehension. *Scientific Studies of Reading*, *10*(3), 323–330.

Georgiou, G. K., Das, J. P., & Hayward, D. (2009). Revisiting the simple view of reading in a group of children with poor reading comprehension. *Journal of Learning Disabilities*, *42*, 76–84.

Gough, P., & Tunmer, W. (1986). Decoding, reading and reading disability. *Remedial and Special Education*, *7*(1), 6–10.

Graesser, A. C., & Goodman, S. M. (1985). Implicit knowledge, question answering and the representation of expository text. In: B. Britton & J. B. Black (Eds), *Understanding expository text* (pp. 109–171). Hillsdale, NJ: Erlbaum.

Guthrie, J. T., Hoa, A. L. W., Wigfield, A., Tonks, S. M., Humenick, M. N., & Littles, E. (2007). Reading motivation and reading comprehension growth in the later elementary years. *Contemporary Educational Psychology*, *32*, 282–313.

Guthrie, J. T., & Wigfield, A. (2000). Engagement and motivation in reading. In: M. L. Kamil, P. B. Mosenthal, P. D. Pearson & R. Barr (Eds), *Handbook of reading research* (Vol. 3, pp. 403–422). Mahwah, NJ: Erlbaum.

Haenggi, D., & Perfetti, C. A. (1994). Processing components of college level reading comprehension. *Discourse Processes*, *17*, 83–104.

Hoover, W. A., & Gough, P. B. (1990). The simple view of reading. *Reading and Writing*, *2*, 127–160.

Johnston, T. C., & Kirby, J. R. (2006). The contribution of naming speed to the simple view of reading. *Reading and Writing*, *19*, 339–361.

Keenan, J. M., Betjemann, R. S., & Olson, R. K. (2008). Reading comprehension tests vary in the skills they assess: Differential dependence on decoding and oral comprehension. *Scientific Studies of Reading*, *12*, 281–300.

Kintsch, W. (1988). The role of knowledge in discourse comprehension: A construction-integration model. *Psychological Review*, *95*, 163–182.

Kirby, J. R., Desrochers, A., Roth, L., & Lai, S. S. V. (2008). Longitudinal predictors of word reading development. *Canadian Psychology*, *49*, 103–110.

Kjærnsli, M., Lie, S., Olsen, R. V., & Roe, A. (2007). *Tid for tunge løft: Norske elevers kompetanse i naturfag, lesing og matematikk i PISA 2006*. [Time for hard work: Norwegian students' competence in science, reading and mathematics in PISA 2006.] Oslo: Oslo University Press.

Klette, K. (2007). Trends in research on teaching and learning in schools: Didactics meets classroom studies. *European Educational Research Journal*, *6*, 147–160.

Klinkenberg, J. E. (2005). *Å bedre barns leseflyt: Twenty-seven variations of repeated reading [Supporting children's reading fluency: Twenty seven variations of repeated reading]*. Oslo: Aschehoug.

LaBerge, D., & Samuels, S. J. (1974). Towards a theory of automatic information processing in reading. *Cognitive Psychology*, *6*, 293–323.

Landi, N. (2005). Behavioral and electrophysiological investigations of the relationship between semantic processing and reading comprehension. *Brain and Language*, *102*, 30–45.

Landi, N., & Perfetti, C. A. (2007). An electrophysiological investigation of semantic and phonological processing in skilled and less-skilled comprehenders. *Brain and Language*, *102*, 30–45.

Lervåg, A., & Aukrust, V. (2009). Vocabulary knowledge is a critical determinant of the difference in reading comprehension between first and second language learners. *The Journal of Child Psychology and Psychiatry* Early View. Retrieved January 12, 2010 from Wiley Interscience.

Leslie, L., & Caldwell, J. (2001). *Qualitative reading inventory-3*. New York, NY: Addison Wesley.

Lyster, S. A. H. (1994). *Språkrelaterte lærevansker hos barn og unge. Kartlegging og tiltak [Language related learning disabilities in children and adolescents. Assessment and intervention]*. Oslo: Gyldendal Akademis.

Lyster, S. A. H. (1998). Preventing reading failure: A follow-up study. *Dyslexia, 4*, 132–144.

Lyster, S. A. H. (2002). The effects of morphological versus phonological awareness training in kindergarten on reading development. *Reading and Writing, 15*, 261–294.

Lyster, S. A. H. (2007). Reading development and reading disabilities: Focus on Norway. In: T. Scruggs & A. M. Mastropieri (Eds), *Advances in learning and behavioral disabilities. Vol. 20: International perspectives* (pp. 21–55). Oxford: Elsevier.

Lyster, S. A. H. (2003). Morphological awareness and reading development. Evidence from a training study. Paper presented at Bangor Dyslexia Conference, Great Britain.

Mastropieri, M. A., & Scruggs, T. E. (1997). Best practices in promoting reading comprehension in students with learning disabilities. *Remedial and Special Education, 18*, 197–216.

Ministry of Education and Research. (2009). *White paper on teacher education "The teacher – the role and the education*" (Report to the Storting No. 11 (2008-2009)). Principal elements. Retrieved 09.09.2009 from http://www.regjeringen.no/en/dep/kd/Documents/Brochures-and-handbooks/2009/factsheet-white-paper-on-teacher-educati.html?id = 545075

Nasjonalt Læremiddelsenter. (1995). *Kartlegging av leseferdighet. 6. klasse* [Testing reading abilities. Grade 6]. Oslo: Nasjonalt Læremiddelsenter.

National Institute for Literacy. (2009). *What is literacy?* Retrieved 01.10.2009 from http://www.nifl.gov/about/faq.html#literacy.

National Reading Panel. (2000). *Teaching children to read* (NIH Pub. No. 00-4754). Washington, DC: National Institute of Health and Human Performance.

National Research Council of the National Academies. (2008). *Early childhood assessment. Why, what, and how*. Washington, DC: The National Academic Press.

OECD and Statistics Canada. (1995). *Literacy, economy and society; Results of the first international literacy survey*. Paris: OECD.

OECD/Statistics Canada. (2000). *Literacy in the information age. Final report of the international adult literacy survey*. Paris: OECD Publication Service.

Olson, R., Kliegel, R., Davidson, B. J., & Foltz, G. (1985). Individual developmental differences in reading disability. In: T. G. Waller (Ed.), *Reading research: Advances in theory and practice* (Vol. 4, pp. 1–64). New York: Academic.

Palincsar, A. S., & Brown, D. S. (1987). Enhancing instructional time through attention to metacognition. *Journal of Learning Disabilities, 20*, 66–75.

Perfetti, C. A. (1985). *Reading ability*. New York: Oxford University Press.

Perfetti, C. A. (1992). The representation problem in reading acquisition. In: P. B. Gough, L. C. Ehri & R. Treiman (Eds), *Reading acquisition* (pp. 145–174). Hillsdale, NJ: Lawrence Erlbaum Associates.

Perfetti, C. A. (2007). Reading ability: Lexical quality to comprehension. *Scientific Studies of Reading, 11*, 357–383.

Perfetti, C. A., & Hart, L. (2002). The lexical quality hypothesis. In: L. Vehoeven, C. Elbro & P. Perfetti (Eds), *Precursors of Functional Literacy* (pp. 189–213). Amsterdam: John Benjamins.

Rasmussen, J. B. (2003). Reading literacy performance in Norway: Current practice and critical factors. *European Journal of Education, 38*, 427–443.

Raven, J. C. (1976). *Standard Progressive Matrices. Sets A, B, C, D & F (Reprinted version)*. Oxford: Oxford Psychologists Press Ltd.

Raven, J. C., Court, J. H., & Raven, J. (1983). *Manual for Raven's Progressive Matrices and Vocabulary Scales (Section 3) – Standard Progressive Matrices (1983 edition)*. London: Lewis.

Saenz, L. M., & Fuchs, L. S. (2002). *Examining the reading difficulty of secondary students with learning disabilities: Expository versus narrative text*. Remedial and Special Education, 23(1), 31+. Retrieved March 31, 2007, from http://www.questia.com/PM.qst?a = o&d = 5000696588

Samuelstuen, M. S., & Bråten, I. (2005). Decoding, knowledge, and strategies in comprehension of expository text. *Scandinavian Journal of Psychology, 46*, 107–117.

Savage, R. (2006). Reading comprehension is not always the product of nonsense word decoding and linguistic comprehension: Evidence from teenagers who are extremely poor readers. *Scientific Studies of Reading, 10*, 143–164.

Savage, R., & Wolforth, J. (2007). An additive simple view of reading describes the performance of good and poor readers in higher education. *Exceptionality Education Canada, 17*, 243–268.

Steelman, J. D., Pierce, P. L., & Koppenhaver, D. A. (1994). The role of computers in promoting literacy in children with severe speech and physical impairments. In: K. G. Butler (Ed.), *Severe communication disorders: Intervention strategies* (pp. 200–212). Gaithersburg, MD: Aspen.

Undheim, J. O. (1978). Wechsler intelligence scale for children-revised: WISC-R manual. In: Norweigian (Ed.), Oslo, Norway: Norsk Psykologforening.

US Department of Labor Employment & Training Administration (1998). *Workforce Investment Act Laws and Regulations*, section 203. Retrieved 25.09.2009 from http://www.doleta.gov/usworkForce/WIA/act.cfm

Vacca, J. A., Vacca, R. T., & Grove, M. K. (2003). *Reading and learning to read*. Boston, MA: Allyn and Bacon.

Van Daal, V., Solheim, R. G., Gabrielsen, N. N., & Begnum, A. C. (2007). PIRLS 2006 – Norsk rapport [PIRLS 2006 – The Norwegian report]. Oslo: Utdanningsdirektoratet.

Venezky, R. L. (1990). Definitions of literacy. In: R. L. Venezky, D. A. Wagner & B. S. Ciliberti (Eds), *Toward defining literacy* (pp. 2–16). Newark, DE: International Reading Association.

Venezky, R. L. (2000). The origins of the present-day chasm between adult literacy needs and school literacy instruction. *Scientific Studies of Reading, 4*(1), 19–39. Reprinted from *Visible Language, 16*(2), 113–136.

Vygotsky, L. S. (1962). *Thought and language*. Cambridge, MA: MIT Press.

Westby, C. E. (2005). Assessing and facilitating text comprehension problems. In: H. W. Catts & A. G. Kamhi (Eds), *Language and reading disabilities* (2nd ed., pp. 154–223). Boston, MA: Allyn & Bacon.

Wiederholt, L., & Bryant, B. (1992). *Examiner's Manual: Gray Oral Reading Test-3*. Austin, TX: Pro-Ed.

Wigfield, A., & Guthrie, J. T. (1997). Relations of children's motivation for reading to the amount and breath of their reading. *Journal of Educational Psychology*, *89*, 420–432.

Woodcock, R. W., McGrew, K. S., & Mather, N. (2001). *Woodcock-Johnson III test of achievement*. Itasca, IL: Riverside.

A LONGITUDINAL STUDY OF THE IMPACT OF EFFECTIVE BEGINNING READING INSTRUCTION FOR ENGLISH LEARNERS: LITERACY, LANGUAGE, AND LEARNING DISABILITIES

Anne W. Graves

ABSTRACT

This study examined literacy instruction in 14 first grade classrooms (9 classrooms in Year One and 5 classrooms in Year Two) of English Language Learners in three schools in Southern California. Pre and posttest measures of reading for 186 first graders across 2 years, representing 11 different native languages yielded outcome data. These data were examined in reference to ratings of the quality of instruction based on the use of the English Learners Classroom Observation Instrument (ELCOI). Students were followed through 6th grade (n = *59). Results indicated a moderately strong correlation* (r = *.65) between teacher rating and oral reading fluency scores of students at the*

Literacy and Learning
Advances in Learning and Behavioral Disabilities, Volume 23, 155–174

ISSN: 0735-004X/doi:10.1108/S0735-004X(2010)0000023008

end of 1st grade and a strong correlation (−.83) between teacher rating and number of students reading below end of 1st grade reading thresholds. Descriptive longitudinal data on passage reading comprehension and oral reading fluency yielded moderately strong correlations in 3rd grade. By 6th grade, correlations between 1st grade literacy practices and reading were weak (r = .016). Students who were labeled with learning disabilities were extremely weak readers without exception, however, several students who performed at benchmark in 1st grade were later labeled. Educational implications and recommendations for future research are discussed.

A survey conducted by the U.S. Department of Education (Kindler, 2002) found that, during the 2000–2001 school year, English learners (ELs) accounted for over 1 in 10 students in elementary schools but the population of ELs in urban areas is much higher. ELs in the United States speak more than 460 different languages. Although Spanish speakers continue to represent the largest group of ELs (79.2%), there are four other groups with large representation. These are Vietnamese, Hmong, Cantonese, and Korean. Combined, they now account for approximately 6% of ELs in U.S. schools. Other languages are spoken by less than 1% of the national population, though there are urban areas with sizable populations of students speaking Tagalog, Somali, Cambodian, Russian, and more recently South Asian and Middle Eastern languages.

In countries other than the United States such as Holland, and urban areas in Canada such as Vancouver and Toronto, multiple language classrooms are the norm (Chiappe, Siegel, & Wade-Woolsey, 2002; Droop &Verhoeven, 2003). Currently in the United States, students who speak languages other than English are often taught in multiple language classrooms with some form of sheltered content instruction designed to develop English language while teaching content area knowledge in reading, mathematics, language arts, and science (Echevarria & Graves, 2011; Graves & Rueda, 2008). Some form of sheltered content instruction is especially prevalent for non-Spanish speakers, but remains the main model used for student from Spanish speaking homes as well. In multilingual classrooms, occasionally, a paraprofessional speaks one of the languages spoken by students, but it is extremely rare that the teacher does (Merickel et al., 2003).

Advancements in reading research in recent years naturally lead to questions about replications of investigations with ELs. Reading skills are the foundation for success in all areas of academic endeavor

(Peregoy & Boyle, 2000). If good reading skills are not acquired in the early elementary grades the failure cycle is initiated (Good, Kaminski, & Hill, 2000). Reading difficulties often lead to special education referral some of which may be avoidable (Snow, Burns, & Griffin, 1998).

Little research has been conducted to provide empirical evidence for primary grade teachers whose central responsibilities include instruction in reading and language arts for ELs (August & Hakuta, 1997; Gersten & Baker, 2000) although this situation has begun to change (Linan-Thompson, Vaughn, Hickman-Davis, & Kouzekanani, 2003). Longitudinal data on ELs as they progress through school is virtually non-existent.

Results from several recent studies in the United States indicate that instructional practices such as small group instruction that is explicit and focused on reading subskills are effective for both Native speakers and English language learners (Gunn, Biglan, Smolkowski, & Ary, 2000; Haager & Windmueller, 2001; Linan-Thompson et al., 2003). Similarly, there have been a series of well-designed studies on second language reading from both Canada (Chiappe et al., 2002; Geva & Wang, 2001; Lesaux & Siegel, 2003; Wade-Woolley & Siegel, 1997) and Holland (Droop &Verhoeven, 2003). This research has been synthesized in a report by the National Reading Panel (2000) and appears to indicate that second language learners can acquire the ability to read at approximately the same rate as native speakers in the early grades; however, we still know little about specific instructional procedures that enhance or impede this process, or factors that lead to long-term success in reading. Some similar insights have emerged from the qualitative research conducted in the United States by Fitzgerald and Noblit (2000) and Weber and Longhi-Chirlin (2001). These served as a point of departure for the original 1st grade study that was the basis for this longitudinal investigation.

In 1999, California developed a Reading and Language Arts Framework (California Department of Education, 1999) that provided Kindergarten to Grade 12 Standards for literacy instruction. The Framework, especially in the primary grades, was strongly based on findings from controlled, rigorous research studies. The state actively encouraged linking English language development with reading and language arts activities for ELs, although initially provided limited guidance on this topic. As a result, a team of researchers in previously reported studies (Gersten, Baker, Haager, & Graves, 2005) studied basic instructional principles and the modulation of instruction with ELs in California (California Reading and Literature Project, 1999). The first step in that work was to begin with systematic observations of beginning reading instruction for ELs followed by the development of a classroom observational instrument reported in Gersten et al. (2005).

In Southern California, the rise in both the number of ELs entering school and the number identified with learning disabilities is often noted (California Department of Education, 1999). In the large urban school district in which this study was conducted approximately 52 languages are spoken in the schools. In this investigation, the student population is referred to as a multiple language group in that 11 native languages are represented as well as a wide variety of cultural groups. The focus is on four 1st grade classrooms across 2 years.

A growing body of research (Gersten et al., 2005; Graves, Plasencia-Peinado, Deno, & Johnson, 2005; Chiappe et al., 2002; Droop &Verhoeven, 2003; Gunn et al., 2000; Haager & Windmueller, 2001; Linan-Thompson et al., 2003) has demonstrated that most of the strategies and approaches that research deems effective for native speakers of a language are effective for ELs as well. In fact, Shanahan and Beck (National Reading Panel, 2000) and Chiappe et al. (2002) found that, in terms of phonemic awareness and word reading, ELs can learn to read as quickly as native English speakers.

The original data for this investigation were drawn from a large study of several urban school districts in Southern California conducted in the context of California Schools Literacy Reform by Russell Gersten and a team of colleagues. Various aspects of the larger research project that combined data from several school districts in Southern California, are reported in numerous published articles (Gersten et al., 2005; Graves, Gersten, & Haager, 2004; Graves et al., 2005; McIntosh, Graves, & Gersten, 2007). The team of researchers on the larger project developed an observational measure, the English Learners Classroom Observation Instrument (ELCOI).

The instrument development study (Gersten et al., 2005) and the original 1st grade study (Graves et al., 2004; McIntosh et al., 2007) consisting of 2 years of data from ELs in 14 first grade classrooms in one large Southern California school district are the first data sources for this chapter. We were investigating nine 1st grade classrooms in Year One and five 1st grade classrooms in Year Two. ELs represented 11 different languages and a wide variety of cultural groups. Another unique feature of the 14 classrooms was that teachers were not required to use a specific core or basal reading series. In fact, in Year One, only one of the nine teachers used such a series consistently; this was her own professional decision. Therefore, in this study it was not possible to examine the effectiveness of reading curricula, programs, or materials in any systematic way. The longitudinal follow-up based on reading assessments at the end of 2nd, 3rd, and 6th grades has been submitted for publication (Graves, submitted for publication).

PURPOSES OF THE LONGITUDINAL STUDY

The primary purpose of this investigation was to follow the students in a descriptive longitudinal study for whom we had abundant 1st grade data ($N = 186$). At the end of 2nd, 3rd, and 6th grades, data on oral reading fluency and passage comprehension were collected for purposes of determining correlations and patterns of performance. Percentages of students labeled with learning disabilities are reported as well. From the beginning of the study, we were interested in determining whether the percentages of students falling below the threshold established for successful grade level reading, for reading correlated with teacher ratings. We wished to explore patterns of performance of the ELs who fell below the threshold and to report patterns in performance for and number of students who were labeled with learning disabilities. Finally, using our qualitative field notes, we wished to describe the characteristics of teachers who produced a large percentage of ELs who met the reading criteria set at the end of 1st grade; and the characteristics of one teacher who produced a large percentage of students who did not meet criteria.

Our research questions are as follows: (1) What is the pattern of performance in reading from 1st to 6th grade in ELs? (2) What is the strength of the relationship between language levels recorded in kindergarten (non-English speaking, limited English speaking, or emerging fluency) and student reading outcomes (oral reading fluency; comprehension)? (3) What is the strength of the relationship between end of 1st grade oral reading fluency and reading scores (oral reading fluency and comprehension) at the end of 3rd and at the end of 6th grades? (4) How many students from the original group have been labeled with learning disabilities and what is the pattern of performance associated with those who are labeled?

METHOD

Participants

Schools

We approached a large urban school district in Southern California with a request for 1st grade classrooms with multiple language students and the request to test those students before observations at the beginning of the year and then once again at the end of the year. We preferred sites that had

Table 1. Information about Multiple Language Classrooms (Year One).

Teachers	Schools (All 100% Free or Reduced Lunch)	Teacher Years Experience	Teacher Speak Language Other than English	Language Spoken by Students	% of Class ELL
Marlene	A	21	No	V, L, Sp., Hmong.	80
Dara	A	25	No	V, C, Sp., Hmong.	90
Cara	A	10	No	So., Sp., L, Hm., V, T, Su	88
Guy	B	2	No	So., Sp., C, V	100
Brenda	B	3	Viet	So., Sp., C, V	100
Cathy	B	3	Korean	Ch., Fr, Sp., V.	100
Jim	C	8	Spanish	Dialects of Spanish	100
Cindy	C	9	No	So., Sp., V, C	100
Abigail	C	16	No	So., Sp., C., V.	100

Note: Fr, French; V, Vietnamese; L, Lao; Sp, Spanish; Hm, Hmong; C, Cambodian; So, Somalian; T, Tagalog; Su, Sudanese; Ch, Cantonese dialect/Chinese.

two or three such classrooms available. Only three schools matched the description, so each school was asked to participate.

Three 1st grade classrooms at each of the schools were defined as multiple language settings in which students spoke at least one of the following: Cambodian, Cantonese dialect of Chinese, English, French, Hmong, Lao, Somalian, Spanish, Sudanese, Tagalog, or Vietnamese. Table 1 presents data for the full sample of teachers and students. Teachers had between 80% and 100% ELs who each received either free or reduced lunch. With the exception of one teacher's (Jim's) class (see Table 1), each of the teachers had speakers of at least four different languages. Jim's class, however, was comprised of students whose families were originally from Guatemala, El Salvador, Southern Mexico, and Northern Mexico; as a result, many dialects and indigenous languages were spoken in this setting.

Teachers

In each school, three 1st grade teachers who were teaching in these multiple language settings in 1st grade agreed to participate totaling nine teachers in Year One (see Table 1). In Year Two, we lost five of the original teachers from Year One due to maternity leave, reorganization, or reassignment; however, we added one teacher who was new to School C (see Table 2) giving us a total of five teachers for Year Two.

Table 2. Information about Multiple Language Classrooms (Year Two).

Teachers	Schools (All 100% Free or Reduced Lunch)	Teacher Years Experience	Teacher Speak Language Other than English	Language Spoken by Students Other than English	% of Class ELL
Marlene	A	22	No	Hmong, Lao, Spanish, Tagalog, Vietnamese	90
Dara	A	26	No	Hmong, Lao, Spanish, Tagalog, Vietnamese	80
Guy	B	3	No	Cambodian, Cantonese dialect, Somoli., Spanish, Vietnamese	100
Bonnie	C	17	No	Cambodian, Somoli., Spanish, Vietnamese	100
Jim	C	9	Spanish	Dialects of Spanish	100

All teachers were fully licensed in California to teach students in 1st grade. They ranged from 2 to 26 years of teaching experience. Though three of the teachers spoke a language other than English, teachers in each of these classrooms taught almost exclusively in English since it provided common ground for all of the students. In the case of the Spanish-only classroom, the teacher (Jim) would occasionally give directions or explain a procedure in Spanish. However, with the extreme dialect differences the language support he could provide was minimal. Native language instruction was a logistical impossibility in most classrooms.

Students

Once each teacher had agreed to participate, he or she assisted us in obtaining permission from the parents and guardians of the students in their respective classes for participation in testing, observations, and gaining access to files for obtaining the language proficiency data. First grade ELs from each of the 14 classrooms were included in Year One ($n = 116$) and Year Two ($n = 70$ students). Class sizes ranged from 17 to 20. However, to be included in the data analyses, each student needed to be present for both pre and posttest (see Tables 3 and 4). Ninety-eight percent of the students in the study were identified as English Language Learners by the school district. At the end of the 1st grade year, we obtained permission from parents to follow students through 6th grade, reassessing their reading skills at the end of each year.

Table 3. Year One Data: Observation Scale Ratings and Number of Students At-Risk at the End of the Year.

Teacher (Number of Students)[a]	Rating on ELCOI	0–18 wpm	18–40 wpm	% Reading Below 40 wpm	Pretest Mean (SD)	Posttest Mean (SD)	Effect Size
Marlene ($n = 15$)	3.75	2	1	20	27.19 (15.76)	62.00 (32.37)	1.45
Dara ($n = 10$)	3.5	0	4	40	26.40 (17.77)	58.50 (26.61)	1.45
Cara ($n = 15$)	2.5	2	4	40	9.79 (10.15)	24.36 (19.84)	0.97
Cathy ($n = 14$)	2.5	5	2	50	15.33 (15.76)	39.94 (18.93)	1.41
Brenda ($n = 18$)	2.5	2	8	55	14.70 (27.52)	23.60 (33.35)	0.29
Guy ($n = 15$)	2.0	9	2	73	12.71 (8.53)	36.86 (19.96)	1.69
Jim ($n = 11$)	2.0	8	1	81	24.07 (26.73)	50.60 (32.15)	0.90
Cindy ($n = 7$)	2.0	5	1	85	5.18 (2.52)	19.36 (22.12)	1.13
Abigail ($n = 11$)	1.0	9	0	81	7.16 (7.28)	24.27 (25.77)	1.04

[a]Students who were present for both pre and posttesting.

Table 4. Year Two Data: Observation Scale Ratings and Number of Students At-Risk at the End of the Year.

Teacher (Number of Students)[a]	Rating on ELC0I	0–24 wpm	24–40 wpm	% Reading Below 40 wpm	Pretest Mean (SD)	Posttest Mean (SD)	Effect Size
Marlene ($n = 17$)	3.75	0	2	11	28.06 (30.18)	77.06 (35.89)	1.48
Dara ($n = 11$)	3.75	0	0	0	22.67 (19.00)	81.92 (25.3)	2.67
Guy ($n = 16$)	3.0	2	0	13	10.16 (6.84)	59.66 (22.35)	3.36
Jim ($n = 15$)	2.5	3	3	40	16.87 (9.89)	53.4 (27.99)	1.92
Bonnie ($n = 11$)	2.0	2	5	64	10.00 (15.90)	41.44 (25.70)	1.51

[a]Students who were present for both pre and posttesting.

Measures

English Language Learners Classroom Observation Instrument (ELCOI)
The ELCOI is a 30 item moderate inference Likert scale (see Table 5). Note that there are six empirically derived subscales. The internal consistency reliability for each subscale ranged from .80 to .95, with a median subscale alpha of .89 (Gersten et al., 2005). The median inter-observer agreement on an item-by-item basis was 74%. This is a conservative estimate of instrument reliability as it is based on item-by-item agreement.

Criterion-related validity was established by correlating scores from each subscale with residualized growth scores in actual reading performance in 20 classrooms. (Six of the 20 in the reliability/validity study were classrooms involved in the current study.) The dependent measure for this analysis was a composite of posttest reading comprehension and oral reading fluency, adjusted for pretest scores in letter naming fluency (Gersten et al., 2005). Criterion-related validity coefficients between classroom ratings and residualized growth scores for each of the six subscales on the ELCOI were consistently in the high moderate range: median coefficient was .60, with a range from .49 to .65. Thus, there is evidence of good internal consistency reliability, reasonable inter-rater reliability (for a rating scale requiring a good degree of inference), and good criterion-related validity.

The four classrooms were observed during the 2.5 h Reading/Language Arts instructional session between 5 and 7 times each year. Based on the extensive observational notes, each observer completed a rating form with the items on the ELCOI (see Table 1) listed to the left of a 1 to 4 point Likert scale in which: 4 = very effective, 3 = partially effective, 2 = moderately effective, and 1 = not effective. If a practice was not observed over the 5 to 7 mornings, the observer filled out "not observed." Field notes included specific examples of each teacher's practices. These notes not only guided the determination of the score on the rating scale, but also provided a source for more open-ended qualitative analysis of the observational data.

After observations were completed and reading assessments conducted, we interviewed each teacher. Questions generated by the field notes were posed by one of the researchers and the teachers asked questions that they had about the research. In all cases, the interviews lasted approximately 30 min.

Reading Measure (Oral Reading Fluency)
We used a measure of oral reading fluency that accompanies the Dynamic Indicators of Basic Early Literacy Skills (DIBELS) (Kaminski & Good, 1996)

Table 5. Six Clusters of Items (Dimensions) on the ELCOI: 30 Items were Moderately to Strongly Correlated with Reading Measures.

Instructional Practices (Cluster One)

1. Models skills and strategies
2. Makes relationships overt
3. Emphasizes distinctive features of new concepts
4. Provides prompts
5. Length of literacy activities is appropriate
6. Adjusts own use of English during lesson

Instruction Geared Toward Low Performers (Cluster Two)

7. Achieves high level of response accuracy
8. Ensures quality of independent practice
9. Engages in ongoing monitoring of student understanding and performance
10. Elicits responses from all students
11. Modifies instruction for students as needed
12. Provides extra instruction, practice, and review
13. Asks questions to ensure comprehension

Sheltered English Techniques (Cluster Three)

14. Uses visuals or manipulatives to teach content
15. Provides explicit instruction in English
16. Encourages students to give elaborate responses
17. Uses gestures and facial expressions in teaching vocabulary and clarifying meaning of content

Interactive Teaching (Cluster Four)

18. Secures and maintains student attention during lesson
19. Extent to which students are "on task" during literacy activities
20. Selects and incorporates students' responses, ideas, examples, and experiences into lesson
21. Gives students wait time to respond to questions

Vocabulary Development (Cluster Five)

22. Teaches difficult vocabulary prior to and during lesson
23. Structures opportunities to speak English
24. Provides systematic instruction to vocabulary development
25. Engages students in meaningful interactions about text

Phonemic Awareness and Decoding (Cluster Six)

26. Provides systematic instruction in phonemic awareness
27. Provides systematic instruction in letter–sound correspondence
28. Provides systematic instruction in decoding

Other Items that were moderately correlated with reading measures but did not load in a cluster in the factor analysis

29. Provides feedback on academic performance
30. Transitions between instructional activities are short and efficient

as a primary tool for assessing reading because the ability to recognize isolated words quickly and accurately has been shown to be necessary for comprehension of connected text (Wolf, Bowers, & Biddle, 2000). Very little research is available on the development of reading fluency in ELs, but Gersten and Baker (2000) reported a moderately strong correlation between ORF and comprehension ($r = .6$) in a study of 229 ELs. We also used the research of Kaminski and Good (1996) who have developed DIBELS ORF benchmark thresholds for *end-of-first grade* reading as follows: students reading below 40 words per minute (wpm) are at *some* risk for reading failure, and students reading 20 wpm or fewer are very likely "*at-risk*."

The passages used in the DIBELS ORF subtest are standardized by grade level and are part of the standard timed readings for 1st grade originally developed by Deno and colleagues at the University of Minnesota (Kaminski & Good, 1996). Although not part of the DIBELS procedure advocated by Kaminski and Good (1996), we pretested the 1st graders on oral reading fluency. This allowed the calculation of gain scores. We did this, in part, because the district did advocate reading and reading related instruction in kindergarten. Thus, kindergarten instruction in reading has intensified in recent years, yielding a small group of students who can read to some extent at the beginning of 1st grade.

Reading Comprehension Measure

At the end of 3rd grade, the Passage Comprehension Subtest of the Woodcock Reading Mastery Test-Revised (WRMT-R; Woodcock & Johnson, 1990) was given as a measure of reading comprehension. The Passage Comprehension Subtest requires the student to use the "cloze" technique to supply a word that makes sense in the text (reliability = .92). The test generally takes students in the 3rd grade between 20 and 30 min to complete and, like other subtests in the WRMT-R, requires six consecutive errors to establish a stopping point. The raw scores were converted to standard scores for each student.

Procedures for Reading Assessment of Students

A team of graduate students, who were not involved in the classroom observations, conducted the ORF assessments. Students read passages at the beginning and then again at the end of the year to determine the number of words read in 1 min. In Year One, pretests were conducted in November and posttests in June. In Year Two, pretests were conducted in September and posttests in June. At the end of 2nd, 3rd, and 6th grades, three 1-minute timings were given with words read correctly per minute recorded. After the three timings, the WRMT-R Passage Comprehension Subtest was administered individually to each student at the end of 3rd grade and at the end of 6th grade.

Language Measure
The *Idea Proficiency Test* (IPT) is a test of oral language in English which was given to the ELs in this study in the beginning of kindergarten or when they entered school in the school district. With permission, we gathered the IPT scores from the files for purposes of correlating them with reading outcomes in the ELs.

The IPT tests four basic areas: vocabulary, comprehension, syntax, and verbal expression. The authors of the IPT include various forms of validity and reliability information about the test. Content validity of the IPT examines six domains including syntax, lexicon, phonology, morphology, comprehension, and oral expression. Item analysis indicated that each of the six categories is adequately represented in both forms; however, syntax and morphology are represented to a lesser degree than the others. Concurrent validity data collected in 1990 by the authors of the IPT indicated strong positive correlations ($N = 1{,}054$) between the independent variables teacher prediction ($r = .67$), teacher opinion ($r = .37$), and district designation ($r = .60$). Test/Retest reliability ranged from .86 to .92. Split-half reliability, however, was problematic; it ranged from .30 to .68.

RESULTS

Descriptive Statistics

Student Language
The correlation between oral reading fluency for ELs at the end of 1st grade and oral language proficiency as assessed by the IPT was weak ($r = .12$). In addition, a two-group independent-samples χ^2 with a multicategory response variable was conducted using IPT scores and oral reading fluency scores at the end of the year. Students were assigned a category of poor (1 on IPT), low (2 on IPT), medium (3 on IPT), or high (4 or 5 on IPT). On oral reading fluency by the end of 1st grade, students who read 40 or below words per minute were rated "low," 40–60 wpm were rated "medium," and above 60 were rated "high" ($\chi^2 = 2.121$, $\mathrm{df} = 6$, $p = .908$). Thus, among the children in this sample, oral reading fluency

at the end of 1st grade did not differ significantly based on language level from the beginning of kindergarten. This is a typical pattern for second language learners (e.g., Chiappe et al., 2002; Droop &Verhoeven, 2003).

Reading Fluency

A comparison of pre to posttest reading fluency scores for all students across the 2 years was conducted. Effect sizes for each individual classroom [d = post–pre/(post SD+pre SD/2)] range from .29 to 3.36 (see Tables 3 and 4). There appear to be some floor effects in that data as teachers produce more students who read with greater fluency but still have a few who remain low the standard deviation is so large that the effect size appears to be held artificially low. Weaker teachers whose students begin low and remain low at the end of the year retain a low standard deviation that will in all likelihood yield a higher than appropriate effect size.

In Year One, when examining oral reading fluency scores of students reading 40 wpm or fewer, a natural break in the data existed between 18 and 26 wpm a yielding natural dividing point. There were a continuous number of students reading 18 wpm or fewer and no students reading between 19 words and 25 wpm in that sample in Year One. Therefore, we divided low readers into two categories: those who read 18 or fewer words per minute and those who read 18–40 wpm. By creating this category of the very lowest readers, we were able to examine how many of the lowest readers each teacher had at the end of the year. Year One teachers rated "2" or lower on the ELCOI had between 71% and 85% of students reading 18 words or fewer by the end of 1st grade.

In Year Two, when examining the students reading 40 wpm or fewer, there was a natural break in the data between 24 and 29 words read per minute, yielding a somewhat higher dividing point in Year Two (Year One was 18) for this lowest group of readers. In Year Two there were a continuous number of students reading 24 or fewer and no students reading between 25 and 29 wpm. Therefore, the natural break in the raw data occurred in two different places for Year One and Year Two.

In light of this concern, using Year Two data, we computed effect sizes based on pre/posttest scores only for those students who were reading below 24 wpm at the *beginning of the year*; 61 students out of the original 70 students in Year Two (see Table 6). The higher ranked teachers demonstrated larger effect sizes for these low readers than did the lower ranked teachers.

Table 6. Year Two Data: Multiple Language Classrooms Effect Sizes on Oral Reading Fluency for Students Reading 24 Words or Lower at the Beginning of the Year ($n = 61$).

Teachers	Rating on ELCOI	Pretest Means (SD)	Posttest Means (SD)	Effect Size
Marlene ($n = 11$)	3.75	8.80 (2.30)	56.60 (22.09)	3.92
Dara ($n = 11$)	3.75	11.00 (5.61)	71.25 (14.63)	5.95
Guy ($n = 18$)	3.0	10.06 (6.84)	59.56 (22.35)	3.36
Jim ($n = 12$)	2.5	12.83 (5.49)	44.67 (22.97)	2.24
Bonnie ($n = 9$)	2.0	8.36 (8.07)	41.11 (17.40)	2.57

Teachers

On a scale of 1–4 with 4 as the highest score, teachers were rated from 1.0 to 3.75 during Year One (see Table 3) on the ELCOI. In Year Two, teachers were rated from 2.0 to 3.75 (see Table 4). The correlation between teacher ratings and gain from pretest to posttest on oral reading fluency is moderately strong ($r = .65$).

Exploring the relationship between observed teaching practice and reading fluency was a major thrust of our research. To provide more details about this relationship an analysis of the number of students reading 40 wpm or lower by the end of first were tallied by classroom and compared to the ELCOI rating for each teacher (see Tables 3 and 4). Teachers rated "3" or higher had 60–100% of students reading above 40 wpm. While teachers who scored "2" or lower had 60–85% of students reading 40 wpm or lower. The correlation between 1st grade teacher ratings in this study to students reading 40 wpm or fewer at the end of 1st grade on oral reading fluency is strong ($r = -88$). It is important to note observed patterns among higher ranked teachers' classrooms. Teachers who scored "2" or lower on the ELCOI had only 15–40% of students reading *above* 40 wpm by the end of 1st grade. The correlation between 1st grade teacher ratings in Year One on the ELCOI and number of students reading fewer than 18 wpm by the end of 1st grade is also strong ($r = -.83$).

Follow-Up Years

By 3rd grade, 113 of the original 186 from the two cohorts were found. As might be expected, a strong correlation was found between end of

3rd grade ORF and 3rd grade passage comprehension ($r = .737$). A moderate correlation was found between end of 1st grade ORF and 3rd grade passage comprehension ($r = .66$).

By 6th grade, 59 of the original 186 from the two cohorts were found. Once again, a strong correlation was found between end of 6th grade ORF and 6th grade passage comprehension ($r = .627$). A low to moderate correlation was found between end of 1st grade ORF and 6th grade passage comprehension ($r = .459$). In addition, there was a moderately strong correlation between end of 3rd grade ORF and end of 6th grade ORF ($r = .605$) and a strong correlation between end of 3rd grade passage comprehension and end of 6th grade passage comprehension ($r = .836$).

Students Labeled with Learning Disabilities

In an analysis of the low readers in Year One and Year Two to provide information about students who were labeled with learning disabilities, two kinds of patterns emerged: all of the students who were labeled with learning disabilities by the end of 2nd grade were low readers; and most of the low readers, hence the students who were labeled, were in lower ranked teachers' classrooms.

From the sample of 116 students in Year One, 42 students were reading 18 wpm or fewer by the end of the school year (see Table 3). Of the 42 low readers, 31 were students in the classrooms of teachers ranked 2.0 or lower (see Table 2). Of the 31 students reading 18 words or fewer in the lower ranked teachers' classrooms, 10 of those read fewer than 10 wpm at the end of the year. Of those 10 students, 5 were referred for special education at the beginning of 2nd grade and all 5 were labeled with a learning disability. Those who were ultimately labeled read 7 or fewer words per minute at the end of the year. Otherwise, to our knowledge no other children from Year One were referred for or labeled with a learning disability before or during the 2nd grade year.

From the sample of 70 students in Year Two, 61 were reading 24 words or fewer at the beginning of the year and by the end of the year only 7 students were reading 24 or fewer words. Table 4 indicates that the higher ranked teachers had fewer students reading 24 words or less per minute by the end of the year. Of the seven students from Year Two who were reading 24 or fewer words by the end of the year, one moved out of the school therefore we lost the ability to track him; four were referred for special education during the 2nd grade and three were ultimately labeled with a learning disability. To our knowledge no other students from Year Two ($n = 70$) were referred for special education before or during the 2nd grade year.

By 6th grade, 7 of the 59 students were labeled with a learning disability (11.9%). Five of the seven read below 20 wpm at the end of 1st grade. All seven read below 80 wpm at the end of 6th grade. The two who were labeled later, who read above 20 wpm at the end of 1st grade, had 1st grade teachers who received high ratings on literacy instruction and these two students did not appear "strongly at-risk" at the end of 1st grade but they declined steadily after 1st grade and were finally labeled at the end of 3rd grade.

DISCUSSION

Though multiple language classrooms exist in increasing numbers throughout the largest cities in the United States, few studies have examined instructional factors that lead to successful outcomes for these students in the United States. We were especially interested in examining the relationship between teacher efficacy and student outcomes to attempt to add to existing research on elements that appear to constitute effective reading instruction for English language learners in multiple language settings. Our results indicate a strong relationship (−.83) between teacher rating in 1st grade and benchmark success in oral reading fluency. This strong relationship coupled with the relatively low correlation between oral reading fluency and the initial English proficiency (IPT scores) of students (.12) point to the complexities of student learning. For the students in this study, reading is more closely associated with the classroom teacher than with individual language proficiency. This lends support to the National Reading Panel (2000), the National Literacy Panel (August & Shanahan, 2006), and to the series of studies conducted in the United States (Gunn et al., 2000; Haager & Windmueller, 2001; Linan-Thompson et al., 2003) and abroad (Chiappe et al., 2002; Droop &Verhoeven, 2003).

Effect sizes present a general overview of the progress students made given specific teachers (see Tables 3, 4, and 6). The strong correlation (−.83) indicates that when teachers have a high score on the ELCOI they produce fewer students who read 40 wpm or fewer at the end of 1st grade it is important to look at patterns across classrooms. Therefore, the data indicating the number of weak readers each teacher had at the end of 1st grade was the most conceptually representative of the correlations between teacher ratings and student performance. Though many of the low readers at the end of 1st grade were extremely low at the beginning of the year as well, the stronger teachers were able to produce dramatic results for other readers who may not have made it with less effective instruction.

As students continued into elementary school up through 6th grade, moderately strong correlations continue between oral reading fluency at the end of 1st grade and oral reading fluency in later grades. Oral reading fluency for this group of ELs continues to be strongly correlated with passage comprehension at each grade level.

Students with Learning Disabilities

Students, who were weak readers in this sample of ELs, appear to have the most likelihood of being labeled with a learning disability. Five students from Year One and three students from Year Two were ultimately labeled in 2nd grade. In Year One, the five students who were labeled each read 7 words or fewer by the end of the year. This information indicates that ELs, like native speakers, are vulnerable to labeling if they are poor readers at the end of 1st grade. The number of students labeled from the Year One group (6.03%) and the Year Two group (4.29%) does not appear to differ substantially from national averages of students being labeled with learning disabilities; ELs from this sample did not appear to be over represented in special education at the end of 2nd grade. However, by 6th grade 11.9% of the sample were labeled and two of the seven students had performed nearly at benchmark at the end of 1st grade.

Limitations

Small sample sizes and lack of an ability to randomly select teachers, limit the generalizability of these results.

The IPT test used to determine language proficiency in this study was given at the beginning of kindergarten for most of the students and did not provide information on how much English students had learned during kindergarten and 1st grade. It is possible if we had a measure of language at the end of 1st grade that the language proficiency of students would be more strongly correlated with reading. In fact, it makes sense that students who read well are likely to be learning English at a faster rate than students who are not reading.

Educational Implications

It appears that the 1st grade experience can be greatly enhanced for all students including those who are learning English. In this particular study,

1st grade teachers produced fewer at-risk students when they focused on phonemic awareness, phonics, modeling strategies, and gearing instruction toward low performers. However, two very strong teachers with over 20 years of experience each adopted very different types of approaches. From this research, teachers can look for the points of similarity between the highly ranked teachers and focus on those skills. The ELCOI seems to be a helpful tool in isolating important variable for effective teaching.

Finally, the descriptive data derived from this longitudinal study of ELs as they progress through school provides much needed information and offers some anecdotal evidence about the consistency with non-ELs on high correlations between oral reading fluency and comprehension through 6th grade. However, the general decline in reading comprehension scores as students progress in school is noteworthy and provides a justification for continued focus on reading comprehension instruction and vocabulary development in elementary school. Finally, the two students who thrived in 1st grade when the instruction was intense and the literacy practices were exemplary and later were labeled with learning disabilities can potentially provide insight into the need for continued intensity of instruction throughout elementary school for some students.

REFERENCES

August, D., & Hakuta, K. (1997). *Improving schooling for language-minority children*. Washington, DC: National Academy Press.

August, D., & Shanahan, T. (2006). *National Literacy Panel*. Washington, DC: National Academy Press.

California Department of Education. (1999). *Reading/language arts framework for California public schools, kindergarten through grade twelve*. Sacramento, CA: California Department of Education.

California Reading and Literature Project. (1999). *Reading professional development institute focusing on results, K-3*. San Diego, CA: California Reading and Literature Project.

Chiappe, P., Siegel, L. S., & Wade-Woolsey, L. (2002). Linguistic diversity and the development of reading skills: A longitudinal study. *Scientific Studies of Reading*, *6*(4), 369–400.

Droop, M., & Verhoeven, L. T. (2003). Language proficiency and reading ability in first- and second-language learners. *Reading Research Quarterly*, *38*, 78–103.

Echevarria, J., & Graves, A. (2011). *Sheltered content instruction: Teaching English-language learners with diverse abilities* (4th ed.). Needham Heights, MA: Allyn & Bacon.

Fitzgerald, J., & Noblit, G. W. (2000). Balance in the making: Learning to read in an ethnically diverse first-grade classroom. *Journal of Educational Psychology*, *92*, 1–20.

Gersten, R., & Baker, S. (2000). What we know about effective instructional practices for English-language learners. *Exceptional Children*, *66*, 454–470.

Gersten, R., Baker, S., Haager, D., & Graves, A. W. (2005). Exploring the role of teacher quality in predicting reading outcomes for first grade English learners: An observational study. *Remedial & Special Education, 26*, 185–200.

Geva, E., & Wang, M. (2001). The role of orthography in the literacy acquisition of young L2 learners. *Annual Review of Applied Linguistics, 21*, 182–204.

Good, R. H., III., Kaminski, R. A., & Hill, D. (2000). *Ruining our predictions: Attaining successful reading outcomes for students at-risk for reading difficulties.* Eugene, OR: University of Oregon, Early Childhood Research Institute on Measuring Growth and Development.

Graves, A. W. (submitted for publication). The effects of beginning reading instruction on English learners with learning disabilities. *Elementary School Journal.*

Graves, A. W., Gersten, R., & Haager, D. (2004). Literacy instruction in multiple-language first-grade classrooms: Linking student outcomes to observed instructional practice. *Learning Disabilities Research & Practice, 19*, 262–272.

Graves, A. W., Plasencia-Peinado, J., Deno, S., & Johnson, J. (2005). Formatively evaluating the reading progress of first-grade English learners in multiple language classrooms. *Remedial & Special Education, 26*, 215–225.

Graves, A. W., & Rueda, R. (2008). Teaching written expression to culturally and linguistically diverse learners. In: G. Troia (Ed.), *Instruction and assessment for struggling writers: Evidence-based practices* (pp. 213–242). New York, NY: Guilford.

Gunn, B., Biglan, A., Smolkowski, K., & Ary, D. (2000). The efficacy of supplemental instruction in decoding skills for Hispanic and non-Hispanic students in early elementary school. *The Journal of Special Education, 34*, 90–113.

Haager, D., & Windmueller, M. (2001). Early literacy intervention for English language learners at-risk for learning disabilities: Student and teacher outcomes in an urban school. *Learning Disability Quarterly, 24*, 235–250.

Kaminski, R., & Good, R. H., III. (1996). Toward a technology for assessing basic early literacy skills. *School Psychology Review, 25*(2), 215–227.

Kindler, A. (2002). *Survey of the states' limited English proficient students and available educational programs and services, 1999–2000 summary report.* Washington, DC: National Clearninghouse for English Language Acquisition and Language Instruction Educational Programs.

Lesaux, N., & Siegel, L. (2003). The development of reading in children who speak English as a second language. *Developmental Psychology, 39*, 1005–1019.

Linan-Thompson, S., Vaughn, S., Hickman-Davis, P., & Kouzekanani, K. (2003). Effectiveness of supplemental reading instruction for second-grade English language learners with reading difficulties. *The Elementary School Journal, 103*, 221–238.

McIntosh, A., Graves, A., & Gersten, R. (2007). The effects of response to intervention on literacy development in multiple language settings. *Learning Disability Quarterly, 30*, 197–212.

Merickel, A., Linquanti, R., Parrish, T., Perez, M., Eaton, M., & Esra, P. (2003). Effects of the implementation of proposition 227 on the education of English learners, K-12: Year 3 report, American Institutes for Research and WestEd.

National Reading Panel. (2000). *Report of the national reading panel: Teaching children to read: An evidence-based assessment of the scientific research literature on reading and its implications for reading instruction.* Washington, DC: National Institute of Child Health and Human Development.

Peregoy, S., & Boyle, O. (2000). English learners reading English: What we know, what we need to know. *Theory Into Practice*, *39*(4), 207–211.

Snow, C. S., Burns, S. M., & Griffin, P. (1998). *Preventing reading difficulties in young children*. Washington, DC: National Academy Press.

Wade-Woolley, L., & Siegel, L. S. (1997). The spelling performance of ESL and native speakers of English as a function of reading skill. *Reading and Writing: An Interdisciplinary Journal*, *9*, 387–406.

Weber, R., & Longhi-Chirlin, T. (2001). Beginning in English: The growth of linguistic and literate abilities in Spanish-speaking first-graders. *Reading Research and Instruction*, *41*, 19–50.

Wolf, M., Bowers, P. G., & Biddle, K. (2000). Naming-speed processes, timing, and reading: A conceptual review. *Journal of Learning Disabilities*, *33*, 387–407.

Woodcock, R., & Johnson, M. (1990). *Woodcock-Johnson psycho-educational battery: Test of achievement*. Chicago, IL: Riverside.

WRITING: UNDERUTILIZED FOR YOUNG CHILDREN WITH DISABILITIES?

M. Susan Burns, Julie K. Kidd and Tamara Genarro

ABSTRACT

Young children write to learn the alphabetic code, take notes to help them remember, and provide meaningful text to others. These are cognitively and linguistically complex processes. Reciprocal relationships among the development of writing, the purposes of writing, and the learners of interest impact instructional approaches and student outcomes. Teachers can increase success when they provide explicit and systematic self-regulation and writing instruction, view children as collaborators in the process, provide scaffolding that gradually shifts the responsibility to the children, and adapt instruction to meet the abilities and interests of the children. Effective instructional practices for young children with disabilities or who are at risk, are presented, for example, scaffolded writing, the use of graphic organizers, and self-regulated strategy development.

As a literacy coach, working to develop young children's writing, I (JKK) spent many hours in countless classrooms modeling ways to promote writing. Having a strong foundation in writers' workshop (Calkins, 1994),

Literacy and Learning
Advances in Learning and Behavioral Disabilities, Volume 23, 175–204

ISSN: 0735-004X/doi:10.1108/S0735-004X(2010)0000023009

I was prepared to share with teachers the importance of writing on a daily basis, having a variety of papers and tools available, providing choice in writing, encouraging children to share their writing, and promoting purposeful writing (Kissel, 2008). I was also well versed in the process approach that emphasized children's rehearsal or planning of their writing; composing, revising, and editing the draft; and publishing the final product (Graves, 1993). I was equipped with a variety of strategies, great organizational skills, and a desire to pass on my love of writing to the teachers and young children with whom I worked. Despite my knowledge and preparation, I quickly discovered that, although important, providing an environment conducive to writing, quality literature as models, instruction on the writing process, and time for children to conference with the teacher and peers (Calkins, 1994; Graves, 1993) were not enough. I soon realized that young children, especially those with disabilities who experience difficulties with writing, need explicit instructions on and practice with specific strategies that will promote their writing development (Lienemann, Graham, Leader-Janssen, & Reid, 2006).

Although writing develops easily for some, for many young children, especially those with disabilities, writing is a challenging task (Graham & Harris, 1989; Saddler & Asaro, 2007). This is evident in the 2002 National Assessment of Educational Progress (NAEP) writing assessment, where only 28% of the fourth graders who took the test scored at or above a proficient level (Persky, Daane, & Jin, 2003). Research indicates that children with learning disabilities encounter more difficulties than peers without learning disabilities with various aspects of writing, including planning, drafting, and revising as well as the mechanics of writing such as grammar, punctuation, and spelling (Newcomer & Barenbaum, 1991). For young children with specific language impairments and high-functioning autism, profiles of strengths and weaknesses in writing may differ but still as a whole writing difficulties are present (Kau, 1995; Myles et al., 2003). This means that even a greater percentage of children, than is reported in the NAEP, experience difficulties with writing when children with disabilities are also considered (Lienemann et al., 2006).

The difficulty children encounter is not surprising when taking into account the cognitive and linguistic complexity of the writing process (Boscolo, 2008). Writing requires "self-regulation, cognitive effort, and attentional control" (Lienemann et al., 2006, p. 66). Writing involves strategic planning and revising in addition to mechanics and transcription skills (Graham, 2006; Saddler & Asaro, 2007). To become effective writers, young children need to become increasingly more knowledgeable about writing and must develop the skills, strategies, and motivation required to become proficient writers (Graham, 2006). In essence, writing is a challenging task that must be addressed with sound instruction in order to provide children with the level of writing abilities they will need for educational achievement as well as for success in their future occupations (NCW, 2003).

Access to higher education and a choice within job placement are important reasons to provide effective writing skills to individuals with disabilities (Eaves & Ho, 2008; Neely-Barnes, Marcenko, & Weber, 2008). Much of higher education relies upon substantial understanding of the code and mechanics of language, effective note-taking strategies, and advanced compositional skills. It is the primary means by which students present their understanding and opinions to instructors and classmates. Without effective writing skills, job placement opportunities may be restricted, thereby reducing choice within an important aspect of an individual's life. Choice is directly related to quality of life for students with disabilities. Writing provides an effective means of increasing the individual's ability to convey choice and provide feedback within the community.

Providing effective writing instruction, especially for children experiencing writing difficulties, is extremely important in the early years (Lienemann et al., 2006). The research literature on teaching writing skills to students with disabilities is limited across all disability categories, particularly for students from pre-kindergarten to third grade, but we do know that students with disabilities need more structure and focused interventions to achieve the complicated and difficult skill of effective writing. An early emphasis on writing will assist in promoting young children's writing development and will reduce the possibilities of later writing difficulties (Graham, Harris, & Mason, 2005), which are more difficult to address when interventions are delayed until later in children's school careers (Slavin, Karweit, & Madden, 1989).

Graham and Harris (2005) found that young children with and without disabilities "can succeed at writing when they are provided with explicit and systematic instruction" (p. 31). This is supported by research indicating that explicit instruction on writing processes, such as planning and revising (Harris, Graham, & Mason, 2006; Lienemann et al., 2006; Saddler & Asaro, 2007) as well as instruction on transcription skills, such as handwriting and spelling (Graham & Harris, 2005), have a positive effect on children's writing, especially for those who experience difficulty with writing. Research clearly suggests that attention paid to writing in the early years will ensure that children have the opportunities to develop knowledge about writing as well as the strategies and skills needed to be effective writers (Graham & Harris, 2005; Graham et al., 2005; Harris et al., 2006; Lienemann et al., 2006; Saddler & Asaro, 2007).

A focus on writing instruction for all children is needed for a variety of reasons. One important reason is that writing promotes reading development. The materialization of the alphabetic code that is present in writing is particularly important to some early learners. Writing also supports learning. It "provides a flexible tool for gathering, remembering, and sharing subject matter knowledge as well as an instrument for helping children explore, organize, and refine their ideas about a specific subject" (Graham & Harris, 2005, p. 19). In addition, writing is an important tool for communicating with others. As inclusion of students with disabilities in regular education classes becomes more common (i.e., up to 25% of students with disabilities receive instruction in general education settings for greater than half of the instructional day), writing strategies need to be used that integrate the student with disabilities as much as possible into the classroom culture while individualizing instruction for the specific needs of the child (De La Paz, 2009; Englert, Raphael, Anderson, & Anthony, 1991; Vaughn, Hughes, Schumm, & Klingner, 1998). While it is easy to get lost in the struggles of trying to meet the challenges and needs of multiple students with disabilities, sometimes a simple answer presents itself not to only get through, but also to enjoy the experience. Consider the following vignette that illustrates the impact of flexible teaching strategies and functional use of writing on student motivation (based on work of Harris, 2007).

Mrs. Miller finds that the second- and third-grade students she sees in the special education resource room do not like to write. She knows she has to think through a method that will engage these students. In conversation and through observation, she notices that several of the students write notes among peers to communicate. Modeling for these students, Mrs. Miller began giving her students notes when making requests related to her needs as their resource room teacher. Examples included, "Please bring the book you are reading in class when you come to the resource room." She then asked that students make similar requests to her in writing whether it was that they wanted to go to the restroom, library, speech therapist, etc. The teacher responded to requests and students' needs were met. Next Mrs. Miller included brief reasons for requests she made of students (she was also willing to help students read her notes if it was necessary). In turn Mrs. Miller required that students include a reason in their written requests. (Mrs. Miller would help with dictation if needed.) Mrs. Miller found that students were quite willing to write notes to participate in this note-writing system to get their requests met. It turned out that students also learned about their own needs in this process. For example, Nate wanted to go to the library but wanted Mrs. Miller to go with him to help him pick out a book on The Plains Indians that he would be able to read and understand and that was required as reading for his general education social studies assignment. In the words of Harris' (2007) description of a teacher of older students, Mrs. Miller found

> lots of students willing to write if they had a reason to do so. ... they were amenable to learning how to improve their skills. Yes, I teach writing successfully with many of the standard methods, but when a student presents a special challenge, I have to be creative and use what works. ... The challenge for the teacher is finding a way to make writing relevant. (Harris, 2007, p. 91)

Incorporating these teaching considerations into early childhood writing instruction may produce greater enjoyment and understanding of writing for young children with learning disabilities.

Despite a need for explicit instruction of writing processes, skills, and strategies in the preschool and primary grades and the call for school reform to focus on writing instruction (NCW, 2003), little attention has been given to the reforms needed to ensure that sound writing instruction is provided in the early years (Graham & Harris, 2005). Teachers need to have knowledge of unique instructional strategies for these students, including those both in and out of inclusive settings. As students progress in education, different types of instruction may be more effective and appropriate. Each disability (e.g., autism, specific language impairment, learning disabilities, and developmental delays) presents itself with different strengths and challenges, yet all of them can respond to systematically and consistently presented interventions targeted toward skills and knowledge that are slightly beyond what is already known by the student (Nelson, 2005). Graham and Harris cited the No Child Left Behind Act (NCLB), which "places little emphasis on writing" (p. 19), as an example of what they describe as "an unfortunate oversight, as writing is critical to school success" (p. 19). This lack of attention to writing is also evident in primary classrooms. Although teachers report spending, on average, 3 h a week on writing, some teachers devote as little as 30 min a week to writing instruction and those who do allocate time for writing spend the majority of the time on transcription skills rather than on the processes of writing (Graham & Harris, 2005).

Even when time is devoted to writing instruction, the quality of the instruction varies from teacher to teacher. In a study of 155 first-, second-, and third-grade general education teachers, Graham and Harris (2005) discovered that most implemented activities commonly found in classroom writing programs, such as mini lessons, modeling, conferencing, and reteaching strategies and skills in addition to teaching basic writing skills, such as mechanics, grammar, spelling, and handwriting. However, when examining the adaptations teachers made, especially those needed for children who experience difficulties with writing, they found that a great percentage of teachers made no or minimal adaptations for children who needed modifications to succeed with writing. When teachers did make adjustments, they often placed restrictions on children's writing that reduced the freedom children had to make choices, interact with classmates, use the computer, and pace themselves. They also concluded, "there was considerable variability in how teachers approached the task of making adaptations for struggling writers" (Graham & Harris, 2005, p. 23).

Given the shortcomings of current instructional practices and the wide variation in the implementation and adaptation of writing instruction (Graham & Harris, 2005), ensuring that teachers are familiar with ways to provide and adapt instruction for all children is an important step in addressing the challenges children face when learning to write. In this chapter, we share what is known about young children and writing first by examining the purposes and development of writing and then by discussing what is known about children with disabilities who experience difficulty with writing. We then examine strategies that promote writing as a way to learn the code and promote reading, writing to take notes and remember information, and writing as a vehicle for providing meaningful text to others.

PURPOSES OF WRITING AND WRITING DEVELOPMENT OF YOUNG CHILDREN

The development of young children's writing is presented within the context of the purpose of writing and the young learners being described. Development differs, given the purpose for writing, for example, whether writing to remember something or writing to tell a story. Individual children with disabilities or those placed at risk for writing problems learn writing skills and concepts in a different manner and have different learning needs and outcomes. Fig. 1 depicts the relationship among the development of writing, the purposes of writing, and the learners of interest. In this section, we address what is known about writing development from the prospective of young children learning about and producing print, how it functions on the page, and as a code. Further, we address writing development from the standpoint of meaning and how children develop meaningful text to share with other readers or self at a future time, whether for the purposes of

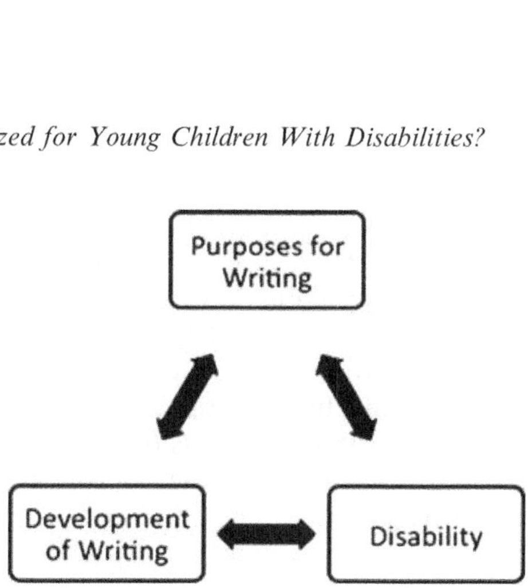

Fig. 1. Simple Path Model in Special Education Writing.

remembering (note-taking), story telling, or providing content-specific information. We then comment on varying trajectories of writing development for young children with disabilities. Although the following information is presented in a linear manner, it continually reflects on the reciprocal impact that one aspect of writing has upon another, as depicted in Fig. 1. Consider, for example, that writing for meaning might be eased in terms of cognitive load (Kester, Lehnen, Van Gerven, & Kirschner, 2006) if the young writer understands punctuation and capitalization, or if the young writer who is impacted by handwriting difficulty due to a disability is given assistive technology to ease the production of print.

Print and Learning the Code

When 3-year-old children are asked to write versus draw, they produce "writing" that resembles letters or symbols (Brenneman, Massey, Machado, & Gelman, 1996) more so than when they are asked to draw. When asked whether a piece of writing is a word or not, 3-year-old children identify those that are conventional looking words, for example, "BEEK" or "BAAK" as words and "BBBB" or "4303" as non-words (Tolchinsky, 2003). With experience, young children learn about many additional aspects of writing such as directionality and other features of space on the paper (e.g., linearity) (Clay, 1988; Levin & Bus, 2003). Before or at the beginning of kindergarten, children know that words include units of sound (Vernon & Ferreiro, 1999), but they do not have the features of specific letters congruent with these sounds. Furthermore, they may not write recognizable letters except in areas where this was specifically taught, such as knowing how to write one's own name (Gentry, 2005).

Throughout the kindergarten year, children are taught more and more recognizable alphabetic letters, they learn to write in an alphabetic language, and gain phonemic knowledge about how alphabetic sound is related to print (Snow, Burns, & Griffin, 1998). They are taught to include spaces between words, punctuation, capitalization, etc. Correct letters are used for some of the sounds in words but additional letters might be included; conventional spelling is used for a few words (Gentry, 2005). To accurately assess meaning of initial writing attempts, the assessment must be derived in the context of the activity, though young children often add drawings and other visual supports to clarify meaning. Gentry (2005) indicates that the writing of first-grade students becomes easier to read phonetically, especially initial and ending sounds, and three-fourths of words used are spelled correctly by the end of first grade. By second grade, conventional spelling is used for all words taught as a function of spelling lessons although this might include looking up misspelled words and making corrections. Spelling in third grade is conventional a great deal of the time. Understanding of prefixes and suffixes, as well as common word patterns helps with spelling. Children actively look for misspelled words in drafts and correct them.

Writing for Remembering (Note-Taking)

Children use words and graphics for remembering, whether it is remembering what they wanted to accomplish during play (e.g., making a sign to remind others to not touch their block construction); taking notes from a book they are reading, then organizing that information so that they remember it; or writing down homework from the board so they know what they need to accomplish that evening. Sequential and integrated note-taking may include highlighting, handwritten notes, underlining text, use of graphic organizers, and student summarization of the preceding note-taking strategies. Levels of complexity in these skills vary with development and learning, but research has demonstrated that children as young as those in third grade can use note-taking to promote learning (Lee, Lan, Hamman, & Hendricks, 2008).

Writing to Provide Meaningful Text

Before children can write conventionally, they combine graphics and word writing in their work, with the interest being the communication of the idea rather than conventionality (Levin & Bus, 2003). Revision has been shown to be a part of this process when learners are given multiple opportunities to readdress a topic (Kissel, 2008). Kindergarten children build upon these skills and generate ideas for simple stories, although they might request help from adults and more capable peers in writing down the stories.

First-grade writers are more competent in using words, phrases, and sentences in meaningful text. They often do not understand the idea of writing to a specific audience but do change writing to clarify points. Second-grade students build upon this and produce more types of writing (e.g., narratives, expository writing, and persuasive essays). They are more likely than younger children to target an audience and produce the sequence, clarity, and details needed for the audience. They reread more closely and make changes based on that rereading. Third-grade writers have a sense of audience. They keep the audience in mind and plan before writing. They reread and think about whether they communicate the intended meaning, and they revise for meaning and mechanics.

It is important to consider that the writing trajectory of specific students at any grade level might actually be qualitatively different from that described above. For example, a child who is visually oriented might develop note-taking most effectively by using visual representations of information rather than relying on conventional note-taking. When teachers account for individual differences of children, they can think of writing instruction and production in terms of development, learning with sophisticated complex visual graphics, or conventional elaborated, yet connected, text. These are noteworthy considerations as we turn our discussion to writing instruction and acquisition for children with disabilities.

What We Know about Writing and Students with Disabilities

At the heart of educational instruction of students with and without disabilities is the goal of helping students become competent and independent in the use of cognitive processes (Nelson, 2005). As students progress through different stages of writing acquisition, they are required to use multiple cognitive processes to facilitate the writing process (Nelson & Van Meter, 2007). In order to construct meaning, students must integrate phonological-orthographic knowledge, syntactic knowledge, semantic knowledge, discourse knowledge, pragmatic knowledge, and prior world knowledge while controlling metacognitive reasoning within the context of the input of stimuli and the output of resulting writing products (Nelson & Van Meter, 2007).

Some authors suggest that writing should progress through the hierarchy of basic to more advanced writing structures (Graham & Harris, 2005). A rationale for first establishing a foundational knowledge of handwriting, spelling, and the written code (i.e., phonological-orthographic knowledge) before progressing to the more advanced features of writing is to control the level of cognitive demand (Nelson, 2005). The idea is to allow the student to gain fluency within lower-level skills so that when higher-level skills are introduced, the student can focus exclusively on the new aspects of instruction. However, Dockrell, Lindsay, Connelly, and Mackie (2007) demonstrated that early writing skills have a direct effect on future spelling, but not on higher-level writing tasks. Moreover, when students are given support at their zone of proximal development, regardless of their current level within the writing hierarchy, students have the ability to acquire higher-level skills with relative ease (Berninger, Abbott, Whitaker, Sylvester, & Nolen, 1995).

When teachers help students incrementally acquire new knowledge and skills, they are scaffolding instruction to assist students in paying attention to the relevant information within each new learning experience (Nelson, 2005). Berninger et al. (1995) and Nelson (2005) suggest that there is not a need to delay higher-level writing instruction for students with disabilities because higher-order skills benefit the learner in having a better holistic understanding of the writing process and the components within it. Knowing story elements can reduce cognitive burden about what to include in a story (Saddler & Asaro, 2007), while it may also increase reading comprehension (Nelson & Van Meter, 2007). A written plan provides external memory where the child can store ideas to reduce cognitive burden when writing. The plan liberates mental resources to engage in other aspects of writing (Harris et al., 2006).

Though diagnostic criteria place individual students in specific disability categories, similar features exist among the categories of learning disabilities, developmental delay, high-functioning autism, and specific language impairment. A common feature for students with these disabilities is evidenced in slower acquisition rates compared to control students. Another common feature for students with differing disabilities is dysgraphia, or graphomotor difficulties. This may negatively affect a student's ability to easily perform the motoric aspects of writing tasks. While it is beyond the scope of this chapter to provide intervention strategies for handwriting, it is noteworthy to consider that when students with disabilities are less fluent with handwriting and the alphabetic code, they are more likely to experience delays or deficits in other domains of educational instruction.

Speech delays, which may be found in any of the disabilities on which we have focused, have a negative impact on writing acquisition and development. Both phonological and nonphonological issues affect the development and complexity of writing (Nelson, 2005). Speech delays can also impact other related domains of literacy such as reading & writing (Dockrell et al., 2007). Of the disability categories presented, students with autism present with the most broad and severe deficits that necessitate further instructional modifications.

Mayes and Calhoun (2007) identified attention, graphomotor skills, and processing speed as comorbid and significant deficits for high-functioning students with autism. In fact, 68% of students had comorbid weaknesses in these three areas, a finding that may provide insight into the percentage of students with high-functioning autism who are instructed in inclusion settings (i.e., 30%). When students have diminished attention spans, the relevance of spoken or written information may be lost. Further, reduced graphomotor skills may prevent students from keeping up with the pace of instruction for note-taking or written assignments. This weakness compounds existing writing deficits. Finally, processing speed is an indicator of how capable a student with autism is in finding relevant information. Slower processing speeds relate to diminished levels of reading and/or listening comprehension skills (Mayes & Calhoun, 2007; Newman et al., 2007).

Educational interventions for children with autism tend to require instruction using established principles and procedures of applied behavior analysis (Odom et al., 2003). It is beyond the scope of this chapter to present all of the teaching principles and procedures, but we encourage teachers to look at the research literature to identify the components of effective educational instruction for students with autism.

Though research on teaching writing to students with autism is extremely limited, some specific strategies that have been presented in the literature for writing interventions have demonstrated efficacy: sentence combining to increase descriptive adjective use (Rousseau, Krantz, Poulson, & Kitson, 1994); delayed cues to teach sound–symbol relationships (Clark & Green, 2004; Quill, 1997); matching printed to spoken words and word construction using movable letter tiles (de Rose, de Souza, & Hanna, 1996); picture, word, or sentence starters that offer a choice based on student preference as an effective tool to prompt story development (Delano, 2007; Fey, Catts, Proctor-Williams, Tomblin, & Zhang, 2004); using written lists as prompts to engage in a sequence of activities

(Stromer, Mackay, McVay, & Fowler, 1998); video, peer, or adult modeling of the desired writing (Marcus & Wilder, 2009; Nikopoulos & Keenan, 2006); and computer-based interventions (Heimann, Nelson, Tjus, & Gillberg, 1995).

Some relative strengths for students with autism include visual performance skills and acquisition of fact-based learning, which may prove useful for expository writing. Deficits in inferential reasoning and theory of mind for children with autism (Happé & Frith, 2006; Loukusa & Moilanen, 2009) may increase the difficulty of other forms of compositional instruction. Even hyperlexia, which occurs in only 5–10% of children with autism, has features that can be used to establish related literacy (Craig & Telfer, 2005; Newman et al., 2007). Overall, despite more access to treatment, outcomes for students with autism are not improving (Eaves & Ho, 2008). This may suggest that quality of instruction has not improved commensurately for this population over time (Eaves & Ho, 2008).

In many cases, students with disabilities need explicit and intensive instruction to master the writing skills and concepts mentioned above. For example, they might need visual organizers and instruction to learn how to plan. In other cases, they may not achieve the fluency in a specific area such as spelling because they have a phonological core deficit that necessitates assistive technology (e.g., spell check word processing programs). The following sections of this paper emphasize effective instructional strategies that can be used for students who have specific language impairments, learning disabilities, high-functioning autism, or who are placed at risk from writing difficulties as a result of poor instruction.

LEARNING THE CODE

In this section we focus on preventative writing instruction for two populations: (1) children who fail to write at grade-level proficiency and (2) children with disabilities (e.g., specific language impairment, learning disabilities, developmental delays, or high-functioning autism). Earlier in the chapter we learned that many children are knowledgeable about the writing code as early as their pre-kindergarten years. For example, when 3-year-old children are asked to write versus draw, they more frequently produce "writing" that resembles letters or symbols (Brenneman et al., 1996) than the picture representations that they are likely to produce when asked to draw. From pre-kindergarten to first grade, they gain mastery of the fundamentals of the writing code. At that time, they understand the sound–letter relationship in words (i.e., the alphabetic principle), which results in more phonetically clear writing of first-grade students, especially with initial and ending sounds (Gentry, 2005; recall Gentry's descriptions of writing development presented earlier in this paper). Application of children's knowledge of sound–letter correspondence can be seen in the writing of their stories and ideas, for example, as they write "I want a dog" on their birthday gift wish list. A pre-kindergarten student's representation of this wish might consist of a long squiggle 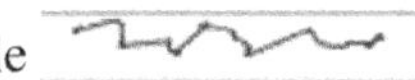 or I , a kindergarten student's representation might be "I w dg," and a first grader writes "I wt a dog." In the second and third grades, spelling becomes more conventional. Similarly, mechanics of print including linearity, directionality, use of space between words, punctuation, and capitalization develop during the early childhood years.

Scaffolded Writing

Scaffolded writing is one approach that has been used successfully to teach not only pre-kindergarten- and kindergarten-aged children to use the alphabetic code in writing, but it also has similarly proven useful for older children with disabilities (Bodrova & Leong, 1998, 2001). Students are provided the "tools" needed to meet the challenge of writing, for example, lines as placeholders for words the children want to write and a "sound map" that helps students associate letters with sounds. At first, the teacher makes the lines as a student dictates what the student wants written. An example is the child saying, "I want to be the waitress in the restaurant." The teacher initially supports the child by making lines with breaks between words, a line representing each word, and ending with a period. "I want to be the waitress in the restaurant" would look like __ ________ ____ ____ ______ _______________ ____ ______ ____________________. The teacher then repeats what the child intended to write on each line and proceeds to help the child write the words on the line. The child takes more and more responsibility for making the lines as he or she learns more about scaffolded writing (Bodrova & Leong, 1998, 2001). The possible progression might look similar to the writing sample in Fig. 2, below. At first the words might be longer squiggles (see Fig. 2(a)) or random letters. The teacher builds upon the child's initial input and moves toward use of letters (see Fig. 2(b)), letter strings with phonemic representations and letter spelling (see Fig. 2(c)), and conventional spelling. In reality, students will have different ideas that they

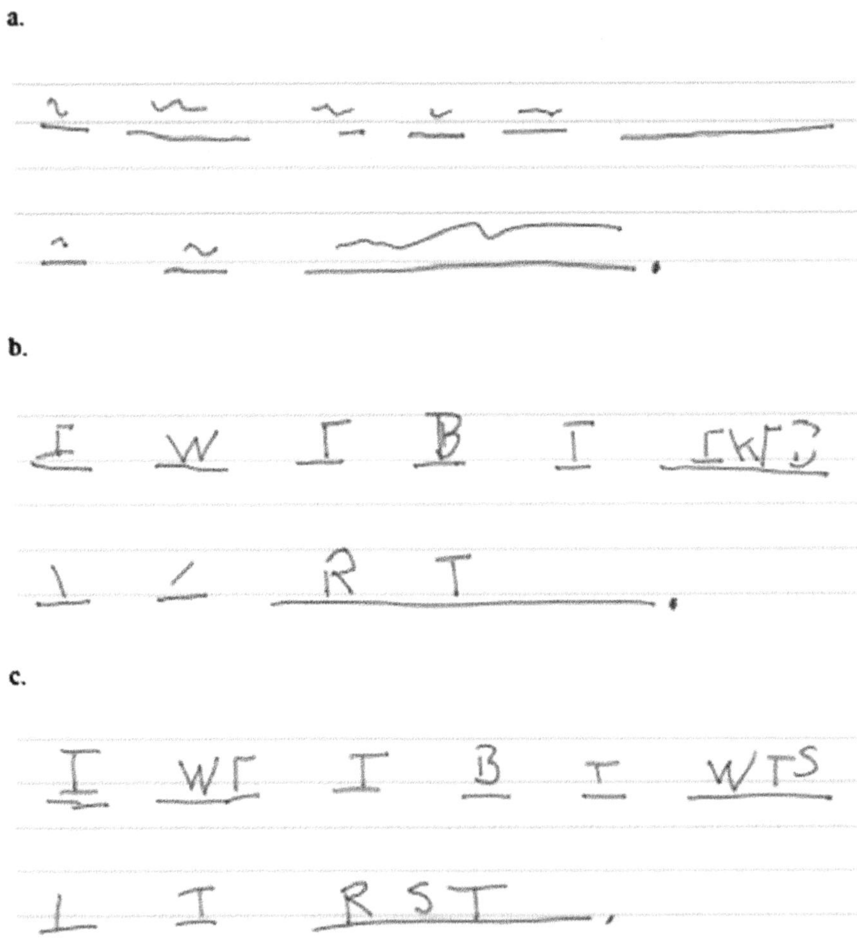

Fig. 2. Hypothetical Examples of (a) Squiggle Letters, (b) Letter Attempts, and (c) Phonemic Letter Strings.

will want to write as they advance within scaffolded writing, but the same sample is written here to highlight the scaffolded writing progression. In the scaffolding process, students are provided the means to understand the association between oral and written language (e.g., by using placeholder lines that are short for words with few letters in them, "__" as a line for "I" and "________________" as a line for "elephant" or by using Elkonin blocks for letter to sound matching (Elkonin, 1963)). More proficient writers are introduced to different forms of a "sound map" that is used to help find words for sounds. A sound map is a special form of an alphabet chart where the letters are not arranged in alphabetic order but in order of how and where sounds are articulated when spoken.

In scaffolded writing, students are provided with contextualized writing that initially has a consequence within a short period of time (i.e., writing a "plan" for learning centers time that defines what the student wants to accomplish during the learning time). What they write stands as the representation that directs their behavior during that time. In Bodrova and Leong (1998) and Gentry's (2005) case studies with "at-risk" kindergarten children and the Barnett et al. (2008) experimental study with "at-risk" pre-kindergarten children, children were found to use phonemic features of writing as a result of scaffolded writing instruction. A similar approach is used in the Book Buddies program (i.e., "Writing for Sounds," developed by Johnson, Invernizzi, & Juel, 1998). Research on Book Buddies with first-grade "at-risk" students produced similar positive results in terms of children increasing their knowledge and skills of the phonemic features of writing (Meier & Invernizzi, 2001). Though this study did not include children with disabilities, participants were chosen based on being the lowest scoring students on the Phonological Awareness Literacy Screening (Invernizzi, Meier, Swank, & Juel, 1998). What is clear in the above studies is that the explicit writing programs mentioned above are all a part of an integrated literacy program. In most instances factors from various parts of that program are impacting children's learning of the code.

In research with struggling writers in early elementary integrated literacy instruction, writing and reading are tied together and children are taught strategies to produce the writing code, including mechanics (Englert, 2009; Englert et al., 1995; Englert & Tarrant, 1995). Englert and Dunsmore (2005) assert that the integration of reading and writing provides the opportunity for intensive, explicit instruction. This supports metacognitive development to help students with disabilities become active writers, who are capable of conveying depth within their ideas. Additional studies of explicit teaching of composition writing are in the upcoming section on writing meaningful connected text.

WRITING FOR REMEMBERING (NOTE-TAKING)

Young children use words and graphics for remembering, whether it is remembering what they wanted to accomplish during play, taking notes from a book, or writing down homework or class work from the board for future use. Much of the information from the previous section on learning the code overlaps with the child's purposes when using writing to remember something. Indeed, scaffolded writing developed by Bodrova and Leong (1998, 2001) was used primarily with young children to make plans for what they wanted to achieve during centers time (i.e., play plans). Note-taking requires fairly sophisticated metacognitive ability; the young learner has to understand that there is a need to write something down to remember it. Note-taking levels of complexity vary with development and learning.

Within their research on effective note-taking instruction with third-grade children, Lee et al. (2008) studied note-taking in science instruction with students receiving either strategic note-taking or partial strategic note-taking compared to a control where students were asked to take notes but not given the strategic note-taking framework. In strategic note-taking, students were given a Strategic Note-Taking Form. On the first page of the form, students were asked to write down what they know about the topic and in addition they were told how to use the next pages on the form. Students were asked the following information numerous times on multiple pages of the form. They were asked to write down (a) the topic of the day, (b) three to seven new main points with details as they were being discussed, (c) new concepts or terms, and (d) a quick description of how the ideas are related. These methods were based on those of Boyle (2001) who worked with older students with mild disabilities.

The third-grade students in Lee et al.'s (2008) study did not include students with learning disabilities but did include students with lower to higher levels of achievement. Students in the strategy groups outperformed those in the control group. There was also a main effect for prior achievement across groups but not interaction between the instructional conditions and achievement. Students who were low achievers gained from the strategy instruction as did the high achievers.

Konrad, Joseph, and Eveleigh's (2009) meta-analysis review of strategic note-taking type of strategies included studies predominantly of students older than those in third grade, but in the studies including fourth-grade students in inclusion classrooms. Positive effects of note-taking strategies on the accuracy of note-taking and learning outcomes were found. The authors qualify their findings regarding younger children noting that the note-taking strategies need to be explicitly taught to the young children.

Younger students may benefit from note-taking but may not yet have the understanding of perspective shifts and main story elements. Nonetheless, introduction of graphic organizers that are modified for student age or grade level may provide scaffolded instruction to allow younger students to prepare to work independently at higher-level writing tasks (Nelson, 2005).

Highlighting textual information, taking handwritten or computer notes, using graphic organizers, and writing student summaries can further facilitate higher-level writing tasks. Students who highlight text and those who take handwritten notes have positive short-term acquisition, but did not have long-term retention of targeted material or develop understanding of relational knowledge within text (Englert, 2009; Kobayashi, 2005). In fact, the literature suggests that underlining written text while reading appears to have a greater impact on short-term retention than either highlighting or taking handwritten notes, It also produces a more thorough critical reading and analysis of the literature (Kobayashi, 2007). Another study suggests that note-taking with note-reviewing produced significantly greater results than note-taking alone or no note-taking on academic achievement (Kobayashi, 2006b).

Graphic organizers can direct attention to particular story elements (Boulineau, Fore, Hagan-Burke, & Burke, 2004), reduce the level of task difficulty (Stull & Mayer, 2007), and provide a relational view of the instructional material (DiCecco & Gleason, 2002), thereby increasing short-term retention. Students can take notes directly on the partially filled-in graphic organizers to identify and elaborate on story or concept elements and themes. Stull & Mayer (2007) looked at the differential effects of author-provided versus learner-generated graphic organizers to determine which of these produced greater benefits in conceptual understanding for the students. The results showed an initial benefit to the author-provided graphic organizers but no statistically significant difference at follow-up, though supplying author-provided graphic organizers decreases cognitive load to allow students to pay attention to the more salient aspects of the lesson (Stull & Mayer, 2007). Similarly, paper-based graphic organizers were equally effective as computer versions in providing writing educational benefit (Kobayashi, 2006a). This is one way to adapt instruction for students who have graphomotor difficulties to facilitate higher-level writing skills and knowledge. Gajria, Jitendra, Sood, and Sacks (2007), Kim, Vaughn, Wanzek, and Wei (2004), and Stull and Mayer (2007) found that while graphic organizers may provide structure to knowledge acquisition and decrease cognitive load, their use does not provide evidence of efficacy for either maintenance or generalization conditions.

Student summaries of highlighted text, handwritten notes, or underlined text, together with graphic organizers provide the longest retention of material. Research shows that writing a summary based on the notes (i.e., either highlighting or handwritten notes) and the graphic organizer transfers the knowledge systematically within the student's zone of proximal development (Pressley, Collins, Gaskins, & Solic, 2006). Given that students will need to acquire academic content across many subjects, their zone of proximal development in each new topic or subject area justifies the indefinite continuation of graphic organizer use (Nelson, 2005).

In summary, note-taking in which strategies are taught and incorporated into practice can improve accuracy and achievement (Kiewra, 1989; Konrad et al., 2009; Lee et al., 2008). Sequential integration of highlighting, handwritten notes, or underlining along with graphic organizers and student-written summaries may facilitate acquisition, maintenance, and, possibly, generalization of metacognitive writing skills. Young children can learn effective note-taking as a part of various uses for writing in the elementary classroom, thereby preventing future problems in this area.

PROVIDING MEANINGFUL TEXT

At a very young age, children begin to develop an understanding that written text is used to convey meaning and share messages with others. This was apparent one afternoon when I gave my cousin's 33-month-old daughter paper and crayons. She occupied herself for quite a while using different colors to scribble on the paper. After a while she looked up and "read" her scribbles, "Mommy, Daddy, Julie!" The next afternoon, she asked for the paper and crayons, sat up at the table, and filled her paper once again with colorful scribbles. This time I asked her what she was writing. She responded by pointing to the scribbles and saying, "A, B, C, D." Her emerging understanding of writing was apparent in these interactions. She understood that through scribbles on paper, she could graphically represent the important people in her life and let someone else know that she was thinking about these people. She also knew that writing involved letters that are somehow captured on paper and then read to others.

The challenge for educators is how to continue to build on these initial explorations of writing in ways that promote more accurate representations of the written word and encourage the use of effective writing strategies to share thoughts, stories, and information with others. An even greater challenge is how to develop writing knowledge, strategies, and skills in children who experience difficulty with learning to write. This section will examine what is involved in creating meaningful text and will identify research-based strategies that develop the knowledge, strategies, and skills that enhance children's writing abilities, especially in children with learning disabilities who experience difficulty with writing. Although we recognize the importance of handwriting and spelling in learning to write to provide meaningful text, these two skills will only be briefly addressed. The focus of this section will be on strategies and skills that support the development of processes that enhance children's writing.

Self-Regulated Strategy Development

Many cognitive demands exist as children write to share meaningful text with others. Effective writers consider their audience, the purpose for writing, the topic, and the form of writing (e.g., narrative, informative, persuasive). They generate and organize their ideas and capture their ideas in writing. While they draft, they make revisions that improve their writing. As they revise, they add and delete text, they make changes to existing text, and rearrange text. During this process, effective writers also attend to mechanics, grammar, and spelling. Writers with learning disabilities who experience difficulty with writing tend to be less forward-thinking than effective writers; they often do not recognize the need to revise, and when they do revision, their approach to revising is often ineffective (Saddler & Asaro, 2007). They often employ a process that involves writing down information retrieved from memory and then using these ideas to generate additional ideas (Graham, Harris, & Larsen, 2001). "With this retrieve-and-write process little attention is directed at the needs of the audience, the constraints imposed by the topic, the development of rhetorical goals, or the organization of text" (Graham et al., 2001, p. 75). Furthermore, revision strategies are often limited; they usually consist of correcting mechanics, substituting words, and writing a final draft that is neater (Graham, 2007; Graham et al., 2001; Saddler & Asaro, 2007). Despite these difficulties, it is evident from recent research that (1) providing primary-age children with direct instruction on writing strategies and (2) scaffolding the use of these strategies can enhance children's writing abilities, including the abilities of those with learning disabilities who have difficulty in writing (Gentry, 2005; Graham & Harris, 2005; Harris et al., 2006; Lienemann et al., 2006; Saddler, 2006; Saddler & Asaro, 2007).

Many teachers and researchers agree that key features of a sound writing program include providing an environment and tools conducive to writing, writing on a daily basis, promoting children's choice and motivation to write, encouraging purposeful and authentic writing, and providing opportunities for interactions with and feedback from teachers and peers (Graham et al., 2001; Kidd & Bromley, 2008; Kissel, 2008). Although these features are key to setting up an effective writing program, it is also important to integrate writing across the curriculum, provide direct instruction and modeling, and adapt instruction to meet the individual backgrounds, experiences, interests, and abilities of the children (Graham et al., 2001; Kidd & Bromley, 2008). Instruction and modeling on specific writing strategies are important aspects of effective writing instruction. Saddler (2006) describes strategies as "plans for accomplishing a task" and further asserts that "effective strategy instruction helps promote active student involvement while engaged in task-specific behavior" (p. 292). Teaching with self-regulated strategy development (SRSD) is one way to provide instruction that evokes effective writing strategies, helps the children identify strategy supports, and naturally creates instructional adaptations to meet the children's needs (Graham & Harris, 2005; Harris et al., 2006; Lienemann et al., 2006; Saddler, 2006; Saddler & Asaro, 2007).

Although initial research on SRSD was conducted with older children, recent studies have targeted students of kindergarten through third-grade who experience difficulty with writing. The current thinking is that early intervention will make a difference in future success with writing tasks (Graham et al., 2001; Saddler, Moran, Graham, & Harris, 2004). One prevalent and effective approach for teaching young children strategies that promote self-regulation is the SRSD approach (Graham & Harris, 2005; Harris et al., 2006; Lienemann et al., 2006; Saddler, 2006; Saddler & Asaro, 2007). In SRSD, strategies are taught in an explicit and systematic manner, with attention given to the skills and information children need to implement the strategies and with an emphasis on ways to help them manage and monitor the writing task (Graham et al., 2005). This approach utilizes a six-stage approach to instruction: (1) "Develop and activate background knowledge," (2) "Discuss the strategy," (3) "Model the strategy," (4) "Memorize the strategy," (5) "Support the strategy," and (6) "Independent performance" (Harris, Graham, Mason, & Saddler, 2002, p. 112–113). SRSD uses four components of self-regulation, combined or in isolation, to promote the acquisition and use of strategies: "self-instruction, goal setting, self-monitoring, self-reinforcement" (Harris et al., 2002, p. 112). It also "allows teachers to use the level of support (e.g., explicit instruction, guided discovery, and/or individualized assistance) needed for student success" (Harris et al., 2002, p. 112). SRSD is successful because the cognitive demands of writing are reduced when children are taught strategies and provided support in the use of these strategies (Graham & Harris, 2005).

Applying strategies independently frees up children to focus their attention on other aspects of their writing.

Teaching Planning and Revising Strategies

Planning and revising are writing processes that are critically important. Using the SRSD approach to teach planning and revising strategies can promote writing development in children with learning disabilities who experience difficulty with writing. Explicit teaching and modeling of planning strategies can improve the length and quality of the writing as well as produce stories that are more complete in the use of story elements (Lienemann et al., 2006; Saddler, 2006; Saddler et al., 2004). It also results in children (a) spending more time on their planning and (b) being more knowledgeable about planning their writing and on the elements they need to include when writing stories and persuasive essays (Harris et al., 2006). A focus on self-regulated planning also was found to increase children's motivation to write (Graham & Harris, 2005). The teaching of planning strategies in combination with the teaching of revising strategies was also found to be effective. Saddler and Asaro (2007) examined the effects of teaching planning and revising strategies using the SRSD approach. They found that when second-grade children were taught to organize their writing, consider what makes a good story, use self-statements to talk about the story, and identify and correct problems, they wrote longer and more complete stories that were of a higher quality.

In the SRSD approach, students are taught to plan and organize their writing as well as generate more ideas as they write. One strategy taught is referred to as POW. POW is one of the mnemonic devices used to help children remember what to do. In this case, POW reminds children that they need to "Pick my ideas," "Organize my notes," and "Write and say more" (Lienemann et al., 2006, p. 71). Teaching children story grammar has proven to be another effective strategy for improving children's writing (Saddler & Asaro, 2007). Children are taught to remember the following mnemonic device: WWW, What = 2, How = 2 (a who question, a when question, a where question, 2 what questions, and 2 how questions). This helps children remember and consider the seven elements of a story and encourages them to ask themselves the following questions when writing a story: "*Who* are the main characters? *When* does the story take place? *Where* does the story take place? *What* do the main characters want to do? *What* happens when the main characters try to do it? *How* does the story end? *How* do the main characters feel?" (Graham & Harris, 2005, p. 27).

Genre-specific strategies are also taught to assist children when writing in a specific genre. For example, when learning to write persuasive essays, children are taught to use a planning strategy with the mnemonic TREE. This strategy encourages children to "Tell what you believe," "give three or more Reasons," "End it," and "Examine" (Graham & Harris, 2005). In other words, young children are taught to state their belief or a claim, support their claim with reasons why they believe this, conclude the argument, and examine their writing to make sure they have included all the parts (Graham & Harris, 2005). For older children, the Es in TREE can prompt them to "Explain reasons" and "End it"; however, this was modified for use with second graders because third graders had difficulty explaining reasons in an earlier study (Graham & Harris, 2005).

In addition to strategy instruction, the effect of teacher behaviors on young children's writing has also been examined. Saddler and Asaro (2007) concluded that effective writing instruction includes a focus on revising and teachers' use of verbal prompting and modeling to encourage children to revise their writing. Teachers model effective writing strategies by showing children how they revise their own writing. This gives children a clear picture of what strategies to use, when to use them, and how to use them. Verbal prompting helps children revise their own writing by drawing attention to places in their writing that can be revised (Saddler & Asaro, 2007). For example, the teacher might prompt a child to add more information or change a word to a more exciting word. Along similar lines, teachers might ask questions about children's writing that help them identify areas of concern. For example, a teacher might ask a child about details in a story that could be added to help children generate more details or questions about what happened first, second, and third to help children organize their writing.

Peer support and assistance was also examined in the research on the SRSD approach. Graham et al. (2005) found in their work with third graders that adding the peer-support component to the approach was beneficial because the peer interactions promoted generalization of strategy use to genres for which there was no instruction, increased the use of story elements in narratives, and increased the time spent in writing informational text (Graham et al., 2005). A study conducted by Harris et al. (2006) with second-grade children had similar results. They concluded that children who participated in the peer-support component incorporated more story elements into their stories, spent more time planning their informative text, knew more about planning, and knew more about the qualities that make a good story and an effective persuasive essay.

Handwriting and Spelling

Although handwriting and spelling are considered lower-level skills of writing, difficulties with handwriting or spelling can have an effect on children's writing (Graham, Berninger, Abbott, Abbott, & Whitaker, 1997; Graham & Harris, 2005; MacArthur, 1999). To attend to the mechanical issues of writing takes cognitive energy that can be used for other processes, such as planning and revising. For example, when children need to attend to mechanical or spelling issues, their attention shifts and may cause them to forget what they planned to write or may result in a less coherent or complex piece of writing (Graham & Harris, 2005). Graham et al. (1997) concluded in their study of children in grades one through six that their "study clearly shows that individual differences in the mechanics of writing, especially handwriting fluency, are predictive of individual differences in compositional fluency and quality" (p. 180). Graham and Harris (2005) concluded in their review of studies in the primary grades that handwriting and spelling instruction contributes to children's abilities to generate content and construct sentences. However, this does not mean that "skills such as handwriting and spelling must be mastered before children are allowed to write" (Graham et al., p. 180). Instead, instruction on handwriting and spelling should be part of a comprehensive program that includes a focus on the higher-level processes of writing.

When considering handwriting and spelling, it is also important to note that the use of technology can make the process of writing easier for some children. Tools such as word processing, spell checkers, grammar checkers, word prediction software can ease the cognitive demands and free children up to focus on the processes of writing (Graham et al., 2001; MacArthur, 1999). Likewise, a software is available that translates print into speech and speech into print. Making use of available tools can provide children who experience difficulty with writing the support they need and influence the way they write (Graham et al., 2001).

Effectiveness of Self-Regulated Strategy Development

The effectiveness of the SRSD approach can be attributed to several factors. In this approach, teachers provide direct instruction on specific strategies like the ones described above that are designed to increase children's independent use of purposeful planning and revising strategies as they write (Graham et al., 2005). They also teach children self-regulation by teaching them how to "use goal setting, self-monitoring, self-instructions, and self-reinforcement to manage their use of the strategy, the task, and their behaviors" (Lienemann et al., 2006, p. 71). They view children as collaborators in the learning process and gradually shift the responsibility for the use of the task-specific and self-regulation strategies from themselves to the children (Graham et al., 2005; Lienemann et al., 2006). Teachers also provide opportunities for children to generalize the strategies to other writing tasks (Graham et al., 2005). For example, children who learned strategies for story and persuasive writing were able to generalize their learning to personal narrative and informative writing even though they did not receive instruction in the latter (Harris et al., 2006). In addition, teachers provide instruction and support that is adapted to meet the needs of individual children and is guided by the degree to which children are able to perform the strategies rather than by time (Lienemann et al., 2006).

The importance of such an approach to teaching writing to young children who experience difficulty with writing was particularly evident in one of the authors' work as a literacy coach in primary classrooms as described here. I can remember one year when I spent a considerable amount of time in the third-grade classrooms where the teachers, including the learning disabilities teacher, and I put much effort into teaching the children to write well-organized and elaborated stories. We taught the students key strategies for planning and revising their stories by sharing with them what they needed to know about the strategy and why they would want to use the strategy. We modeled writing and self-regulation strategies, provided opportunities to implement strategies with varying levels of scaffolding, gave them feedback on their strategy use, and encouraged them to collaborate with peers. The learning disabilities teacher followed up each lesson with additional instruction adapted to provide the children with the information, practice, and support that they personally needed. As a whole, the third-grade children's writing was quite remarkable, including the students with identified learning disabilities in writing. At the end of the year, I warned them that I knew what they could do and would expect them to use their strategies in fourth grade. When I walked into one of the fourth-grade classroom at the beginning of the year, the children greeted me with choruses of "We remember, we remember." And one of the children with an Individualized Education Plan (IEP) in writing proceeded to tell the class exactly what I prepared to review with them about writing stories using organized and elaborated paragraphs. It was the first year in my work as a literacy coach that I did not have to spend the first month of school reviewing everything the children learned in third grade. Amazingly, they did remember.

SUMMARY

Young children write to learn the alphabetic code, take notes to help them remember, and provide meaningful text to others. As their writing develops, they gain phonemic knowledge about the relationship between sounds and letters (Gentry, 2005: Snow et al., 1998) and become more proficient at writing to learn information (Lee et al., 2008). They also become more knowledgeable about the purposes and forms of writing and ways to convey ideas to others (Kidd & Bromley, 2008). In addition, they develop knowledge about the processes of writing, such as planning and revising, and become more adept at engaging in the writing processes (Saddler & Asaro, 2007).

However, learning to write is a cognitively and linguistically complex process (Boscolo, 2008) that requires "self-regulation, cognitive effort, and attentional control" (Lienemann et al., 2006). To learn to write and use writing for a variety of purposes, children with disabilities who experience difficulty with writing need opportunities to learn effective writing strategies, apply them with support, and perform them independently (Harris et al., 2002). This chapter discussed a variety of ways by which teachers can support the writing development of young children who experience difficulty with writing – including scaffolded writing, the use of graphic organizers, and SRSD. The underlying premise is that young children who experience difficulty with writing can find success, independence, and enjoyment when engaging in writing for a variety of purposes. Teachers can increase opportunities for success when they provide explicit and systematic self-regulation and writing instruction, view children as collaborators in the process, provide scaffolding that gradually shifts the responsibility to the children, and adapt instruction to meet the abilities and interests of the children. When teachers devote instructional time to promote writing and use sound approaches to teach writing, young children who experience difficulty with writing can become more effective and motivated writers.

REFERENCES

Barnett, W. S., Yarosz, D. J., Thomas, T., Hornbeck, A., Stechuk, R., & Burns, M. S. (2008). Educational effectiveness of a Vygotskian approach to preschool education: A randomized trial. *Early Childhood Research Quarterly*, *23*, 299–313.

Berninger, V. W., Abbott, R. D., Whitaker, D., Sylvester, L., & Nolen, S. B. (1995). Integrating low- and high-level skills in instructional protocols for writing disabilities. *Learning Disability Quarterly*, *18*, 293–309.

Bodrova, E., & Leong, D. J. (1998). Scaffolding emergent writing in the zone of proximal development. *Literacy Teaching and Learning*, *3*(2), 1–18.

Bodrova, E., & Leong, D. J. (2001). *Tools of the mind: A case study of implementing the Vygotskian approach in American early childhood and primary classrooms*. Geneva: UNESCO.

Boscolo, P. (2008). Writing in primary schools. In: C. Bazerman (Ed.), *Handbook of research on writing: History, society, school, individual, text* (pp. 293–309). New York: Erlbaum.

Boulineau, T., Fore, C., Hagan-Burke, S., & Burke, M. D. (2004). Use of story-mapping to increase the story-grammar text comprehension of elementary students with learning disabilities. *Learning Disability Quarterly*, *27*, 105–121.

Boyle, J. R. (2001). Enhancing the notetaking skills of students with mild disabilities. *Intervention in School and Clinic*, *36*, 221–225.

Brenneman, K., Massey, C., Machado, S. F., & Gelman, R. (1996). Young children's plans differ for writing and drawing. *Cognitive Development*, *11*, 397–419.

Calkins, L. (1994). *The art of teaching writing*. Portsmouth, NH: Heinemann.

Clark, K., & Green, G. (2004). Comparison of two procedures for teaching dictated-word/symbol relations to learners with autism. *Journal of Applied Behavior Analysis*, *37*, 503–507.

Clay, M. S. (1988). *What did I write? Beginning writing behaviour*. Portsmouth, NH: Heinemann.

Craig, H., & Telfer, A. (2005). Hyperlexia and autism spectrum disorder: A case study of scaffolding language growth over time. *Topics in Language Disorders*, *25*, 364–374.

Delano, M. (2007). Use of strategy instruction to improve the story writing skills of a student with Asperger syndrome. *Focus on Autism and Other Developmental Disabilities*, *22*, 252–258.

De La Paz, S. (2009). Rubrics: Heuristics for developing writing strategies. *Assessment for Effective Intervention*, *34*, 134–146.

de Rose, J., de Souza, D., & Hanna, E. (1996). Teaching reading and spelling: Exclusion and stimulus equivalence. *Journal of Applied Behavior Analysis*, *29*, 451–469.

DiCecco, V., & Gleason, M. (2002). Using graphic organizers to attain relational knowledge from expository text. *Journal of Learning Disabilities*, *35*, 306–320.

Dockrell, J., Lindsay, G., Connelly, V., & Mackie, C. (2007). Constraints in the production of written text in children with specific language impairments. *Exceptional Children*, *73*, 147–164.

Eaves, L., & Ho, H. (2008). Young adult outcome of autism spectrum disorders. *Journal of Autism and Developmental Disorders*, *38*, 739–747.

Elkonin, D. B. (1963). The psychology of mastering the elements of reading. In: B. Simon & J. Simon (Eds), *Educational psychology in the U.S.S.R.* Stanford, CA: Stanford University Press.

Englert, C. (2009). Connecting the dots in a research program to develop, implement, and evaluate strategic literacy interventions for struggling readers and writers. *Learning Disabilities Research and Practice*, *24*, 104–120.

Englert, C., & Dunsmore, K. (2005). Tenets of sociocultural theory in writing instruction research. In: J. Fitzgerald, C. MacArthur & S. Graham (Eds), *Handbook of writing research* (pp. 208–221). New York: Guilford.

Englert, C., Raphael, T., Anderson, L., & Anthony, H. (1991). Making strategies and self-talk visible: Writing instruction in regular and special education classrooms. *American Educational Research Journal*, *28*, 337–372.

Englert, C. S., Garmon, A., Mariage, T., Rozendal, M., Tarrant, K., & Urba, J. (1995). The Early Literacy Project: Connecting across the literacy curriculum. *Remedial and Special Education, 18*, 253–275.

Englert, C. S., & Tarrant, K. L. (1995). Creating collaborative cultures for educational change. *Remedial and Special Education, 16*, 325–336.

Fey, M. E., Catts, H. W., Proctor-Williams, K., Tomblin, J. B., & Zhang, X. (2004). Oral and written story composition skills of children with language impairment. *Journal of Speech, Language, and Hearing Research, 47*, 1301–1318.

Gajria, M., Jitendra, A., Sood, S., & Sacks, G. (2007). Improving comprehension of expository text in students with LD: A research synthesis. *Journal of Learning Disabilities, 40*, 210–225.

Gentry, J. (2005). Instructional techniques for emerging writers and special needs students at kindergarten and grade 1 levels. *Reading and Writing Quarterly: Overcoming Learning Difficulties, 21*, 113–134.

Graham, S. (2006). Writing. In: P. A. Alexander & P. H. Winne (Eds), *Handbook of educational psychology* (pp. 457–478). Mahwah, NJ: Erlbaum.

Graham, S. (2007). Executive control in the revising of students with learning and writing difficulties. *Journal of Educational Psychology, 89*, 223–234.

Graham, S., Berninger, V. W., Abbott, R. D., Abbott, S. P., & Whitaker, D. (1997). Role of mechanics in composing of elementary school students: A new methodological approach. *Journal of Educational Psychology, 89*, 170–182.

Graham, S., & Harris, K. R. (1989). A components analysis of cognitive strategy training: Effects on learning disabled students' compositions and self-efficacy. *Journal of Educational Psychology, 81*, 353–361.

Graham, S., & Harris, K. R. (2005). Improving the writing performance of young struggling writers: Theoretical and programmatic research from the Center on Accelerating Student Learning. *Journal of Special Education, 39*, 19–33.

Graham, S., Harris, K. R., & Larsen, L. (2001). Prevention and intervention of writing difficulties for students with learning disabilities. *Learning Disabilities Research and Practice, 16*, 74–84.

Graham, S., Harris, K. R., & Mason, L. (2005). Improving the writing performance, knowledge, and self-efficacy of struggling writers: The effects of self-regulated strategy development. *Contemporary Educational Psychology, 30*, 207–241.

Graves, D. (1993). *Writing: Teachers & children at work*. Portsmouth, NH: Heinemann.

Happé, F., & Frith, U. (2006). The weak coherence account: Detail-focused cognitive style in autism spectrum disorders. *Journal of Autism and Developmental Disorders, 36*, 5–25.

Harris, J. (2007). Making a move. In: R. Stone (Ed.), *Best practices for teaching writing: What award-winning classroom teachers do* (pp. 91–93). Thousand Oaks, CA: Corwin Press.

Harris, K. R., Graham, S., & Mason, L. H. (2006). Improving the writing, knowledge, and motivation of struggling young writers: Effects of self-regulated strategy development with and without peer support. *American Educational Research Journal, 43*, 295–340.

Harris, K. R., Graham, S., Mason, L., & Saddler, B. (2002). Developing self-regulated writers. *Theory Into Practice, 41*, 110–115.

Heimann, M., Nelson, K., Tjus, T., & Gillberg, C. (1995). Increasing reading and communication skills in children with autism through an interactive multimedia computer program. *Journal of Autism and Developmental Disorders, 25*, 459–480.

Invernizzi, M., Meier, J., Swank, L., & Juel, C. (1998). *Phonological awareness literacy screening (PALS)*. Charlotte, VA: UVA Printing Services.

Johnson, F. R., Invernizzi, M., & Juel, C. (1998). *Book buddies: Guidelines for volunteer tutors of emergent and early readers*. New York: Guilford Press.

Kau, I. (1995). The assurance of things hoped for: Coping behavior of children with language disorders in a process-writing environment. *Journal of Learning Disabilities*, *28*, 560–568.

Kester, L., Lehnen, C., Van Gerven, P., & Kirschner, P. (2006). Just-in-time, schematic supportive information presentation during cognitive skill acquisition. *Computers in Human Behavior*, *22*, 93–112.

Kidd, J. K., & Bromley, K. (2008). Promoting writing with reading and learning. In: S. B. Wepner & D. S. Strickland (Eds), *The administration and supervision of reading programs* (4th ed., pp. 157–169). New York: Teachers College Press.

Kiewra, K. A. (1989). A review of note-taking: The encoding-storage paradigm and beyond. *Educational Psychology Review*, *1*, 147–172.

Kim, A., Vaughn, S., Wanzek, J., & Wei, S. (2004). Graphic organizers and their effects on the reading comprehension of students with LD: A synthesis of research. *Journal of Learning Disabilities*, *37*, 105–118.

Kissel, B. (2008). Apples on train tracks: Observing young children re-envision their writing. *Young Children*, *63*(2), 26–33.

Kobayashi, K. (2005). What limits the encoding effect of note-taking? A meta-analytic examination. *Contemporary Educational Psychology*, *30*, 242–262.

Kobayashi, K. (2006a). Combined effects of note-taking/-reviewing on learning and the enhancement through interventions: A meta-analytic review. *Educational Psychology*, *26*, 459–477.

Kobayashi, K. (2006b). Conditional effects of interventions in note-taking procedures on learning: A meta-analysis. *Japanese Psychological Research*, *48*, 109–114.

Kobayashi, K. (2007). The influence of critical reading orientation on external strategy use during expository text reading. *Educational Psychology*, *27*, 363–375.

Konrad, M., Joseph, L. M., & Eveleigh, E. (2009). A meta-analytic review of guided notes. *Education and Treatment of Children*, *32*, 421–444.

Lee, P., Lan, W., Hamman, D., & Hendricks, B. (2008). The effects of teaching notetaking strategies on elementary students' science learning. *Instructional Science*, *36*, 191–201.

Levin, I., & Bus, A. G. (2003). How is emergent writing based on drawing? Analyses of children's products and their sorting by children and mothers. *Developmental Psychology*, *39*, 891–905.

Lienemann, T. O., Graham, S., Leader-Janssen, B., & Reid, R. (2006). Improving the writing performance of struggling writers in second grade. *The Journal of Special Education*, *40*, 66–78.

Loukusa, S., & Moilanen, I. (2009). Pragmatic inference abilities in individuals with Asperger syndrome or high-functioning autism. A review. *Research in Autism Spectrum Disorders*, *3*, 890–904.

MacArthur, C. (1999). Overcoming barriers to writing: Computer support for basic writing skills. *Reading and Writing Quarterly*, *15*, 169–192.

Marcus, A., & Wilder, D. (2009). A comparison of peer video modeling and self video modeling to teach textual responses in children with autism. *Journal of Applied Behavior Analysis*, *42*, 335–341.

Mayes, S., & Calhoun, S. (2007). Learning, attention, writing, and processing speed in typical children and children with ADHD, autism, anxiety, depression, and oppositional-defiant disorder. *Child Neuropsychology, 13*, 469–493.

Meier, J., & Invernizzi, M. (2001). Book buddies in the Bronx: Testing a model for America Reads and National Service. *Journal for the Education Placement of Students Placed At-Risk, 6*, 319–333.

Myles, B., Huggins, A., Rome-Lake, M., Hagiwara, T., Barnhill, G., & Griswold, D. (2003). Written language profile of children and youth with Asperger syndrome: From research to practice. *Education and Training in Developmental Disabilities, 38*, 362–369.

National Commission on Writing. (2003). *The Neglected "R": The Need for a Writing Revolution*. Princeton, NJ: College Entrance Examination Board.

Neely-Barnes, S., Marcenko, M., & Weber, L. (2008). Does choice influence quality of life for people with mild intellectual disabilities? *Intellectual and Developmental Disabilities, 46*, 12–26.

Nelson, N. (2005). The context of discourse difficulty in classroom and clinic: An update. *Topics in Language Disorders, 25*, 322–331.

Nelson, N., & Van Meter, A. (2007). Measuring written language ability in narrative samples. *Reading and Writing Quarterly: Overcoming Learning Difficulties, 23*, 287–309.

Newcomer, P., & Barenbaum, E. M. (1991). The written composing ability of children with learning disabilities: A review of the literature from 1980–1990. *Journal of Learning Disabilities, 24*, 578–593.

Newman, T., Macomber, D., Naples, A., Babitz, T., Volkmar, F., & Grigorenko, E. (2007). Hyperlexia in children with autism spectrum disorders. *Journal of Autism and Developmental Disorders, 37*, 760–774.

Nikopoulos, C., & Keenan, M. (2006). *Video modelling and behaviour analysis: A guide for teaching social skills to children with autism*. London: Jessica Kingsley.

Odom, S., Brown, W., Frey, T., Karasu, N., Smith-Canter, L., & Strain, P. (2003). Evidence-based practices for young children with autism: Contributions for single-subject design research. *Focus on Autism and Other Developmental Disabilities, 18*, 166–175.

Persky, H. R., Daane, M. C., & Jin, Y. (2003). *The nation's report card: Writing 2002*. Washington, DC: US Department of Education, Institute of Education Sciences.

Pressley, M., Gaskins, I., Solic, K., & Collins, S. (2006). A portrait of benchmark school: How a school produces high achievement in students who previously failed. *Journal of Educational Psychology, 98*, 282–306.

Quill, K. (1997). Instructional considerations for young children with autism: The rationale for visually cued instruction. *Journal of Autism and Developmental Disorders, 27*, 697–714.

Rousseau, M., Krantz, P., Poulson, C., & Kitson, M. (1994). Sentence combining as a technique for increasing adjective use in writing by students with autism. *Research in Developmental Disabilities, 15*, 19–37.

Saddler, B. (2006). Increasing story-writing ability through self-regulated strategy development: Effects on young writers with learning disabilities. *Learning Disability Quarterly, 29*, 291–305.

Saddler, B., & Asaro, K. (2007). Increasing story quality through planning and revising: Effects on young writers with learning disabilities. *Learning Disability Quarterly, 30*, 223–234.

Saddler, B., Moran, S., Graham, S., & Harris, K. R. (2004). Preventing writing difficulties: The effects of planning strategy instruction on the writing performance of struggling writers. *Exceptionality*, *12*, 3–17.

Slavin, R., Karweit, N., & Madden, N. (1989). *Effective programs for students at-risk*. Boston, MA: Allyn and Bacon.

Snow, C. E., Burns, M. S., & Griffin, P. (Eds). (1998). *Preventing reading difficulties in young children*. Washington, DC: National Academy Press.

Stromer, R., MacKay, H., McVay, A., & Fowler, T. (1998). Written lists as mediating stimuli in the matching-to-sample performances of individuals with mental retardation. *Journal of Applied Behavior Analysis*, *31*, 1–19.

Stull, A., & Mayer, R. (2007). Learning by doing versus learning by viewing: Three experimental comparisons of learner-generated versus author-provided graphic organizers. *Journal of Educational Psychology*, *99*, 808–820.

Tolchinsky, L. (2003). *The cradle of culture and what children know about writing and numbers before being taught*. Mahwah, NJ: Lawrence Erlbaum.

Vaughn, S., Hughes, M. T., Schumm, J. S., & Klingner, J. (1998). A collaborative effort to enhance reading and writing instruction in inclusion classrooms. *Learning Disability Quarterly*, *21*, 57–74.

Vernon, S. A., & Ferreiro, E. (1999). Writing development: A neglected variable in the consideration of phonological awareness. *Harvard Educational Review*, *69*, 395–415.

TEACHING STUDENTS WITH LD TO USE READING COMPREHENSION STRATEGIES

Alison Gould Boardman, Janette K. Klingner, Amy L. Boelé and Elizabeth Swanson

ABSTRACT

While weaknesses for students with learning disabilities (LD) may exist in basic reading skills, difficulty understanding text goes beyond reading the words on the page. The complex nature of reading requires educators to provide struggling readers with reading strategies that support active engagement with text, comprehension monitoring, and a means to organize their understanding before, during, and after reading. In this chapter we describe collaborative strategic reading (CSR), a multi-component model for teaching reading comprehension strategies. CSR has been associated with reading gains for students with LD as well as low- and high-achieving students, and English language learners. We provide information about teaching reading strategies as well as suggestions for overcoming possible stumbling blocks to implementation.

Students with learning disabilities (LD) and struggling readers often have difficulty understanding what they read. While weaknesses may exist in

Literacy and Learning
Advances in Learning and Behavioral Disabilities, Volume 23, 205–235

ISSN: 0735-004X/doi:10.1108/S0735-004X(2010)0000023010

basic reading skills such as phonological processing, the alphabetic principle, decoding, fluency, and vocabulary, difficulty understanding text seems to go beyond the ability to read the words on the page. In fact, many teachers are surprised when students with adequate word reading ability struggle with comprehension (Edmonds et al., 2009; Englert & Thomas, 1987; Williams, 1998, 2000). Students should be provided with a comprehensive reading program that involves instruction in areas in which remediation is warranted. Yet the complex nature of reading requires educators to go beyond word reading instruction to provide struggling readers with reading strategies that support active engagement with text, comprehension monitoring, and a means to organize their understanding before, during, and after reading both in the younger grades (NICHD, 2000) and in middle and high school (e.g., Kamil et al., 2008).

In this chapter we describe collaborative strategic reading (CSR; Klingner & Vaughn, 1996; Klingner, Vaughn, Dimino, Schumm, & Bryant, 2001b), a multicomponent model for teaching reading comprehension strategies. CSR has been associated with reading gains for students with LD, students at risk for reading difficulties, as well as average- and high-achieving students (e.g., Bryant et al., 2000; Klingner, Vaughn, & Schumm, 1998; Vaughn et al., 2000), and English language learners (ELLs; Klingner & Vaughn, 1996). During more than 15 years of research and practice with CSR, we have observed that teaching multicomponent reading comprehension strategies reflects both the depth and scope of reading comprehension. Simply laying out the steps for instruction does not seem to be enough to facilitate high quality classroom implementation. For this reason, in addition to providing a practice guide that includes how to teach CSR, we also address some of the reality factors associated with teaching and learning to use reading strategies. We include information about overcoming barriers to implementation, addressing ways to provide feedback to support learning during group work, and supporting students whose work shows that they are not yet proficient at strategy use. These practical issues and solutions are intended to connect research to practice and thus maximize student understanding and growth in reading.

READING STRATEGIES

A strategy can be thought of as an approach or a procedure for carrying out an activity. Yet any plan or strategy is only effective if you know *what it is*, *why use it*, *how to use it*, and *when*. Consider a recipe for lemon chiffon pie that requires the cook to separate six eggs and beat the whites. There is quite a bit of information needed to carry out these instructions. The cook must understand that "separate" means to remove the egg yolk from the egg white (*what*). Then a procedure must be used to remove the yolk (*how*) she must also infer *when* to employ the yolk separating process, that the eggs must be separated prior to beating them. And still, if the cook does not know *why* separating eggs is important in this recipe, perhaps she will choose to skip that part to save time. Providing the directions for making a pie and then simply evaluating the end product is similar to the way reading comprehension is taught in many classrooms (Durkin, 1978–79; Klingner, Urbach, Golos, Brownell, & Menon, 2008; Pressley, 2006). In numerous studies of reading instruction, researchers have observed that teachers more commonly than not, do little more than mention a strategy and then assess the product. For example, a teacher may tell students that the main idea is a short statement that contains only the most important information (*what*). Next she directs students to write a main idea, and later she evaluates how well they were able to carry out this task. What both our cook and our students are missing is the explicit strategy instruction needed to carry out their tasks. While the teacher explained what makes up a main idea, she failed to communicate why the main idea is important, how to find the main idea, and when.

Without explicit teaching in main idea or other reading strategies, many students hear the same directions year in and year out, without ever figuring out how to accomplish the components that will help them become better readers. Certainly, teachers can help students understand the content of "Where the Red Fern Grows" or a textbook chapter on photosynthesis. But, reading is about learning strategies that will help students with LD and struggling readers know what to do to understand and remember texts every time they read, in school and outside.

This explicit teaching is facilitated by teacher modeling and many opportunities to practice. High quality teachers of reading comprehension provide this extensive instruction in strategies that are used before, during, and after reading and combine them into a reading routine that students learn to apply in a variety of reading situations.

COLLABORATIVE STRATEGIC READING

Collaborative strategic reading (Klingner & Vaughn, 1996; Klingner et al., 2001b) is one of several multicomponent reading comprehension instruction models that include strategies for summarizing information, asking and answering questions, comprehension monitoring, and peer discussion (see e.g., Palincsar & Brown, 1984; Palincsar, 1986; Pressley et al., 1992; Pressley, Brown, El-Dinary, & Afflerbach, 1995). In CSR, students learn to use the following reading strategies: First, students *preview* a passage before reading. They connect what they glean from a quick look at the title, headings, pictures, and the like to their prior knowledge during brainstorm. Students also make predictions about what they might learn. During reading, students monitor their understanding by recording *clunks*, or unknown words or concepts. They stop after each short section of text (usually one or a few paragraphs) to use fix-up strategies to figure out the meaning of their clunks and to write a brief *gist* (main idea) statement. After reading, students *wrap up* by asking and answering questions and by writing down one or two of the most important ideas from the passage. CSR's plan for strategic reading is presented in Fig. 1 and discussed in more detail later.

CSR is unique in its emphasis on structuring peer discussion through the use of cooperative learning roles and procedures. In their cooperative groups, students are given expert roles so that each member is responsible for guiding the learning as the groups utilizes their before, during, and after

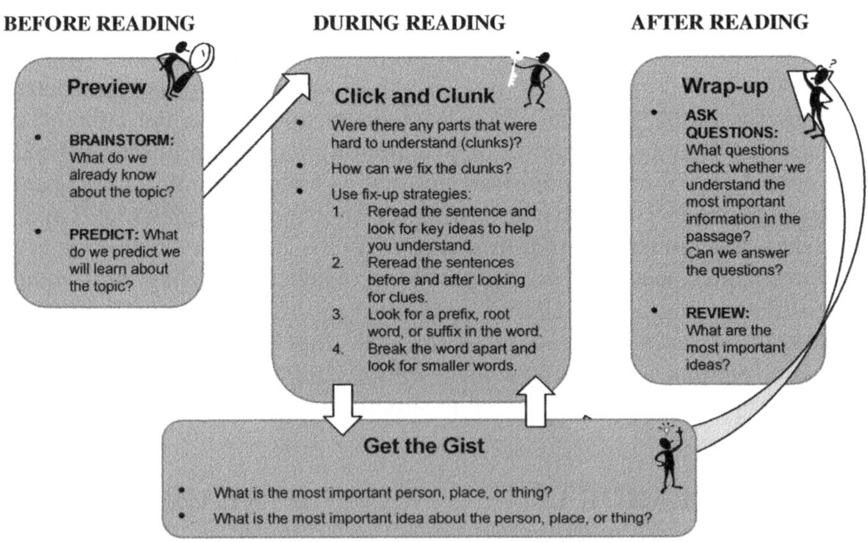

Fig. 1. CSR's Plan for Strategic Reading Includes Before, During, and After Reading Strategies. Reprinted with Permission from Sopris West Educational Services (Klinger et al., 2001b).

reading strategies. Cue cards are used to prompt students as they take the lead in their designated role. While group discussion and shared ideas are important aspects of CSR group work, there is also particular attention paid to individual accountability. For each strategy, students first think of and record an individual response, and then they discuss their ideas with the group. While students are free to help each other, each is responsible for having his or her own ideas. The learning logs also become an important forum for teacher feedback. The teacher can glance quickly at students' learning logs during the lesson in order to provide in-the-moment feedback or she can assess understanding after the lesson is over and use that information to inform planning. Fig. 2 contains a sample of a CSR learning log.

RESEARCH SUPPORT FOR CSR

Studies over the past decade have supported CSR's effectiveness among students with diverse needs. We will briefly discuss CSR's effectiveness when implemented by researchers and teachers, and then describe facilitators and barriers to implementation.

Researcher-Implemented Effectiveness

Researcher-implemented studies are an important first step in determining the effectiveness of classroom interventions. Indeed, the following studies established initial evidence that CSR produces gains in comprehension and vocabulary when implemented with high levels of fidelity. In the first CSR study (Klingner et al., 1998), researchers taught CSR to a group of fourth grade ELLs daily during an 11-day history unit, while the comparison group received typical instruction. CSR had a moderate effect on a measure of comprehension (effect size = .44). In the following study (Klingner & Vaughn, 2000), researchers modeled all CSR strategies for students before teachers assumed instruction. Here, CSR was implemented two to three times per week for four weeks over the course of two science units. ELLs and low-, average-, and high-achieving students made gains in target vocabulary over time.

Teacher-Implemented Effectiveness

To establish evidence regarding CSR's effectiveness when implemented in school settings with classroom teachers, a series of studies (Bryant et al., 2000;

CSR Learning Log

Name:______________________________Date:______________________________
Topic:____

BEFORE READING: Preview

Brainstorm : Connections to prior knowledge

Predict : What I might learn about the topic

DURING READING: Section 1

Clunks:	Fix-up Strategies
__________ = ____________________	1 2 3 4
__________ = ____________________	1 2 3 4
__________ = ____________________	1 2 3 4

Gist:

DURING READING: Section 2

Clunks:	Fix-up Strategies
__________ = ____________________	1 2 3 4
__________ = ____________________	1 2 3 4
__________ = ____________________	1 2 3 4

Gist:

DURING READING: Section 3

Clunks:	Fix-up Strategies
__________ = ____________________	1 2 3 4
__________ = ____________________	1 2 3 4
__________ = ____________________	1 2 3 4

Gist:

AFTER READING: Wrap-Up

Questions: Write Questions and Answers

Review : Write one or two of the most important ideas in this passage.
Be prepared to justify your ideas.

Fig. 2. CSR's Student Learning Log Promotes Individual Accountability and Helps Students Keep a Record of What They Have Learned.

Klingner, Vaughn, Arguelles, Hughes, & Leftwich, 2004; Vaughn et al., 2000) was conducted where teachers were provided with varying degrees of professional development and coaching support as they implemented CSR. Whether teachers were trained in a group of reading strategies, CSR being one of them (Bryant et al., 2000), or were trained solely in CSR (Klingner et al., 2004; Vaughn et al., 2000), students made small gains in reading comprehension, with effect sizes ranging from .19 to .22. However, when growth patterns in reading comprehension for students with LD who received CSR instruction were investigated, findings were more impressive, with robust gains in reading comprehension reported (Vaughn et al., 2000; effect size = .83). Thus, CSR is effective in promoting gains in reading comprehension, particularly among students with LD, when instruction is provided in classroom settings by researchers or teachers.

Facilitators and Barriers to Implementation

As teachers and instructional leaders consider CSR, it is important to capitalize on reported facilitators to implementation and to work to prevent the barriers. As part of a restructuring plan for special education services on two elementary school campuses, seven teachers were provided with professional development in a set of research-based interventions (CSR, partner reading, the writing process, and making words) and were asked to identify facilitators and barriers after the first, third, and fifth years of implementation (Klingner, Arguelles, Hughes, & Vaughn, 2001a; Klingner, Vaughn, Hughes, & Arguelles, 1999; Vaughn, Hughes, Schumm, & Klingner, 1998). Following, we report facilitators and barriers that persisted over the five-year period as well as those identified by teachers in a study that we are currently conducting in middle school language arts and reading classrooms (Swanson, Boardman, Klingner, & Vaughn, in preparation).

Several facilitators were consistently reported by teachers who successfully implemented CSR. First, student acceptance of the strategy was critical to implementation success. One teacher noted, "I find the [ELLs] love it [CSR]," (Klingner et al., 2001a, p. 230). Another teacher helped her students with LD understand how CSR would increase their ability to understand what they read. She said, "Creating buy-in [for CSR] among my students was a must for my success," (Swanson et al., in preparation, Teacher interview, April 23, 2009). Similarly, as teachers realized their students benefited from CSR, their implementation levels rose. A recent CSR teacher told us,

> I wasn't as much of a believer in the whole process as I am now … It was probably mid-fall … [when] I saw the caliber of what they were producing … and the reading teacher in me went 'whoa,' this is something I haven't been able to elicit before through other things I've tried. (Teacher interview, May 5, 2009)

Teachers cited lesson modeling and general support from colleagues as important facilitators as well. After one year of implementation, a teacher reported, "When you have support, be it from the whole staff or from another teacher that comes into your room, it makes a big difference," (Klingner et al., 1999, p. 269). Another teacher said, "When Heidi … came in, I told her my problem [with CSR] … and Heidi said, 'Try this.' … It made a world of difference to me," (Klingner et al., 2001a, p. 231).

The opportunity to adapt and modify the strategy to meet student need was also cited as a facilitator. For example, one teacher spoke about modifying CSR to address her students' inability to work effectively in groups: "I think it should be teacher-directed. We tried at first to have students do it on their own, but there was a lot of confusion," (Klingner et al., 2001a, p. 231).

Solutions to several barriers should be considered as well. For some teachers, the wide range of student needs hindered their ability to fully implement CSR. In one case, with mostly low performing students, it became difficult to identify a leader for the cooperative group, thus resulting in unproductive group work (Vaughn et al., 1998). CSR works best when heterogeneous groups are created, such that groups comprise students of a variety of reading levels and social skills. When this is not possible, the teacher may choose to maintain the leadership role throughout group work time until students become proficient enough to take on the role of the leader. Then instruction in role-alike groups can help transition students to taking on the role of the leader.

An intense pressure to cover content is cited by teachers in both elementary and middle school settings. Teachers acknowledged that with CSR, students learned the material, but the time to cover the topic with that much depth was a luxury they could not afford (Klingner & Vaughn, 1999). One teacher said, "It works alright for a 3-paragraph article in the Weekly Reader, but it would take all day to do a chapter in science," (Vaughn et al., 1998, p. 66). Teachers who received administrative support were able to overcome this barrier. One teacher spoke of the "finish the book" atmosphere at her school until her principal gave teachers "permission" to focus on quality instead of quantity (Klingner et al., 2001). When content coverage is an issue, teachers may choose portions of required readings, selecting parts that are difficult or those containing important content information, to use with CSR while providing more traditional reading experiences with other sections.

Another pressure was preparing for standardized testing. In short, some teachers felt uncomfortable spending time establishing proficient use of CSR, instead choosing to focus on "test ready" booklets for several weeks prior to the exam while everything else was put on hold (Boardman & Woodruff, 2004; Klingner et al., 1999; Swanson et al., in preparation). Yet, some teachers view test preparation differently. As one teacher stated:

> I think that's really odd that people would see CSR as being ... in opposition to [state test] instruction. ... it was like, 'I don't have to give them tricks on how to take the test now. I can give them some solid thinking about what is going on in those passages' ... most of the questions ask students to identify the main idea or define words. My students use CSR to answer the questions. (Teacher interview, May 5, 2009)

We find that when teachers are concerned with high stakes assessment, they tend to be in favor of CSR when they perceive that CSR strategies are aligned with test preparation and can improve results. Thus, in situations where teachers are under great pressure to see gains in test scores, providers of professional development and coaches may need to make connections clear so that teachers see that the components of CSR support the same reading comprehension goals they are working toward with their students. In our efforts to support teachers who are learning CSR, we have found that working closely with teachers to overcome potential barriers can result in improved implementation.

HOW TO TEACH CSR

Our thoughts about how to teach CSR have changed somewhat over the years. We used to advise teachers to first teach CSR's reading comprehension strategies to the whole class and practice them until students could apply them proficiently on their own. We suggested that once students knew the strategies well, then teachers should teach students how to implement CSR while working collaboratively in cooperative learning groups. In other words, we thought of this process as sequential: first students learned the strategies and then they learned their cooperative learning roles. Now we think that it may work better to teach CSR's strategies and group roles simultaneously. Therefore, our descriptions of how to teach the CSR strategies include opportunities to practice each one in pairs or in small groups.

The First Day

On the first day, the primary purposes are to introduce CSR to students and to provide them with an overview of the entire CSR process so that they can get a sense for what CSR will look like once it is up and running. We explain to students that they will be learning strategies, or tactics, that will help them understand and remember what they read. These strategies are what many good readers do automatically when they read, perhaps without even realizing it. We ask students what reading is, and then emphasize the importance of reading as thinking. We show CSR's plan for strategic reading (see Fig. 1) and briefly go over the strategies. If time permits, we use a "think aloud" procedure to model how to use the strategies, verbalizing what we are thinking while we apply each of the strategies while reading through a short sample passage. Here is an example of one teacher's "think aloud" while using the "click and clunk" strategy to figure out an unknown word.

> I don't understand the word "biodegrade." Let me see if there are any clues that can help me figure it out. I'll try rereading the sentence the word is in and thinking about what would make sense. "And, after a short time, the (paper six-pack) rings fall apart, or *biodegrade*." It looks like the definition is right there in the sentence, "fall apart." That makes sense, because paper rings can fall apart if they get wet. I'll write that in my Learning Log.

Teaching the Strategies

Whether students learn the CSR strategies before learning CSR's cooperative group roles or at the same time, it is important to follow certain procedures for teaching each strategy (Klingner, Morrison, & Eppolito, in press):

- Tell students what the strategy is.
- Explain how to implement the strategy, step by step.
- Emphasize the importance and potential benefits of using the strategy.
- Model the strategy for the students using a think aloud procedure.
- Provide multiple opportunities for guided practice in the strategy, as a whole class, in small groups, or in pairs. Support students by prompting them to complete steps they might have missed or by assisting them to complete steps. Reexplain steps of the strategy as needed.

- Give students opportunities to practice the strategy independently, with feedback and support as needed. Gradually fade assistance until students can apply the strategy on their own.
- Make available a list or chart of the steps of the strategy as a reminder, if needed. In CSR, cue cards can serve this purpose. Chart-sized versions of the cue cards can be posted on the wall.
- Ask students to self-evaluate how well the strategy works for them.

Preview

We introduce previewing by asking students if they have ever been to the movies and seen a "sneak preview." We prompt them to think about what they learn when they watch a preview, such as what the movie is about, who the main characters are, and when and where the movie takes place. We explain to students that previewing a passage they are going to read is somewhat similar, except that they develop their own preview by skimming the text. We suggest that they look at: (a) the title, headings, and subheadings; (b) words that are italicized, bold, or underlined; (c) pictures, tables, and graphs; and (d) any questions or key information highlighted in the columns. They are trying to find out (Klingner & Vaughn, 1999):

- *what* the passage is mainly about
- *who* the passage is mostly about
- *when* the events in the passage take place
- *where* the events in the passage take place.

We teach students that once they have a sense for what a passage is about, they *brainstorm* what they already know about the topic, perhaps from something else they have read, or from watching television, or from personal experiences, or something they have learned in school. When we can make connections between new knowledge and prior knowledge, it helps us better understand and remember what we are learning.

We explain that the final step when previewing is to *predict* what we think we will learn. When we predict, we make an educated guess about what we think we will find out, just as meteorologists predict what the weather will be. Our prediction does not have to be accurate to be a good prediction. We discuss how predicting what we will learn can help us to be more interested in a topic because we want to read to find out if our prediction was correct.

When teaching students how to preview, make them write their brainstorms and predictions in their CSR learning logs. Then ask them to share their responses with another student while working in pairs or with a small group of students. Students should not need much time to do this. We suggest 1 ½ min to record brainstorms and about another 2 min to share responses, and then 1 ½ min to write down predictions and 2 min to share them, for a total of no more than 7 min. The CSR Leader's cue card (see Fig. 4) has prompts to help Leaders guide their groups in completing these activities.

Click and Clunk

We emphasize how important it is for students to monitor their understanding while reading, and to take steps to fix their comprehension when it breaks down. That is exactly what the click and clunk strategy is all about. When we understand what we are reading, everything is "clicking" along smoothly. It is sort of like skateboarding on a sidewalk with smooth cracks; we move right along, click, click, click… When we do not understand, clunk, we hit an obstacle that stops us, or changes our course slightly in some way. When reading, clunks are words, concepts, or ideas that are unclear to us. When that happens, we use fix-up strategies to figure out the words or ideas:

(a) Reread the sentence and look for key ideas to help you understand.
(b) Reread the sentences before and after looking for clues. Think about what would make sense.
(c) Look for a prefix, root word, or suffix in the word.
(d) Break the word apart and look for smaller words you know.

One positive aspect of click and clunk that many teachers have shared with us over the years is that they see their students using the strategy in other subject areas, with other readings. Students say to each other, for example, "Wait, I have a clunk. Do you know the meaning of this word?" Encourage students to use this strategy, as well as the other CSR strategies, throughout the day.

We have developed practice sentences with highlighted clunks for students to use while learning this strategy. We recommend that students work in pairs or small groups to: (a) figure out the meaning of a clunk, and (b) determine which of the fix-up strategies was most useful for figuring out the clunk. Fig. 3 presents examples of teacher-created sentences that can be used to practice the fix-up strategies.

When teaching students how to use the click and clunk strategy while working in small groups, explain that one of the CSR roles is a Clunk Expert (see Fig. 4). The Clunk Expert helps the group figure out the meaning of an unknown or confusing word by first asking if anyone already

1. A snake's body is very <u>supple</u>. It can bend easily and can fit in small spaces.
2. In the summer the birds <u>molt</u>, or lose their feathers.

Fig. 3. Students First Practice Using the Fix-Up Strategies with Teacher-Created Sentences.

knows the meaning of someone's clunk and can explain it, or, if not, by suggesting which fix-up strategies to use to try to figure out the word. Once the group has agreed on a plausible definition for a word, the Clunk Expert directs students to write this definition in their CSR learning logs. If the group cannot figure out the word or come to a consensus about its meaning, it is the Clunk Expert's role to ask the teacher for assistance.

Get the Gist

We teach students that when they get the gist, they are figuring out the main idea or the most important information in a section of text they have just finished reading (e.g., one or two paragraphs). We emphasize that getting the gist is different from identifying the topic sentence in a paragraph. Rather, it involves deciding what the most important points are about a topic and paraphrasing them in a brief sentence, or gist statement, that is typically 10 words or less (Fuchs, Fuchs, Mathes, & Simmons, 1997). Students learn to distinguish between important or main ideas and supporting details, and to omit details from their gists. We explain that getting the gist helps us check to make sure we understand what we are reading, and helps us remember important ideas. We follow these steps to get the gist:

- What is the most important who or what in this section?
- What are the most important ideas we have read about this who or what?
- How can we condense these ideas into a gist statement?

One of the CSR roles is that of Gist Expert (see Fig. 4). It is the Gist Expert's role to help groupmates come up with a good gist. First the group must agree on the most important who or what in the section of text. Then each person in the group independently identifies the most important ideas in the section and tries to incorporate these into a good gist statement. Students write their gists in their CSR learning logs. Once everyone has recorded their gists, the Gist Expert asks students to share their gists. The group then discusses the merits of each gist and tries to come up with one gist statement they agree is a good one.

We have found that coming up with good gist statements can be quite challenging. We have seen teachers try different activities over the years to help their students hone their skills. For example, some teachers ask the Gist Experts to write their groups' best gists on a chalkboard, whiteboard, overhead transparency, or projected computer screen (one per group). Then the teacher guides students in analyzing each gist and selecting the ones they think are the best. Students' CSR learning logs provide teachers with a way to check students' gists to make sure they are of high quality.

Wrap Up

We teach students that they wrap up after reading an entire passage as a way to make sure they understand the most important ideas they have learned. The first part of wrap-up is to generate questions about what they have read. Asking and answering questions helps students to identify main ideas, summarize text, monitor their understanding, integrate information from different parts of the text, apply higher-level thinking skills (e.g., making inferences), and remember what they have learned. We teach students to start their questions with who, what, when, where, why, or how ("5 W's and an H"), and tell them that their questions should be like those a teacher would ask on a test to find out what students have learned.

There are different ways to generate questions. We have taught some teachers to use question stems, such as those recommended by Rosenshine and Meister (1992):

- How were _______ and _______ the same? Different?
- What do you think would happen if _______?
- What do you think caused _______ to happen?
- How would you compare and contrast _______?
- What might have prevented the problem of _________ from happening?
- What are the strengths and weaknesses of _________?

We have encouraged other teachers to teach their students to generate questions using question–answer relationships (Raphael, 1986). We suggest teaching three question types:

- *Right There*: The answer is easy to find in the reading. The words used to make up the question and the words used to answer the question are *right there* in one place, in the same sentence.
- *Think and Search*: The answer to the question is in the passage. The answer is made up of information that comes from more than one

sentence or paragraph. Thus, finding the answer requires synthesizing information from different parts of the reading.

- *The Author and You*: The answer to the question is in your head and in the passage. To respond entails connecting your understanding of what the author has written with your prior knowledge about the topic.

When providing students with opportunities for guided practice, have them work in pairs or with a small group. Students can take turns being the Question Expert and reminding each other of the different types of questions they should come up with and write in their CSR learning logs. Students generally learn to write "right there" questions rather easily, but take longer to learn to write "think and search" and "author and you" questions. Students' learning logs provide a record for teachers to examine so that they can provide individual students with specific feedback about their questions.

The question generation strategy lends itself well to post-CSR follow-up activities. Some teachers distribute index cards to CSR groups and ask students to write one or two of their best questions on one side of the card and the answers on the other side. Students can then pass these cards from group to group. Or teachers can use the questions to play a Jeopardy-type game in which the three different question types are assigned different point values. Teachers might also use student-generated questions on quizzes or end-of-the-unit tests.

The second part of wrap-up is the review strategy. We teach students to write down the most important ideas they learned from the day's reading assignment in their CSR learning logs. We also ask students to be ready to justify why they think the information they recorded is important. Reviewing important information in this way helps students remember what they have read. Asking them to justify their responses helps them to be more active, engaged readers, and to use higher-level thinking skills.

As with the other CSR strategies, students can practice reviewing with partners or in small groups. The CSR Leader's card includes prompts for carrying out this strategy. Students should take turns as the Leader, prompting their classmates to write the most important ideas they have learned in their CSR learning logs and to share their ideas.

Implementing CSR in Cooperative Groups

Cooperative learning groups are an essential feature of CSR. In other words, without group work, the strategies applied in CSR would not really be part of "Collaborative Strategic Reading." When teaching students how to use the CSR strategies while working in cooperative learning groups, we suggest emphasizing that they have two responsibilities: to make sure they understand what they are reading and to help their groupmates do likewise (Johnson & Johnson, 1989).

We suggest spending time making sure students are familiar with all of the CSR cooperative group roles. One way to do this is to have students participate in "role-alike" groups in which all the students who have been assigned a particular role gather and discuss their responsibilities and the importance of their role in helping CSR to function well. Another support to group roles is the use of expert role cue cards. Students use the role cards to remind them what to say in their group and also to prompt them of the features of each strategy. Fig. 4 presents samples of cue cards. CSR roles include:

Leader: Leads the group in the implementation of CSR by indicating what to read next and which strategy to apply. Calls on students to respond; keeps students on task.
Clunk Expert: Uses clunk cards to remind the group of the steps to follow when trying to figure out a difficult word or concept.
Gist Expert: Guides the group toward the development of a gist and determines that the gist contains the most important idea(s) but no unnecessary details.
Question Expert: Guides the group in generating questions to make sure they understand the most important ideas they have learned.
Timekeeper: Keeps track of time and lets the group know how much time they have for each strategy or section of text.
Encourager: Watches the group and gives feedback. Encourages all group members to participate and assist one another. Evaluates how well the group has worked together and gives suggestions for improvement.

Monitoring Group Work

Teaching how to implement CSR never stops. Once students have learned the strategies and their roles and are generally working well in cooperative learning groups, the teacher should still circulate among groups and provide assistance as needed (Klingner & Vaughn, 1999). Teachers can help by clarifying misunderstandings about clunks, checking students' gists, questions, or review statements, prompting students to focus on particular information in the passage, and encouraging them to participate. The teacher might pay particular attention to individual students who could be in need of extra assistance or who have had difficulties working in their

Leader	Clunk Expert	Gist Expert
BEFORE READING **Preview** ▪ We know that today's topic is_____. ▪ Let's brainstorm. In your learning logs, write everything you already know about the topic. ▪ Who would like to share their ideas? ▪ Look at the title, pictures, and headings. ▪ Now let's predict. In your learning logs, write what you think you will learn about. ▪ Who would like to share their best ideas? DURING READING **Read** ▪ Who would like to read the next section? **Click and Clunk** ▪ Write your clunks in your learning log. ▪ Clunk expert, please help us out. **Get the Gist** ▪ It's time to get the gist. Gist expert, help us out. [Repeat steps for each section] AFTER READING **Wrap-Up** ▪ It's time to ask questions. Question expert, please help us out. ▪ It's time to review. Write down one or two of the most important ideas from the passage. ▪ Let's share our most important ideas.	DURING READING ▪ What is your clunk? ▪ Does anyone know the meaning of the clunk? **If YES:** ▪ Please explain the clunk. ▪ Does everyone understand now? **If NO:** **1.** Reread the sentence without the word. Think about what would make sense. **2.** Reread the sentence with the clunk and the sentences before or after the clunk looking for clues. **3.** Look for a prefix, suffix, or root in the word. **4.** Break the word apart and look for smaller words you know.	DURING READING ▪ Everyone think of a gist and write it in your learning log. ▪ Name the most important who or what in this section. Then write the most important information about the who or what. Your gist is 10 words or less. ▪ Who would like to share their gist? **Question Expert** DURING READING **Wrap-Up** ▪ Now let's think of some questions to check whether we understood what we read. Write your questions and answers in your learning logs. ▪ Who would like to share his or her best question? ▪ Who would like to answer that question? ▪ Where did you find the information to answer that question?

Fig. 4. Expert Role Cue Cards Prompt Students to Guide Group Members through CSR. *Note:* Samples of Some of the CSR Roles are Provided Here. *Source:* Adapted from Klingner et al. (2001b) with permission from Sopris West Educational Services.

groups. One especially useful technique is to ask for the attention of the whole class when it seems as though multiple groups are struggling to understand a difficult clunk or having trouble generating a succinct gist. Teachers might ask one group to explain how they figured out a clunk or a gist, or they might model how to do it themselves.

The teacher's role in assisting students is especially important when the class is reading about a new topic or learning challenging academic content. Teachers should sometimes conduct whole-class previews to help introduce new material and ensure that students are making connections to their prior knowledge. They should also regularly carry out whole-class wrap-ups to review what was learned. Additional suggestions for teacher support are provided in the following section.

PROVIDING EFFECTIVE FEEDBACK TO STUDENTS DURING GROUP WORK

Struggling readers often do not learn reading strategies easily or quickly. The frequency and quality of teacher feedback may be a key factor in how well students learn to use and apply strategies and ultimately, in how well they understand what they read. "Feedback can significantly improve learning processes and outcomes 'if delivered correctly'" (Shute, 2008, p. 154). Feedback can take a variety of forms such as one-to-one interactions, whole-class activities, written feedback on assignments, and scores and comments on assessments. Here we focus on recommendations that enhance a teacher's potential to increase student performance during CSR group work by the nature of feedback that she provides.

Provide Feedback that Is Specific

Teachers who provide specific feedback that focuses students quickly on the correctness of their responses are more successful at supporting students in achieving learning goals (Shute, 2008). This feedback also helps students understand (a) the goal they are trying to reach, (b) how they are doing so far, and (c) what they need to do next to reach their goal (Hattie & Timperley, 2007).

For example, teachers can approach a group and quickly glance at one or more student learning logs. The teacher then asks guiding questions that focus on errors in student work. "Your gist says 'Volcanoes can cause mud slides.' I agree that 'volcanoes' is the most important who or what, but your gist is a *detail* about volcanoes." This initial feedback lets the students know that they have made an error because their gist is a detail. The feedback is clear and specific. The teacher goes on to provide guidance about how to move forward. A teacher might then say something such as, "Go back to the section and *combine those important details* together to come up with the most *important information about the who or what.*" This feedback lets the student know where they need to go to meet their goal of producing an accurate gist (Hattie & Timperley, 2007). We have observed that questions such as "How is it going?" or "Is everyone on track?" are too general and often lead to easy responses from the students such as "Yes, we're fine." Even content-related comments that are general may not provide enough information to support students. For example, "I'm not sure about that gist. Why don't you take another look at it?" In these situations, students often fail to see what the teacher hopes they will notice with another look at their incorrect response.

Provide Feedback that Connects to CSR Strategies

Many reports of ineffective feedback are related to providing support that is inconsistent with what students need. Once teachers understand what has gone wrong, they can use the explicitness of the CSR strategies to provide feedback. Students learn steps for each strategy as well as why it is important and when and how to use the strategy. Thus, when giving feedback, teachers are the most effective when they bring students back to these specific definitions. In the following exchange, students have confused brainstorm with predict. The teacher redirects students to think about the distinctions between the two components of preview and asks questions that engage students in explaining their understanding and applying it to their reading. This feedback is effective because it focuses specifically on the errors the students have made, it brings the students directly back to when and how to use the CSR components that students have learned, and it involves students in identifying the correct response.

In this excerpt from a CSR lesson, students are sharing their responses during preview. The teacher approaches the group and realizes that students are confusing brainstorm (connect to prior knowledge) with predict (what you think you will learn). She asks an initial question that reveals students' misunderstandings:

Teacher: Are you all brainstorming or predicting?
Student #1: Brainstorming.
Student #2: I thought they were predicting.
Teacher: Did that sound like a prediction to you?
Student #3: I was thinking sharing the ideas.

After listening to a few students share their incorrect brainstorms she realizes that students do not agree on what they are doing because they have confused prediction and brainstorm. This initial fact-finding is important because it helps the teacher understand why the students' responses are incorrect. This is a task-level problem related to distinguishing between two strategies and knowing when to apply each one. Once the teacher understands the problem, she is able to provide appropriate feedback to students.

> Teacher: Can I just clear this up one more time. Okay? When we brainstorm, we are sharing what?
> Students: What we already know.
> Teacher: What we already know. When you brainstorm, have you read this article?
> Students: No.
> Teacher: No, all you have done is looked at it briefly for some clues and then asked yourself 'What do I already know about this?' Okay, so who can tell me the difference between brainstorm and predicting?
> Student #3: When you brainstorm it is what is already in your mind and predicting
> Student #4: And predicting is like, what you think it is about.
> Teacher: So predicting – have you read it yet?
> Students: No. [some students begin to erase and rewrite responses.]
> Teacher: No. Again, brainstorm is what is in your head already before you read and predicting is still in your head but it's based on what you think you are going to learn. What does it seem like it's pointing to? Okay. All right so you all can carry on. (Classroom observation, May 22, 2009)

The teacher has successfully guided the students to go back to their brainstorms and to their predictions to make sure they have categorized each correctly. Student work gathered at the end of this lesson indicated that all students in this group correctly demonstrated brainstorming and predicting in their learning logs.

Connect Strategy Use with Comprehension Goals

The purpose of teaching comprehension strategies is to equip students with tactics for understanding what they read. However, there is a delicate balance between strategy use and comprehension. Students must learn that using strategies is more than following a set of procedures. Similarly, completing the learning log is not the same as filling out a worksheet. The utility of strategy use is to support students' active engagement with text (Kamil et al., 2008). Thus, when understanding breaks down, feedback should support strategy use and also encourage students to engage with the text. Teachers should ask themselves, "What am I doing to help students as I monitor groups?"

Teachers who find themselves spending much of their time explaining the content of a reading, providing definitions of clunks, and thinking of levels of questions when students have difficulty generating their own may be falling back into old habits. Continue to support students to use the strategies thoughtfully and to help them see the link between active engagement and understanding.

Encourage Students to Provide Feedback to Each Other

The power of teachers to provide important feedback that can move students forward in their understanding and application of reading strategies is undeniable. Yet, students provide a great deal of feedback to one another as they work together in their CSR groups. This feedback loop is integral to the CSR model. After students individually complete a component of CSR, they go on to share their responses and to solve problems and provide feedback to one another. When groups work well together, this feedback provides the in-the-moment evaluation and elaboration that a teacher may not be able to deliver to each student. Furthermore, students are often able to explain their thinking in kid-friendly language that gets just the right information across. The click and clunk strategy is a component with built-in group problem solving. Consider the following example of an exchange that occurred between students in a group of four working together to come up with a definition for the word "noxious" they had encountered in their reading.

Student #1: My clunk is noxious.
Student #2: (Clunk Expert): Does anyone know the meaning of the word?
Student #1: Isn't it a feeling you get where like
Student #3: That's nauseas.
Student #4: Isn't it a chemical that kills?
Student #2: (Clunk Expert): Okay let's re-read the sentence. 'Cotton plants for instance, are often smothered with noxious chemicals to keep away insects and weeds.'
Student #3: So it's something that kills bugs and weeds.
Student #4: It's something that kills.
Student #1: It's bad for the environment.
Student #3: It's not good.
Student #2: (Clunk Expert): It's a danger to the environment.
Student #1: Okay, I've got it. (Classroom observation, April 21, 2009)

Having agreed on the meaning of the word, students write their definitions in their learning logs. Students working effectively in small groups are notable for their high levels of commitment to the task. In CSR, students are concerned both with applying reading strategies correctly as well as the larger goal of understanding what they read. Through the use of "expert" roles, individual accountability, and group work skills students may be especially receptive to feedback from each other and from their teacher because they care about what they are doing and they want to do well (Hattie & Timperley, 2007). Student commitment to the task coupled with just-right feedback from their teacher and peers provides students with the means to improve on their strategy use in CSR and their comprehension of what they read.

MAXIMIZE STUDENT LEARNING BY ATTENDING TO LEARNING LOGS

In the previous section we focused on ways to provide feedback during group work. While teachers can look at learning logs during lessons to get a sense for a student's comprehension, analysis of learning logs can also be used to monitor student progress and to guide planning for future lessons. Many teachers choose to use a CSR scoring rubric to help them evaluate students' proficiency at the strategies and to identify individual and common areas of confusion or error (see Table 1). In the following section we highlight regular areas in need of attention based on learning logs from a CSR research study and provide suggestions for organizing instruction to capitalize on opportunities for student learning.

Brainstorm Errors

Brainstorm and Prediction Statements are the Same

Many teachers report that previewing is the easiest CSR component to teach. Yet when they analyze the learning logs, teachers are surprised to find that their students have written prediction statements instead of brainstorm statements that connect prior knowledge to the text topic. In this case, it is important to be explicit. As we noted earlier, feedback can sometimes be provided in-the-moment during group work. During a subsequent lesson, a teacher can provide a few examples of prepared brainstorm statements and prediction statements and plan an activity in which the students have to distinguish between the two. To gain a deep understanding of any reading strategy, students must understand not only

Table 1. The CSR Learning Log Evaluation Rubric can be Used to Measure Students' Growth in Using CSR Strategies.

	Proficient (3)	Becoming Proficient (2)	Not Proficient (1)	Score and Comments
Before				
Brainstorm	• Brainstorm is directly related to the topic • Includes clear evidence of the student's prior knowledge of the topic	• Brainstorm is *somewhat* related to the topic • Includes ambiguous evidence or superficial connection to the student's prior knowledge	• No evidence of prior knowledge • Brainstorm provides unrelated prior knowledge • The brainstorm is a prediction • Text appears to be copied	___
Predict	• Use of topic, title, subheadings, and pictures to formulate prediction • Consistent with text • Prediction is correct	• Prediction is derived only from brainstorm • Does not appear to relate to or is only superficially related to text or topic	• No evidence of use of passage topic, characteristics, or brainstorm in formulating prediction • Prediction is clearly unrelated	___
During				
Clunks	• Clunk is listed • Brief definition is given • Definition is mostly correct	• Clunk is listed • Brief definition is given • Definition is mostly incorrect	• Lists clunk with no definition • Clunk box is blank	___ ___ ___
Get the gist	• Names who/what and most important information of who/what • Gist captures overall idea of section • Gist is paraphrased and is approximately 10 words	• Names who/what but focuses on details rather than the main idea • Part of gist appears to be copied from the text • Gist is partially correct	• Incorrectly names who/what and focuses on details rather than the main idea • Gist appears to be copied exactly from the text • Section is blank	___ ___ ___

Table 1. *(Continued)*

	Proficient (3)	Becoming Proficient (2)	Not Proficient (1)	Score and Comments
After				
Ask and answer questions	• Various types of questions are written • Important ideas from text are captured in the questions • Questions are written in question format • Answers can be found by looking in the text	• Various types of questions are written • Important ideas are inconsistently captured in the questions • Answers can be found by looking in the text	• Only one question type is given when more are expected • Important ideas are not captured in the questions • Questions are written as statements • Questions are not related to the text	___
Review	• Statement reflects important information • Brief but complete sentence(s)	• Reflects important information, but is detail focused or too vague	• Lacks important information • Detail focused or overly vague • Possibly copied from the text	___
Notes				Total

Source: Boelé, Boardman, Klingner, and Annamma (2009).

how to perform the component, but also why it is important. Students who understand both the importance of brainstorming and why they are utilizing this strategy are more likely to brainstorm correctly.

Brainstorms are Too Vague
Many times it is difficult to get a sense for the prior knowledge a student is accessing because it is not evident from his or her learning log entry. For example, a student may write, "Fabrics are involved" for the topic *earth-friendly fabrics*. Teachers can tell students that they need to be convincing about what they know about the topic. The various text features (title, subheadings, pictures, captions, keywords) can all be used to stimulate prior knowledge. When a student's brainstorm is vague or an incomplete thought, it is likely that he is having trouble accessing his prior knowledge of the topic. During the few minutes when students are writing their brainstorms, teachers can facilitate the process by asking the whole class leading questions. For example, "What do you already know about things that are "earth-friendly?" What do you know about fabrics?" or "Look at the sub-heading that says 'Made from Waste.' When things are made from waste, they are recycled. What do you already know about recycling?"

Prediction Errors

Predictions are Based Only on the Title
Students may make superficial predictions based only on the title when they have not previewed the passage. Alert students to first look at the headings, pictures, captions, bold words, and other features that stand out in the text and to use that information to formulate their predictions. Tell them that they will gain much more insight into the content of the text if they look beyond the title, which will ultimately help them monitor their comprehension. Make an overhead transparency (or use an LCD projector) to display the text. Spend 5 min of whole-group instruction time having a few student volunteers point to the place in the text that led them to their prediction. Another option is to do a similar activity in small groups. After each prediction is stated, the rest of the group members try to "guess" the place in the text that led to that particular prediction. For each activity, students are drawn back to the text to make predictions that are connected to the text.

Clunks and Fix-Up Strategies Errors

Students Do Not Have any Clunks

Sometimes students do not encounter any unknown words in a section of text. However, it is more likely that students leave the clunk box blank in their learning logs for other reasons, the most common being that they are not carefully monitoring their understanding while they read. To identify a clunk, students must be able to recognize that they have a breakdown in understanding. Especially during the preliminary stages of fix-up strategy instruction, it is helpful to ask students to find at least two or three clunks per section or even to have students use fix-up strategies for preselected clunks. This alleviates any discomfort students may have with admitting to their peers that they do not know a word. It also provides practice with using the strategies for those who may already know a word's meaning, as well as for those who may partially know a word's meaning. Students must learn what type of word becomes a clunk. For example, a student might say they know the word *misappropriation*, but when asked to explain the meaning, they are unable to provide a definition or understand the meaning of the sentence in which the word was used. Teachers can demonstrate the different levels of "knowing" a word so that students learn to apply fix-up strategies for words that they may be familiar with but unclear about their definition in the text.

It can be difficult to gain insight into clunk fix-up strategy usage solely from the learning logs. Group observations and asking questions to individual students are also essential for assessing these skills.

Gist Errors

Gist Is Detail Focused

Learning how to synthesize detailed information into a larger, more global idea can be difficult for many students. When planning gist lessons, especially in the early stages of gist instruction, it is helpful to use text that is conducive to locating a main idea. Before asking students to generate a gist statement, the teacher might try writing one herself. If the section does not lend itself to a gist statement (e.g., the paragraph is simply a list of factual information), a different paragraph or piece of text may be needed for instructional purposes.

Teachers might consider presenting a mini lesson that aims to "prove" one gist as better than another. With a section of text projected for students to see, a teacher can present two or three prepared gists, and assign different colors to each gist. Then, she can highlight sections of the text that support each gist. Students should visually see that the color that is most prevalent represents the best gist.

Gist Lacks Important Information

Many students begin their gists by writing, "It's about how…" They likely begin this way because they are answering the question in their minds, "What is the section mostly about?"; however, such an answer typically leads to an incomplete gist. In this case, it is important to emphasize the need for a gist that is comprised of two parts: (1) the most important who or what, and (2) the most important thing about the who or what. Students first need practice with writing simple sentences that begin with the most important who or what (the subject) and end with the most important thing about the who or what (the predicate) before writing gists with more complex sentence structures. Gists should always be written in a complete sentence. Some teachers ask students to agree in their small groups on the most important who or what in the passage before going on to write their individuals gists. This way, students work together and have some prediscussion about the section's meaning before working on their gist statements.

Another reason for incomplete gists is an overemphasis on word count. Students may first need very flexible word count limits (5–15) before implementing more stringent limits (8–12).

Question Generation Errors

Questions Are Not Varied

Students first need to understand the differences between question types before being able to write varied questions. If students are only writing "right there" questions when they have been asked to write different types of questions, then it is likely that they need further instruction on other types of questions. In the same way, students who always begin a question the same way (e.g., What is a…?) can be encouraged to use other question stems and be provided with additional instruction as needed.

Questions Lack Important Information

Questions should focus on important information that was learned from the text. Other CSR strategies may be helpful in determining important information, especially the gist strategy. Looking back to the gists can help with question writing. Generating gists garner similar synthesis skills as those used to come up with higher-level, teacher-type questions. As students are beginning to develop their understanding of questions, it may be helpful for them to write their gist as a question. The words "how" and "why" are generally good sentence starters for higher-level questions. Once students are familiar with question writing, they can move away from using gist statements and write more creative, original questions.

Answers to Questions Cannot be Found in the Text
It is fairly common for students to write questions that require additional sources of information to answer. Whereas these questions may be interesting and thought provoking, they do not usually facilitate comprehension of the information presented in the passage itself. Teachers can remind students that the purpose of writing and answering questions in CSR is to help them understand and remember what they have read. For this reason, questions should "stay with" the text. After students write their questions, they can highlight the places in the text where the information can be found for answering each question. By highlighting the text and writing an answer to their own questions, students will become aware of questions that may need to be revised. Questions that go beyond the text can be saved for use in follow-up activities.

Review Errors

Review Only Reflects Information Gained from a Preview
The purpose of review is to identify the critical information across a large section of text. A review that reflects information gained from the preview is not incorrect; it is just likely incomplete. Similar to previously mentioned activities, students can practice locating the sources of information in their reviews by highlighting, circling, pointing, or talking with others. They can be made aware that in doing so, they are demonstrating more in-depth comprehension. A key component of the review strategy is to have students provide evidence for why their review statements reflect the most important information in the text.

Review Is a "Fun Fact"
It is important to celebrate with students when they find information from their reading that is interesting or fun. Although a review statement is

intended to help students create overall meaning from the passage, students should not feel discouraged from writing "fun facts." They can write two review statements, one that captures the big ideas and one that reflects merely interesting information. However, if students write both statements, they should be able to say which contains the most important ideas and which contains the "fun fact."

Review Statements Are Incorrect

If students are misunderstanding the general content of the passage, then it is likely that they are struggling to effectively use the other CSR strategies. A teacher may need to review the previous sections of the learning log and determine if other strategies need attention in conjunction with the review.

Student learning logs are a rich source of information that provides teachers with insight into students' understanding of the CSR strategies. When only one or a small group of students is struggling with a strategy, teachers can target individual or small group focus lessons to provide additional support. When teachers recognize common areas in need of attention, they can use this information to plan for the class in ways that will deepen students' reading skills, providing students with access to broader scopes of literature.

FINAL THOUGHTS

To address the multidimensional nature of teaching and learning to use reading comprehension strategies, we have gathered questions and issues that have come up through hours of classroom observations, coaching, and conversations with teachers who have shared their experiences of working with students to improve their reading comprehension. For teachers who have provided excellent instruction in literature, the content areas, or in the components of basic reading skills, but who have not yet taught specific comprehension strategies, CSR may require a shift in thinking about reading instruction. But these same teachers, their students, and the results of numerous research studies continue to demonstrate that CSR can be an effective and rewarding model to implement in classrooms. We hope that by providing specific information about the realities of teaching and learning to use CSR, educators will be better equipped to use strategy instruction to increase reading outcomes.

REFERENCES

Boardman, A. G., & Woodruff, A. L. (2004). Teacher change and "high-stakes" assessment: What happens to professional development? *Teaching and Teacher Education*, *20*, 545–557.

Boelé, A. L., Boardman, A. G., Klingner, J. K., & Annamma, S. (2009). *CSR rubric*. Unpublished document, School of Education, University of Colorado, Boulder, CO.

Bryant, D. P., Vaughn, S., Linan-Thompson, S., Ugel, N., Hamff, A., & Hougen, M. (2000). Reading outcomes for students with and without reading disabilities in general education middle-school content area classes. *Learning Disability Quarterly*, *23*, 238–252.

Durkin, D. (1978–1979). What classroom observations reveal about reading comprehension instruction. *Reading Research Quarterly*, *14*, 481–533.

Edmonds, M. S., Vaughn, S., Wexler, J., Reutebuch, C., Cable, A., Tackett, K. K., & Schnakenberg, J. W. (2009). Synthesis of reading interventions and effects on reading outcomes for older struggling readers. *Review of Educational Research*, *79*, 262–300.

Englert, C. S., & Thomas, C. C. (1987). Sensitivity to text structure in reading and writing: A comparison between learning disabled and non-learning disabled students. *Learning Disability Quarterly*, *10*, 93–105.

Fuchs, D., Fuchs, L. S., Mathes, P., & Simmons, D. (1997). Peer-assisted learning strategies: Making classrooms more responsive to student diversity. *American Educational Research Journal*, *34*, 174–206.

Hattie, J., & Timperley, H. (2007). The power of feedback. *Review of Educational Research*, *77*, 81–112.

Johnson, D. W., & Johnson, R. (1989). *Cooperation and competition: Theory and research*. Edina, MN: Interaction Book Company.

Kamil, M. L., Borman, G. D., Dole, J., Kral, C. C., Salinger, T., & Torgesen, J. (2008). *Improving adolescent literacy: Effective classroom and intervention practices: A practice guide* (NCEE#2008-4027). Washington, DC: National Center for Education Evaluation and Regional Assistance, Institute of Education Sciences, US Department of Education. Retrieved from http://ies.ed.gob/ncee/wwc

Klingner, J., Arguelles, M. E., Hughes, M. T., & Vaughn, S. (2001a). Examining the school-wide "spread" of research-based practices. *Learning Disability Quarterly*, *24*, 221–234.

Klingner, J., Urbach, J., Golos, D., Brownell, M., & Menon, S. (2008, April). How do special education teachers promote reading comprehension? Paper presented at the annual meeting of the American Educational Research Association, New York, NY.

Klingner, J. K., Morrison, A., & Eppolito, A. (in press). Metacognition to improve reading comprehension. In: R. O'Connor & P. Vadasy (Eds), *Handbook of reading interventions*. New York: Guilford.

Klingner, J. K., & Vaughn, S. (1996). Reciprocal teaching of reading comprehension strategies for students with learning disabilities who use English as a second language. *Elementary School Journal*, *96*, 275–293.

Klingner, J. K., & Vaughn, S. (1999). Promoting reading comprehension, content learning, and English acquisition through collaborative strategic reading (CSR). *The Reading Teacher*, *52*, 738–747.

Klingner, J. K., & Vaughn, S. (2000). The helping behaviors of fifth graders while using collaborative strategic reading during ESL content classes. *TESOL Quarterly*, *34*, 69–98.

Klingner, J. K., Vaughn, S., Arguelles, M. E., Hughes, M. T., & Leftwich, S. A. (2004). Collaborative strategic reading: Real world lessons from classroom teachers. *Remedial and Special Education*, *25*, 291–302.

Klingner, J. K., Vaughn, S., Dimino, J., Schumm, J. S., & Bryant, D. (2001b). *Collaborative strategic reading: Strategies for improving comprehension*. Longmont, CO: Sopris West.

Klingner, J. K., Vaughn, S., Hughes, M. T., & Arguelles, M. E. (1999). Sustaining research-based practices in reading: A 3-year follow-up. *Remedial and Special Education, 20*, 263–274.

Klingner, J. K., Vaughn, S., & Schumm, J. S. (1998). Collaborative strategic reading during social studies in heterogeneous fourth-grade classrooms. *The Elementary School Journal, 99*, 3–22.

National Institute of Child Health and Human Development. (2000). *Report of the National Reading Panel: Teaching children to read: An evidence-based assessment of the scientific research literature on reading and its implications for reading instruction: Reports of the sub-groups*. Washington, DC: US Department of Health and Human Services, National Institute on Health.

Palincsar, A. S. (1986). The role of dialogue in providing scaffolded instruction. *Educational Psychologist, 21*, 73–98.

Palincsar, A. S., & Brown, A. L. (1984). The reciprocal teaching of comprehension-fostering and comprehension-monitoring activities. *Cognition and Instruction, 1*, 117–175.

Pressley, M. (2006). *Reading instruction that works: The case for balanced teaching* (3rd ed.). New York: The Guilford Press.

Pressley, M., Brown, R., El-Dinary, P. B., & Afflerbach, P. (1995). The comprehension instruction that students need: Instruction fostering constructively responsive reading. *Learning Disabilities Research and Practice, 10*, 215–224.

Pressley, M., El-Dinary, P. B., Gaskins, I., Schuder, T., Bergman, J., Almasi, J., & Brown, R. (1992). Beyond direct explanation: Transactional instruction of reading comprehension strategies. *The Elementary School Journal, 92*, 513–555.

Raphael, T. E. (1986). Teaching question answer relationships, revisited. *The Reading Teacher, 39*, 516–522.

Rosenshine, B., & Meister, C. (1992). The use of scaffolds for teaching higher-level cognitive strategies. *Educational Leadership, 49*, 26–33.

Shute, V. J. (2008). Focus on formative feedback. *Review of Educational Research, 78*, 153–159.

Swanson, E., Boardman, A. G., Klingner J. K., & Vaughn, S. (in preparation). Middle school language arts and reading intervention teachers' experiences implementing Collaborative Strategic Reading during a multi-site randomized control trial study.

Vaughn, S., Chard, D. J., Bryant, D. P., Coleman, M., Tyler, B., Linan-Thompson, S., & Kouzekanani, K. (2000). Fluency and comprehension interventions for third-grade students. *Remedial and Special Education, 21*, 325–335.

Vaughn, S., Hughes, M. T., Schumm, J. S., & Klingner, J. K. (1998). A collaborative effort to enhance reading and writing instruction in inclusion classrooms. *Learning Disability Quarterly, 21*, 57–74.

Williams, J. P. (1998). Improving comprehension of disabled readers. *Annals of Dyslexia, 48*, 213–238.

Williams, J. P. (2000). *Strategic processing of text: Improving reading comprehension for students with learning disabilities* (Report No. EDO-EC-00-8). Reston, VA: Council for Exceptional Children. (ERIC Document Reproduction Service No. ED 449596).

PERSUADING STUDENTS WITH EMOTIONAL DISABILITIES TO WRITE: A DESIGN STUDY

Margo A. Mastropieri, Thomas E. Scruggs, Yojanna Cuenca-Sanchez, Nancy Irby, Sara Mills, Linda Mason and Richard Kubina

ABSTRACT

An exploratory study was undertaken to examine the implementation of strategy instruction in persuasive writing with a class of 10 adolescent students with severe emotional/behavioral disabilities (EBD). Several learner characteristics were observed to interact with curriculum and instructional variables. Modifications were made, on an ongoing basis, to respond to these student characteristics. After approximately four months of instruction, findings indicated that all students had mastered the components of effective persuasive essay writing, and performed competently on criterion writing measures, greatly different from performance at the beginning of instruction. Although the design of this investigation does not allow for definitive causal explanations, insights were gained regarding the interaction between EBD characteristics and strategy instruction. Implications for further research are discussed.

Literacy and Learning
Advances in Learning and Behavioral Disabilities, Volume 23, 237–268

ISSN: 0735-004X/doi:10.1108/S0735-004X(2010)0000023011

Students with serious emotional/behavioral disabilities (EBD) face significant learning challenges in school (Lane, 2004); among these challenges is developing proficient expressive writing skills. Writing skills are of critical importance because of their emphasis on organized, rational thinking, considering the perspectives of others, and clearly communicating facts and opinions to others – skills that are of great potential value for students with EBD (Regan, Mastropieri, & Scruggs, 2008). Unfortunately, relevant research in this area is very limited. In a review of academic interventions for students with EBD, Lane (2004) stated, "academic interventions targeting written expression…represent, by far, the least developed instructional area of the three [i.e., reading, writing, math] examined in this chapter" (p. 475).

Unfortunately, students with emotional and behavioral disabilities are at a great disadvantage with respect to writing skills. Lane, Wehby, Little, and Cooley (2005a) reported that mean achievement in written language in self-contained elementary and secondary schools for students with EBD was below the 10th percentile. In a following study, these low scores were seen to decline over time (Lane, Wehby, Little, & Cooley, 2005b). Lane, Barton-Arwood, Nelson, and Wehby (2008) reported that written expression among students with EBD in self-contained schools was at the 15th percentile, and that these scores were associated with behavioral variables (e.g., school adjustment, externalizing, and internalizing; Furlong, Morrison, & Jimerson, 2004). Nelson, Benner, and Rogers-Adkinson (2003) reported that sample of students with EBD and co-morbidity in language disorders produced mean scores of 18th–25th percentile on written language measures. Nelson, Benner, Lane, and Smith (2004) also reported that a random sample of students with EBD scored at the 15th percentile in broad writing, and that these scores were associated with externalizing behaviors. Results of earlier investigations (e.g., Epstein & Cullinan, 1983; Scruggs & Mastropieri, 1986), and reviews of relevant research conducted over time (Reid, Gonzalez, Nordness, Trout, & Epstein, 2004) suggest that these deficits are perennial and consistently observed.

Some research, however, has been conducted recently in the area of writing. One promising instructional approach, that has successfully improved written performance with students with learning disabilities, is the Self-Regulated Strategy Development Model (SRSD) (Harris, Graham, Mason, & Friedlander, 2008). The SRSD instructional approach provides supports in self-regulation such as goal setting, self-monitoring, and self-instruction while explicitly teaching strategies to facilitate writing performance. SRSD has been successfully implemented in a very extensive body of research (e.g., Rogers & Graham, 2008; Graham & Harris, 2003;

Graham & Perrin, 2007; Santangelo, Harris, & Graham, 2008). However, until very recently, little was known whether such instruction could impact learning of students with serious emotional disabilities.

Mason, Harris, and Graham (2002) described one application of the SRSD model with one third grade student described as having attention, learning, and behavioral disabilities. The SRSD model was implemented using the planning and organizing strategy POW (P = Pick my idea, O = Organize my notes, W = Write and say more) and the strategy for writing stories: WWW, What = 2, How = 2 (Who is the main character? When does the story take place? Where does the story take place? What does the main character do? What happens? How does the story end? How do the characters feel? Mason et al., p. 498). Mason et al. provided writing samples to indicate how the student had progressed in writing. More systematic evidence was provided by Adkins (2005), who taught three second and third grade students with EBD, in 19–25 sessions, to use the planning and story writing strategy, using a multiple baseline design. All students improved in number of story elements, number of words written, and overall quality indices on post intervention, maintenance, and generalization probes.

More recently, Lane et al. (2008) extended the Adkins study using the same SRSD writing strategy in teaching six second grade students who were at risk for EBD how to plan and draft a story. Students were taught individually in one of three legs of intervention implementation using the SRSD model over 10–15 sessions. All students improved at post intervention and maintenance assessment periods on number of story elements, quality, and total number of words written over baseline performance. Finally, Mason and Shriner (2008) reported that expressive writing performance was enhanced when six elementary aged students with EBD, or at risk for EBD, and served largely in inclusive settings, were presented with one-to-one SRSD strategy instruction by trained graduate students. These authors selected a strategy for teaching persuasive essays, referred to as POW + TREE (Topic sentence, Reasons – three or more-, Ending, Examine; see Harris, Graham, & Mason, 2006). After instruction, all students gained substantially in their abilities to create a persuasive essay.

To date, some evidence supports the use of SRSD as a positive strategy for improving writing in students with EBD; however, that evidence at present is largely confined to a relatively small number of primary or upper elementary students with, or at risk for EBD, served largely in general education classes, and taught in one-to-one settings. It is presently unknown whether, or how, such a model can be employed effectively in whole-class instruction with a population of secondary students with very serious EBD who receive services in special, separate settings. This appears to be a significant limitation of the literature to date, since students with EBD, frequently characterized as deficient in communication skills, perspective taking, reflective thinking, articulate self-expression, and using language in social situations (e.g., Furlong et al., 2004; Kauffman & Landrum, 2008), could potentially benefit enormously from increased written expression skills. Further, an increased ability to make a thoughtful, considered argument in writing, of the sort directly taught with the SRSD "POW + TREE" strategy, could be of particular benefit.

The present investigation was undertaken to determine how previous research using SRSD could be adapted for middle school aged students with serious emotional disabilities. This implementation took place in a separate setting school for students with serious emotional disabilities, and involved direct, daily classroom interaction with the students over an extensive time period. This paper describes the iterative decision-making process and development procedures employed, during the process of learning how to adapt instruction and instructional procedures to meet the needs of these students.

The present investigation employed quantitative and qualitative methods to study the processes of classroom instruction over time, as well as the outcomes associated with this instruction. This approach included many elements of "design experiment" or "design study" methodology (Brown, 1992; Collins, 1999; Palinscar, 2005), which is "based strongly on prior research and theory and carried out in educational settings, [and] seeks to trace the evolution of learning in complex, messy classrooms and schools…and produce instructional tools that survive the challenges of everyday practice" (Shavelson, Phillips, Towne, & Feuer, 2003, p. 25). Of particular interest in this investigation were the interactions between learner characteristics and instructional methods and materials; this methodological approach allowed us to make changes throughout the instructional period as needed, in order to study the learning process as it proceeded through several classroom and instructional modifications.

RESEARCH QUESTIONS

Specifically, the research questions addressed in the current investigation were:

1. Can the SRSD model of instruction for the POW + TREE persuasive writing strategy, used successfully in previous research with students with

learning disabilities, be adapted for middle school students with serious emotional and behavioral disorders served in a separate setting?
2. How do the characteristics of adolescent students with EBD interact with SRSD instruction?
3. What supports, inputs, interactions, and modifications are required to implement this SRSD POW+TREE strategy effectively with a population of adolescents with significant EBD?
4. What outcomes in writing performance are associated with SRSD instruction?

A design study-type approach was employed to address these research questions, because there was a need to explore the circumstances under which SRSD instruction could be effective, as well as to evaluate the potential effectiveness of the strategy itself. That is, given the student population, we were uncertain how many instructional sessions would be necessary, what structural arrangements would be needed, and what modifications or adjustments would be needed in order to facilitate optimal learning. We were also interested in observing the characteristics of the student population, and determining how these characteristics interacted with SRSD instruction as it was being implemented. With this design, we could not draw unequivocal causal conclusions; however, it was hoped that we would be able to gather evidence of importance to the implementation of SRSD instruction with adolescents with severe EBD, and to provide implications for further research with this population.

METHOD

Setting

This study was conducted in a specialized middle school for students with emotional and behavioral disorders in a large public school district in the eastern United States. This center was the most restrictive environment placement in the public school district of well over 100,000 students. All academic classes were taught by special education teachers and paraprofessionals who received training in the very explicit school-wide behavior management system. In addition, school counselors were present to provide ongoing counseling services to students. The middle school included seventh and eighth grade classes, and the class size ranged from 3 to 10 students per teacher and assistant. Students participated in four core classes

(English, science, math, and history), physical education, and two elective classes per day. All students participated in the state-wide high stakes testing and their scores were returned to their home schools. At the time of this investigation, there were approximately 68 students enrolled. Eighty-one percent were male and 18.82% were female. Ethnic and racial backgrounds of students were: 45.9% Caucasian, 27.1% African American, 17.7% Hispanic, 3.5% Asian, and 5.9% other. Forty-eight percent of the students participated in free and reduced lunch, and 22.4% were characterized as limited English proficient.

A positive behavioral support system using a point system and daily vouchers was consistently used throughout the school. Vouchers (individual point sheets) were tailor-made to identify idiosyncratic behaviors targeted for each student; generally, points were earned for preparedness, properly participating in classroom activities, appropriately asking for and accepting help, respecting others and property, and promoting emotional and physical safety. Vouchers were completed at the end of every class period by teachers. Teachers discussed with students why or why not points were received. Points earned daily accumulated and students earned participation privileges in end-of-week special activities.

Another way in which the school managed behavioral issues was through the use of time-out (Lewis, Lewis-Palmer, Newcomer, & Stichter, 2004), implemented when students were experiencing extreme difficulties controlling their behaviors. Students who were especially volatile were also provided with "flash passes" which could be used at any time during the day as a pass to the Crisis Response Center (CRC), where students could go when they were in crisis. Students were sent to CRC for fighting, drugs, gang-related activities, racial comments, stealing, or sexual comments. When this happened, students met with the CRC counselor and a determination was made regarding whether school detention or suspension was warranted. In-school detention and suspension also took place in CRC.

The school also provided the Pet Center, which housed various animals in a separate area within the school, and after-school programs such as art, video games, pets, *taekwondo*, fooze ball, and air hockey. Parent involvement also was an important part of the school's policy.

Sample

Students served in this special middle school had a wide range of behavioral and emotional needs. Some students had significant psychiatric issues, including depression, bipolar disorder, thought disorders, anxiety, oppositional defiant disorders, antisocial behavior, and Attention Deficit Hyperactivity Disorder (ADHD). It is common for students to have several co-existing disorders. For example, the majority of students were dually diagnosed with a psychological and a conduct disorder or ADHD; others had probation officers because of infractions with the legal system, in addition to their emotional and behavioral disorders. According to the principal, approximately 60–70% of the students were on some type of medication.

Ten, eighth grade students classified as having serious emotional disabilities were participants. Students were selected by the building administrators as needing assistance with explicit writing instruction. All students had been diagnosed with a variety of serious emotional and behavioral disabilities, including serious anxiety disorders. The sample included eight males and two females. Five students were Caucasian, three were African American, one was Hispanic, and one was from a mixed racial/ethnic background. Two of the students had emigrated from other countries. One student was dropped from the study because he was expelled from school for exhibiting aggressive behaviors toward his teachers during the course of the investigation. Another student's placement was changed to a less restrictive environment to his home school during the study, but this student still participated in posttesting. Students' pretest writing levels ranged from a third to an eleventh grade level on the Woodcock Johnson Writing Fluency subtest ($M = 6.5$, SD = 2.6) of the Woodcock Johnson III Tests of Achievement (WJ-III; Woodcock, McGrew, & Mather, 2001a, 2001b). Other WJ-III subtest standard scores similarly reflected below average mean performance, with wide variability: Written Language, 95.4 (SD = 14.0, range = 77–116); Math, 94.5 (SD = 12.7, range = 80–120); Broad Reading, 93.4 (SD = 13.2, range = 72–117); and Total Score, 93.8 (SD = 17.0, range = 75–120). Written essay performance, as assessed by the essay pretest (see Table 3), was low, with much less variability, across a number of criteria. Additional individual student demographic data obtained from school records are presented in Table 1.

Teacher

The middle aged African American female teacher was a fully licensed special education teacher with seven years experience working at this school. She had a master's degree in special education and a strong reputation in the school as a caring, supportive teacher who arranged successful class environments for students, while holding students to behavioral and

Table 1. Student Characteristics.

Student	Gender	Ethnicity	Age	Co-Morbidity with EBD	Problem Behaviors	Behavioral Goals
Alice	Female	African American	13.8	ADHD, and depression[1]	Externalizing and Internalizing	Interpersonal skills; tolerance level; and anger management
George	Male	Caucasian	14.8	Maladjustment[2]	Internalizing	Self-control (verbal and physical); participation in school tasks and activities
Richard	Male	African American	13.7	Negative moods[3]	Internalizing	Improve: appropriate interaction, keeping hands to himself, and accept teacher assistance and comply with teachers
Albert	Male	Multiracial	13.9	Autism, LD, OHI, and negative moods[1,2]	Externalizing and Internalizing	Develop age appropriate work behavior and improve: following directions, and interacting appropriately with adults and peers
Maria	Female	Caucasian	13.9	LD, anxieties, and depression[3,4]	Internalizing	Increase positive and respectful interactions with peers and adults
Sam	Male	Caucasian	14.3	LD and ADHD, depression, sleep disorders, and noncompliance[5,6]	Externalizing	Improve: accepting feedback, complying with teachers, develop appropriate ways of interacting, and reduce disruptive behaviors
Edward	Male	African American	14.0	Hyperactivity, depression, and aggression[2,3]	Externalizing and Internalizing	Decrease disruptive behaviors and participate responsibly in class
Tom	Male	African American	14.1	ADHD, and depression[7,8]	Externalizing and Internalizing	Improve and use coping strategies to comply with school routine and procedures
Bruno	Male	Caucasian	13.3	LD, SPL, and OHI, ADHD, depression, and anxieties[1,2]	Externalizing and Internalizing	Improve peer interactions and social skills
Jose	Male	Hispanic	13.7	Depression[3]	Internalizing	Maintain school appropriate interactions with peers, and keep body to self, and accept teacher assistance.

Notes: LD, Learning Disability; SPL, Speech and Language Disabilities; OHI, Other health Impairments; ADHD, Attention Deficit Hyperactivity Disorder.
[1]Children's Depression Inventory.
[2]Behavior Assessment System for Children, 2nd edition.
[3]Reynolds Adolescent Depression Scale.
[4]Revised Manifest Anxiety Scale.
[5]Conners Parent Rating Scale-Revised.
[6]Personality Inventory for Children, 2nd edition.
[7]Sentence Completion Test.
[8]Thematic Apperception Test.

curriculum standards. She was the assigned English teacher for these students and as such, had experience teaching writing to conform to the state standards of learning and regularly implemented writing instruction to students.

Project Staff

Project staff included a team of four university researchers, consisting of one Caucasian female faculty member and three advanced graduate students, all female (two Caucasian, one Hispanic), all of whom had experience working with individuals with disabilities in various settings and were enrolled in doctoral programs. All staff received extensive training in implementing SRSD prior to beginning the study.

Materials

All materials were based on those developed by Graham and Harris (e.g., 2005) and as modified by Mason and Shriner (2008) to work with students with EBD. The SRSD (Harris et al., 2008) provides supports in self-regulation such as goal setting, self-monitoring, self-instruction, and self-reinforcement while explicitly teaching strategies to facilitate writing performance. The specific SRSD strategy taught was the planning and writing for persuasive essays: POW+TREE, in which P = Pick my idea; O = Organize my notes; W = Write and say more; and T = Topic sentence – tell what you believe; R = Reasons (write three or more) – why do I believe this and will my readers believe this?; E = Ending – wrap it up; and E = Examine – do I have all my parts?

Student Materials

Student materials included notebook computers and paper folders that contained all student materials used throughout the project. The student materials included a student contract for learning, a POW+TREE chart containing all steps in the strategy, a graphic organizer of the POW+TREE strategy that contained spaces for students to write in their persuasive essay notes prior to writing the essay (see Fig. 1), a sheet containing transition words which could be used to assist in generating transitions while writing, a self-statement sheet which was used to help students reflect on ways to think of good ideas, what do think while working and when checking their work, self-evaluation essay charts, and copies of student printed essays. Students also all had wireless notebook PCs which were connected to a school-wide

TOPIC Sentence
Tell what you believe!

Yes__________

No__________

POW + TREE

Transition Words	R Reasons -3 or More Why do I believe this? Will my readers believe this?	E EXPLAIN Reasons Say more about each reason

E **ENDING**
Wrap it up right! DID YOU? __________
E **EXAMINE DID YOU?** __________

Fig. 1. Graphic Organizer.

network and were used throughout the study during all phases of writing the essays. Since all students used notebook PCs for all writing tasks before and after the study, this was not considered a new variable introduced in this project. When students experienced difficulties with their own notebook PCs, they used a larger PC located in the back of the room, or occasionally used paper and pencil.

Training Materials and Procedures
Teaching materials included all student materials as well as a detailed notebook containing all lesson plans for learning how to implement the

POW+TREE strategy based on those implemented in previous research (e.g., Mason & Shriner, 2008). Steps in the instructional sequence included the recommended SRSD stages of instruction, such as developing background knowledge and discussing it, modeling the strategy, memorizing the strategy, supporting the strategy with guided practice, and independent practice.

All teaching and project staff met together for training with experts in SRSD instruction. During this training, all materials from the lesson plans and notebooks were described, and videotaped model lessons from previous research studies were viewed. Instructors role played implementing lessons until criterion performance in implementing SRSD was obtained, by all project staff and the teacher. During instruction it became necessary sometimes to modify lessons based on student performance. When this happened, changes were discussed and shared electronically and in person with the teacher and all staff. An electronic web site was used to house copies of all lesson plans and any changes. Project staff met daily to review SRSD components, along with student performance and progress. Project staff also met four days a week with the teacher and periodically with building administrators who expressed a desire to be kept up to date with the study's progress. During teacher meetings all student performance data were reviewed, lessons and specific lesson components covered were addressed, specific issues with progress or lack of academic progress with specific students, and any behavioral issues were discussed. During meetings with the building administrators student progress was discussed, as well as any issues or upcoming schedule modifications due to field trips or school assemblies.

Procedures

After obtaining relevant Institutional Review Board approvals and student, parent and teacher consent, teacher and staff training, student pretesting took place, followed by instructional lessons, posttesting, and maintenance testing. Prior to the initiation of the research, project staff were in the school observing classes and students. This was done at the suggestion of the school administrators and teachers, to provide students with an opportunity to become familiar with the individuals who would be working with them in their classes. Instruction occurred approximately four days per week, from October through the last week in February, during a 29-min school-wide remediation period for a total of 55 sessions, or a total of 26.6 h of instruction over more than four months. (This implementation period was considerable longer than we had originally planned). Individual students received a mean number of 42.2 (SD = 5.8) days of instruction, with a range of 33.5–50 days. When students were not present in class for instruction they were frequently in school, but participating in other activities, such as the school crisis resource center, school suspension, play practice, meetings with mentors, student counsel association meetings, or meetings with other teachers.

The model of SRSD instruction was implemented to teach students how to write persuasive essays. Initially, the assigned classroom teacher delivered the instruction; however, over time project staff assumed more and more instructional responsibilities, until project staff were heavily involved in all of the daily instruction. This arrangement appeared more suitable to helping students move through the content to reach criterion and the independent stage of instruction. During instruction, project staff made continuous modifications and adjustments based on the individual emotional, behavioral, and learning needs of these students as described in the following text.

SRSD Instructional Procedures

SRSD instruction included the six phases of instruction: Develop Background Knowledge, Discuss It, Model It, Memorize It, Support It, and Independent Performance, while emphasizing throughout self-regulation, independent use, and student ownership. The instructional goal was to have students internalize self-regulation strategies and write persuasive essays independently. Initially instruction was delivered and lessons directed by the teacher. However, instruction was carefully scaffolded to have students gradually gain ownership of the strategy. During stage 1, students acquired the knowledge for using the POW+TREE strategy to write persuasive essays. The POW component consisted of a general planning and organizing strategy, while the TREE component provided specific steps for writing a persuasive essay. Students practiced learning the planning and writing strategy acronym, what it represented and discussed background knowledge. During the second stage of instruction: Discuss it, students continued with learning the specific acronym of POW+TREE, remembering what each component represented. Sample persuasive essays were reviewed and students practiced identifying sections of model essays.

During the third stage of instruction, Model it, the teacher modeled the entire planning and writing process using self-statements and the graphic organizer. The teacher modeled think aloud self-statements while she planned out each step involved in using POW+TREE from selecting the topic, to generating ideas for the organizer, to beginning writing.

For example, the teacher used statements, such as "What do I believe?" "What is the next step I have to do?" "Did I answer all the questions?" And "I like that idea." to model planning, self-evaluation, and self-reinforcement throughout the process. Students also completed their own self-statement charts that could be referred to during subsequent lessons. During the planning, a large graphic organizer was placed on the board, and students assisted with generating ideas that were written on the organizer. Goal setting was also introduced and students were taught that part of the goal for persuasive essay writing was to ensure that all components (topic sentence, three or more reasons, explanations for reasons, and ending) of the essay were completed.

During the fourth stage of instruction, Memorize it, students demonstrated that they had learned what the strategy steps were for writing persuasive essays. In this case, all students were required to state POW+TREE and describe what each component represented.

The fifth stage of instruction: Support it, consisted of collaborative writing. During this stage, students worked collaboratively with the teacher and writing was monitored by both students and teacher. At first, the class selected an essay prompt from two options, but as instruction moved to the independent stage students selected their own essay prompts from the two provided.

Initial Days of Instruction

The first day of instruction, the teacher introduced the study, explained what would happen, and presented students with learning contracts to sign. The "Writing to Persuade Learning Contract" contained students' names, the date with target completion dates, the goal, how to meet the goal, signatures of both the student and teacher for the initial contract, and signature lines for both students and teachers and completion dates when instruction was successfully completed.

During the first day of instruction, all 10 students were present. The desks were spaced in rows on the left and right hand side of the room, but shaped into a large semicircle with several students sitting in the back row across the room. The teacher's desk was in the front left corner of the room and the paraprofessional's desk was in the back right side of the room. There were several personal computers along the back wall of the room, an overhead projector, and notebook computer projector at the front of the room, and white board across the front classroom wall. This general seating arrangement remained constant across the majority of the study. Students kept their assigned seats while in this room.

Collaborative Decision-Making

Since the project goal was to have students learn to use the POW+TREE strategy independently, all discussions and decision-making were focused on how to improve student learning and performance. Project staff met daily after instruction, and with the teacher and school administrators on a regular basis, to assess student learning and performance. Daily field notes, observational data, attendance records, student performance data, and videotaped records were used to assess procedures, methods, and materials. When student learning appeared to be progressing at a slower than expected rate, decisions were made to modify and adjust instruction. A collaborative decision-making process was employed, whereby all parties participated in, and agreed on instructional modifications. For example, when students had not yet achieved criterion level performance within the originally scheduled study completion date, administrators agreed to, and facilitated re-scheduling of classes to allow the instruction to proceed beyond the originally agreed-upon completion date. In order to accomplish this, project staff met with teachers and administrators, all student performance data and progress to date was reviewed, and discussion was held on how to best meet the original goal of having students meet criterion with the writing strategy. Also, the teacher's input was considered in delaying student re-grouping until a time when it was thought re-grouping would be less intrusive.

Data Sources and Scoring

All students were pre- and posttested on the Writing Fluency subtest of the Woodcock Johnson III (WJ-III), as well as the Oral and Written Language Scales (OWLS) (Carrow-Woolfolk, 1996). Prior to and subsequent to instruction, students were also provided with two essay prompts, asked to select one and write essays in response to the prompts. A delayed posttest was also administered to assess maintenance, approximately 12 weeks subsequent to posttesting. All essay testing procedures were identical. In addition, students were individually interviewed regarding their knowledge of the POW+TREE strategy, their perceptions of the strategy instruction, and generalized use of the writing strategies.

Essay Scoring

Four independent scorers read and scored each essay individually. Scorers met to assess inter-rater reliability, and discussed disagreements until they were resolved. The resulting inter-rater reliability was 98%. Each essay was scored using a holistic rubric with a scale from 0 to 10. A score of 0 was given for no essay parts, and 10 for a complete essay. A complete essay had to include the following components: (a) topic sentence; (b) more than three reasons with explanations; (c) ending sentence; and (d) a logical sequence of writing, including at least one counter argument. In addition, each essay was scored by number of words, paragraphs, transition words, and parts of the essay, including: topic sentence, each reason, each explanation, each counterargument, and an ending sentence.

On-Task Behavior

A time sampling procedure (Alberto & Troutman, 2008) was used to record students' on and off-task behaviors during 30-s intervals for 15 min of most class periods. When the class was split into two separate groups later in the implementation period, each class was observed for 10-min intervals, at varying times throughout the period. Trained observers sat in the front of the room where they could see the faces of all students, and used handheld devices with earphones to listen to audio recordings of "tapping sounds" every 30-s to prompt accurate coding. Coding was completed using handheld devices and/or paper-pencils. In addition, since there was a great deal of mobility in and out of the room by individual students, time individual students were out of the room was also coded. Students could be out of the room during the period for a number of reasons, including being in time-out or seeing a counselor or another teacher, or even attending student council meetings. Student attention to task was operationally defined as the following:

(a) student is in designated area of room,
(b) student is manually engaged with appropriate materials,
(c) student is reading/writing to the writing prompts,
(d) student refrains from making derogatory comments about task/other,
(e) student asks relevant question(s) to adult(s), as needed,
(f) student maintains focus on appropriate task and/or the writing tools, and
(g) student may appear in thought by intermittently and quietly looking away from material and not writing (engaged only with self not with others).

Other Data Sources

Throughout the implementation period, video cameras were employed daily to create a visual record of class activities. These recordings were reviewed regularly by project staff to assist with understanding the instructional process. In addition, copious field notes were taken throughout the investigation to document characteristics of the students, and their responses to instruction. Staff met daily to make reflections on these data sources. Teacher, student, and administrator interviews were also conducted, to gain further insights on the implementation of SRSD instruction, and for triangulation with other data sources.

Fidelity of Treatment Implementation
Fidelity of treatment checklists during instructional lessons were used by trained observers. The checklists were designed to match the original lesson plans and contained all of the critical elements for each lesson. For example, for Lesson 1 (POW+TREE), the fidelity checklist contained elements relevant to the five components of the lesson: (a) state purpose and define "persuade"; (b) Describe and discuss POW; (c) Discuss what makes writing to persuade powerful; (d) Introduce TREE – uncover the rest of the chart; (e) Read and examine all elements of a writing to persuade paper; and (f) Lesson wrap-up and return materials. Examination of checklists indicated that the instruction had been delivered with a high degree of fidelity ($M = 96$, range 90–100%).

Data Analyses

Qualitative Analysis
Video recordings, field notes, notes of group meetings, and interviews were analyzed in order to determine how the student characteristics appeared to interact with instructional methods and materials in this investigation. All data were examined recursively using techniques of analytic induction and the constant comparative method. Analytic induction "involves scanning the data for categories of phenomena and for relationships among such categories, developing working typologies and hypotheses upon an examination of initial cases, then modifying and refining them on the basis of subsequent cases" (LeCompte & Preissle, 1993, p. 254). These processes were undertaken in order to generate general concepts or themes that characterized writing strategy instruction with this sample of students with severe emotional and behavioral disorders.

Quantitative Analysis
Pretest, posttest, and maintenance measures of achievement tests and essay writing were compared statistically by means of the Wilcoxon

matched-pairs, signed ranks test (Siegel & Castellan, 1988). Nonparametric were employed throughout, as the criterion of homogeneity of variance was frequently not met, largely because of apparent floor effects on pretests. For this reason also, effect size data for criterion measures were calculated using posttest or maintenance standard deviations. On-task data were analyzed descriptively.

RESULTS AND DISCUSSION

This investigation was implemented over a considerable portion of the school year, and involved ongoing data collection involving a variety of measures. Results are reported and discussed in the following sections with respect to (a) structural classroom modifications undertaken throughout the implementation period; (b) ongoing modifications made as a consequence of observed student characteristics; (c) results of observational data; (d) results of outcome measures including standardized tests and criterion essay measures; (e) descriptive writing outcomes; (f) student strategy scores; and (g) student, teacher, and administrator reports. Each is described, in sequence, as follows.

Structural Classroom Modifications

The present implementation was intended to determine and describe the optimal conditions for delivery of SRSD instruction with adolescents with severe EBD; consequently, a number of modifications in instruction were made on an ongoing basis in response to classroom situations. These modifications included adaptations in instruction, materials, and activities. That is, instruction began as conducted by the regularly assigned classroom teacher. However, due to the fact student learning was not proceeding as rapidly as felt necessary, after about five weeks, it was determined that instruction would be undertaken by the university research team, on a whole-class basis. Later, after about 12 total weeks of instruction, it was determined that it would be more appropriate to divide the class into two groups, using an additional available classroom, again led by the university research team. This was done to address the substantial heterogeneity in academic skills in the group, and also to create two separate groups that would interact more appropriately. Specifically, one individual student frequently exerted a negative influence on the behavior of several of the lower-achieving students during whole-class instruction, often encouraging off-task and noncompliant behavior. However, when moved to a smaller, more homogeneous group of higher-achieving students, this student participated much more appropriately. This revised instructional model was then followed throughout the remainder of the investigation.

Modifications were also made on instructional materials. For example, the graphic organizer used by all students was modified to include a column for "explanations." Also, essays were written with missing parts, for students to identify missing essay elements. This was done to provide an "identification" level of learning essay parts, to provide an additional step and further facilitate later acquisition of the strategy on the "production" level (Mastropieri & Scruggs, 2009).

Finally, one major structural modification made during this investigation was to extend the instructional period approximately two months beyond the original target date for completion of the project (before winter recess). This modification was made because students, although learning, were not moving as rapidly through the lessons as originally anticipated. The reasons for the slower overall pace of instruction were thought to be related to observed student characteristics, as described in the following section.

Student Characteristics and Instructional Modifications

Many instructional modifications were made throughout the course of the investigation, in response to the presenting characteristics of the students in this investigation. These characteristics, and corresponding modifications as they evolved throughout the investigation, are described in the following paragraphs.

Cognitive Organization

Similar to the students with learning disabilities on which much prior SRSD research is based (Graham & Harris, 2003), students in the present investigation demonstrated relative deficits in organized conceptual thinking relevant to composing a persuasive essay. Although this finding may have been a manifestation of a more generalized academic deficit common in students with EBD (Lane, 2004), examination of pretest essay scores revealed substantial limitations in number of essay parts, transition words, and number of paragraphs written, all of which are indicative of a lack of careful, organized thinking, and which led to the overall low holistic writing score at pretest (see pretest data in Table 3). Lack of clear and comprehensive thinking about a topic may also lead to a minimal number of words written. For example, one student wrote the following for his pretest essay: "Kids my age should be able to have cell phones because we can use it for emergencies or to call friends." Although sensible, this pretest represents a simple and rather obvious statement rather than an essay, and, beyond simple sentence and semantic structure, contains virtually no organization as a persuasive presentation. In response to the prompt, "Should students your age go to school in the summer?", another student wrote, "Because they should enjoy the summer time they earned it. I'm not sure but not in school because they should learn in school."

SRSD as applied in this investigation seemed particularly appropriate for addressing this characteristic, since the strategy (in this case, POW+TREE) directly targets cognitive organization in the conceptualization and execution of the persuasive essay. However, given other characteristics of this student population, additional modifications to implementation were necessary.

Disorders of Anxiety and Affect

Also described as internalizing disorders (Gresham & Kern, 2004), problems with anxiety or affect interacted negatively with instruction throughout this investigation. For example, some students were so quietly withdrawn it was often unclear whether they were covertly participating in the lesson. As project staff circulated the room to answer individual questions and to assist with task completion, it became clear that some students became anxious and did not want "teachers" very close to them. For example, Albert frequently made statements such as, "You are too close to me!" Other students appeared shy and unsure of their work. For example, Tom frequently put his arms over his work, closing his computer and covering everything he had written, whenever the teacher or staff approached, and sometimes swearing at university staff when they approached. On occasion, he deliberately manipulated his computer to make it freeze. Such behaviors were addressed throughout the investigation by allowing students sufficient personal space for their comfort when necessary, while still maintaining expectations of individual effort. At the same time, alternative times were identified for target students when it was possible to examine students' work and provide feedback with less discomfort to the student.

Other disorders of anxiety seemed less pronounced. For example, George was typically very quiet and withdrawn. He made no eye contact, and frequently appeared not to be listening. However, with some degree of patience on the part of teacher and staff, George was observed re-visiting his paper and making changes after re-direction, but without speaking.

Albert repeatedly exhibited discomfort with the video camera, although it appeared to influence his work less as the investigation progressed over time. Albert did, however, obsessively sharpen pencils, keeping them in the pencil sharpener until reduced to only small stubs.

Disorders of mood also played a significant role in instruction. When asked to work, Maria once replied, "Okay, but you know it depends on how I feel behavior-wise." Her affect often became negative, and directly inhibited her willingness to work. She brooded about perceived injustices for extensive time periods. For example, one day she was denied a small reward because of inappropriate behavior during writing instruction, and for the next two months she repeatedly brought up this perceived injustice to project staff. Another example is seen in an entry from class field notes:

> Maria was beginning a new graphic organizer. After filling in the first line, she said, "I messed up," and crumpled up the paper. We looked at the paper later and saw that she had written the topic sentence in the space for Reason 1. On the bottom of the paper she had scrawled, "Son of a bitch."

When it was announced that the writing instruction was going to be extended beyond that originally planned, Maria demanded to speak with the principal, and made empty threats.

Sam's affect often inhibited his writing performance. He once reported, "I have a lot on my mind and it is hard to focus." The teacher and project staff accommodated disorders of mood by developing a sense, over time, of when to allow students time to regain their composure, and when to direct students to return to task. Students themselves also accommodated these moods, sometimes asking to go to "time-out" to calm themselves.

Disorders of Perception

Disorders of perception in the form of fantasies or unrealistic thinking can have a significant inhibiting impact on student learning (see Kauffman, 2005; Kauffman & Landrum, 2008). Although a less common classroom problem in this investigation, one student in particular frequently exhibited disorders of perception of reality, often drifting into fantasy and speaking openly of a bizarre "outer world"; much of his thinking and schoolwork revolved around details of life on an imaginary planet. Such thinking served to prevent the student from focusing his attention on his writing assignments, and also at times served to separate him from other students in the class. This fantasizing was responded to by teacher and staff with understanding, inhibiting ridicule of other students, and frequently encouraging the student to retain focus on the writing task, and to re-direct his thinking to "real world" topics.

Disorders of Aggression

Aggressive conduct disorders are among the most difficult problems exhibited by students with EBD (Furlong et al., 2004). These characteristics were frequently observed in most classroom sessions, were exhibited by most students on different occasions, and included expressions of anger, animosity, noncompliant behavior, and aggression against other students or teachers. One student, in fact, was removed from the setting during the course of this investigation as a consequence of violent, aggressive behavior exhibited toward other teachers in the school. Many of the students spoke aggressively to other students or teachers, refused to do schoolwork, or acted aggressively toward others. Sam, for example, exhibited erratic behavior, and frequently moved or re-arranged materials on Alice's desk, simply because Alice became very upset when others touched her possessions. Following is an entry from class field notes:

> Alice came into the classroom, and called Maria, "little bitch." Maria responded, and Richard got involved. Alice disrupted the class throughout the whole period. The teacher had to stay with Alice in the hallway while she screamed, kicked the door, and made derogatory remarks. Maria and Richard were arguing with her from inside the classroom. Tom, who was working diligently, became frustrated and angry because he could not concentrate. The same happened with Albert. Alice's behavior was so outrageous that she got everyone off task and anxious.

Aggressive behaviors exerted a substantial negative influence on academic engagement, and the aggressive behaviors of an individual student often resulted in several other students, or the entire class, losing focus on academics. Teachers and staff intervened on aggressive behavior in several different ways, including looking for "triggers" that predicted aggressive behavior and taking preventative measures, allowing students space and time to calm down when appropriate, allowing students to refer themselves to time-out, allocating additional levels of teacher or staff supervision, and removing students from the classroom to meet with counselors when necessary. For example, at the beginning of one class period, Alice spent most of the class time wandering around the room, talking loudly, misbehaving, and disrupting others. After several minutes of this behavior, research staff sat with her and encouraged her to work. As a consequence, in time Alice was able to finish her prompt, label the essay parts, graph her progress, and begin brainstorming for the next prompt. Although extensive in terms of the staff resources allocated to Alice in this situation, this level of supervision, with research staff sitting right next to her, allowed her to stay in class and complete her work, rather than simply being sent out of the classroom.

Implications

Although the cognitive, affective, and behavioral characteristics of the students in the class were accommodated effectively and relatively efficiently by the teacher and project staff, the overall impact on overall academic engagement was substantial, as described in the following section. In large part, these characteristics all contributed to the extensive allocated time period necessary for the students to learn and master the SRSD strategy for writing persuasive essays.

On-Task Data

Students were observed throughout the investigation for on-task behavior, and time spent out of the room. Reliability of observation was .95 as calculated by agreements divided by total observations. Overall, it was noted that the proportion of on-task behavior was adequate ($M = 86\%$; $SD = 21\%$; range $= 68$–99%) during the time students spent in class. However, the amount of time students spent out of the classroom, largely because of time-out, CRC, or absences, was quite substantial ($M = 32\%$; $SD = 42\%$; range $= 10$–50%), and represented a significant challenge. Overall, mean student on-task behavior, counting time spent out of class, was 62% ($SD = 17\%$). Given the established relation between academic time-on-task and academic achievement (e.g., Mastropieri & Scruggs, 2004), this level of academic engagement clearly played an inhibiting role in instruction. The degree to which on-task data taken during writing instruction differed from student engagement at other periods of the school day is uncertain; however, according to teacher reports, amount of time spent out of the classroom was similar throughout the day.

Standardized Tests

Student standardized test scores, and corresponding statistics, are presented in Table 2. As can be seen, students made statistically significant gains on the fluency subtest of the WJ-III, with a moderate effect size (ES) of .67. Although a small descriptive gain was observed on the OWLS measure

(ES = .15), this difference was not statistically significant. This lack of reliable gain on the OWLS was attributed to the relatively low level of concordance between the measure and the strategy being taught, with only a single item on the measure of direct relevance.

Criterion Writing Tests

Scores on the criterion measures of essay components demonstrated large, statistically significant effects on nearly all measures, as presented in Table 3. Students' posttest and three-month maintenance test scores indicated large and consistent increases over pretest scores on measures of number of words written, number of essay parts, number of paragraphs, number of transition

Table 2. Achievement Data Results.

Test	Pretest Mean (SD)	Posttest Mean (SD)
Woodcock Johnson Fluency	18.40 (5.04)	21.78 (4.99)[a]
OWLS	88.40 (11.89)	89.88 (8.13)

[a]Significantly greater than pretest, $p<.05$, according to the Wilcoxon Matched-Pairs, Signed Ranks Test.

Table 3. Essay Results.

Essay Components	Pretest Mean (SD) ($N = 10$)	Posttest Mean (SD) ($N = 9$)	Maintenance Mean (SD) ($N = 6$)
Number of words	82.80 (67.75)	230.78 (115.78)[b] ES[a] = 1.28	174.17 (83.25)[c] ES = 1.10
Number of parts	3.90 (1.52)	7.61 (2.52)[b] ES = 1.47	6.50 (1.23)[c] ES = 2.11
Number of paragraphs	1.16 (.95)	4.78 (1.47)[b] ES = 2.46	3.42 (1.39)[c] ES = 1.63
Transition words	1.50 (1.51)	10.33 (5.00)[b] ES = 1.77	3.50 (3.02) ES = .66
Holistic scoring	3.2 (1.40)	5.44 (1.67)[c] ES = 1.40	4.67 (1.86)[c] ES = .79

[a]ES, Effect size using posttest or maintenance SD.
[b]Significantly greater than pretest, $p<.01$, according to the Wilcoxon Matched-Pairs, Signed Ranks Test.
[c]Significantly greater than pretest, $p<.05$, according to the Wilcoxon Matched-Pairs, Signed Ranks Test.

words, and on holistic scoring of the quality of the essay. Effect sizes were generally quite large, with an overall mean of 1.47 (range = .66–2.46). These values correspond favorably to a standardized mean effect size of 1.15 overall for SRSD instruction, in a meta-analysis reported by Graham and Perrin (2007).

Descriptive Results

In addition to the quantitative results of the SRSD intervention, some very obvious results of the strategy can be observed in the examination of student written products prior to and subsequent to the instruction. These differences were obvious with all students in this investigation. As an example, Table 4 presents Maria's first essay, followed by her essay written after instruction in the SRSD POW+TREE strategy. In this example, the

Table 4. Maria's Pre- and Posttest Writing Samples.

First Essay ("Should students have cell phones?"):

Children from the ages 10 and up should have cell phones. When children need to call there parents or 911 they need to have a cell phone. Like if I broke my leg, And couldn't move what would I do sit there? I would need help and what would I do if no one else was around. I would need too call for support or help. All these reasons and more are why we need a cell phone.

Second Essay ("Would you rather be given a sweater or a gift card as a gift?"):

I would rather receive a 30$ gift card than a sweater as a present because, you have more options, it's less humiliating, cooler, more ordinary, and gift cards are more popular.

First, with a gift card you have more options. You can get what you want. You can get more than just a sweater. Plus, you can spend it on what you want rather than have someone pick you out a tacky sweater.

Second, getting a gift card is a lot less humiliating. Because, when you get a sweater from your grandmother, you are going to get laughed at rather you like it or not by all your friends. You are defiantly going to look and feel weird. Plus, everyone in school is going to criticize you.

Third, gift cards are a lot cooler that stupid sweaters. You can use the gift cards with your friends if you want. Then you can use the gift card just about anywhere. Plus, with a sweater you don't have to feel pressured to tell everyone that your grandmother got you the stupid sweater and that she made you were it to school.

Fourth, a gift card is a normal gift. A sweater is not. Plus, gift cards don't itch you to death like stupid sweaters do. Then gift cards don't suffocate you I swear that who ever designed the sweater made it as a touchier device.

Fifth, gift cards are very popular. Everyone has had a gift card at leased once in there lives. So, you don't have to feel out of date with the times. Plus, if you have no use for it you can give it to someone else without feeling embarrassed about it.

In conclusion, give a gift card as a gift not a sweater. There great to have and they won't embarrass you. Therefore, gift cards are much better gifts than sweaters.

very substantial difference in essay length (in this case, 78 vs. 313 words), organization, and quality is clearly represented, and is similar to the differences observed on all students in this investigation. (See also two additional examples in the appendix.)

Strategy Data

Subsequent to writing final essays, students were interviewed on their strategy knowledge. Eight students were available for these interviews for the posttest, and six for the delayed maintenance test. In the post interview, seven of eight students were able to retell all seven components of the strategy, and the eighth student was able to retell all components with prompting. When asked to re-create the graphic organizer, four students re-created all components, three re-created all except one component, and the eighth student re-created all except two components. When asked whether they had applied elements of this strategy in other situations, two students reported they had done so in science class, two in English class, and four reported applying the strategy in multiple classes.

In the surprise maintenance interview, conducted approximately three months after the end of instruction, five of six students were able to retell all seven components of the strategy, and the sixth student was able to retell all components with prompting. When asked to re-create the graphic organizer, three students re-created five components, one re-created four components, and two students re-created three components. When asked whether they had applied elements of this strategy in other situations, three students reported they had done so in multiple classes, two reported employing the strategy for personal use, and one reported not employing the strategy elsewhere.

Student, Teacher, and Administrator Interviews

There was general agreement on the part of all participants that the SRSD strategy had been effective in improving the writing skills of students in the class. For example, in interviews, Edward reported, "[POW+TREE] has helped me to get done with my work faster...You can think and look back at your notes. You don't have to think while you're typing." Maria stated, "[POW+TREE] has helped me get less stressed out. It has helped me organize my thoughts...[POW+TREE] changed my opinion [about writing]. Before, writing was just like a hobby, something I liked to do. Now, I can see actually being able to get a job with writing…I use [my organizer] in every period now." For example, describing writing a paper on energy in science class, Maria stated, "Everybody was having trouble and I explained [POW+TREE] to Jay. Jay liked it." Edward stated, "[It] made me explain my sentences more better for people to understand. Also to make sure I read through my work and check to see if I made any mistakes and to make corrections, to see if it makes sense to me and to others." All student comments were generally positive about the writing strategy they had been taught.

The teacher and administrator reports were similarly positive. The teacher stated, "Without question, POW TREE helped weak writers by giving them a structured format for essays. For on-grade level writers, it helped them know where they needed to expand their supporting details and how to organize the information." The administrator also acknowledged the importance of the SRSD strategy, and its potential for all students in the school.

CONCLUSIONS

The results of this investigation provided preliminary evidence for the challenges of teaching SRSD strategies to middle school students with significant EBD, as well as the very substantial positive benefits that may result from these strategies, appropriately taught. In this investigation, in spite of numerous affective and behavioral challenges, students learned the POW+TREE writing strategy and employed it to significantly improve their writing of persuasive essays. Students improved in all elements of essay writing, including number of words written, number of paragraphs written, number of transition words, number of essay parts, and overall quality of writing as measured by holistic scoring. In addition, students gained statistically on a standardized measure of writing fluency, although scores on another standardized writing measure were apparently not influenced. Reports of all participants related the observed gains to the instruction, and all indicated the particular strengths of the writing strategy.

Results of student scores on standardized and criterion measures represent gain over time, without reference to a control or comparison group. For this reason, final causal conclusions can not be drawn. However, it seems probable, if not certain, that the observed gains were associated with instruction in the SRSD strategy, for the following reasons:

1. Large, statistically significant gains were observed in nearly all relevant test scores, coupled with a high degree of concordance between the structure of the essays produced and the strategy taught.
2. Students were able to describe, discuss, and apply the strategies when asked.
3. Teacher, administrator, and student reports supported the efficacy of SRSD instruction.
4. Outcomes of the present intervention were closely aligned with those of previous SRSD research with typically achieving students and students with learning disabilities (e.g., Graham & Harris, 2003).

Research literature has consistently documented the academic deficits of students with EBD, although the reasons for these deficits are not entirely clear. However, it seems possible that problems with cognitive organization, anxiety and affect, perceptions of reality, and aggressive conduct disorders interact negatively with opportunities to learn, on an ongoing basis, resulting in lower achievement in many academic areas. Indeed, such difficulties were observed continuously throughout this investigation, and seemed very directly linked to the substantial time spent off-task, or out of the classroom altogether. Although the teacher and project staff were able to accommodate these characteristics to a great extent, considerable instructional time was lost in the process. The strategy was very successfully taught, and learned, by the end of this intervention; however, students' affective and behavioral characteristics contributed to the necessity for extending the instruction considerably beyond the amount of time usually allocated to other students (e.g., students with learning disabilities) to learn the same strategies (see Harris, Graham, Brindle, & Sandmel, in press). Such results provide a possible explanation for the consistent findings of low academic achievement scores of students with EBD (Lane, 2004; Lane et al., 2008; Scruggs & Mastropieri, 1986).

A moderate level of task engagement (86%) was obtained during the time students were in class, possibly assisted by the number of teachers, and small group instruction employed throughout the investigation. However, overall engagement was lowered significantly by student absences from class, often because of disruptive behavior; this lowered level of overall engagement probably contributed substantially to the overall slowed pace of instruction. Clearly, SRSD instruction in itself did not resolve these longstanding behavior problems. However, it also became clear that behavioral self-control in itself was not the immediate cause of observed student deficiencies in written expression. All students demonstrated substantial limitations in ability to structure and organize a persuasive argument, and to present a clearly expressed opinion in writing to a reader. The structured, systematic training embedded in the SRSD strategy was observed to interact very positively with these characteristics, and to provide opportunities for substantial improvement in cognitive organization and writing skills.

In light of the relative shortage of research on writing instruction for students with EBD (Lane, 2004), the present results contribute substantially to our knowledge of writing instruction with this population, and how the characteristics of the students interact with the characteristics of instruction. Although the present results seemed very positive, the one-group design leaves open the question whether a different method of instruction might have been even more effective, or whether alternative means of addressing behavioral challenges would have resulted in superior outcomes. Future research, including experimental models with random assignment and comparison conditions, could provide further information on instruction to improve writing of persuasive essays, or other types of writing, by students with EBD. Future research could also consider instruction on an individual or more homogeneous small-group level, to determine whether this is more efficient. Finally, since some decrement was observed on the three-month maintenance scores, relative to posttest scores, a brief review or booster session implemented prior to maintenance testing might demonstrate the extent to which strategy use may be enhanced over time. At present, however, it can be argued that the SRSD strategies for writing, with appropriate supports, hold considerable promise for improving the academic skills of students with emotional or behavioral disorders.

ACKNOWLEDGMENTS

Partial support for this research was provided by grants: Grant No. R324A070199-07 from the U.S. Department of Education, Institute of Educational Sciences, awarded to The Pennsylvania State University with a subcontract to George Mason University and Grant No. H325D070008 from the U.S. Department of Education, Office of Special Education Programs awarded to George Mason University.

REFERENCES

Adkins, M. H. (2005). *Self-regulated strategy development and generalization instruction: Effects on story writing among second and third grade students with emotional and behavioral disorders* (Unpublished doctoral dissertation). University of Maryland, College Park (AAT 3202407).

Alberto, P. A., & Troutman, A. C. (2008). *Applied behavior analysis for teachers* (8th ed.). Upper Saddle River, NJ: Prentice Hall.

Brown, A. L. (1992). Design experiments: Theoretical and methodological challenges in creating complex interventions. *Journal of the Learning Sciences*, *2*, 141–178.

Carrow-Woolfolk, E. (1996). *Oral and written language scales: Written expression scale manual*. Circle Pines, MN: American Guidance Service.

Collins, A. (1999). Toward a design science of education. In: E. Scanlon & T. O'Shea (Eds), *New directions in educational technology*. New York: Springer-Verlag.

Epstein, M. H., & Cullinan, D. (1983). Academic performance of behaviorally disordered and learning-disabled pupils. *Journal of Special Education*, *17*, 303–307.

Furlong, M. J., Morrison, G. M., & Jimerson, S. R. (2004). Externalizing behaviors of aggression and violence and the school context. In: R. B. Rutherford, M. M. Quinn & S. R. Mathur (Eds), *Handbook of research in emotional and behavioral disorders* (pp. 243–261). New York: Guilford Press.

Graham, S., & Harris, K. R. (2003). Students with learning disabilities and the process of writing: A meta-analysis of SRSD studies. In: H. L. Swanson, K. R. Harris & S. Graham (Eds), *Handbook of learning disabilities* (pp. 323–344). New York: Guilford Press.

Graham, S., & Harris, K. R. (2005). *Writing better: Effective strategies for teaching students with learning difficulties*. Baltimore, MD: Brookes.

Graham, S., & Perrin, D. (2007). A meta-analysis of writing instruction for adolescent students. *Journal of Educational Psychology*, *99*, 445–476.

Gresham, F. M., & Kern, L. (2004). Internalizing behavior problems in children and adolescents. In: R. B. Rutherford, M. M. Quinn & S. R. Mathur (Eds), *Handbook of research in emotional and behavioral disorders* (pp. 262–281). New York: Guilford Press.

Harris, K. R., Graham, S., Brindle, M., & Sandmel, K. (in press). Metacognition and children's writing. In: D. J. Hacker, J. Dunlosky & A. C. Graesser (Eds), *Handbook of metacognition in education*. Mahwah, NJ: Lawrence Erlbaum Associates.

Harris, K. R., Graham, S., & Mason, L. H. (2006). Improving the writing performance, knowledge, and motivation of struggling writers in second grade: The effects of self-regulated strategy development. *American Educational Research Journal*, *42*, 295–340.

Harris, K. R., Graham, S., Mason, L. H., & Friedlander, B. (2008). *Powerful writing strategies for all students*. Baltimore, MD: Brookes.

Kauffman, J. M. (2005). *Characteristics of emotional and behavioral disorders of children and youth* (8th ed.). Upper Saddle River, NJ: Pearson/Merrill Prentice Hall.

Kauffman, J. M., & Landrum, T. J. (2008). *Characteristics of emotional and behavioral disorders of children and youth* (9th ed.). Upper Saddle River, NJ: Prentice Hall.

Lane, K. L. (2004). Academic instruction and tutoring interventions for students with emotional/behavioral disorders: 1990 to present. In: R. B. Rutherford, M. M. Quinn & S. R. Mathur (Eds), *Handbook of research in emotional and behavioral disorders* (pp. 462–486). New York: Guilford Press.

Lane, K. L., Barton-Arwood, S. M., Nelson, J. R., & Wehby, J. (2008). Academic performance of students with emotional and behavioral disorders served in a self-contained setting. *Journal of Behavioral Education, 17*, 43–62.

Lane, K. L., Harris, K. R., Graham, S., Weisenbach, J. L., Brindle, M., & Morphy, P. (2008). The effects of self-regulated strategy development on the writing performance of second-grade students with behavioral and writing difficulties. *Journal of Special Education, 41*, 234–253.

Lane, K. L., Wehby, J. H., Little, M. A., & Cooley, C. (2005a). Academic, social, and behavioral profiles of students with emotional and behavioral disorders educated in self-contained classrooms and self-contained schools: Part I – Are they more alike than different? *Behavioral Disorders, 30*, 349–361.

Lane, K. L., Wehby, J. H., Little, M. A., & Cooley, C. (2005b). Students educated in self-contained classrooms and self-contained schools: Part II – How do they progress over time?. *Behavioral Disorders, 30*, 363–374.

LeCompte, M. D., & Preissle, J. (1993). *Ethnography and qualitative design in educational research* (2nd ed.). New York: Academic/Elsevier.

Lewis, T. J., Lewis-Palmer, T., Newcomer, L., & Stichter, J. (2004). Applied behavior analysis and the education and treatment of students with emotional and behavioral disorders. In: R. B. Rutherford, M. M. Quinn & S. R. Mathur (Eds), *Handbook of research in emotional and behavioral disorders* (pp. 523–545). New York: Guilford Press.

Mason, L. H., Harris, K. R., & Graham, S. (2002). Every child has a story to tell: Self-regulated strategy development for story writing. *Education and Treatment of Children, 25*, 496–506.

Mason, L. H., & Shriner, J. (2008). Self-regulated strategy development instruction for six elementary students with emotional behavioral disorders. *Reading and Writing: An Interdisciplinary Journal, 21*, 71–93.

Mastropieri, M. A., & Scruggs, T. E. (2004). Effective classroom instruction. In: C. Spielberger (Ed.), *Encyclopedia of applied psychology* (pp. 687–691). Oxford, UK: Elsevier.

Mastropieri, M. A., & Scruggs, T. E. (2009). *The inclusive classroom: Strategies for effective instruction* (4th ed.). Upper Saddle River, NJ: Prentice Hall.

Nelson, R. J., Benner, G. J., Lane, K., & Smith, B. W. (2004). Academic achievement of k-12 students with emotional and behavioral disorders. *Exceptional Children, 71*, 59–73.

Nelson, J. R., Benner, G. J., & Rogers-Adkinson, D. L. (2003). An investigation of the characteristics of k-12 students with comorbid emotional disturbance and significant language deficits served in public school settings. *Behavioral Disorders, 29*, 25–33.

Palinscar, A. S. (2005). Working theory into and out of design experiments. *Learning Disabilities Research and Practice, 20*, 218–220.

Regan, K. S., Mastropieri, M. A., & Scruggs, T. E. (2008). Advances in literacy practices for students with emotional and behavioral disabilities. In: T. E. Scruggs & M. A. Mastropieri (Eds), *Policy and practice: Advances in learning and behavioral disabilities* (Vol. 22, pp. 317–339). Bingley, UK: Emerald.

Reid, R., Gonzalez, J. E., Nordness, P. D., Trout, A., & Epstein, M. H. (2004). A meta-analysis of the academic status of students with emotional/behavioral disturbance. *The Journal of Special Education, 38*, 130–143.

Rogers, L., & Graham, S. (2008). A meta-analysis of single subject design writing intervention research. *Journal of Educational Psychology, 100*, 879–906.

Santangelo, T., Harris, K. R., & Graham, S. (2008). Using self-regulated strategy development to support students who have "trubol giting thangs into werds". *Remedial and Special Education, 29*, 78–89.

Scruggs, T. E., & Mastropieri, M. A. (1986). Academic characteristics of behaviorally disordered and learning disabled children. *Behavioral Disorders, 11*, 184–190.

Shavelson, R. J., Phillips, D. C., Towne, L., & Feuer, M. J. (2003). On the science of education design studies. *Educational Researcher, 32*(1), 25–28.

Siegel, S., & Castellan, N. J. (1988). *Nonparametric statistics for the behavioral sciences.* New York: McGraw Hill.

Woodcock, R. W., McGrew, K. S., & Mather, N. (2001a). *Examiner's manual. Woodcock–Johnson III Tests of Achievement.* Itasca, IL: Riverside Publishing.

Woodcock, R. W., McGrew, K. S., & Mather, N. (2001b). *Woodcock–Johnson III.* Itasca, IL: Riverside Publishing.

APPENDIX. PRE–POST WRITING SAMPLES

Jose's Pretest

Kids my age should be able to have cell phones because we can use it for emergencies or to call friends.

Jose's Posttest

I would have a $30 gift card as a gift. My first reason is that I could use it to buy gifts for people I care about. Another reason is to use it to buy some movies or some video games.

My next reason is to save the money for something special.
My first reason is that I could use it to buy gifts for people I care about. If I go to the store and I see something nice that someone would like, then I would get it in secret.

Like the time I saw a beautiful ring that my mom would like I gave it to her as a present for Christmas. Also try to get it as cash and send it to my grandfather he'll need it more than me.

Another reason is to use it to buy video games. If there is a real cool game that is the store I'd go buy it and play it when I have time. Or maybe a new movie just came out I would ask my parents if they can they take me to the store, and buy it to watch it with them. Save up for a game that I want so when I save enough I can get.

My final reason is to save that money for something special. Like buying stuff for my cousins back home. Also buying stuff for camp, the summer, the pool, a party, or for winter and snow. Maybe just saving it for something cool that might come out like a movie or a game. Or to buy a gift for a very special girl that I care about a lot.

This is why I would get a gift card as a gift. It's important to be careful for the things you buy or get. If you are not careful you may get mad or very upset so be careful.

Bruno Pretest

Kids should NOT go to school during the summer because I think that thay should have a bigger brake.

Bruno Posttest

I will choose a digital camera

Which would you rather have to take a picture with a digital camera, film (35 mm) camera or a disposable camera? First a digital camera is better because you can see the picture you took.

Second you can have more options like for example the numbers of pictures you take. Third you can take the memory card anywhere you go.

First. A digital camera is better because you can see the picture you took. Also you change the cameras settings like for example Black and white settings.

Second you can have more options like for example the numbers of pictures you take. The more memory the more pictures you can take.

Third you can take the memory card anywhere you go. Another the digital camera are much better then any other camera in the world.

This is why I should get a digital camera.

COMPONENTS AFFECTING EXPRESSIVE WRITING IN TYPICAL AND DISABLED WRITERS

Cesare Cornoldi, Francesco Del Prete, Anna Gallani, Francesco Sella and Anna Maria Re

ABSTRACT

This paper examines the role of some basic variables that may be critical in children with difficulties in expressive writing. Preliminary data demonstrating the role of a series of variables are presented. In particular, based on these data, a model was derived using structural equations showing how orthography, neuropsychological functions (idea generation and planning), and revision affect the performance of tasks requiring children to describe the content of pictures. These variables appeared to significantly discriminate between children with good and poor expressive writing skills.

Writing is a frequent cause of concern in schools worldwide. Teachers frequently report that over half their students do not meet classroom writing requirements, at all grade levels, including higher education (Rogers & Graham, 2008). However, not enough attention has been devoted to the characteristics of children who present severe difficulties in producing

Literacy and Learning
Advances in Learning and Behavioral Disabilities, Volume 23, 269–286

ISSN: 0735-004X/doi:10.1108/S0735-004X(2010)0000023012

adequate texts, or to intervention techniques. This is still true even in our technological society, where writing can be the gateway to success at school and work alike, since people are expected to produce written documents of many different types. Moreover, writing can give support to emotions and reasoning.

This paper examines how expressive writing (EW) – used here as roughly synonymous with production of written texts or composition – can be studied, and the role of some basic variables that may be critical for children with writing difficulties. An overview of the literature is given, along with preliminary data demonstrating the role of these variables collected as part of the Padua Expressive Writing Disabilities Project.

MODELS OF EXPRESSIVE WRITING

The 'modal' model in the field was proposed by Hayes and Flower (1980), who described EW as a problem-solving task involving a series of operations, in particular retrieval of knowledge from memory, planning, translation of ideas into written form, self-monitoring, and revision. Berninger and Swanson (1994) developed the model, observing that distinction should be made between text generation and text transcription, the latter being the main source of problems for 'young' writers. They also stressed that general linguistic factors, such as discourse, syntax, morphology, lexicon, and phonology are critical for writers to succeed. Berninger (1999) stressed how working memory may affect a child's writing. Specifically, if a child has not mastered the rapid process of transcription, working memory capacity is devoted to the acts of handwriting and spelling rather than higher-level composition skills.

Subsequently, Berninger, Abbott, Abbott, Graham, and Richards (2002) considered the relationship between reading and writing based on a series of different approaches and models. In particular, one of their approaches considered the case of a learning disability in reading and writing; 23 psychometric measures were collected from a group of children with learning disabilities (LD) and their relatives. The authors found that, for the children, only the orthographic and phonological factors had direct paths to reading accuracy, spelling and composition factors. In the case of affected adults, only the orthographic factor (and IQ) had a direct path.

Focusing on the basic deficits in children with severe LD and young children with LD, however, may overlook the importance of cognitive–neuropsychological processes underlying EW. A model describing how different factors

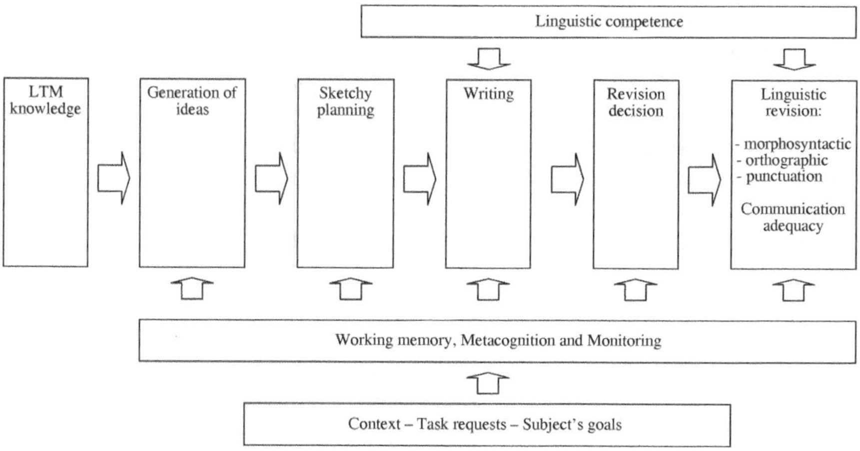

Fig. 1. A Model Describing the Main Variables Affecting Success in Expressive Writing.

may contribute to successful writing is presented in Fig. 1. EW is considered the result of a series of general factors (e.g., knowledge, language, working memory, and metacognition) that affect the specific processes involved in writing, within the contextual constraints. The specific processes involved in writing are: (a) basic cognitive–neuropsychological processes (idea generation, sketchy planning); (b) transposition (largely affected by linguistic competence and spelling); and (c) revision.

Idea generation seems to be dependent on the degree of pertinent elements stored in long-term memory (knowledge) and on the ease with which this information is accessed (semantic fluency). Van den Bergh and Rijlaarsdam (2007) suggested that idea generation may be present throughout the whole writing process, though with different characteristics and implications. However, a main phase of idea generation is represented by the initial retrieval from long-term memory and its combination with contextual cues in order for the writer to make a sketchy plan of the text and start writing. This phase is particularly amenable to treatment as it can be treated in a specific way. That is, teaching the child that knowledge should be used in the most effective way, where all possible elements that might be included in a text are considered.

As with idea generation, text planning and organization are also processes developed throughout the whole writing process. However, when starting to write, children must have made a sketch plan of what and how they want to write and must create the basis for organization of the text.

Transposition is the process most strongly affected by the child's linguistic competence, and includes lexical, syntactic, and paragraph-producing expertise.

Revision is a complex process that involves checking the linguistic properties of the text ("Editing" or "Linguistic revision") and checking the general adequacy of the text produced ("Is it really meeting the required goals?"). Linguistic revision is also affected by the child's linguistic competence, including grammar knowledge. In fact, Hayes, Flower, Schriver, Stratman, and Carey (1987) observed that only good writers focus their attention, while revising, on both local problems (at sentence level or below) and global problems. To pay attention at this level, the writer has to use comprehension processes that rely strongly on working memory while reading for revising (see also Hayes & Chenoweth, 2007). Wallace and Hayes (1991) demonstrated that a very short instructional session was sufficient to change the attitudes of a group of freshmen, improving global revision and quality of text.

LEARNING DISABILITIES IN WRITING

As in the similar case of persistent difficulties in mathematics, a distinction should be made between more general difficulties (partly modifiable, and also due to motivational and instructional factors) and severe disabilities (which, in the case of EW, may be associated with other forms of reading and writing disorders).

Berninger and Hart (1992) distinguished between different types of writing difficulties, concluding that, in a group of 300 primary grade children, around 2% had problems in written narrative. Obviously, the estimate of the percentage of children with EW problems can vary according to age and school demands, ranging from this relatively low value to high values (6–22%) for middle school students, as suggested by Hooper, Montgomery, and Brown (1993).

Students with EW disability can be considered as a group, and their general characteristics can be studied. For example, Gregg, Coleman, Stennett, and Davis (2002) examined the discourse complexity (in an expository text produced in a 30-min period) of college students with a diagnosis of LD and/or ADHD. These groups had similar performance on both general (e.g., holistic rating and length, two highly correlated variables) and specific (based on a classification system developed by Biber, 1995) for examining output related with different types of text writing ability measures. Additionally, both groups performed lower than a control group on these measures. Text length was approximately 290 words for the students with disabilities and about 340 (SD = 89.08) for the controls. Gregg et al. (2002) found that all writers emphasized some basic functions, such as verb tense, reference through use of relative pronouns, reduction of the text by using pronouns and "do" instead of a richer verb, and frame elaboration through use of attributive adjectives and adverbs. Examination of the specific features of the output of the different groups showed that, in general, the clinical groups were poorer than the controls. Interesting findings from Biber's study concern the greater use of first-person pronouns and hedges, and the less frequent use of time adverbials in the LD group than in the pure ADHD group and controls.

A diagnosis of EW disability is related to the assessment procedures and identification of both the main aspects of EW and the aspects that can be dissociated when considering learning disabled individuals. If the different aspects of writing are considered, rather than using an overall holistic assessment, then different subtypes can be observed. For example, Roid (1994) assessed six traits (ideas, organization, word choice, sentence fluency, etc.) and found 11 cluster solutions. Focusing on children with difficulties, Sandler et al. (1992) found a large group of children with fine motor and linguistic deficits, another group with spatial deficits, and two small groups, one with attention/memory deficits, and the other with sequencing deficits.

A major study regarding differentiation between the various subtypes of EW difficulties was carried out by Wakely, Hooper, de Kruif, and Swartz (2006). Taking a sample of 276 fourth- and fifth-graders, these authors asked them to write two stories prompted by an initial sentence. They collected one holistic score and one series of analytical and metacognitive scores. These showed six clusters, based on five main scores (of understandability, grammar, semantics, spelling, and reading): children who were (a) average, (b) skilled, or (c) poor in grammar, (d) poor in semantics, (e) poor in text quality, and (f) poor in spelling–reading. Children poor in grammar (7% of the sample) were mainly characterized by morphosyntactic errors. Children with poor text quality (23% of the sample) did not make a particularly high number of errors, but received a low holistic rating, due to the paucity of offered information and lack of communicative power. It is possible that these children, by paying attention to the syntactic and orthographic aspects of their output, did not save working memory space for activating and organizing relevant content. Children in the Low Semantics subtype (12% of the sample) made a considerable number of understandability errors, owing to missing words, words in the wrong order or misused, ambiguous references. Finally, the Low Spelling–Reading subtype (5% of children) was characterized by poor reading comprehension and a high percentage of spelling errors (with an average around 20%).

TREATMENT

Determining which variables are of particular relevance to EW requires care, especially when considering provision of treatment to children with disabilities. Educational approaches in writing instruction can clearly strike a variety of different chords (as illustrated in the book edited by Graham, MacArthur, & Fitzgerald, 2007), including motivation, thinking, communication, awareness of goals, contexts, genre familiarity, and so on. Cutler and Graham (2008) surveyed the classroom instructional practices in writing of 178 primary school teachers in the United States. Most teachers reported eclectic use of process writing (emphasizing the communicative role of writing) and skills instruction (based on systematic teaching of handwriting, spelling, sentence construction, grammar, punctuation, capitalization, and so on). However, the teachers also reported specific instructional practices. The authors concluded with some general recommendations, including a higher integration between school and home, increasing motivation for writing, and the use of computers.

If we consider specific treatment that goes beyond typical classroom work, studies in the literature put forward various approaches and criteria for measuring the outcomes, typically focusing on improvement in the holistic impression offered by the written text. However, some research has focused on specific dependent variables, which are targets of the intervention and considered particularly relevant. For example, McCurdy, Skinner, Watson, and Shriver (2008) used a specific Comprehensive Writing Program (CWP), including a series of behavioral techniques, which focused on three target skills regarding production of: (1) complete sentences, (2) compound sentences, and (3) sentences containing adjectives.

An implication of the influential model of Hayes and Flower (1980) is that some writing programs have addressed the underlying neuropsychological processes (e.g., planning). This approach has been criticized (e.g., Berninger, 1994) because it brings the risk of underestimating the importance of language functions necessary for writing. However, a large body of evidence (Graham & Perin, 2007) has confirmed its efficacy. Furthermore, the approach has the advantage of identifying some basic mechanisms that could be targeted by specific, relatively short programs designed to enhance children's EW abilities, used in association with the classical linguistic experience children gather over time. In this respect, one approach of particular relevance is the Self-Regulated Strategy Development (SRSD) model, proposed by Graham and Harris (1997) and focused on metacognitive abilities. Page-Voth and Graham (1999) showed that a strategy facilitating goal attainment (for enhancing the production of arguments and counterarguments supporting a premise) increased the quality of the texts produced by seventh- and eighth-graders with writing problems. Hooper, Wakely, de Kruif, and Swartz (2006) treated 73 fourth- and fifth-graders in a 20-lesson program aimed at neuropsychological and metacognitive components, and found positive effects and some initial evidence of specific effects related to subtypes of EW disability. Re, Caeran, and Cornoldi (2008) showed that a procedural facilitation, supporting organization of planning, increases the quality of texts produced by ADHD children.

According to Rogers and Graham (2008), very few studies have examined group effects of writing programs. The authors found positive effects from 12 different procedures, the most effective being as follows (ranked according to impact): teaching strategies for planning, revising, and editing; teaching written summarization; using peer tutoring for specific components; establishing specific goals; teaching the requisite writing skills (handwriting, spelling, and typing); using word processors; teaching students to write complex sentences; and establishing a process approach to writing (see also Graham & Perin, 2007). In their meta-analysis of single-subject treatments, Rogers and Graham (2008) examined which intervention methods produced a PND (percentage of non-overlapping data) with mean and median values above the recommended level of 50% (Scruggs, Mastropieri, Cook, & Escobar, 1986). Data confirmed the efficacy of teaching strategies for planning and drafting both narrative and expository texts, followed by grammar teaching, setting specific goals, and teaching strategies for editing. Based on this evidence and a model of EW, Re, Cazzaniga, Pedron, and Cornoldi (2009) developed a program designed to enhance EW abilities of children with difficulties. The program, entitled "*Io scrivo*" ("I write") targets four of the main EW components – idea generation, planning, revision, and working memory.

THE PRESENT STUDY

The main goal of the present study was to examine the role of some of the critical variables in producing a successful written text (see Fig. 1).

In particular, we concentrated on variables that might be easiest to treat in a program for children with disabilities (Re et al., 2009). In the first phase we examined how these variables might affect the performance of a random sample of children. In the second phase we focused on a subset group of children who had low performance on the writing tasks. The data were collected using a series of new tasks or adaptations that are currently undergoing psychometric analysis within the Padova Expressive Writing Project.

The Tasks

Expressive Writing Measures

The measures were derived from the Tressoldi and Cornoldi (1990) Writing Battery, which requires the subject to produce one descriptive text and one narrative text based on given illustrations (see also Re, Pedron, & Cornoldi, 2007). Two scores were obtained:

(1) Holistic ratings. Two raters gave holistic ratings of both texts. The high correlations (always above 0.85) found between the two raters showed that the ratings were reliable; and
(2) Productivity. The text length in number of words (segmented elements) was computed. The index has proven to be strongly related, in primary grades, to the other indices of text quality.

Spelling

The percentage of words incorrectly written were computed for both of the passages produced.

Cognitive–Neuropsychological Processes

Two tasks were administered to measure cognitive–neuropsychological processes (see the appendix for a descriptions of the tasks). First, for the idea generation task, the child was asked to make a list of all the elements s/he could include in a description of his/her home. Second, for the sketch planning task (Butterflies), the child was given a scrambled series of elements that could be included in a text describing butterflies' wings (butterflies = "farfalle" in Italian) and asked to put them in order to give a reasonable structure for a text on the topic. The number of correctly reordered elements was determined.

Linguistic Revision

Three different texts were given to the child, containing morphosyntactic (e.g., inappropriate plural), spelling, and punctuation errors, respectively. For each passage the child was asked to underline the errors. We determined the omissions made in detecting errors for the morphosyntactic task (i.e., number of non-omissions in morphosyntactic task) and the orthographic task (i.e., number of non-omissions in orthographic task). For the punctuation text, we determined the punctuations that had been correctly eliminated (i.e., number of punctuations correctly eliminated) and those correctly added (i.e., number of punctuations correctly added).

Phase 1: Relationship between the Variables Affecting EW in a Group of 150 Third- to Fifth-Graders

The first phase tested the model described in Fig. 1, assessing the role of some of the variables assumed to be critical in EW. In order to include the role of spelling competence, which can affect how fluent the child is and is not overloaded during transposition (see Berninger, 1994), spelling measures were also considered. With respect to the model described in Fig. 1, we distinguished between text productivity, often considered a measure of text quality, and a more comprehensive estimation of the quality of the text. Therefore, performance in EW was considered on the basis of the holistic ratings given by expert judges to the texts written by children. It was assumed that these overall ratings were affected by productivity and that the latter one is influenced by the basic cognitive processes of idea generation and organization in planning.

Subjects

Participants were 161 children attending a primary school in the suburbs of a medium-sized town in north-east Italy. They were mainly Italian in origin, and from medium sociocultural-level families. Participants fell in roughly equal numbers of third-, fourth-, and fifth-graders (nine classes were involved, three per grade), and of males and females.

Procedure

Children were administered all tasks in their own classroom in a single session lasting 70–90 min during school hours.

Results

The pattern of relationships between variables was investigated using structural equations based on the model described in Fig. 1 and computed via LISREL. The derived model is based on the covariance matrix between the observed variables.

Two preliminary steps were: (a) change of the sign of variables describing errors, in the direction of positive performance, in order to have only positive links in the model; and (b) standardization of all the measured variables introduced in the model, in order to have a unique unit of measure.

Productivity for the descriptive and narrative texts produced the endogenous observed variables (*Number of written words in descriptive text* and *Number of written words in narrative text*) measuring the first endogenous latent "*Productivity*." *Descriptive text global impression* and *Narrative text global impression* were the endogenous observed variables measuring the first endogenous latent variable "*Holistic ratings*."

The other exogenous observed variables measured the three latent exogenous variables. In particular, percentages of correctly written words for the two texts (*Percentage of correct words in narrative text* and *Percentage of correct words in descriptive text*) measured spelling competence; idea generation (*Number of ideas*, and *Number of categories in idea production*) and sketchy planning (*Butterflies*) measured the basic cognitive–neuropsychological processes; the other variables measured the child's linguistic revision ability. The basic cognitive–neuropsychological processes measured the latent endogenous variable describing Productivity, where Spelling and Linguistic Revision Ability measured the latent endogenous variable describing Holistic ratings.

The fitness indices were good, as the RMSEA (0.016) was much lower than the usual critical value of 0.08 and the relationship between χ^2 and degrees of freedom was less than 1 (i.e., lower than the typical critical value of 2.5). The Normed Fit Index (NFI) and the Non-Normed Fit Index (NNFI) were also good (NFI = 0.93 and NNFI = 0.96) (see Fig. 2).

The goodness of the model was also supported by the residuals, which were uniformly low. Thus the model confirmed our assumption that three different main latent variables – basic cognitive abilities (via productivity), spelling competence, and linguistic revision – affect EW performance.

Phase 2: Study of a Group of Children with Difficulties in EW

The second step was to examine how far the variables thus defined actually discriminated between a specific subgroup of children who, according to

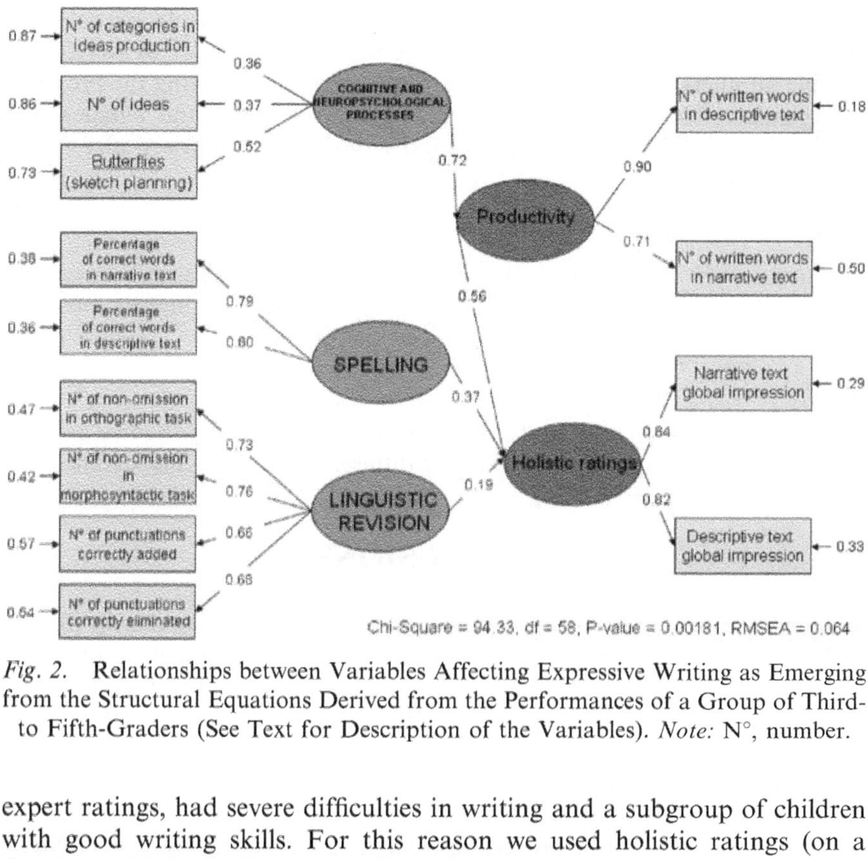

Fig. 2. Relationships between Variables Affecting Expressive Writing as Emerging from the Structural Equations Derived from the Performances of a Group of Third- to Fifth-Graders (See Text for Description of the Variables). *Note:* N°, number.

expert ratings, had severe difficulties in writing and a subgroup of children with good writing skills. For this reason we used holistic ratings (on a 5-point scale) for both passages from the two experts.

The two groups were compared on all the above-mentioned variables as well as in writing speed. According to Berninger (1994), writing speed can affect the difficulties encountered by poor writers.

Subjects

The experts' ratings, which were highly correlated based on interrater reliability, and the similarity of the mean scores for the two texts (Pearson's $r = 0.87$) were used to identify a subgroup of children considered to be "poor writers" (summed rating for the two texts ≤ 4). The 32 children belonging to this category were approximately 20% of the sample, with unequal split between males ($n = 25$) and females ($n = 7$). This disproportionality provides further support to the presence of a gender effect in learning outcomes associated with language. These children were compared to the group of children with good writing skills. A cut-off summarized rating score of ≥ 7 was used to define good writers in order to have comparable numbers of children in each group. Further supporting the presence of a gender effect, in this case the proportion of males and females was exactly the opposite. The group of good writers was comprised of 7 males and 25 females

Tasks
The tasks were as described above. In addition, the children carried out a speed-writing task, which required them to write the highest possible number of numbers words (one, two, etc.) in 1 min.

Results
Fig. 3 (see also Table 1) presents the mean scores obtained by the two groups. Student's t-test comparisons showed all differences to be highly significant.

CONCLUSIONS

Despite the impact of EW difficulties on academics and success in life, as well as their potential influence on psychological development, writing has not received the same attention as decoding and spelling. The present study revisits models of writing based on identification of a series of distinct components. On the basis of a revised model of EW, we have identified a series of critical components and devised procedures for their assessment (see Figs. 1 and 2).

Administration of these procedures to a group of primary school children showed that the predicted variables did indeed affect success on two writing tasks, as measured by the children's productivity. In particular, a structural equation analysis found that an empirical model derived from our general model had a good fit. The model showed how basic cognitive functions of idea generation and planning affect productivity. Moreover, the latter, together with revision and spelling, affect the overall quality of the text. Furthermore, analysis of a group of children rated by experts as poor text-producers confirmed that all the procedures identified had successfully distinguished between children with good and poor written output.

The fact that many different trainable variables appear to affect failure in EW implies that children with EW difficulties might benefit from an intervention focused on one or more of these variables. Given the role of the cognitive–neuropsychological variables we have identified, targeted

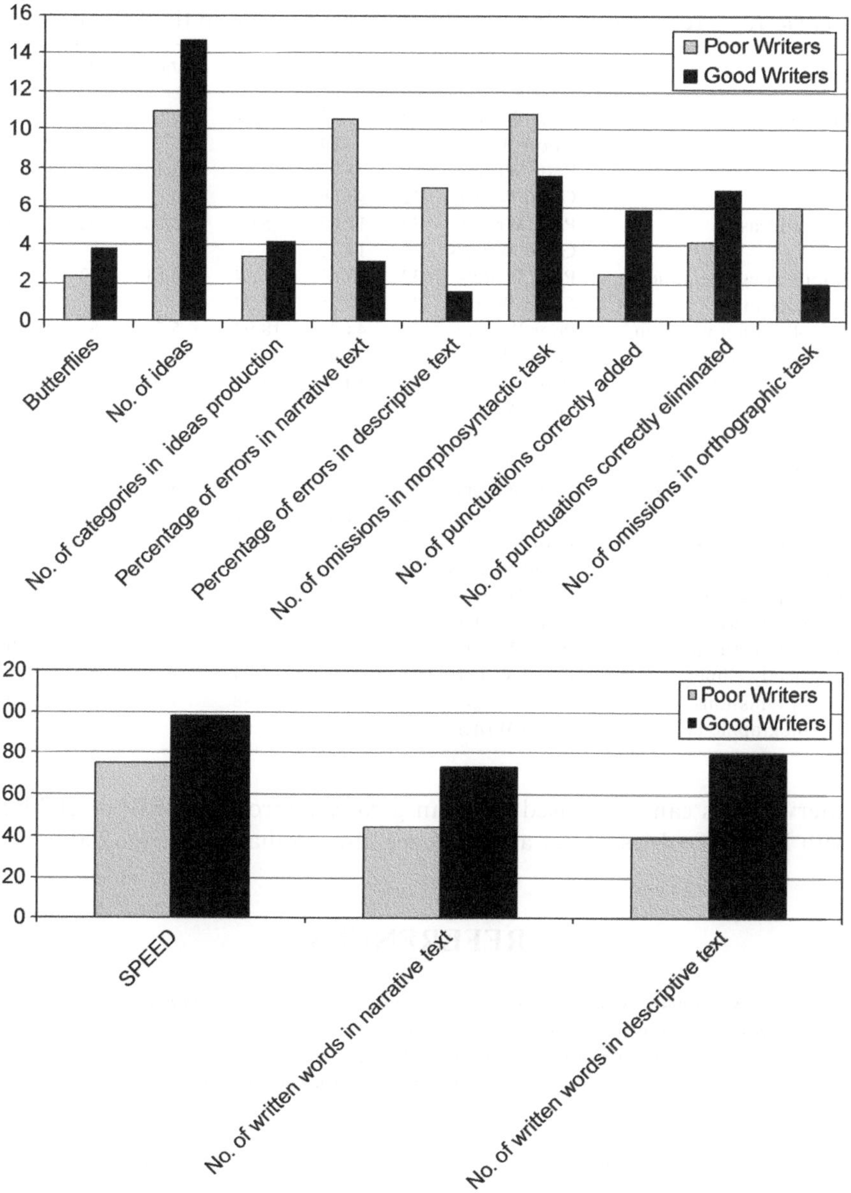

Fig. 3. Differences in Performance between a Group of Good (Black) and Poor (Gray) Writers (Speed = Numbers Words Written in 1 min). The Scores for Speed and Productivity are Reported Below as the Scale of the Measures was Different. *Note:* No, number.

Table 1. Mean Scores Obtained by the Two Groups in the EW Battery.

Tasks	Groups	*N*	Mean	SD	*t*-Value	df	*p*
Butterflies	Poor Writers	30	2.43	1.71	−3.515	60	<0.001
	Good Writers	32	3.84	1.43			
Speed	Poor Writers	32	75.72	18.98	−5.158	62	<0.001
	Good Writers	32	98.56	16.34			
No. of ideas	Poor Writers	32	11.03	5.05	−2.801	62	0.007
	Good Writers	32	14.72	5.46			
No. of categories in ideas production	Poor Writers	32	3.47	1.24	−2.512	62	0.015
	Good Writers	32	4.25	1.24			
No. of written words in narrative text	Poor Writers	32	44.31	18.97	−5.214	62	<0.001
	Good Writers	32	73.97	25.98			
Percentage of errors in narrative text	Poor Writers	32	10.65	6.83	5.687	62	<0.001
	Good Writers	32	3.14	3.00			
No. of written words in descriptive text	Poor Writers	32	39.50	20.25	−6.786	62	<0.001
	Good Writers	32	79.84	26.84			
Percentage of errors in descriptive text	Poor Writers	32	7.00	5.40	5.313	62	<0.001
	Good Writers	32	1.67	1.71			
No. of omissions in morphosyntactic task	Poor Writers	32	10.94	2.79	5.326	62	<0.001
	Good Writers	32	7.72	1.97			
No. of punctuations correctly added	Poor Writers	32	2.50	2.07	−7.157	62	<0.001
	Good Writers	32	5.91	1.71			
No. of punctuations correctly eliminated	Poor Writers	32	4.16	2.93	−4.881	62	<0.001
	Good Writers	32	6.94	1.34			
No. of omissions in orthographic task	Poor Writers	32	5.96	2.38	7.768	62	<0.001
	Good Writers	32	2.00	1.62			

interventions can be devised that can greatly improve the EW of children with EW difficulties (Re et al., 2009; see also Graham & Perin, 2007).

REFERENCES

Berninger, V. (1994). *Reading and writing acquisition. A developmental neuropsychological approach*. Madison, WI: Brown & Benchmark.

Berninger, VW. (1999). Coordinating transcription and text generation in working memory during composing: Automatic and constructive processes. *Learning Disability Quarterly, 22*, 99–112.

Berninger, V. W., Abbott, R. D., Abbott, S. P., Graham, S., & Richards, T. (2002). Writing and reading: Connections between language by hand and language by eye. *Journal of Learning Disabilities, 35*, 39–56.

Berninger, V. W., & Hart, T. M. (1992). A developmental neuropsychological perspective for reading and writing acquisition. *Educational Psychologist, 27*, 415–434.

Berninger, V., & Swanson, H. L. (1994). Modifying Hayes and Flowers' model of skilled writing to explain beginning and developing writing. In: E. Butterfield (Ed.), *Children's writing: Toward a process theory of development of skilled writing* (pp. 57–81). Greenwich, CT: JAI Press.

Biber, D. (1995). *Dimensions of register variation: A cross-linguistic comparison.* Cambridge, UK: Cambridge University Press.

Cutler, L., & Graham, S. (2008). Primary grade writing instruction: A national survey. *Journal of Educational Psychology, 100*, 907–919.

Graham, S., & Harris, K. R. (1997). Self-regulation and writing: Where do we go from here?. *Contemporary Educational Psychology, 22*, 102–114.

Graham, S., MacArthur, C. A., & Fitzgerald, J. (Eds). (2007). *Best practice in writing instruction.* New York: Guilford Press.

Graham, S., & Perin, D. (2007). What we know, what we still need to know: Teaching adolescents to write. *Scientific Studies of Reading, 11*, 313–335.

Gregg, N., Coleman, C., Stennett, R. B., & Davis, M. (2002). Discourse complexity of college writers with and without disabilities: A multidimensional analysis. *Journal of Learning Disabilities, 35*, 23–38.

Hayes, J. R., & Chenoweth, N. A. (2007). Working memory in an editing task. *Written Communication, 24*, 283–294.

Hayes, J. R., & Flower, L. S. (1980). Identifying the organization of writing processes. In: L. W. Gregg & E. R. Steinberg (Eds), *Cognitive processes in writing* (pp. 3–30). Mahwah, NJ: Lawrence Erlbaum Associates.

Hayes, J. R., Flower, L., Schriver, K., Stratman, J., & Carey, L. (1987). Cognitive processes in revision. In: S. Rosenberg (Ed.), *Advances in applied psycholinguistics, Volume II: Reading, writing, and language processing* (pp. 176–204). Cambridge, UK: Cambridge University Press.

Hooper, S. R., Montgomery, J. W., & Brown, T. T. (1993). Prevalence of writing problems across 3 middle school samples. *School Psychology Review, 22*, 610–622.

Hooper, S. R., Wakely, M. B., de Kruif, R. E. L., & Swartz, C. W. (2006). Aptitude–treatment interactions revisited: Effect of metacognitive intervention on subtypes of written expression in elementary school students. *Developmental Neuropsychology, 29*, 217–241.

McCurdy, M., Skinner, C., Watson, S., & Shriver, M. (2008). Examining the effects of a comprehensive writing program on the writing performance of middle school students with learning disabilities in written expression. *School Psychology Quarterly, 23*, 571–586.

Page-Voth, V., & Graham, S. (1999). Effects of goal setting and strategy use on the writing performance and self-efficacy of students with writing and learning problems. *Journal of Educational Psychology, 91*, 230–240.

Re, A. M., Caeran, M., & Cornoldi, C. (2008). Improving expressive writing skills of children rated for ADHD symptoms. *Journal of Learning Disabilities, 41*, 535–544.

Re, A. M., Cazzaniga, S., Pedron, M., & Cornoldi, C. (2009). *Io scrivo: Valutazione e potenziamento delle abilità di espressione scritta.* Firenze: Editore Giuntiscuola.

Re, A. M., Pedron, M., & Cornoldi, C. (2007). Expressive writing difficulties in children described by their teachers as exhibiting ADHD symptoms. *Journal of Learning Disabilities, 40*, 244–255.

Rogers, L. A., & Graham, S. (2008). A meta-analysis of single subject design writing intervention research. *Journal of Educational Psychology, 100*, 879–906.

Roid, G. H. (1994). Patterns of writing skills derived from cluster analysis of direct-writing assessments. *Applied Measurement in Education, 7*, 159–170.

Sandler, A. D., Watson, T. E., Footo, M., Levine, M. D., Coleman, W. L., & Hooper, S. R. (1992). Neurodevelopmental study of writing disorders in middle childhood. *Journal of Developmental and Behavioral Pediatrics, 13*, 17–23.

Scruggs, T. E., Mastropieri, M. A., Cook, S. B., & Escobar, C. (1986). Early intervention for children with conduct disorders: A quantitative synthesis of single-subject research. *Behavioral Disorders, 11*, 260–271.

Tressoldi, P. E., & Cornoldi, C. (1990). *Batteria per la valutazione della scrittura e delle competenze ortografiche nella scuola dell'obbligo*. Firenze: Organizzazioni Speciali.

Van den Bergh, H., & Rijlaarsdam, G. (2007). The dynamics of idea generation during writing: An online study. In: G. Rijlaarsdam (Series Ed.) and M. Torrance, L. van Waes, & D. Galbraith (Volume Eds), *Writing and cognition: Research and applications* (Vol. 20). Studies in writing (pp. 125–150). Amsterdam: Elsevier.

Wakely, M. B., Hooper, S. R., de Kruif, R. E. L., & Swartz, C. (2006). Subtypes of written expression in elementary school children: A linguistic-based model. *Developmental Neuropsychology, 29*, 125–159.

Wallace, D. L., & Hayes, J. R. (1991). Redefining revision for freshmen. *Research in the Teaching of English, 25*, 54–66.

APPENDIX. THE IDEA GENERATION TASK

Instructions:

- List all the elements you could include in a description of your home.

Scoring:

(a) number of reproduced ideas
(b) number of categories represented out of the 11 predefined

Predefined categories and examples of responses classified within each category:

1. **THE PLACE** (indirizzo, punti di riferimento…) "*vicino alla mia casa c'è un pista ciclabile,*"
2. **OUTDOORS** (giardino, tetto, terrazza, colore) "*…circondata da alberi che fanno molta ombra,*"
3. **INDOORS** (numero e tipologia delle stanze…) "*la mia casa è composta dalla cucina, dalla taverna, dal salotto, dal garage, le camere da letto e la sauna*"
4. **FURNITURE** "*ho anche un pianoforte e due tavolini di cristallo*"
5. **ESTHETIC JUDGEMENT** "*la mia casa è molto bella*"

6. **SPECIFIC EMOTIONS** "*... e quando devo fare la nanna mi sento al sicuro, e quindi dormo tranquilla*"
7. **PETS** "*ho una tartaruga che si chiama Scorza e ha 4 anni. Ho anche un pesce che si chiama Oliver e ha 6 anni*".
8. **HISTORY** "*abbiamo appena finito di ristrutturare la casa perché era molto vecchia...è stata costruita da mio nonno*"
9. **RELEVANT DETAILS** "*c'è perfino un ripostiglio dove c'è sempre freddo perché c'è sempre la finestra aperta*"
10. **ACTIONS** "*io a casa gioco a nascondino*"
11. **WISHES** "*vorrei una mia stanza da letto perché fino adesso la sto condividendo con mia sorella Alice*"

THE PLANNING TASK

Correct Structure

1. *Introduction*: Butterflies' wings, etc.
2. *Specification of the introduction*: The color of the wings
3. *Specific feature*: The colored powder is easily lost
4. *Example*: The powder remains on your hands if you touch them
5. *Introduction to the explanation*: There are many explanations
6. *Specific explanation*: It is a defence against a spider's web
7. *Conclusion*: The instance of the powder loss reveals how

Order of Sentence Presentation

1. Specific feature
2. Example
3. Specific explanation
4. Conclusion
5. Introduction
6. Introduction to the explanation
7. Specification of the introduction

Instructions:

- Imagine that you have to write a composition on "Butterflies' wings."
- Reorder the following sentences to give the best structure to your composition.

- Note: The seven sentences (not syntactically connected) refer to the different parts of a well-organized text.

Scoring: 1 point for each sentence following a sentence that precedes it in the correct order (1 point is always awarded for the first sentence given).

LINGUISTIC REVISION TASKS

(1) Morphosyntactic
(2) Orthographic
(3) Punctuation

Instructions: Imagine you are your teacher. Correct the text(s), which contain a series of errors.

Scoring: Number of correctly detected errors (for "Punctuation" include the number of appropriately added or deleted punctuations).

DYSLEXIA: A CATEGORICAL FALSEHOOD WITHOUT VALIDITY OR UTILITY

Simon Gibbs and Julian Elliott

ABSTRACT

Children's failure to develop proficiency in reading and writing continues to challenge educationalists, parents and carers. In this chapter we argue that the concept of dyslexia as an explanation for failure or as a starting point for intervention is fatally flawed. Our argument is that the concept is a socially constructed category with no scientific basis. Hence quasi-medical differential diagnosis is invalid and educationally divisive. We question this phenomenon that persists despite the protestations of Stanovich (1994, 2005) and others, through a brief survey of work in the fields of social categorisation, cognitive psychology and neuroscience. In summary our view is that whilst there are some 'natural' tendencies to categorise, with regard to literacy there is no identified objectively defined and unambiguous discontinuity between skilled and unskilled reader. There is, therefore, no support for the persistence of a distinctive category of dyslexia. Further, the notion of 'dyslexia' in itself does not support appropriate intervention.

Literacy and Learning
Advances in Learning and Behavioral Disabilities, Volume 23, 287–301

ISSN: 0735-004X/doi:10.1108/S0735-004X(2010)0000023013

Despite the ubiquitous nature of the concept of dyslexia, typically used to describe a failure to acquire sound decoding skills, fierce argument continues to rage in many countries around the world as to the scientific and clinical validity of this construct. At its simplest level, debate has centred upon whether dyslexia 'exists', or is, alternatively, a conceptual artefact that serves to exculpate those who fail to provide an appropriate educational experience. Others have argued that such a debate is meaningless (Elliott & Gibbs, 2009), for while there are clearly many children who encounter significant difficulty in acquiring literacy, independent of the tuition they receive, subdividing this population into dyslexics and non-dyslexics is inappropriate, invalid and potentially discriminatory.

In this chapter we do not intend to underplay the experience and consequences of difficulty in acquiring fluent literacy. We fully appreciate that children and adults may be significantly distressed by failure in literacy (either or both spelling and reading). Such problems entail serious challenges for those who have responsibility for the education and emotional well being of children and young people. For us, problems arise from two sources. One relates to fundamental problems with definition and the other is about the practicalities of providing support to those who are struggling to acquire proficiency in literacy.

As we will argue later in the chapter, there is a lack of any scientifically objective line of demarcation to determine in a consistent and rigorous fashion who will benefit from different and more specialised treatment by virtue of being 'dyslexic'. Not only is there no clear line of demarcation, the notion or label of 'dyslexia' does not in itself indicate any specific form of treatment. As a result, educational administrators are forced to use arbitrary, ad hoc, definitions of dyslexia (such as the widely discredited IQ-reading level discrepancy measure) to allocate resources and, in so doing, not only differentiate between children arbitrarily but also allocate specialised treatment and resources in an unfair and discriminatory fashion.

We do, however, recognise the considerable advances in understanding gained from research into factors associated with the development of reading development (see, for instance, Snowling & Hulme, 2005) and work that has shown the efficacy of appropriate forms of intervention (e.g., Hatcher et al., 2006). While these advances are reassuring for parents, educators and children, a consequence of this is the widespread belief that a diagnosis of dyslexia will be key to ensuring that appropriate educational steps are taken. Drawing upon the medical model: diagnosis is the key to determining treatment, and a diagnosis of dyslexia points to appropriate means of remediation. One of our aims in this chapter is to challenge the hegemony of quasi-medical categorisation – or diagnosis – of children exhibiting difficulties with literacy. We wish to emphasise that, in our view, the categorisation of some children as 'having' dyslexia, whilst others are alternatively conceived as 'garden-variety' poor readers (cf. Stanovich, 1988), is scientifically and socially problematic. Our purpose here is quite clear: to highlight evidence that illustrates the conceptual flaws in the conception of dyslexia as a distinct, differentially diagnosable condition, and to demonstrate how, perversely, this leads to damaging educational consequences for many.

Thus, our contention is that dyslexia is not a distinct and distinguishable category of impairment. We suggest that dyslexia is falsely reified, and is indistinguishable from the generality of reading difficulties. [This is, however, not a new assertion. Stanovich (1994) demonstrated very clearly that there is no valid means to dissociate dyslexia from other forms of reading retardation.] In order to support greater educational and social inclusion, as well as ensuring greater equality of opportunity, we will, therefore, argue that the maintenance of dyslexia as a differentially diagnosed condition is divisive and unfair. In short we will argue that dyslexia – as a differential term – is a social construct with arbitrary definition.

INITIAL CONFUSION

Let us start by noting that, despite Stanovich's (1994) paper and his demonstration that a discrepancy definition of dyslexia has no basis in science, a range of arbitrary definitions of dyslexia persists. Thus, for example, The American Psychiatric Association's diagnostic manual (DSM-IV, American Psychiatric Association, 1994) provides the following criteria for the diagnosis of dyslexia:

- Reading achievement substantially below that expected for the person's age, measured intelligence and age-appropriate education.
- The disturbance in reading ability interferes with academic achievement or activities of daily living that require reading skills.
- If a sensory deficit is present, the reading difficulties are in excess of those usually associated with the specific sensory deficit.

Co-morbid 'symptoms' of dyslexia are often considered to include difficulties with: speech and language, short-term memory, ordering and sequencing, clumsiness, a sense of rhythm, rapid information processing, concentration, inconsistent hand preference, verbal fluency, phonic skills, frequent letter reversals (d for b, for example), mental calculations, self-image, and anxiety when being asked to read aloud. However, as Rice and Brooks (2004, p. 11) noted:

> There is no consensus … as to whether dyslexia can be distinguished in practice from other possible causes of … literacy difficulties. Many 'signs of dyslexia' are no less characteristic of non-dyslexic people with reading skills deficits. In our present state of knowledge, it does not seem helpful for teachers to think of some literacy learners as 'dyslexics' and others as 'ordinary poor readers.'

Rice and Brooks (p. 11) also noted that at the broader theoretical level, similar ambivalence prevails:

> There are many definitions of dyslexia but no consensus. Some definitions are purely descriptive while others embody causal theories. It appears that 'dyslexia' is not one thing but many, in so far as it serves a conceptual clearing house for a number of reading skills deficits and difficulties, with a number of causes.

In light of the above, important questions to be asked, therefore, are: 'what creates or perpetuates the notion of dyslexia as a distinct entity?', 'what purpose might it serve?', but most importantly, 'is the notion at all helpful?'

We will approach the questions in stages. Firstly, by considering the social construction and categorisation of children as 'dyslexic'; secondly, by considering literature that deals with putative diagnoses of dyslexia and the scientific ideas and methods associated with such discriminations; finally, by addressing the utility of the concept.

SOCIALLY CONSTRUCTED CATEGORISATION

In general terms, it is apparent that psychological development depends on the uniquely individual interaction between brain and environment or, as Ferrari (2002) noted, development (normal and abnormal) depends on the socio-cultural context. More pertinent to our argument is the view of Pennington and Olson (2005, p. 453) that "Dyslexia is an interesting example of the intersection between an evolved behaviour (language) and a cultural invention (literacy)."

As we will detail later, there seems to be no naturally evolved human cognitive mechanism to deal specifically with the codes of written language (see Wolf, 2008). Byrne (2005) described the complexity of the tasks involved in acquiring literacy. The enormity of the task is particularly evident for those seeking to acquire literacy in a language such as English where the relationship between phonological representation and orthography is anything but straightforward [and further complicated over time by the vagaries of writers and printers – see Crystal (2004)].

Thus, as the characteristics of the dominant oral language, the phonological structures within the language, and the relationships these have with their orthographic (written) representations vary from culture to culture (Caravolas, 2005; Seymour, 2005), incidence rates for supposed dyslexia also vary considerably. It is important to note that there is, therefore, no consistency in the definition or incidence of dyslexia across cultures.

Given the complexity of the task, it might be regarded as somewhat miraculous that literacy is acquired at all. But, once acquired, literacy is self-evidently a powerful social tool. It enables communication over distance and time. In comparison to the timescale of human evolution, however, the emergence of literacy as a communicational tool is very recent (Wolf, 2008). In evolutionary terms, literacy (in Western society at least) was, in the earliest stages, only available to a powerful elite, and was used as a means to both acquire and to maintain religious, social, cultural and political power. The ensuing aspiration and requirement that all should become literate emerged more recently. Cook-Gumpertz (2006) has suggested that the transition from a societal position in which unauthorised attempts to acquire literacy were viewed as dangerously radical to the converse in which illiteracy was seen as the social and political danger, did not take place until the late 19th century. Once universal literacy is posited as an important social and educational aim, as Goody and Watt (1968) suggested, it follows that shades or gradations of literacy and illiteracy (almost inevitably requiring some form of label) may follow. Goody and Watt also highlighted the ensuing serious implications for schools – as '*key institutions of society*' – if they are deemed to be unsuccessful in inculcating successful literacy. (In the United Kingdom, for instance, schools are currently rated and compared on a range of indicators that include measures of children's literacy.) In such circumstances, it seems likely that schools would come to regard themselves as insufficiently knowledgeable, skilful or resourced and either attribute failure to innate characteristics of children (as being, for instance, 'dyslexic') or for other reasons, discriminate between such children and other, more able readers [for a discussion of issues related to teachers' attitudes regarding their motivation to include see also: Ferri and Connor (2005) and Gibbs (2007)]. The alternative rationale, outlined above, located in relation to the idea that 'literacy' is an artefact of the interaction between human linguistic capabilities and random social constructs, is rarely invoked. Thus, in ways that are analogous to the phenomenon of 'categorical perception' (Harnad, 1987), children are placed in socially constructed categories, in this case, as being literate or not. Within the latter category there has been a further unjustifiable categorisation, as Stanovich (1994, 2005) and others have persistently argued, in which some children are seen as 'dyslexic' and others are perceived merely as poor readers.

In all of our social interactions, how we deal with people depends on how we perceive them – as well as how they are in themselves (Eiser & Streobe, 1972). For reasons set out above, the issue of how we perceive and deal with people becomes particularly focussed and sharply dichotomised in the field of literacy. We will now discuss particular aspects of these social processes, specifically the social construction of categories, and in particular how this relates to the phenomenon that has been labelled as dyslexia.

The Social Purpose of Classification or Category Creation

In general, knowledge development is a social activity (Berger & Luckmann, 2002) with social purposes. Classification or categorisation is, certainly in western scientific orthodoxy, central to the development of knowledge (Estes, 1994; Jenkins, 2000). Within this paradigm, in order to be able to classify or categorise elements of a group, it is first necessary to be able to specify differences and similarities between members and non-members. Whilst for the purposes of scientific research it may be helpful and legitimate to partition groups using researcher-defined criteria (e.g., a reading age two years below chronological age), such arbitrary distinctions are highly questionable in relation to the allocation of educational provision. As we will seek to demonstrate, in the case of reading difficulty there is no clearly delineated dividing line between what is and is not, dyslexia.

The Act of Social Category Creation

There is now a substantial literature in the fields of sociology and psychology that addresses theories and features of social categories. Social categories are defined or created by others (Jenkins, 2000). Harnad (1987) noted that categorisation requires the reliable detection of features that distinguish members of a category from 'confusable non-members'. However, Rothbart and Taylor (1992), for instance, argued persuasively that many social categories are treated by laypeople as if they are natural categories with clearly identified biological underpinnings, as well as being historically and culturally invariant (see also Medin & Ortony, 1989). This 'essentialist' view has been challenged by Haslam, Rothschild, and Ernst (2000) who reported finding a two-factor structure to social categories. One factor corresponding to the concept of natural kinds as delineated by Kripke (1980) and Quine (1977) is characterised by specific and necessary properties of immutability, discreteness and historical stability. The other, corresponding to the concept of reification, is suggestive of 'entitivity' (Campbell, 1958) in seeming to have homogeneity and coherence as a meaningful entity that is itself informative, uniform and exclusive. Haslam et al. suggested that although "social categories, like artefacts, reflect historically situated human desires, needs and conventions" (p. 114), they come to be treated as though they have an underlying essence.

We suggest that this is the situation with regard to 'dyslexia' since, as we have argued above, dyslexia lacks historical and cultural consistency.

It would, however, not be logical to simply propose that the converse was necessarily valid and that something treated as a category with a natural 'essence' but evidently lacking discreteness, immutability, homogeneity and coherence, was merely a social category. It is also necessary to indicate that the category has no clearly defined biological underpinning discriminants.

In order to examine possible biological accounts for dyslexia we therefore now turn to experimental and scientific investigations.

THE SCIENTIFIC AND DIAGNOSTIC TREATMENT OF THE PHENOMENON

As already noted, psychological and experimental studies have revealed much of value in understanding the course of development or the failure to acquire skills in literacy (see Snowling & Hulme, 2005). However, the study of biological factors (see Fischer, Bernstein, & Immordino-Yang, 2007) whilst providing many related insights, do not yet provide any evidence of substantive organic or biological entities underpinning literacy per se. Further, and more crucially, it is less clear whether these findings are of use in determining whether or not someone may be categorised as dyslexic, and if so, what the practical consequences of such a description might be. Whilst, as we have already implied, the distinguishing characteristics (the phenotype) of dyslexia may seem obvious, it is almost certain that we should regard reading generally (and those features that may lead to a diagnosis of dyslexia in particular) as having significant phenotypic plasticity – for the psycho-linguistic reasons adduced above.

We first review evidence from biological, brain-based and cognitive studies before returning to the persistent issue of the use of IQ/ability tests in the assessment of dyslexia.

Biological and Genetic Factors

Given the quasi medical status that dyslexia appears to have, it is, perhaps, understandable why considerable resources have been devoted to discovering the underlying biological essence of this condition (see, e.g., Fischer et al., 2007; Mody & Silliman, 2008).

Functional magnetic resonance imaging (fMRI) studies show great promise and have, to date, yielded interesting findings that have helped improve current models and theories (see, for instance Richards et al., 2005; Shaywitz & Shaywitz, 2005; Temple et al., 2003). However, it needs to be noted that, in essence, current findings can only be regarded as correlational and not indicative of causal relationships (see Paré-Blagoev, 2007; Schulte-Körne et al., 2007).

At the yet more fundamental level of genetics, whilst it seems there may be some evidence of heritability (Grigorenko, 2001), it is most likely this relates to underlying language development (see also Bishop & Snowling, 2004; Duff et al., 2008). However, even if the genotype could be detected (and that seems highly problematic: see, Grigorenko & Naples, 2009; Thomas & Karmiloff-Smith, 2002), as we have already shown, environmental factors (for instance host language and culture) would seem to be obvious compounding influences. Critically, as Grigorenko and Naples (2009) and Wolf (2008) indicated, it is highly unlikely that hypothesised mechanisms would be related solely to the development of reading. This is hardly surprising given the relatively (in terms of human evolution) very recent emergence of writing and reading as communicational tools (Wolf, 2008).

At the level of neurological and anatomical brain structures, therefore, it seems quite improbable that structures or mechanisms directly and uniquely implicated in reading could be found. We can, therefore, dismiss claims for immutable biological underpinnings.

Cognitive Factors

Although a number of competing theories about the cognitive processes underlying literacy have been proposed, the dominant account now supports the role of phonology. This perspective recognises that while language and speech are natural human abilities, reading and writing are parasitic on language and have to be taught (Mattingly, 1972; Shaywitz & Shaywitz, 2005). Thus, in order to acquire proficiency in literacy, one needs to be able to recognise different sounds in spoken language and relate this to the orthographic symbols that represent the language in writing. Whilst this appears to be the most complete and coherent available theory at present (Torgesen, 2007), it is acknowledged that it does not provide a full account (Snowling, 2008; Torgesen, 2007) and there is still debate about whether phonological awareness is the key determinant of success or failure in literacy (Vellutino, Fletcher, Snowling, & Scanlon, 2004).

Cognitive accounts demonstrate how the task of becoming literate (Byrne, 2005) is complex, irregular and dependent on other linguistic and cognitive abilities. What these accounts do not show, however, is any clear evidence of a distinctive discontinuity in the dimensionality of reading and associated cognitive abilities. To reiterate, measures of word literacy and underlying skills lie on a continuum (Shaywitz & Shaywitz, 2005). On this basis we can, therefore, dispense with the concept of dyslexia as a distinct entity with clearly defined boundaries. With reference to the literature on categorisation, dyslexia does not, therefore, satisfy the criteria of essentialism in that it does not possess clearly defined "biological underpinnings ... [and is not] historically invariant and culturally universal ... [with sharp] boundaries ... not susceptible to sociocultural shaping" (Haslam et al., 2000, p. 114).

The Use of IQ in the Identification of Dyslexia

"Developmental dyslexia is defined as unexpected difficulties in learning to read in children of average or above average intelligence." (Nicolson & Fawcett, 2007, p. 135; see also the DSM-IV criteria cited above.)

This type of definition has for too long been dominant and widespread (McNab, 1994; Presland, 1991). Despite the case against its use, and the real-world implications for those who struggle to acquire literacy, it is puzzlingly persistent. For advocates of inclusive education, the issue is particularly critical since the use of the IQ-discrepancy model can serve to exclude children from specialised intervention (Catts, Hogan, & Fey, 2003; Francis et al., 2005; Stanovich, 2005).

Stanovich (1994, 2005), Coltheart and Jackson (1998), Vellutino, Scanlon, and Lyon (2000), Vellutino et al. (2004) and others, have long argued against the continued use of IQ-discrepancy definitions of learning difficulties, specifically dyslexia. As Stanovich (1994) contended, dyslexia has so many empirically unverified connotations and assumptions, the term should be abandoned. This argument is supported by empirical studies. Thus, Stanovich and Siegel (1994) were unable to find significant differences between 'dyslexic' (defined as having significant IQ-reading discrepancies) and other poor readers on a range of tests of phonology and non-word reading. Similarly, Hatcher and Hulme (1999), in a longitudinal study of predictors of response to intervention found no effects on word reading accuracy of IQ, although, perhaps unsurprisingly, there was evidence of a relationship between aspects of verbal IQ and reading comprehension. Stuebing et al. (2002) conducted a meta-analysis and found substantial evidence of overlap in the functioning of 'IQ-discrepant' and 'IQ-consistent' readers. More recently, Francis et al. (2005) have shown how the practice of imposing an arbitrary cut-off on the distribution of scores (which is embodied by the IQ-discrepancy approach) leads to instability in groups and invalid decisions for individual children.

In simple terms, therefore, no absolute categorical boundary can be legitimately set on the basis of IQ-achievement discrepancies, or on any other basis, between those who can and those who cannot (whether or not such individuals are labelled as dyslexic). Measures of word reading/spelling and underlying and requisite skills lie on a continuum (Shaywitz & Shaywitz, 2005). Academic researchers may still allocate children to 'normal' and 'non-normal' groups on the basis of arbitrary researcher-defined criteria in order to test for patterns of functioning that discriminate between groups, *post hoc*. For academic psychologists, distinguishing between groups of readers/non-readers on the basis of intelligence *may* shed light on underlying cognitive mechanisms (e.g., Snowling, 2008). However, the situation for educationalists and administrators is rather different and, as indicated above, there is no theoretical or ethical reason for making use of a discrepancy definition of non-readers as do, for example, Nicolson and Fawcett (2007).

Setting All the Above Critiques to One Side (Momentarily) Could 'Dyslexia' Have Educational Utility?

One may ask whether, if it were possible to identify clearly, reliably, validly a child with dyslexia, to differentially diagnose dyslexia from other forms of reading failure, would that in itself be helpful?

We suggest that if the label has any utility it should differentially indicate what treatment or resources should result. As Stanovich (2005, p. 104) wrote:

> ... the summary model of difficulties in reading that is generally accepted [due to difficulties with phonology] ... provides no support for differentiating poor readers on the basis of IQ. 'Consider that:
>
> 1. The primary subcomponent of reading that is problematic for children with severe reading problems is word recognition.
> 2. The primary psychological process underlying the word-recognition difficulties of reading disabled individuals is a problem in phonological coding due to weak segmental language skills.
> 3. Both the distal processing problem in the phonological domain and the proximal word-recognition problem can in part be remediated with intensive intervention.
>
> 'The problem for the discrepancy assumption that is so foundational ... is: *none of these facts correlate at all with IQ!*'' (Emphasis in the original.)

Likewise, Vellutino et al. (2004, p. 31) urged that practitioners should relinquish assessment that attempted to provide categorical labels "in favor of assessment that would eventuate in educational and remedial activities tailored to the child's individual needs."

With regards to work in the field of neuroscience, whilst this may have illuminated some of the underlying processes implicated in reading, the techniques are neither theoretically or practically capable of providing a differential decision (Schulte-Körne et al., 2007).

More generally, there continues to be no clear evidence that there is a particular form of intervention that is more suitable for some poor readers than others (Stanovich, 1991; Vellutino et al., 2000). Rather, it seems that the approach advocated for dyslexics (consisting of highly structured work to develop phonological awareness linked to successful practice with reading) is equally appropriate for other poor readers (Hatcher & Hulme, 1999; Rice & Brooks, 2004; Shaywitz, Fletcher, Holahan, & Shaywitz, 1996), although there is some evidence that an intervention that is successful for most may not necessarily be successful for all (Hatcher et al., 2006). It also seems that whether classified as dyslexic or poor reader, children's responses to intervention are indistinguishable (Brooks, Burton, Cole, & Szczerbin'ski, 2007).

SUMMARY AND CONCLUSION

We have argued that although there is a natural social inclination to locate people in categories this does not necessarily validate the category as having innate distinctiveness. In the case of children with developmental reading difficulties that are typically linked to underlying difficulty with the phonological and orthographic representations of the oral language, there is no identified natural and unambiguous discontinuity between skilled and unskilled reader – or on any dimension of the underlying cognitive associates. Equally, there is no clear-cut evidence to support differential assessments on the basis of scientific findings. There is, therefore, no support for the maintenance of a distinctive category of 'dyslexia'. Furthermore, the notion of 'dyslexia' in itself does not support differential intervention.

However, the notion of 'dyslexia' persists. As stated at the start of the chapter, it is clear that too many children (and adults) struggle with, and are distressed by, problems with literacy. This is a puzzling phenomenon that continues to thwart many endeavours to enable children to engage successfully with education. Interestingly, a recent UK Government Report, *Identifying and Teaching Children and Young People with Dyslexia and Literacy Difficulties* [Department for Children, Schools, and Families (DCSF), 2009] attests to the value of the dyslexia construct, yet notes that difficulties lie on a continuum, with no clear cut boundaries. One is left to ponder whether this key qualification too will find its way into the public vernacular and be reflected in everyday understandings and practice. Unless such recognition can be achieved, it is likely that many poor readers who lack the ability to obtain the cherished dyslexic label will continue to be vilified as lazy, ignorant or unintelligent and, concomitantly, be perceived as less needy of specialised reading intervention.

REFERENCES

American Psychiatric Association. (1994). *DSM-IV-TR: Diagnostic and statistical manual of mental disorders (diagnostic & statistical manual of mental disorders)*. Arlington, VA: American Psychiatric Association.

Berger, P. L., & Luckmann, T. (2002). The social construction of reality. In: C. J. Calhoun (Ed.), *Contemporary sociological theory* (pp. 42–65). Chichester, UK: Wiley-Blackwell.

Bishop, D. V. M., & Snowling, M. J. (2004). Developmental dyslexia and specific language impairment: Same or different? *Psychological Bulletin*, *130*, 858–886.

Brooks, G., Burton, M., Cole, P., & Szczerbin'ski, M. (2007). *Effective teaching and learning reading*. London: National Research and Development Centre for Adult Literacy and Numeracy.

Byrne, B. (2005). Theories of learning to read. In: M. J. Snowling & C. Hulme (Eds), *The science of reading: A handbook* (pp. 104–119). Oxford, UK: Blackwell.

Campbell, D. T. (1958). Common fate, similarity, and other indices of the status of aggregates of persons as social entities. *Behavioural Sciences, 3*, 14–25.

Caravolas, M. (2005). The nature and causes of dyslexia in different languages. In: M. J. Snowling & C. Hulme (Eds), *The science of reading: A handbook* (pp. 336–355). Oxford, UK: Blackwell.

Catts, H. W., Hogan, T. P., & Fey, M. E. (2003). Subgrouping poor readers on the basis of individual differences in reading-related abilities. *Journal of Learning Disabilities, 36*, 151–164.

Coltheart, M., & Jackson, N. E. (1998). Defining dyslexia. *Child Psychology and Psychiatry Review, 3*, 12–16.

Cook-Gumpertz, J. (2006). Literacy and schooling. In: J. Cook-Gumpertz (Ed.), *The social construction of literacy* (2nd ed., pp. 19–49). Cambridge, UK: Cambridge University Press.

Crystal, D. (2004). *The stories of English.* London: Allen Lane.

DCSF. (2009). *Identifying and teaching children and young people with dyslexia and literacy difficulties.* London: HMSO.

Duff, F. J., Fieldsend, E., Bowyer-Crane, C., Hulme, C., Smith, G., Gibbs, S., & Snowling, M. J. (2008). Reading with vocabulary intervention: Evaluation of an instruction for children with poor response to reading intervention. *Journal of Research in Reading, 31*, 319–336.

Eiser, J. E., & Streobe, W. (1972). *Categorization and social judgement.* London: Academic Press.

Elliott, J. G., & Gibbs, S. (2009). Does dyslexia exist? In: R. Cigman & A. Davis (Eds), *New philosophies of learning* (pp. 115–130). Chichester, UK: Wiley-Blackwell.

Estes, W. K. (1994). *Classification and cognition.* Oxford, UK: Oxford University Press.

Ferrari, M. (2002). Development is also experienced by a personal self who is shaped by culture. *Behavioural and Brain Sciences, 25*, 755–756.

Ferri, B. A., & Connor, D. J. (2005). Tools of exclusion: Race, disability, and (re) segregated education. *Teachers College Record, 107*, 453–474.

Fischer, K. W., Bernstein, J. H., & Immordino-Yang, M. H. (Eds). (2007). *Mind, brain and education in reading disorders.* Cambridge, UK: Cambridge University Press.

Francis, D. J., Fletcher, J. M., Stuebing, K. K., Lyon, R., Shaywitz, B. A., & Shaywitz, S. E. (2005). Psychometric approaches to the identification of LD: IQ and achievement scores are not sufficient. *Journal of Learning Disabilities, 38*, 98–108.

Gibbs, S. (2007). Teachers' perception of efficacy: Beliefs that may support inclusion or segregation. *Educational and Child Psychology, 24*, 47–53.

Goody, J., & Watt, I. (1968). The consequences of literacy. In: J. Goody (Ed.), *Literacy in traditional societies* (pp. 27–58). Cambridge, UK: Cambridge University Press.

Grigorenko, E. L. (2001). Developmental dyslexia: An update on genes, brains and environments. *Journal of Child Psychology and Psychiatry, 42*, 91–125.

Grigorenko, E. L., & Naples, A. J. (2009). The devil is in the detail: Decoding the genetics of reading. In: P. McCardle & K. Pugh (Eds), *Helping children learn to read: Current issues and new directions in the integration of cognition, neurobiology and genetics of reading and dyslexia* (pp. 135–150). New York: Psychological Press.

Harnad, S. (1987). *Categorical perception: The groundwork of perception.* Cambridge, UK: Cambridge University Press.

Haslam, N., Rothschild, L., & Ernst, D. (2000). Essentialist beliefs about social categories. *British Journal of Social Psychology, 39*, 113–127.

Hatcher, P. J., & Hulme, C. (1999). Phonemes, rhymes, and intelligence as predictors of children's responsiveness to remedial reading instruction: Evidence from a longitudinal study. *Journal of Experimental Child Psychology*, *72*, 130–153.

Hatcher, P. J., Hulme, C., Miles, J. N. V., Carroll, J. M., Hatcher, J., Gibbs, S., Smith, G., Bowyer-Crane, C., & Snowling, M. (2006). Efficacy of small group reading intervention for beginning readers with reading-delay: A randomized controlled trial. *Journal of Child Psychology and Psychiatry*, *47*, 820–827.

Jenkins, R. (2000). Categorization: Identity, social process and epistemology. *Current Sociology*, *48*, 7–25.

Kripke, S. (1980). *Naming and necessity*. Cambridge, MA: MIT Press.

Mattingly, I. G. (1972). Reading, the linguistic process, and linguistic awareness. In: J. F. Kavanagh & I. G. Mattingly (Eds), *Language by ear and by eye: The relationship between speech and reading* (pp. 133–147). Cambridge, MA: MIT Press.

McNab, I. (1994). *Specific learning difficulties: How severe is severe? BAS Information Booklet*. Windsor, UK: NFER-Nelson.

Medin, D. L., & Ortony, A. (1989). Psychological essentialism. In: S. Vosniadou & A. Ortony (Eds), *Similarity and analogical reasoning* (pp. 179–195). New York: Cambridge University Press.

Mody, M., & Silliman, E. R. (Eds). (2008). *Brain, behaviour, and learning in language and reading disorders*. New York: The Guilford Press.

Nicolson, R. I., & Fawcett, A. J. (2007). Procedural learning difficulties: Reuniting the developmental disorders? *Trends in Neurosciences*, *30*, 135–141.

Paré-Blagoev, J. (2007). The neural correlates of reading disorder: Functional magnetic resonance imaging. In: K. W. Fischer, J. H. Bernstein & M. H. Immordino-Yang (Eds), *Mind, brain and education in reading disorders* (pp. 148–167). Cambridge, UK: Cambridge University Press.

Pennington, B. F., & Olson, R. K. (2005). Genetics of dyslexia. In: M. J. Snowling & C. Hulme (Eds), *The science of reading: A handbook* (pp. 296–315). Oxford, UK: Blackwell.

Presland, J. (1991). Explaining away dyslexia. *Educational Psychology in Practice*, *6*, 215–221.

Quine, W. O. (1977). Natural kinds. In: S. P. Schwarz (Ed.), *Naming, necessity and natural kinds* (pp. 155–175). New York: Cornell University Press.

Rice, M., & Brooks, G. (2004). *Developmental dyslexia in adults: A research review*. London: National Research and Development Centre.

Richards, T., Berninger, V., Nagy, W., Parsons, A., Field, K., & Richards, A. (2005). Brain activation during language task contrasts in children with and without dyslexia: Inferring mapping processes and assessing response to spelling instruction. *Educational and Child Psychology*, *22*, 62–80.

Rothbart, M., & Taylor, M. (1992). Category labels and social reality: Do we view social categories as natural kinds? In: G. R. Semin & K. Fiedler (Eds), *Language and social cognition* (pp. 11–36). London: Sage.

Schulte-Körne, G., Ludwig, K. U., Sharkawy, J., Nöthen, M. M., Müller-Myhsok, B., & Hoffman, P. (2007). Genetics and neuroscience in dyslexia: Perspectives for education and remediation. *Mind, Brain and Education*, *1*, 162–172.

Seymour, P. H. K. (2005). Early reading development in European orthographies. In: M. J. Snowling & C. Hulme (Eds), *The science of reading: A handbook* (pp. 296–315). Oxford, UK: Blackwell.

Shaywitz, B. A., Fletcher, J. M., Holahan, J. M., & Shaywitz, S. E. (1996). Discrepancy compared to low achievement definitions of reading disability: Results from the Connecticut longitudinal study. *Journal of Learning Disabilities, 25*, 639–648.

Shaywitz, S. E., & Shaywitz, B. A. (2005). Dyslexia (specific reading disability). *Biological Psychiatry, 57*, 1301–1309.

Snowling, M. J. (2008). Specific disorders and broader phenotypes: The case of dyslexia. *The Quarterly Journal of Experimental Psychology, 61*, 142–156.

Snowling, M. J., & Hulme, C. (Eds). (2005). *The science of reading: A handbook*. Oxford, UK: Blackwell.

Stanovich, K. E. (1988). Explaining the differences between the dyslexic and the garden-variety poor reader: The phonological core variable difference model. *Journal of Learning Disabilities, 21*, 590–604.

Stanovich, K. E. (1991). Discrepancy definitions of reading disability: Has intelligence led us astray? *Reading Research Quarterly, 26*, 7–29.

Stanovich, K. E. (1994). Annotation: Does dyslexia exist? *Journal of Child Psychology and Psychiatry, 35*, 579–595.

Stanovich, K. E. (2005). The future of a mistake: Will discrepancy measurement continue to make the learning disabilities field a pseudoscience? *Learning Disability Quarterly, 28*, 103–106.

Stanovich, K. E., & Siegel, L. S. (1994). Phenotypic performance profile of children with reading disabilities: A regression based test of the phonological-core variable-difference model. *Journal of Educational Psychology, 86*, 24–53.

Stuebing, K. K., Fletcher, J. M., LeDoux, J. M., Lyon, G. R., Shaywitz, S. E., & Shaywitz, B. A. (2002). Validity of IQ-discrepancy classifications of reading disabilities: A meta-analysis. *American Educational Research Journal, 39*, 469–518.

Temple, E., Deutsch, G. K., Poldrack, R. A., Miller, S. L., Merzenich, M. M., & Gabrieli, J. D. E. (2003). Neural deficits in children with dyslexia ameliorated by behavioral remediation: Evidence from functional MRI. *Proceedings of the National Academy of Sciences of the United States of America, 100*, 2860–2865.

Thomas, M., & Karmiloff-Smith, A. (2002). Are developmental disorders like cases of adult brain damage? Implications from connectionist modelling. *Behavioral and Brain Sciences, 25*, 727–788.

Torgesen, J. K. (2007). An educational/psychological perspective on the behaviours of three children with reading disabilities. In: K. W. Fischer, J. H. Bernstein & M. H. Immordino-Yang (Eds), *Mind, brain and education in reading disorders* (pp. 243–251). Cambridge, UK: Cambridge University Press.

Vellutino, F. R., Fletcher, J. M., Snowling, M. J., & Scanlon, D. (2004). Specific reading disability (dyslexia): What have we learned in the past four decades? *Journal of Child Psychology and Psychiatry, 45*, 2–40.

Vellutino, F. R., Scanlon, D. M., & Lyon, G. R. (2000). Differentiating between difficult-to-remediate and readily remediated poor readers: More evidence against the IQ achievement discrepancy definition of reading disability. *Journal of Learning Disabilities, 33*, 223–238.

Wolf, M. (2008). *Proust and the squid: The story of science and the reading brain*. London: Icon.

THE STUDY OF HUMAN EXCEPTIONALITY: HOW IT INFORMS OUR KNOWLEDGE OF LEARNING AND COGNITION☆

Margo A. Mastropieri and Thomas E. Scruggs

ABSTRACT

This chapter describes a number of research experiences of the authors, directed to increasing our understanding of exceptional individuals, most typically those with learning or behavioral disabilities. A number of examples is presented, to demonstrate how a research emphasis on exceptional persons can help to advance our understanding of human learning and cognition, and how such findings can contribute to the development of an overall, adequate theory of learning and instruction. Several general points from these experiences are presented, generally that the study of human exceptionality (a) can help to clarify our understanding of what we learn, and why we should learn it, (b) can enhance our understanding of what is "possible," (c) demonstrate that what we do is more important than who we are, (d) demonstrate that we

☆This chapter is based upon a presentation made by the first author for the Vision Series of lectures sponsored by George Mason University, Fairfax, VA, October, 2009.

Literacy and Learning
Advances in Learning and Behavioral Disabilities, Volume 23, 303–319

ISSN: 0735-004X/doi:10.1108/S0735-004X(2010)0000023014

learn best by doing, and that our experience informs our understanding, and (e) demonstrate that we are all *exceptional cases.*

The first summer job of the first author involved teaching swimming lessons at a town swimming pond in Massachusetts. One morning, a mother approached her after the classes and asked if she could also teach her son, who had developmental disabilities. She agreed, but soon found out that special permission was necessary to teach this boy – because "students like that" were not allowed to enroll in swimming classes. That experience provided several important lessons, for example that children with developmental disabilities could be taught how to swim – even though many said he could not learn – and that he could learn how to swim, in spite of the opinion of others. This was the starting point of her career in teaching, and helped fuel her passion for education, and for working and studying those with special needs. This journey included teaching at the elementary, high school, and university levels, and working with special individuals, including those with exceptional needs.

Our research interests have developed directly from our teaching experiences, and what we would characterize as some initial failures at helping individuals learn to reach their potential. These interests include cognition and learning, memory-enhancing strategies, science education, peer mediation (or socially mediated instruction), literacy skills and test-taking skills, especially as these are associated with special learning needs.

Throughout this period, we have been most interested in those children and youth who represent the exception to those we consider "typical," "average," or "normally functioning." This population has included those with significant learning problems, intellectual challenges, social/emotional disabilities, sensory/physical impairments, and even those we call intellectually precocious, or "gifted." We have been interested in the attitudes, cognition, skills, emotional/behavioral dispositions, and, particularly, learning characteristics of these populations, and how such individuals could be encouraged to meet their highest potential.

We have been asked whether, in doing this, we have been limiting our understandings by focusing on as little as 5 or 10% of the population. Of course, we have always held an abiding interest in those considered somehow "different," what makes them tick, and how they can best be assisted, when assistance (rather than, e.g., understanding) is what is needed. But in a larger sense, by studying exceptional cases, we can uncover important insights about the human condition, including human functioning, capabilities, and behavior. For example, by studying those who learn or process information more slowly than others, insights can be revealed regarding how we all acquire new information. Children who become violent and aggressive in response to very little provocation provide insights into how we all manage our emotions and solve our problems. Students who do not seem able to master a basic skill like reading, and yet present little difficulty in other areas, provide us with insights on this intricate and complex processes we all take for granted, and how the process can become derailed.

In the school context, individuals with special needs can also provide us with insights about our own ideas of learning and achievement, and enrich our understandings of human development in social contexts. The purpose of this chapter is to demonstrate how a research emphasis on exceptional persons can advance our understanding of human learning and cognition, and how this can contribute to the development of an overall, adequate theory of learning and instruction. We will describe in this chapter several general points that we believe have contributed to our own understandings.

1. EXCEPTIONAL CASES CAN HELP TO CLARIFY OUR UNDERSTANDING OF *WHAT* WE LEARN, AND *WHY* WE SHOULD LEARN IT

Several years ago, we were involved in a project to examine science learning in students with disabilities, part of this project involved the identification of exemplary science programs across the county, and how they were able to accommodate special needs.

In one school district in Illinois, we encountered a 4th grade science classroom undertaking a "small things" unit, for which microscopes were frequently employed. This particular class included a girl who was totally blind. The well-meaning teachers early on had suggested this student be excused from this unit of study. However, her parents – rightly, we think – refused this suggestion, and insisted that their child be taught alongside her peers. As a happy consequence, this situation required teachers to rethink the objectives of their instructional unit, to make a clear discrimination between the mechanics versus the content of science learning, and to carefully prioritize the importance of this content – in other words, to focus on what was really important in the unit.

As physical representations of small things and accompanying explanations were constructed, it became clear that such reflective consideration of course content improved instruction for all students. For example, a projecting microscope can be used to project onto a larger screen a visual representation of the specimen under study, such as a mosquito. The larger mosquito can then be copied using raised glue so that a blind child can feel with her fingertips what the other students were seeing with their eyes. What can became readily apparent in such instances is that all other students appear to gain more knowledge about the overall structure of the mosquito from seeing and touching the raised large version as well (see Scruggs & Mastropieri, 1994a).

When it also became clear that a student with some fine motor difficulties could not easily stain specimens and prepare slides, the previously prioritized objectives (the relative importance of slide staining vs. understanding cellular structure) were helpful in dealing with this issue. We also came across the Brock microscope (Brock Magiscope®), which simplified access to microscopes typically used in classes. This scope had a lumirod which eliminated the need for electrical cord and lights, and a sliding rod which was used to focus the scope, thereby simplifying the process. This microscope was also made of cast iron which made it seem virtually indestructible, which could also be an asset when using with children who may tend to drop things (see www.magiscope.com).

These examples provided an insight, not simply for students with disabilities, but also for understanding of the nature of science. Science has always been concerned with advancement in understanding beyond the sensory and physical limitations that affect and challenge us all – not simply those with disabilities. To advance our knowledge it has always been important for us to develop adaptations and enhancements to our own senses and physical abilities; these adaptations have helped us develop our ability to think and to imagine; and to continue to seek rational and logical explanations for the observed universe. Seen in this way, significant adaptations are needed for all of us, not just those characterized as exceptional (Scruggs, 2004).

2. EXCEPTIONAL CASES CAN ENHANCE OUR UNDERSTANDING OF WHAT IS POSSIBLE

In the state of Utah, we were concerned with training students with significant learning and behavior problems to meet the often complex format demands of standardized achievement tests. As part of our training, we included a typical exercise, taken from an actual standardized test (at that time). In this test, there was a passage to read, followed by a number of questions to answer about the passage. Since many of our young students had substantial difficulty with reading, they were not surprisingly unenthusiastic about approaching comprehension tests of passages they could barely read. So, we deleted the reading passage entirely, leaving only the questions at the bottom. We told the students, "Well, then, if this test is difficult, let's make it absolutely impossible and see how well you can do!!"

The first item asked what the passage was about, admittedly very difficult for those who had not read the passage to answer, although one of the answer choices ("the water will stretch") could probably be eliminated. The second item asked about the consequences of a physical condition of water (e.g., melts, freezes, boils), and also is difficult to answer without reading the passage. The third item asks for the type of class that would address this issue. In this case, "science" seems a very likely choice, given the previous two questions. The fourth item asked what should *not* be done with a glass bottle of water. Three of the choices were benign (refrigerator, closet, ice container); the fourth (freezer) was not only likely, but suggested strongly the answers to the first two items ("freezes," "bottle will break"). At the end of the exercise, we were able to tell students, "You just scored 100% on a reading comprehension test, and you didn't read the passage!"

Exercises like this helped us show students with a history of failure (as well as ourselves) how things may seem impossible may not be so at all, if you try hard and you know how to proceed. Here's another example:

> A secondary student with language learning problems approached his special education teacher with a list of Italian words for a test next period, saying it was impossible for him to pass this class. Here are some of the words:
>
> Rana
> Scarpe
> Roccia
> Mela
> Coniglio

In order to help students with learning difficulties learn and remember difficult verbal information, we employed a method known as the *keyword method* to strengthen the connections between familiar and unfamiliar, new information (e.g., Mastropieri, Scruggs, Levin, Gaffney, & McLoone, 1985c). To use the keyword method, we identify a familiar, acoustically similar proxy for the unfamiliar word, and show it interacting with the definition. For example, the Italian word *rana* means *frog*. The keyword for *rana* is *rain*, since it sounds like rana and you can picture it. Next we show a picture of a frog sitting in the rain. When asked for the meaning of "rana," they think of the keyword, rain, think of the picture with the rain in it, remember there is a frog in the rain, and provide the answer, *frog*. For another example, consider the Italian word *scarpe*, which means *shoes*. We show students a picture of *scars* (keyword for scarpe) on shoes. When asked for the meaning of scarpe, they think of the keyword, scars, remember scars were on shoes, and provide the answer, shoes. Students with learning disorders taught in this way have been seen to double or triple the amount they are able to learn (e.g., Mastropieri & Scruggs, 1989; Mastropieri, Scruggs, & Levin, 1985a, 1985b). So, we found that what students need to learn, is *connections*. And if they do not make them automatically, we can supply them. And what might seem impossible can be made possible.

This previous example was created to demonstrate how the keyword method works, and how effective it can be. Following is an actual example from our own experiences: In Indiana, we worked with a student who needed to learn all 50 states and capitals in order to pass into 8th grade, and he was having a very difficult time doing it, having failed this test several times. We showed him keyword strategies for learning this information. For example, to remember that Annapolis is the capital of Maryland, remember this picture of *apples* (keyword for Annapolis) getting *married* (keyword for Maryland). When I ask for the capital of Maryland, you think of the keyword, marry, remember the apples were getting married, remember apples is the keyword for Annapolis, retrieving the correct answer. This strategy is complicated, nevertheless this student with significant learning problems acquired it and learned all his states and capitals. So he took the test the last time, and earned 100% correct this time. Unfortunately, the teacher gave him an "F," reasoning that it would be impossible for him to learn this well in such a short time! Fortunately, we were able to convince the teacher that the student's learning gains were real, and he passed to 8th grade. At any rate, we had another example of how things thought to be impossible can actually be accomplished (see Mastropieri, Scruggs, Bakken, & Brigham, 1992).

In one of the first research projects we were associated with, we were asked to determine whether a preschool student had normal hearing. This might seem easy enough, however, this particular little boy had severe autism, and although he was bright and attractive looking, he did not respond reliably to any sound, loud or soft. So our problem was: How do you test the hearing of someone who does not respond to sound? The implications were important: if he truly could not hear, he would need a very different type of training, including language training, than if we had normal or near-normal hearing. Since traditional methods of hearing assessment were not possible, we employed a different method: we created an apparatus whereby the little boy placed earphones on his head, and then, in separate trials, learned to push one button when he heard a sound, and another button when he did not hear a sound. This training took quite a bit of time, since we found he also had to learn to sit in his seat, and to wear headphones without tearing them off. In time, however, he learned, not only to demonstrate his (apparently normal) hearing on the task, he also learned to sit in a chair, attend to directions, and respond to requests on cue (Scruggs, Prieto, & Zucker, 1981).

Work with students considered to be exceptional in some way can lead to a very different view of the impossible. Like many special education teachers, clinicians, and researchers in this area today, we are frequently led to think, "Isn't there another way? If we can't succeed this way, *how else* can we succeed?" And, as I try to tell myself in my own life, to go from "I can't do this" to "I can't do this, this way," to, "Well then, what way *can* I do it?"

3. EXCEPTIONAL CASES DEMONSTRATE THAT WHAT WE DO IS MORE IMPORTANT THAN WHO WE ARE

A number of years ago, we studied basic learning processes in students characterized as "gifted," or "academically precocious," and how these processes might differ from more typical students. Academically precocious students, in this case, had, as 7th or 8th graders, scored higher than college bound seniors on the SAT. Over three experiments, we gave them a list of pairs of nonmeaningful and meaningful words (e.g., MEARDON – ZUMAP, see Noble, 1952), under differing circumstances. After students had completed the task, we asked them to describe how they had learned each pair, and we received reports that we could code in seven categories (cf. Martin, Boersma, & Cox, 1965), in increasing order of complexity. That is, a response of "don't know" was scored "1"; repetition (e.g., "I said them over and over") was scored "2"; use of single letter cues (e.g., "Tried to remember L-B") was scored "3"; use of multiple letter cues (e.g., for BODKIN – NOSTAW, "Thought of BO-NO") was scored "4"; use of whole word cues (e.g., "NOSTAW" is Watson backwards") was scored "5"; use of syntactical cues (e.g., for SAGROLE – POLEF, "Sargeant – Police") was scored "6"; and a "superordinate" linking strategy (e.g., for NEGLAN – GOKEM, "If someone neglects you, you go get'im!") was scored "7." If you consider simply the performance data, it is clear that the academically precocious students greatly outperformed more average learners on all aspects of the task, with respective means of, for example, 72% and 44%, respectively for academic precocious and more typical learners (Scruggs & Mastropieri, 1985). However, if you look at the learning data by type of strategy the students reported, a very different picture emerges. When matched for type of strategy employed, performance of the different groups is very similar (Scruggs & Cohn, 1983; Scruggs & Mastropieri, 1985). In most cases, what seems to separate "gifted" and "non-gifted" students on this task is the strategy they applied to learning it ("what they do"), as much as some structural, unchangeable characteristic ("who they are").

In a similar investigation, we found that students with learning disabilities applied much less effective strategies on achievement tests. However, across all types of students, we found much the same information: Appropriate strategies applied to achievement tests resulted in similar performance (Scruggs, Bennion, & Lifson, 1985; Scruggs & Mastropieri, 1988).

Based upon this and similar investigations, including investigations demonstrating the impoverished strategies employed by students with learning disabilities and other special needs, we began a number of investigations in which these students were either provided, or taught to develop, effective cognitive strategies to improve their learning. For example, when we trained students with learning and behavioral problems to use effective test-taking strategies, we found their achievement improved as much as 11 percentile points on some subtests, even though we had not taught them any of the content on the tests (Scruggs & Mastropieri, 1985; Scruggs, Mastropieri, & Veit, 1986).

In one of our mnemonic investigations we taught 3rd grade students with and without learning disabilities important vocabulary for a story they were reading. We taught them in three conditions: in one, we showed the word and definition only (*jettison* = "to throw overboard"). In the second, we showed the word and definition with a related picture. In the third, we used the mnemonic keyword method that we just practiced with the Italian vocabulary, in this case a picture of a *jet* (keyword for jettison) throwing something overboard. Notice, in this instance, the only difference was the explicit verbal link (the keyword) between the target word and its definition. Results showed all students, but particularly those with learning disabilities, performed most poorly in the condition with the descriptive picture. We think this is because the picture distracted the students from the important verbal information. Students performed a little better in the no-picture condition; but all students performed best in the keyword condition, where you can see that the students with (supposedly) learning problems learned at least as well as (or even a little better than) their normally achieving peers (Uberti, Scruggs, & Mastropieri, 2003).

Throughout our program of research, we have applied this thinking in my investigations of exceptional individuals, and they have demonstrated time and again that the way you approach life, the strategies you choose for success, and the effort you invest, can lead you more directly to success in life than the categories we are placed in, or the categories in which we place ourselves.

4. EXCEPTIONAL CASES DEMONSTRATE THAT WE LEARN BEST BY DOING; AND THAT OUR EXPERIENCE INFORMS OUR UNDERSTANDING

In a number of investigations, we interviewed children with intellectual challenges about their understanding of scientific concepts. In some cases, we were surprised with the responses we were given. Here are some examples from our interviews with some children with intellectual challenges, when we asked them what they knew about air:

> Interviewer: What is air? What do you know about air?
> Martin: Umm...It's cold...It's winny.
> Int: It's what? Windy?
> Martin: It's cold and windy outside. (Scruggs, Mastropieri, & Wolfe, 1994–1995, p. 227)

In another example, Bill provided an unexpected explanation:

> Bill: You can make air.
> Int: How can you make air?
> Bill: With wind and sand.
> Int: What:
> Bill: With sand.
> Int: You mean like wind blowing on sand?
> Bill: Yeah. (Scruggs, Mastropieri, & Sullivan, 1994–1995, p. 228)

At first, these answers seem like a kind of puzzle. However, the literature on the development of scientific understandings suggests that preschool age children do not conceptualize air as a material substance, but think of air as existing only as cold or a draft, similar to the 8–10 year olds in our example, who would certainly be at a disadvantage to their peers in a general science class (see Driver, Asoko, Leach, Mortimer, & Scott, 1994). We set up the appropriate experiences for these students, in the form of testing to determine whether air has weight. In this case, we had our students follow the model of Aristotle, who filled a container (in our case, a balloon) with air and placed it on a balance with the same container without air. With a little coaching and direction, all students came to the shared understandings about the properties of air:

> Int: Let's look here. These two empty balloons, do they weight the same:
> Anna: Yeah.
> Int: What is going to happen when I put this blown up balloon in that cup over there? Which one is heavier, the one I put air in or the one I didn't blow up?
> Anna: [indicates the uninflated balloon]
> Int: [places balloon on the balance] Do you think air has weight now that you told me the balloon with air weighs more?
> Anna: [nods yes] Because it's close to the ground and heavier.
> Int: So we can weigh air?
> Anna: Yes.
> Int: Air has weight?
> Anna: Uh huh. (Scruggs et al., 1994–1995, p. 234)

Based in part on these studies, we conducted a series of investigations in which we compared coaching students with disabilities to think with directly teaching the explanations and not providing explanations. A sample of the coaching is illustrated here. In this example, we elicited the correct response from the student by simply asking questions based upon a provided fact, such as the following:

> Experimenter: The anteater has long claws on its front feet. Why does it make sense that the anteater would have long claws on its front feet?
> Student: I don't know.
> Experimenter: Well, let's think about it together. What does the anteater eat?
> Student: Ants?
> Experimenter: Ants, good. Anteaters eat ants. And where do ants live?
> Student: They live in the ground, in holes.
> Experimenter: In holes in the ground. So why would it make sense that the anteater would have long claws on its front feet?
> Student: Oh – to help it dig for ants.
> Experimenter: Yes, exactly, to help it dig for ants. Good. (Scruggs, Mastropieri, & Okolo, 2008, p. 6)

In a second condition, students were directly provided this information, as follows:

> Experimenter: The anteater has long claws on its front feet, to help it dig for ants. What does the anteater have?
> Student: It has long claws on its front feet.
> Experimenter: Yes, the anteater has long claws on its front feet. Good. And why does it have these long claws?
> Student: To help it dig for ants.
> Experimenter: To help it dig for ants. Good. (p. 8)

A third condition provided only the factual information, as a test of whether would elaborate information themselves without coaching or provision of information. Results from these studies indicated that students with learning disabilities and developmental disabilities scored highest in the condition in which they were never explicitly told the information, but were asked to reason through it themselves (Mastropieri et al., 1996; Scruggs et al., 1994; Sullivan, Mastropieri, & Scruggs, 1995).

We were surprised to encounter a student with normal intelligence and physical disabilities in an elementary science class, unable to answer a question about the contents of an egg. When we asked him about this, we found out that, growing up in his house, because of his disability, he had never been allowed in the kitchen! From this we can see that students may be similar with respect to learning potential, but if they have very different experiential backgrounds, their performance may be very different. In some approaches to learning, all students are provided with relevant experiences upon which to base their thinking.

We have used the acronym PORC (predict, observe, record, and compare) with children in our science research as the basic model for asking and answering questions (e.g., Mastropieri et al., 1998). We have used prediction and discrepant events with children and adults. Discrepant events surprise or puzzle you. Predictions often turn out differently from the results when tested. Such activities are great ways to increase motivation, but also provide relevant experiences. One example is the question, "When does gum weigh more, before or after you chew it?" This question surely gets everyone involved in thinking and predicting. And whenever this has been used even with adults, the results are surprising.

In some approaches to science learning, students all work directly with concrete materials, directly relevant to the science concepts they are studying (Mastropieri & Scruggs, 1994). This type of approach provides all students with relevant experiences, rather than assuming they have all had sufficient experience to associate with the textbooks they are reading. We worked in an experimental 4th grade general science classroom in Indiana that also included students with a variety of disabilities: learning disabilities, intellectual disabilities, emotional/behavioral disorders, and physical disabilities. In this classroom, we introduced a hands-on unit on Ecosystems that had recently been developed by the National Science Resources Center at the Smithsonian Institution in Washington, DC (National Science Resources Center, 2003). Using these materials, students in small groups create self-contained ecosystems, referred to as "Eco-columns," made from 2-L soda bottles. The bottom bottle is the aquarium, and it contains water, duckweed, elodea (waterweed), snails, and guppies. The system is self-contained because the sunlight from the outside provides light for plant photosynthesis, the plants are consumed by the guppies, and waste products are consumed by snails. On top of the aquarium is a plastic sleeve from another soda bottle, and then a third soda bottle that houses the terrarium. The terrarium contains dirt, three kinds of grasses, isopods (pill bugs or "rollie-pollies"), and crickets. When placed together, the water from the aquarium evaporates up through the terrarium, and feeds the grass plants. The crickets eat the grass, and the isopods eat the waste matter. The water evaporates on top of the eco-column, and then filters back down into the aquarium. The entire eco-column can continue indefinitely, and helps enforce the concept of and ecosystem, a place where living and nonliving things affect and depend upon each other. In the second part of the unit, students pair their eco-columns, and introduce a change into one: either road salt, excess fertilizer, or a mild vinegar solution to approximate acid rain. They then record and describe how this intrusion affects the entire system, in comparison to their "control" eco-column. Here are some pictures of student eco-columns.

We implemented this unit in the inclusive 4th grade science class, and compared student performance with that of two other 4th grade classes, who were studying ecosystem units in their textbooks (Mastropieri et al., 1998). What we found was that students in the hands-on condition scored better on the textbook multiple choice test than students in the textbook condition, even though the experimental students had never studied the textbook. In addition, on a performance-based test of ecosystems, students in the experimental class scored very much higher, and particularly when we counted how many words they wrote in response to the questions. We also found that, in all three cases, the average performance of the students with disabilities in the experimental class exceeded the performance of the normally achieving students in the textbook condition.

As an example, consider an answer by a student to the following selected questions [writing errors in original, in each case]:

1. Tell me everything you can about an ecosystem.
   – living and nonliving effects each other
5. How can acid rain affect an ecosystem?
   – polluts almost everything
   How do you know your answer is true?
   – I just know
6. Design an experiment to test whether liquid soap is harmful to an ecosystem.
   – pore it all over an insect it would kill it

Interestingly, these answers were written by a normally achieving student in a textbook-condition class. Now consider some answers to those same questions, provided by a student with disabilities in the experimental class:

1. Tell me everything you can about an ecosystem.
   – An ecosystem is a place were living and nonliving thin effect and depend on each other. The living parts of an ecosystem is the plants animal The nonliv parts are te soil, water, air, light, also and ecosystem.
5. How can acid rain affect an ecosystem?
   – acid rain gets on plants. The acid goes to work and start killing thins and makes water cloudy.

How do you know your answer is true?
   – I know because I read and observe

6. Design an experiment to test whether liquid soap is harmful to an ecosystem.
   – How das liquid soap harm and ecosystems. We will add 25 mL of the stuff every day. We will observe every day and write down. and we will compare with our control

This investigation, and others like it (e.g., Scruggs & Mastropieri, 1994b; Scruggs, Mastropieri, Bakken, & Brigham, 1993), demonstrated to us that students may differ very much in background experience, yet if experiences that students share in together can be equated, the amount that all children can achieve can be greatly increased.

We have recently been involved in large-scale 4-year research grant intended to teach persuasive writing to middle school age students with serious emotional disabilities. We are using strategy instruction based on teaching self-regulation skills, of self-monitoring and self-regulation, concomitantly with a generic writing organizing strategy and a genre-specific – persuasive essay writing strategy. This chart shows the basic strategies we have implemented during our instruction. POW is an organizational strategy and TREE is a genre-specific persuasive essay strategy. POW describes the overall strategy for writing:

Pick my idea,
Organize my notes
Write and say more
TREE represents the steps in composing a persuasive essay:
Topic sentence – tell what you believe.
Reasons – three or more.
Ending – wrap it up right!
Examine – do I have all the parts? (see Harris, Graham, Mason, & Friedlander, 2008).

As you might expect, not all students enjoy writing; this is particularly true for many students with serious emotional disabilities. Following is a recent response from one student when asked to write:

> I hate writing.
> Writing and me have nothing in common.
> I am not writing.

Following is an example of an exchange between one student and the first author during writing class....

> MAM (approaching student): Hi Maria, do you need some help getting started with your essay?
> Maria (looking right at MAM): Something smells.
> MAM: Oh?? Well, let's look at your paper...
> Maria (still looking right at MAM): No, I mean something really smells. Real bad.
> MAM: Well, anyway, what is your topic sentence...
> Maria: Don't you get it? Smells.

Following are some examples of the student written products. The first is an example of a student written response at baseline or pretesting. In response to the essay prompt, "Should parents restrict what type of music you listen to?" the student responded:

> Should parents restrict what type of music you listen to I think not. I think we should be able to listen to any type of music we want to.

Following is an example of the same student's writing at post testing, in response to the prompt, "Should students your age be allowed to go to the home Redskins games alone?" [errors in original]

> Students my age should be allowed to go to the Redskins home games alone. Because every one likes football, someone older might not be able to take them, it's the Redskins they rule, and kids my age are responsible.
>
> To begin student my age should be able to go to the Redskins home games. Because every one likes football and would like to go alone. I would love to go to a Redskins home game. Also some football fans like to watch the game alone or with kids there age.
>
> Plus some older people might not be able to take you. They might have to do some work. Plus they should trust you to go alone. I know if my parents could not take me some were I would go by my self. One Time they could not take to the skatepark so they let me and my brother skate up there.
>
> Also it's the Redskins the[y] rule. The Redskins are a fun team to watch. Some of my favorit Redskins players are Portis, Cooly, Moss, and Randle EL. The skins hate the cowboys and so do I. The Redskins are 6-5 five I would love to watch them go 7-5.
>
> Finaly kids my age are very responsible. We would go to the game and come right back. We would know were to go. We would be on are best behavior. Also we are at that age where we need to so some stuff on our own.

> All things considered students my age should be able to go to a Redskins home game alone because every one likes football, some one older might not be able to take you, it's the Redskins, and kids my age are responsible.

Overall, all students improved significantly from their pretest performance (see Mastropieri et al., 2010; Mastropieri et al., in press). Finally, in interviews conducted post instruction revealed students not only understood the learning, but saw the benefits of the strategic instruction for themselves and their struggling classmates. This illustrates how intensive, recursive, and relentless instruction with students who are characterized as very difficult to teach, improved significantly over time when provided with appropriate strategies and the relevant guided experiences.

5. EXCEPTIONAL CASES DEMONSTRATE THAT WE ARE ALL EXCEPTIONAL CASES

This chapter is concerned with some of our investigations over the years, involving human exceptionality, and has focused generally on individuals that have been characterized as exceptional. However, this term is a subjective one, and probably broad enough, in all of its manifestations, to include nearly everyone. One thing years of studying human differences has demonstrated is, we all have all those elements in us that make us unique, that make us ourselves, and that at the same time may be characterized as a "difference" or "deficit." In fact, all individuals, whether or not we remember, were completely helpless babies at one time, in need of the assistance of others for virtually every life activity. If we are fortunate enough to reach old age, we are virtually guaranteed to be considered "handicapped" or with disabilities in one way or another, at one time or another. So when we consider who are the exceptional people out there, the "special" individuals in need of compassion and individual consideration, those who are in some way "different" from the rest, we are pleased to suggest that it is all of us!

We conclude by inviting everyone to celebrate the wonderful diversity of human life around us always, to appreciate the gifts of uniqueness we all have been given, and to think of ourselves, and of others as truly "special." Let us celebrate our collective "special-ness," work to achieve together, and learn to appreciate from one another the great gifts of uniqueness we all have to give.

REFERENCES

Driver, R., Asoko, H., Leach, J., Mortimer, E., & Scott, P. (1994). Constructing scientific knowledge in the classroom. *Educational Researcher*, *23*(7), 5–12.

Harris, K. R., Graham, S., Mason, L. H., & Friedlander, B. (2008). *Powerful writing strategies for all students*. Baltimore, MD: Brookes.

Martin, C. J., Boersma, F. J., & Cox, D. L. (1965). A classification of associative strategies in paired-associate learning. *Psychonomic Science*, *3*, 455–456.

Mastropieri, M. A., & Scruggs, T. E. (1989). Constructing more meaningful relationships: Mnemonic instruction for special populations. *Educational Psychology Review*, *1*, 83–111.

Mastropieri, M. A., & Scruggs, T. E. (1994). Text-based vs. activities-oriented science curriculum: Implications for students with disabilities. *Remedial and Special Education*, *15*, 72–85.

Mastropieri, M. A., Scruggs, T. E., Bakken, J. P., & Brigham, F. J. (1992). A complex mnemonic strategy for teaching states and capitals: Comparing forward and backward associations. *Learning Disabilities Research & Practice*, *7*, 96–103.

Mastropieri, M. A., Scruggs, T. E., Cuenca-Sanchez, Y., Irby, N., Mills, S., Mason, L., & Kubina, R. (2010). Persuading students with emotional disabilities to write: A design study. In: T. E. Scruggs & M. A. Mastropieri (Eds), *Literacy and learning: Advances in learning and behavioral disabilities* (Vol. 23, pp. 237–268). Bingley, UK: Emerald.

Mastropieri, M. A., Scruggs, T. E., Hamilton, S. L., Wolfe, S., Whedon, C., & Canevaro, A. (1996). Promoting thinking skills of students with learning disabilities: Effects on recall and comprehension of expository prose. *Exceptionality*, *6*, 1–11.

Mastropieri, M. A., Scruggs, T. E., & Levin, J. R. (1985a). Maximizing what exceptional students can learn: A review of research on the keyword method and related mnemonic techniques. *Remedial and Special Education*, *6*(2), 39–45.

Mastropieri, M. A., Scruggs, T. E., & Levin, J. R. (1985b). Mnemonic strategy instruction with learning disabled adolescents. *Journal of Learning Disabilities*, *18*, 94–100.

Mastropieri, M. A., Scruggs, T. E., Levin, J. R., Gaffney, J., & McLoone, B. (1985c). Mnemonic vocabulary instruction for learning disabled students. *Learning Disability Quarterly*, *8*, 57–63.

Mastropieri, M. A., Scruggs, T. E., Mantzicopoulos, P. Y., Sturgeon, A., Goodwin, L., & Chung, S. (1998). "A place where living things affect and depend on each other": Qualitative and quantitative outcomes associated with inclusive science teaching. *Science Education*, *82*, 163–179.

Mastropieri, M.A., Scruggs, T.E., Mills, S., Irby, N., Cuenca-Sanchez, Y., Allen-Bronaugh, D. et al. (in press). Persuading students with emotional disabilities to write fluently. *Behavioral Disorders*.

National Science Resources Center. (2003). *Leading science education reform*. Washington, DC: Author.

Noble, C. E. (1952). An analysis of meaning. *Psychological Review*, *59*, 421–430.

Scruggs, T. E. (2004). *Science education for students with disabilities: Good for students, good for science!* U.S. Department of Education, Research and Statistics (see Presentations). Available at: http://www.ed.gov/rschstat/research/progs/mathscience/scruggs.html?exp = 2

Scruggs, T. E., Bennion, K., & Lifson, S. (1985). An analysis of children's strategy use on reading achievement tests. *The Elementary School Journal*, *85*, 479–484.

Scruggs, T. E., & Cohn, S. J. (1983). Learning characteristics of verbally gifted students. *Gifted Child Quarterly*, *27*, 169–172.

Scruggs, T. E., & Mastropieri, M. A. (1985). Spontaneous verbal elaboration in gifted and non-gifted youths. *Journal for the Education of the Gifted*, *9*, 1–10.

Scruggs, T. E., & Mastropieri, M. A. (1988). Are learning disabled students 'test-wise'?: A review of recent research. *Learning Disabilities Focus*, *3*, 87–97.

Scruggs, T. E., & Mastropieri, M. A. (1994a). Refocusing microscope activities for special students. *Science Scope*, *17*, 74–78.

Scruggs, T. E., & Mastropieri, M. A. (1994b). The construction of scientific knowledge by students with mild disabilities. *Journal of Special Education*, *28*, 307–321.

Scruggs, T. E., Mastropieri, M. A., Bakken, J. P., & Brigham, F. J. (1993). Reading vs. doing: The relative effectiveness of textbook-based and inquiry-oriented approaches to science education. *Journal of Special Education*, *27*, 1–15.

Scruggs, T. E., Mastropieri, M. A., & Okolo, C. (2008). Science and social studies for students with disabilities. *Focus on Exceptional Children*, *41*(2), 1–24.

Scruggs, T. E., Mastropieri, M. A., & Sullivan, G. S. (1994). Promoting relational thinking skills: Elaborative interrogation for mildly handicapped students. *Exceptional Children*, *60*, 450–457.

Scruggs, T. E., Mastropieri, M. A., & Veit, D. (1986). The effects of coaching on the standardized test performance of learning disabled and behaviorally disordered students. *Remedial and Special Education*, *7*(5), 37–41.

Scruggs, T. E., Mastropieri, M. A., & Wolfe, S. (1995). Scientific reasoning of students with mental retardation: Investigating preconceptions and conceptual change. *Exceptionality*, *5*, 223–244.

Scruggs, T. E., Prieto, A. G., & Zucker, S. H. (1981). Classroom hearing assessment: An operant training procedure for the non-verbal, autistic child. *Monographs in Behavior Disorders*, *4*, 89–95.

Sullivan, G. S., Mastropieri, M. A., & Scruggs, T. E. (1995). Reasoning and remembering: Coaching thinking with students with learning disabilities. *Journal of Special Education*, *29*, 310–322.

Uberti, H. Z., Scruggs, T. E., & Mastropieri, M. A. (2003). Keywords make the difference! Mnemonic instruction in inclusive classrooms. *Teaching Exceptional Children*, *35*(3), 56–61.

Printed and bound by CPI Group (UK) Ltd, Croydon, CR0 4YY

13/09/2026

14961029-0003